International Space Law and Space Laws of the United States

International Space Law and Space Laws of the United States

Steve Mirmina

Adjunct Professor of Space Law, Georgetown University Law Center and Senior Attorney, NASA Headquarters, Office of the General Counsel, Washington, DC, USA

Caryn Schenewerk

Adjunct Professor of Space Law, Georgetown University Law Center and Vice President of Regulatory and Government Affairs, Relativity Space, Washington, DC, USA

 Edward Elgar
PUBLISHING

Cheltenham, UK • Northampton, MA, USA

Cover image: Greg Rakozy on Unsplash.

Published by
Edward Elgar Publishing Limited
The Lypiatts
15 Lansdown Road
Cheltenham
Glos GL50 2JA
UK

Edward Elgar Publishing, Inc.
William Pratt House
9 Dewey Court
Northampton
Massachusetts 01060
USA

Paperback edition 2023

A catalogue record for this book
is available from the British Library

Library of Congress Control Number: 2022941176

This book is available electronically in the **Elgar**online
Law subject collection
http://dx.doi.org/10.4337/9781788117890

Printed on elemental chlorine free (ECF)
recycled paper containing 30% Post-Consumer Waste

ISBN 978 1 78811 788 3 (cased)
ISBN 978 1 78811 789 0 (eBook)
ISBN 978 1 0353 1894 0 (paperback)

Printed and bound in the USA

Contents

Figures

Acknowledgements

This book would not have happened without the support and encouragement of our friends and colleagues. Without a moment of hesitation, we are humbly indebted to our amazing research assistants, Almudena Azcárate Ortega, Laura Cummings, and Ramzi Masri-Elyafaoui. We would not have completed this project without them. They are stellar individuals who launched themselves into research, writing, and footnoting while successfully starting their space legal careers. They, like all the aspiring space lawyers we have taught, mentored, and hope to inspire with this book, fuel our joy for the topic.

Although any mistakes in the book are attributable solely to the authors, in our effort to deliver a broad and practical text, we relied on substantial contributions from numerous, highly qualified space law professionals. In this vein, we are grateful for their generosity of spirit and time in donating to us dozens if not hundreds of hours of their labor.

Listed only in the order in which these chapters appear in our book, deep and heartfelt thanks go out to:

Albert Lai, for his teaching us about the history of the Outer Space Treaty (OST).

Almudena, for her work on the International Law Primer and the Other Treaties chapter.

Ramzi, for his work on the OST chapter:

Ramzi and Laura, for their work on the Domestic Law Primer.

Sabrina Jawed, for her expertise regarding the FAA's regulation and licensing of human space flight.

Laura, Glenn Tallia, and Derek Hanson, for their contributions concerning NOAA.

Laura, David Goldman, and Christian Hatten, for their expertise on FCC issues.

John Goehring, for his encyclopedic knowledge of the DOD's activities in space.

Gabriel Swiney and Emily Pearce, for their sharing information about the State Department's role in outer space.

Mike Sinclair, for his in-depth knowledge of the Coast Guard's activities in space.

Almudena, for her expertise and UN experience in the fields of national security and military uses of outer space; and **Bryce Poole**, for his editorial prowess; and finally,

David Koplow, for his informed and fascinating legal analyses of planetary defense issues. If an asteroid is coming straight for us, we are putting him on speed dial.

Finally, the authors express their immeasurable appreciation for their families and loved ones whom they were compelled to neglect for hundreds (and hundreds) of hours, to bring this book from the inside of their heads, through their fingers, and into your hands. We put a lot of thought into the book, and we hope you enjoy it.

Steve and Caryn

PART I

Introduction

1. An introduction to international space law and space laws of the United States

INTRODUCTION

Outer space. There is no clear line as to where it starts, and there is no indication that it ever ends. Outer space is beyond the limits of any one nation's jurisdiction, yet all nations rely on outer space for their economies, banking, agriculture, tourism, navigation, and public health. Outer space has fascinated humans for millennia, and ancient civilizations ranging from the Chinese,[1] to the ancient Egyptians,[2] to the Mayans,[3] were proficient in engineering and astronomy and demonstrate fascination with, and detailed knowledge of, celestial bodies.

Outer space also offers a unique perspective on humanity's role in the universe, answering profound questions that humans have asked for millennia as well as raising new questions that humans have not yet thought to ask.

While outer space is immeasurable,[4] the regions of outer space on which humankind most depends are finite. As vast as outer space is, given our level

---

[1] Chinese astronomers constructed the Taosi Observatory in China more than 4,000 years ago. It was only discovered about 2003–2004. *See,* Jia Bi Wu et al., *Astronomical Function and Date of the Taosi Observatory,* 52 SCI. CHINA SERIES G: PHYSICS, MECHANICS & ASTRONOMY 151–158

[2] Abu Simbel Temple, built about 3,200 years ago on the Nile River, was designed so that the sun illuminated the face of King Ramses II deep in the temple twice each year – on the date of his birth and on the date of his coronation. Joshua J. Mark, *Abu Simbel,* WORLD HIST. ENCYCLOPEDIA (May 9, 2018), https://www.worldhistory.org/Abu_Simbel/.

[3] You can still see current references to the 2,000+-year-old Olmec-Mayan Long Count Calendar on monuments in Central America. *The Maya Calendar System,* Smithsonian Museum Am. Indian (2021), https://maya.nmai.si.edu/sites/default/files/resources/The%20Maya%20Calendar%20System.pdf.

[4] Although many people claim that the universe is infinite, it is more accurate to describe it as ever expanding. As far as we know, the universe has been expanding for about 13.8 billion years – therefore, since it's not infinitely old, it is not infinitely big. For another fun fact, because the universe is expanding, the objects we can see from

of technological development and the laws of physics – and setting aside (for now) their intrinsic value – only certain regions in space are of current practical use to humankind. These uses include telecommunications, weather forecasting, advances in science and technology, navigation, and defense. Unfortunately, many of those regions in space are facing risks from over-crowding, radio frequency interference, and space debris.[5] To ensure that outer space remains useful to humans, as well as for reasons of national security and economic prosperity, countries have agreed on various international laws to govern outer space. Efforts to create such laws began in the 1960s, though space flight began a few years earlier. A short synopsis of outer space explora-tion and outer space law are provided below.

EARLY SPACE FLIGHTS

The modern history of space flight began during the Second World War. In Nazi Germany, a team of rocket scientists, including Wernher von Braun, began working on a new weapons delivery system that used rockets instead of planes. Their work culminated in the creation of the V-2 rocket. The project did not gain traction until August 1941, but then it became one of Germany's top technological and engineering priorities.[6] This development began an entirely new weapons delivery system, one that did not need to endanger the lives of pilots or plane crews. With an altitude range of 88 kilometers, a V-2 rocket entered the mesosphere[7] during its flight path.

After World War II ended in Europe, both the United States of America (U.S.) and the Union of Soviet Socialist Republics (U.S.S.R.) acquired hard-ware from the V-2 project, and many of the scientists involved in the German program moved to those countries to work on their military and nascent space programs. For example, Wernher von Braun went on to become the chief

---

13.8 billion years ago are now actually 46 billion light years away. *See*, Korey Haynes, *Is the universe infinite?*, ASTRONOMY (Mar. 3, 2020), https://astronomy.com/news/2020/03/is-the-universe-infinite.

[5]   As of 2018, approximately 20,000 pieces of debris larger than 10 centimeters in size (about the size of a baseball) and 900,000 pieces of approximately 1 centimeter are orbiting the earth. Given the high velocity at which matter travels in outer space, a col-lision with a 10-centimeter piece of debris would completely destroy a satellite. https://cosmosmagazine.com/space/using-asteroid-science-to-track-space-debris.

[6]   GUY HARTCUP & B. LOVELL, THE EFFECT OF SCIENCE ON THE SECOND WORLD WAR 153 (St. Martin's Press, eds., 2000).

[7]   The mesosphere is a layer of Earth's atmosphere. It is directly above the strat-osphere and extends from about 50 to 85 km (31 to 53 miles) above our planet. *The Mesosphere*, UCAR (2021), https://scied.ucar.edu/learning-zone/atmosphere/mesosphere.

architect of the National Aeronautics and Space Administration's (NASA) Saturn V program, which enabled the U.S. to beat the U.S.S.R. in landing humans on the Moon.[8]

Although spaceflight research continued after World War II, there was not much need for law in outer space before the launch of the first artificial satellite, Sputnik 1, into orbit by the U.S.S.R. on October 4, 1957.[9]

Prior to Sputnik, the question of outer space law remained mostly in the realm of academics and intellectuals, who sought to institute space laws before space capabilities were established. The U.S. perspective was to allow technological achievements to dictate best practices. In the 1950s, U.S. President Dwight D. Eisenhower walked a fine line between appeasing both the intellectuals and the military. Eisenhower largely agreed with the intellectuals and promoted peace in outer space through his speeches; but in his actions, he conceded to the military. In his 1957 State of the Union Address, he said, '[o]ur continuing negotiations in this field [of outer space] are a major part of our quest for a confident peace in this atomic age.'[10] By utilizing outer space as a conduit through which there would be peace between the U.S. and the U.S.S.R., Eisenhower was hoping to prevent a 'nuclear Pearl Harbor' with the U.S.S.R.

The U.S.'s attitude towards outer space regulation changed when the U.S.S.R. launched Sputnik 1. The launch of Sputnik 1 created consternation among many across the globe. Sputnik 1 was the first move in the Space Race, and it was followed quickly by competition between the U.S.S.R. and the U.S. to achieve increasingly complex space capabilities. Essentially overnight, the international image of the U.S.S.R. changed. The U.S.S.R. exercised global leadership in the field of space exploration. And three months later, they did it again – this time, Sputnik 2 launched a dog, 'Laika,' into outer space.

Other nations generally did not initiate space-related activities until considerably later. In Europe, for example, the idea of setting up a space agency was born in 1958, and the two agencies that would later become what we now know as the European Space Agency (ESA), were not established until 1962: the European Launch Development Organisation (ELDO), which had the mission of developing launch systems, and the European Space Research

---

[8]   Saturn V rockets, which were launched 13 times, carried 24 humans to the Moon, the only humans to venture beyond low Earth orbit. *Saturn V Rocket*, CRADLE OF AVIATION MUSEUM & EDUC. CTR. (2021), https://www.cradleofaviation.org/history/history/saturn-v-rocket.html.

[9]   Sputnik 1 operated for about three weeks before its batteries died, after which it orbited Earth for about two more months. After that, Earth's gravity pulled it back down towards the planet, and it burned up in the atmosphere.

[10]   Dwight D. Eisenhower, State of the Union Address (Jan. 10, 1957).

Organisation (ESRO), to develop spacecraft. ESRO's first successful satellite launch did not take place until 1968,[11] while NASA was getting ready to land the first human on the Moon, a feat that they achieved only a year later.

Synopsis of Sixty Years of U.S. Space Exploration

The U.S.'s Sputnik moment

While Sputnik's launch marked the beginning of the 'Space Age,'[12] it also marked the beginning of U.S. space exploration. The fact that the U.S.S.R. was able to launch a satellite before the U.S. created a serious national concern that the U.S. may be vulnerable to a nuclear missile attack due to its inferior scientific and technological capabilities.[13] This galvanizing realization is often referred to as the U.S.'s 'Sputnik moment,' a term now commonly used to describe 'a rapid national response that quickly mobilizes major policy change as opposed to a response of inaction or incremental policy change.'[14]

The U.S.'s immediate response to its 'Sputnik moment' laid the foundation for its space programs. Within 10 months after Sputnik's launch, the 85th Congress and the Eisenhower Administration:

- established the Senate Special committee on Space and Astronautics, and the House Select committee on Science and Astronautics – the first time since 1892 that both the House and Senate created standing committees on an entirely new subject,
- established the National Aeronautics and Space Administration (NASA) through the National Aeronautics and Space Act,
- established the Defense Advanced Research Projects Agency (DARPA) within the Department of Defense (DOD) through DOD Directive 5105.15 and National Security – Military Installations and Facilities,
- increased appropriations for the National Science Foundation to $134 million, nearly $100 million higher than the previous year, and
- passed the National Defense Education Act to reform elementary, secondary, and postsecondary science and mathematics education and provide incentives for American students to pursue science, technology, engineering, and mathematics (STEM) postsecondary degrees via fellowships and loans.[15]

---

[11] *History of Europe in Space*, ESA https://www.esa.int/About_Us/ESA_history/History_of_Europe_in_space (last visited July 20, 2021).

[12] *Birth of the Space Age*, NASA (Oct. 4, 2010), https://www.nasa.gov/multimedia/imagegallery/image_feature_1773.html.

[13] Deborah D. Stine, Cong. Research Serv., RL34263, *U.S. Civilian Space Policy Priorities: Reflections 50 Years After Sputnik* (May 27, 2009).

[14] *Id.* at 3.

[15] *Id.* at 2.

Less than a week after NASA's creation, Project Mercury, the U.S.'s first human spaceflight program, was officially approved on October 7, 1958.[16] Project Mercury's goal was to put a man into Earth orbit and return him safely,[17] which the Mercury capsule did on February 20, 1962, when astronaut John Glenn made three orbits around the Earth.[18]

In the early 1960s, the Eisenhower Administration conceived the Apollo program as a follow-up to Project Mercury.[19] However, the Apollo program was not taken seriously until the U.S.S.R. launched cosmonaut Yuri Gagarin, who became the first person to fly in space on April 12, 1961.[20] The following month, President Kennedy addressed a joint session of Congress saying that the U.S. 'should commit itself to achieving the goal, before this decade is out, of landing a man on the Moon and returning him safely to the Earth.'[21]

Apollo's mission of landing humans on the Moon by the end of 1969 involved the largest commitments of resources ever made by any nation in peacetime.[22] From 1960 to 1973, the program cost the U.S. nearly $24 billion, or approximately $283 billion when adjusted for inflation, employed around 400,000 Americans and was supported by over 20,000 industrial firms and universities.[23] Among many noteworthy events of the Apollo program, the landing of humans on the Moon in 1969 stands out as a singular achievement in both U.S. and world history.

After the Apollo program ended in the 1970s, the U.S. introduced the Space Shuttle program in 1981. The five Space Shuttles flew a total of 135 missions, launched numerous scientific and technological missions, and were essential to the construction of the International Space Station (ISS). The ISS is governed by an international treaty, often referred to as the 'IGA,' which is short

---

[16] *Project Mercury Overview – Introduction*, NASA (Nov. 30, 2006), https://www .nasa.gov/mission_pages/mercury/missions/overview-intro.html.

[17] *Project Mercury Overview – Objectives and Guidelines*, NASA (Nov. 30, 2006), https://www.nasa.gov/mission_pages/mercury/missions/objectives.html.

[18] *Mercury Crewed Flights Summary*, NASA (Nov. 30, 2006), https://www.nasa .gov/mission_pages/mercury/missions/manned_flights.html.

[19] *Manned Space Flight*, NASA, https://history.nasa.gov/SP-4402/ch4.htm (last visited July 20, 2021).

[20] Deborah D. Stine, Cong. Research Serv., RL 34645, *The Manhattan Project, the Apollo Program, and Federal Energy Technology R&D Programs: A Comparative Analysis* (June 30, 2009).

[21] John F. Kennedy, Address to Joint Session of Congress (May 25, 1961).

[22] Bob Allen, *NASA Langley Research Center's Contributions to the Apollo Program*, NASA (Apr. 22, 2008), https://www.nasa.gov/centers/langley/news/ factsheets/Apollo.html.

[23] *Id.*

for the Intergovernmental Agreement.[24] As of the date of writing, 243 individuals from 19 countries have visited the ISS,[25] which has been continuously occupied since November 2000. The crew of six people live and work while traveling at a speed of five miles per second (about 18,000 mph), orbiting Earth about every 90 minutes. In 24 hours, the space station makes 16 orbits of Earth, traveling through 16 sunrises and sunsets. This microgravity laboratory has hosted more than 2,700 research investigations from researchers in more than 103 countries.

In this 60-year period, nine countries have developed the ability to reach outer space: U.S.S.R./Russia, U.S., France, Japan, China, India, Israel, Iran and North Korea. Together, these countries have launched more than 8,900 satellites. About 5,000 of those remain in orbit, and of those 5,000, approximately 2,787 are functional.[26]

THE DEVELOPMENT OF SPACE LAW

Between Sputnik's launch in 1957 and today, space law has seen progressive development.

United Nations Committee on the Peaceful Uses of Outer Space (COPUOS)

In 1958, one year after Sputnik 1, the United Nations (UN) created an Outer Space Affairs Division. That was later transformed into the Office of Outer Space Affairs, now located in Vienna, Austria. Also in 1958, the UN convened a Committee on the Peaceful Uses of Outer Space (COPUOS), which was made a permanent committee of the UN General Assembly one year later and still functions. COPUOS has been the primary source for the drafting of international space law.

---

[24] The Agreement among the Government of Canada, Governments of the Member States of the European Space Agency, the Government of Japan, the Government of the Russian Federation and the Government of the United States of America Concerning Cooperation on the Civil International Space Station (1998). U.N. Doc. A/AC.105/C.2/2013/CRP.24, https://www.unoosa.org/pdf/limited/c2/AC105_C2_2013_CRP24E.pdf.

[25] Mark Garcia, *Visitors to the Station by Country*, NASA (July 12, 2021), https://www.nasa.gov/feature/visitors-to-the-station-by-country/.

[26] *UCS Satellite Database*, UNION CONCERNED SCI., https://www.ucsusa.org/resources/satellite-database (last updated May 1, 2021).

The UN Outer Space Treaties

COPUOS began drafting a series of UN General Assembly resolutions in the early 1960s regarding outer space, culminating in what crystallized in 1967 as the Treaty on Principles Governing the Activities of States in the Exploration and Use of Outer Space, including the Moon and Other Celestial Bodies (Outer Space Treaty, or OST).[27] More than 100 States are party to the OST,[28] including all major spacefaring nations. The OST is the primary international legal instrument governing activities in outer space. This Treaty also provides the impetus for most nations around the world to draft their own domestic space laws and regulations.

The Treaty establishes several fundamental principles:

- the exploration and use of outer space shall be carried out for the benefit and in the interests of all States and shall be the province of all humankind;
- outer space shall be free for exploration and use by all States;
- outer space is not subject to national appropriation by claim of sovereignty, by means of use or occupation, or by any other means;
- States shall not place nuclear weapons or other weapons of mass destruction in orbit or on celestial bodies or station them in outer space in any other manner;
- the Moon and other celestial bodies shall be used exclusively for peaceful purposes;
- astronauts shall be regarded as the envoys of humankind;
- States shall be responsible for national space activities whether carried out by governmental or nongovernmental entities;
- States shall be liable for damage caused by their space objects; and
- States shall avoid harmful contamination of space and celestial bodies.

Chapter 3 examines the terms of the Outer Space Treaty in detail. The OST was followed by four additional space law treaties over the next 13 years. These instruments, discussed in Chapter 4, expound upon and provide greater details of the principles laid out in the OST. The four additional treaties are

---

[27] Treaty on Principles Governing the Activities of States in the Exploration and Use of Outer Space, including the Moon and Other Celestial Bodies (1967), 610 U.N.T.S. 205, 18 U.S.T. 2410.

[28] The list on the status of international agreements relating to activities in outer space is compiled and distributed by the United Nations Office for Outer Space Affairs, available online at https://www.unoosa.org/oosa/en/ourwork/spacelaw/treaties/status/index.html.

concerned with the rescue and return of astronauts and objects;[29] the liability of launching states;[30] the registration of spacecraft;[31] and the Moon.[32]

Other Relevant Law

Apart from these five space law treaties (also sometimes referred to as the *core* space law treaties), customary international law, and UN 'soft law' are also relevant to space law, as are several bilateral and multilateral treaties and other agreements. At the domestic level, national space laws and regulations also exist pertaining to space-related activities. The domestic laws of the U.S. are discussed extensively in the second half of this book.

Terrestrial law applicable to outer space
One of the most important (and often overlooked) articles of the Outer Space Treaty is Article III. That article requires States Parties to carry out the exploration and use of outer space 'in accordance with international law, including the Charter of the United Nations....' Article III confirms that international law applies to activities in outer space, just as it does to activities on Earth. Examples of international law that apply *mutatis mutandis*[33] in outer space include the principle of *pacta sunt servanda*,[34] humanitarian law or the 'laws of armed conflict,' human rights, and international environmental law. International humanitarian law (also sometimes referred to as the laws of war) thus applies in space, even apart from the UN Charter, which gives a new perspective on the Universal Declaration of Human Rights. Elements

---

[29]   Agreement on the Rescue of Astronauts, the Return of Astronauts, and the Return of Objects Launched into Outer Space (1968), 672 U.N.T.S. 119; 19 U.S.T. 7570.

[30]   The Convention on International Liability for Damage Caused by Space Objects (1972), 961 U.N.T.S. 187; 24 U.S.T. 2389.

[31]   Convention on Registration of Objects Launched into Outer Space (1974), 1023 U.N.T.S. 15; 28 U.S.T. 695.

[32]   Agreement Governing the Activities of States on the Moon and other Celestial Bodies (1979), Article 3, 1363 U.N.T.S. 21; 18 U.S.T. 2410.

[33]   *Mutatis mutandis* is a Latin phrase found in the field of law that means, more or less, 'changing those things that need to be changed.' So, a maxim may be applicable to a certain situation, but it just may need to be tweaked a bit to fit the circumstances. There is no specific English equivalent, so it is used in its Latin form and italicized.

[34]   *Pacta sunt servanda* is another Latin phrase used in international law to mean 'agreements are binding.' This is a fundamental principle that forms the basis for all international law. In general, it means that States (meaning countries) must perform the obligations they agree to in Treaties and must do so in good faith. *See, e.g.*, I.I Lukashuk, *The Principle Pacta Sunt Servanda and the Nature of Obligation Under International Law*, 83 AM. J. INT'L L. 513–518 (1989).

of international environmental law also apply to outer space activities, such as: Principle 21 of the Stockholm Declaration on the Human Environment regarding transboundary harm,[35] the principle of common but differentiated responsibilities,[36] the principle of intertemporal law,[37] and intergenerational equity.[38] These are just a few examples: other areas of international law also are applicable to outer space activities through the terms of Article III.

United Nations General Assembly resolutions

Since 1980, the UN General Assembly has adopted four Declarations of Principles on space matters. Three have had significant effect. These deal with remote sensing (1986),[39] use of nuclear power sources in space (1992),[40] and space benefits (1996).[41] A 1982 resolution on direct broadcasting satellites has

---

[35] Stockholm Declaration Principle 21 provides: 'States have, in accordance with the Charter of the United Nations and the principles of international law, the sovereign right to exploit their own resources pursuant to their own environmental policies, and the responsibility to ensure that activities within their jurisdiction or control do not cause damage to the environment of other States or of areas beyond the limits of national jurisdiction.' Stockholm Declaration on the Human Environment, Principle 21, Dec. 15, 1972, A/RES/2994.

[36] *See*, 1992 Rio Declaration on Environment and Development, Principle 7, June 6, 1992, UN Doc. A/Conf. 151/126, 31 ILM 874: 'States shall co-operate in a spirit of global partnership to conserve, protect and restore the health and integrity of the Earth's ecosystem. In view of the different contribution to global degradation, States have common but differentiated responsibilities. The developed countries acknowledge the responsibility they bear in the international pursuit of sustainable development in view of the pressures their societies place on the global environment and of the technologies and financial resources they command.'

[37] The principle of intertemporal law provides that, in questions involving the environment (at least), new norms of international law must be taken into account even with respect to continuing activities governed by existing international agreements. Gabčikovo-Nagymaros Project, Hungary v. Slovakia, Judgment, 1997 I.C.J. Rep. 88, ¶ 140 (Sep. 25, 1997).

[38] The principle of intergenerational equity or intergenerational justice refers to the preservation of natural resources and the environment (here, the space environment) for the benefit of future generations. *See*, Edith Brown Weiss, *In Fairness to Future Generations*, Am. U. Int'l. L. Rev. 8, 19–26 (1992).

[39] *Principles relating to remote sensing of the Earth from outer space*, GA Res. 41/65 (Dec. 3, 1986).

[40] *Principles Relevant to the Use of Nuclear Power in Outer Space*, GA Res. 47/68 (Dec. 14, 1992).

[41] *Declaration on International Cooperation in the Exploration and Use of Outer Space for the Benefit and in the Interest of All States, Taking into Particular Account the Needs of Developing Countries*, G.A. Res. 51/122 (Dec. 13, 1996). The Space Benefits declaration focuses on strengthening international cooperation in outer space

had little substantive effect.[42] Beyond these adopted resolutions, the General Assembly has adopted a series of hortatory resolutions making clarifications and recommendations on the existing treaties.[43] Despite these resolutions' non-legally binding nature, spacefaring States have generally acted in accordance with their provisions.

International Telecommunications Union

Other international law relevant to outer space is found in the International Telecommunications Union (ITU). The ITU is a separate intergovernmental organization with a wide-ranging portfolio including regulating radio-frequency spectrum and satellite orbits. The ITU's Radio Regulations are the key procedures for regulating how satellites and ground stations communicate.[44] The ITU Radio Regulations comprise thousands of pages of detailed international agreement for using the radio-frequency spectrum. They are discussed more fully in Chapter 9, which addresses telecommunications.

Bilateral and multilateral agreements

Additionally, since 1979, bilateral and multilateral international agreements have also moved to the forefront of space law. An important example is the 1998 International Space Station (ISS) Intergovernmental Agreement (IGA), which has 15 States Parties[45] and established the legal framework for cooperation on the ISS.

This framework was further expanded by bilateral memoranda of understanding, various implementing arrangements, and numerous contractual agreements. There are thousands of other binding and nonbinding bilateral and multilateral arrangements ranging from international agreements enabling individual space missions, to others creating working groups or collabora-

---

as well as the sharing of mutual benefits from space exploration, in the interest of all countries, irrespective of their degree of economic or scientific development.

[42]   *The Principles Governing the Use by States of Artificial Earth Satellites for International Direct Television Broadcasting*, GA Res. 37/92 (Dec. 10, 1982).

[43]   *See, e.g., Application of the concept of the 'launching state'*, GA Res. 59/115 (Dec. 10, 2004).

[44]   Even though they are called 'regulations,' the ITU Radio Regulations, as well as the ITU Constitution and Convention are considered treaties under international law. *See, Radio Regulations*, ITU Library & Archive Service, Vol. 1, (2016), http://search .itu.int/history/HistoryDigitalCollectionDocLibrary/1.43.48.en.101.pdf.

[45]   The 15 States Parties to the ISS IGA are: the United States of America, Canada, Japan, the Russian Federation, and 10 Member States of the European Space Agency (Belgium, Denmark, France, Germany, Italy, The Netherlands, Norway, Spain, Sweden, Switzerland, and the United Kingdom). *See, supra* note 24.

tion on specific issues (e.g., the Inter-Agency Space Debris Coordination Committee).[46]

SPACE LAWS OF THE UNITED STATES

To implement the international obligations undertaken pursuant to the Outer Space Treaties, the U.S. has drafted domestic laws and regulations to implement its internationally legally binding commitments into its domestic legal system. Article VI of the OST requires States to authorize and supervise the activities of their nationals in outer space.

The U.S. supervises the activities of its nationals in outer space through a combination of statutes and regulations. Congress passes federal laws which empower various agencies to elaborate and provide greater details of those laws through their agency-level regulations.[47]

There are numerous federal statutes that govern activities in outer space. For example, the Commercial Space Launch Competitiveness Act (CSLCA), which governs commercial space launch and reentry activities, is examined in Chapter 7.[48] Other statutes examined in greater detail in this book include the Land Remote-Sensing Policy Act, which governs commercial remote-sensing regulations by the Department of Commerce's National Oceanic and Atmospheric Administration (NOAA) and the 1934 Communications Act, which created the Federal Communications Commission (FCC), discussed in Chapters 8 and 9, respectively.

These various statutes authorize regulations that are found in the Code of Federal Regulations (CFR) and dictate the process for obtaining U.S. licenses to conduct space activities from the FAA, NOAA and FCC. U.S. space activities are also overseen by NASA and the Department of Defense (DOD), neither of which regulate commercial activities, though they do promulgate regulations governing their own activities. As will be examined in Chapter 5, U.S. agencies can only do that which they are specifically authorized to do by Congress. U.S. agency regulations easily exceed tens of thousands of pages.[49] Our hope is that this volume will help you digest some of the relevant organic

---

[46] There is no central 'repository' of all these international agreements; individual States and space agencies maintain their own files. NASA alone has concluded several thousand agreements in its 60-year history, more than 800 of which are active as of this writing.

[47] This is elaborated more fully in Chapter 5.

[48] *See e.g.*, 51 U.S.C. §§ 50902–50923.

[49] In one recent rulemaking procedure, an agency's proposed rule was over 700 pages. *See, Streamlined Launch and Reentry License Requirements*, 85 Fed. Reg. 79566 (Dec. 10, 2020).

statutes and their related implementing regulations governing various space activities.

LOOKING TO THE FUTURE

Space-related investment and activities were dominated by States for the first several decades of space exploration, and States continue to be active. As of 2022, several States are planning major activities in space, including robotic and human visits to the Moon, visits to Mars, mineral exploitation of asteroids and other celestial bodies, and military activities. In addition to major players in space such as China, France, Germany, Italy, India, Japan, Russia, and the U.S., numerous other States are increasingly active in space, including New Zealand, Israel, Nigeria, South Africa and Mexico.

Private activities in space are playing an increasingly important role. Such activities have existed since the early 1960s, when private enterprises conducted experiments on State-launched satellites, or operated satellites on behalf of governments, but the nature and number of commercial activities are expanding dramatically. Private enterprises are involved in: launching satellites for States and for themselves; supplying and carrying personnel and cargo to the ISS; creating and operating communications systems in space, including constellations of thousands (or tens of thousands) of small satellites; contracting to take tourists into space, including around the Moon; contracting to survey the Moon's surface on behalf of States; and attempting or planning to exploit mineral resources on asteroids and the Moon.

These developments are also driving a debate about the need for new laws for outer space. Those who see a clear need note that all five space treaties described above assume that space is dominated by States rather than also engaged in by private entities – a situation that is rapidly evolving. They further note that there are lacunae (gaps) in space law because of technological progress that was unforeseen (and unforeseeable) when the OST entered into force over 50 years ago and the sheer increase in the number and types of space activities. Questions exist regarding the legality of, or liability associated with, certain outer space activities, both present and future, how to resolve conflicting claims to resources and how disputes may best be resolved. Examples of issues about which legal norms could be useful include: ownership of resources such as water or mineral resources on the Moon; asteroid mining; space tourism; private companies (as contrasted with States) launching rockets; hotels in space; criminal law in space; piracy in space; one-way trips to Mars; rights to intellectual property created in space; settlement of disputes between rival resource-gathering entities (whether private or State-owned); governance of human settlements in space; extradition; military operations in space; protection of historical or natural sites such as the site of the first human landing on the Moon; inorganic or organic pollution of celestial bodies; and, of course, other environmental concerns of the types that arise everywhere humans go.

In addition to expanding the principles contained in existing space treaties, several other areas of law provide possible models that can serve as starting points for addressing these questions. These models include the Antarctic regime,[50] the Law of the Sea, and the International Telecommunications Union. Only time will tell what details emerge as the outer space legal regime evolves.

What does seem certain is that, because outer space is beyond any State's national jurisdiction, future international agreements will be required to address issues such as these, as well as questions humans have yet to imagine. Being or becoming a 'space lawyer' will be fascinating for many years to come.

STRUCTURE OF THIS BOOK

As suggested by the title, this book has two main areas: international space law; and space laws of the United States. The first part of this book provides a general overview of most international space law with which a practitioner should be familiar. It discusses the primary space law treaties; the treaty-making process in the United Nations; and many of the bilateral and multilateral legal agreements. The second part of the book addresses the space laws of the United States. The U.S. has more extensive legislation and regulation than all other countries on Earth (perhaps even put together). This book will address both the statutes (created by Congress) and the regulations (created by the U.S. executive branch agencies) regarding governmental and commercial spaceflights.

What makes this book different from all other books about space law, however, is that it is written by two space law practitioners for the space law practitioner (and aspiring practitioners). One of the book's authors has worked as a lawyer at NASA Headquarters for more than 20 years practicing international space law for a living; the other author has worked for leading 'new space' companies (including SpaceX), practiced law on Capitol Hill, and worked in the White House Office of Management and Budget (OMB). Both authors understand how space law functions on the international level as well as how Washington works. In addition, the two authors have more than 20 years' combined experience teaching space law.

---

[50]   *See, e.g.*, Antarctic Treaty (1961), 402 U.N.T.S. 71; 12 U.S.T. 794.

One goal of this book is to serve as a practitioner's guide. When, one day, a client walks in and asks what they might need to do to get a license to launch an object into outer space, or what to do when an object in outer space has fallen upon them, this book will serve as a roadmap for the answer. To effectuate that goal, meet Ruth. Ruth is a junior attorney working at a nameless, but well-heeled, law firm in Washington, D.C. On a chapter-by-chapter basis, Ruth's interactions with her senior partner at the law firm, friends, and family will involve legal research assignments, curious scenarios, and friendly banter regarding the laws that govern space-related activities. Ruth will inspire both law students and space law practitioners who need to research the answers to Space Law questions raised by their clients. Armed with this book, space law practitioners should be able to answer clients' space law questions at least as well as Ruth does.

PART II

International space law

2. International space law primer

Ruth's father's birthday is one of those rare occasions when her whole family gathers together. Her dad is a stellar cook and every year organizes a big family get-together around delicious food. It feels great to escape D.C. and be surrounded by loved ones for a couple of days.

As she passes the bread to her cousin Ramzi, she asks, 'How is law school going?' He had just started in September, and she was eager to hear how he was enjoying it.

'So far it's great! Some classes are challenging, but I've met amazing people. And after hearing about your space law practice, I decided to join the Space Law Society. You made space law sound so cool that I decided to explore it for myself.'

'That's amazing! I'm so happy you're interested in space law; it's a fascinating field. Tell me, how can I help?' She smiles at him, excited and humbled.

'The Space Law Society advisor suggested taking International Law as a 2L, if I am interested in space.' He reaches for his drink and continues: 'I am pretty sure I'll be practicing law in the U.S., so why should I study International Law? How is it related to space law?'

'That is actually a great question. I took International Law during my 2L year, and then, as a 3L, when I took Space Law, it was very relevant.' She smiles briefly, remembering how much she liked her Space Law professor. 'I discovered that Space Law and International Law are intrinsically linked. Let me explain...'

THE INTERNATIONAL LEGAL SYSTEM

Understanding space law requires a basic understanding of international law. After all, space is an inherently international domain – and it is beyond the jurisdiction of any nation. The first UN treaty on outer space entered into force in 1967,[1] two years before humans took their first steps on the moon. About 15

---

[1]   Also known as the 'Outer Space Treaty.' Treaty on Principles Governing the Activities of States in the Exploration and Use of Outer Space, Including the Moon and Other Celestial Bodies, *opened for signature* Jan. 27, 1967, 610 U.N.T.S. 205, T.I.A.S. No. 6347 [*hereinafter* OST].

years later, individual nations, beginning with the U.S., began enacting their own domestic space legislation.

Defining International Law

Sometimes called 'public international law,' international law mostly comprises a set of restrictions and entitlements agreed upon by countries (known as 'States' in this context). Generally, States create international law by concluding treaties either to govern transactions with one another or to carry out activities that transcend national borders or implicate core human values.[2]

While international law began as a 'law of nations' where only States were subject to it, this notion has evolved over the last century. Nowadays, while States continue to be the primary subjects of international law, institutions, individuals, nongovernmental organizations, business associations, and other non-State actors can find themselves subject to it, illustrating one way in which domestic and international law work together.[3] International law is also distinct from domestic laws in significant ways – it does not have a supreme law maker like a congress or a parliament; it does not have a supreme law enforcer, such as a military or an executive; and it does not have much of a law interpreter or judiciary, like a supreme court or constitutional court.[4] However, this view does not take into account an essential characteristic of international law: it exists to serve the interests of the global community, which encompasses myriad peoples with different legal traditions and cultures.[5] It is not intended to function as a carbon copy of, or substitute for, any domestic legal system.[6]

---

[2] DAVID J. BEDERMAN & CHIMÈNE I. KEITNER, INTERNATIONAL LAW FRAMEWORKS 3 (4th ed. 2016).

[3] *Id.* at 9. *The Paquete Habana* was a landmark U.S. Supreme Court case concerning the seizure of fishing vessels in violation of customary international law. The Court famously stated: 'international law is part of our law,' and as it is integrated with U.S. law, it is binding as such. Paquete Habana; The Lola, 175 U.S. 677, 700 (1900).

[4] BEDERMAN & KEITNER, *supra* note 2, at 10.

[5] *Id.* at 11.

[6] The origins of international law as we now know it can be traced to the sixteenth-century Spanish theologian and jurist Francisco de Vitoria, who became concerned with the Spanish colonization of America and the colonizers' treatment of the native peoples. He sought to create a system of law that could be used regulate relations between societies – Native Americans and Spanish – that had very different cultural orders and understandings of propriety and governance. *See* Antony Anghie, *Francisco De Vitoria and the Colonial Origins of International Law*, 5 SOC. & LEGAL STUD. 321, 322 (1996). While Grotius undoubtedly played an important role in shaping international law as we understand it today, his work owes much to a long list of notable precursors, such as Francisco de Vitoria and others from the 'School of Salamanca.' *See generally* Thomas Izbicki & Matthias Kaufmann, *School of Salamanca*, STAN.

One of the core principles of international law is the maxim that agreements are binding, *pacta sunt servanda*. It is precisely this concept that helps promote compliance with international law. Does everyone obey international law? No, but 'almost all nations observe almost all principles of international law and almost all of their obligations almost all of the time.'[7] It is in a nation's self-interest to comply with international law, since disregard for the international regime can result in being shunned by the international community, due to a State's reputation for lacking reliability or trustworthiness.

Historically, there have been several proposals to create an international adjudicatory body to address a State's noncompliance with international law.[8] Right after World War II, as part of the UN's creation in 1945, the UN Charter established the International Court of Justice (ICJ), to serve as the principal judicial body of the UN. The ICJ's role is to settle legal disputes between States amicably and to give advisory opinions on legal questions referred to it by UN organs and specialized agencies.[9]

Sources of International Law

To properly understand the sources of international law, it is important to consider the 1969 Vienna Convention on the Law of Treaties (VCLT). The VCLT is, in essence, a treaty on treaties. The VCLT addresses a series of topics that are essential to understanding and properly interpreting the functioning of treaties. It incorporates rules related to: the conclusion and entry into force of treaties (Part II); the observance, application and interpretation of treaties (Part III); the amendment and modification of treaties (Part IV); and the invalidity, termination and suspension of the operation of treaties (Part V), amongst others. Although the U.S. has not ratified the VCLT, it considers its provisions to be reflective of customary international law, and it therefore complies with them.

SOURCES OF INTERNATIONAL LAW

ENCYCLOPEDIA PHIL. (2019), https://plato.stanford.edu/cgi-bin/encyclopedia/archinfo .cgi?entry=school-salamanca (on the School of Salamanca and its role in establishing international law).

7   LOUIS HENKIN, HOW NATIONS BEHAVE 47 (1979).

8   *See History*, INT'L CT. JUST. (2021), https://www.icj-cij.org/en/history.

9 · *The Court*, INT'L CT. JUST. (2021), https://www.icj-cij.org/en/court. Its functioning and organization is regulated in the Statute of the International Court of Justice, of which all UN Member States are parties by virtue of their ratification of the UN Charter.

The ICJ Statute highlights in its Article 38(1) – perhaps its most quoted article – the sources of international law, comprising:
a) 'international conventions, whether general or particular, establishing rules expressly recognized by the contracting states', also known as treaties;
b) 'international custom, as evidence of a general practice accepted as law', also known as customary international law or 'CIL';
c) 'the general principles of law recognized by civilized nations', known simply as general principles; and
d) 'judicial decisions and the teachings of the most highly qualified publicists of the various nations, as subsidiary means for the determination of rules of law.'

VCLT Article 2 provides that a treaty is an 'international agreement concluded between States in written form and governed by international law, whether embodied in a single instrument or in two or more related instruments and whatever its particular designation.' Although not covered by the VCLT, international organizations (such as the UN or the European Space Agency (ESA)) can also enter into binding agreements with other organizations or with States.

Customary international law (CIL) generally consists of rules of law derived from the consistent behavior of States acting out of the belief that the law required them to act in a certain manner. At least two elements of customary international law will always be required to see if CIL has been formed: (1) the widespread repetition of international acts by several States over time, referred to as 'State practice'; and (2) the requirement that the acts must occur out of a sense of legal obligation, referred to as '*opinio juris*.'[10] It is actually very important to note that the VCLT itself, at least for the U.S., is an example of something not legally binding on the U.S. (as a treaty) but nevertheless is binding on the U.S. because its provisions are considered CIL.

When an international lawyer cannot locate applicable treaty law or CIL, she would normally look for any applicable general principles of law. These general principles are used as gap fillers when there are neither explicit treaties nor easily identifiable CIL. General principles boil down to a notion of law that is so fundamental that it is found in essentially all legal systems. Examples

---

[10] While State practice and *opinio juris* are considered the two essential elements of CIL, as recognized by the International Court of Justice. *Legality of the Threat or Use of Nuclear Weapons,* Advisory Opinion, 1996 I.C.J. Rep. 66 (July 8). The third element indicates that there must be a certain uniformity in the acceptance of a practice for CIL to emerge. *See Draft Conclusions on Identification of Customary International Law, with Commentaries,* [2018] 2 Y.B. INT'L L. COMM'N, U.N. Doc. A/73/10.

of general principles are good faith performance of obligations, the *pacta sunt servanda* principle, equality of States, and independence of judges.

Finally, reference can also be made to judicial decisions and the writings of legal scholars. While ICJ decisions are only binding on the parties involved in that particular case, they are still important to the creation of *opinio juris*, as well as in the formation of State practice, both of which are needed for the establishment of customary international law. While there is no '*stare decisis*'[11] in international law, the ICJ and legal scholars will look to its previous opinions for guidance. Even the U.S. Supreme Court has opined on the importance of examining 'teachings of the most highly qualified publicists' and legal scholarship to find evidence of international law.[12]

SPACE LAW AS AN INHERENTLY INTERNATIONAL LEGAL REGIME: THE BIRTH OF SPACE LAW AT THE UN

The Committee on the Peaceful Uses of Outer Space[13]

Fearful that the rivalry that existed on Earth between the U.S. and Soviet Union (U.S.S.R.) would also extend to space, the UN established the initially *ad hoc* Committee on the Peaceful Uses of Outer Space (COPUOS) on December 13, 1958,[14] to develop rules to govern the use of outer space and ensure peace.[15]

---

[11] *Stare decisis* is Latin for 'to stand by things decided.' The full Latin phrase is 'stare decisis et non quieta movere—stand by the thing decided and do not disturb the calm.' *See* James C. Rehnquist, *The Power That Shall Be Vested in a Precedent: Stare Decisis, The Constitution, and the Supreme Court*, 66 B.U. L. Rev. 345, 347 (1986).

[12] In *The Paquete Habana*, the Supreme Court stated that 'where there is no treaty and no controlling executive or legislative act or judicial decision, resort must be had to the customs and usages of civilized nations, and as evidence of these, to the works of jurists and commentators who by years of labor, research, and experience have made themselves peculiarly well acquainted with the subjects of which they treat.' Paquete Habana, 175 U.S. at 700.

[13] For more information on COPUOS and its role in formulating the OST, *see* Albert K. Lai, The Cold War, the Space Race, and Law of Outer Space: Space for Peace (Routledge eds., 2021).

[14] G.A. Res. 1348 (XIII), Question of the Peaceful Use of Outer Space (Dec. 13, 1958); Von Hardesty & Gene Eiseman, Epic Rivalry: The Inside Story of the Soviet and American Space Race 77, 79, 85–7 (2007); Asif A. Siddiqi, Challenge to Apollo: The Soviet Union and the Space Race, 1945–1974 at 171–74 (NASA SP-2000-4408, 1966); Walter Sullivan, Assault on the Unknown 84–98 (1961).

[15] *See* Lai, *supra* note 13. The international community favored the United States' proposal for an ad hoc COPUOS, as it felt that linking the exploration of outer space with disarmament would paralyze the former without advancing the latter, and so the

During its initial years, COPUOS had a slow start, as its creation was also an issue of contention between the U.S. and the U.S.S.R.: on November 7, 1958, the Soviet Union introduced a draft resolution at the UN proposing to 'ban the use of cosmic space for military purposes.' The Soviet proposal, however, had a condition. In return for banning the military use of outer space, the Soviet Union demanded 'the elimination of foreign military bases on the territory of other countries.' 'Foreign military bases' was a not so veiled reference to American bases in allied nations that ringed the Soviet Union from Western Europe, to Turkey, and to Japan. The United States proposed a different approach by asking that the UN declare 'itself on the separability of the question of the peaceful uses of outer space from that of disarmament.'

The UN General Assembly tasked COPUOS with reviewing international cooperation in peaceful uses of outer space, studying space-related activities that could be undertaken by the UN,[16] encouraging space research programs, and studying legal problems arising from the exploration of outer space.[17] The five UN space treaties discussed in Chapters 3–4 were largely drafted within the COPUOS.

The UN Office for Outer Space Affairs

The UN Office for Outer Space Affairs (OOSA) is the office within the UN Secretariat charged with promoting international cooperation in the peaceful uses of outer space as well as the utilization of space science and technology for sustainable economic and social development.[18] OOSA provides substantive secretariat and translation services to COPUOS's two subcommittees. In addition, OOSA maintains the UN Register of Objects Launched into Outer Space.[19] Like COPUOS, OOSA only deals with issues related to the peaceful

---

UN established the ad hoc COPUOS over the Soviet Union's objection, which caused the Soviet Union and its allies to boycott it for several years. COPUOS eventually became a permanent UN committee in 1961, with the Committee work divided between two subsidiary bodies: (i) the Scientific and Technical Subcommittee; and (ii) the Legal Subcommittee.

[16]   G.A. Res. 1721 (XVI), International Co-Operation in the Peaceful uses of Outer Space (Dec. 20, 1961).

[17]   *See Office for Outer Space Affairs*, U.N. (2021), https://www.unoosa.org/oosa/en/ourwork/copuos/index.html.

[18]   *See About Us*, U.N. (2021), https://www.unoosa.org/oosa/en/aboutus/index.html.

[19]   *United Nations Register of Objects Launched into Outer Space*, U.N. Off. Outer Space Aff. (2021), https://www.unoosa.org/oosa/en/spaceobjectregister/index.html. Further elaboration on the registration of space objects may be found in Chapter 4.

uses of outer space. Matters concerning the militarization of outer space are dealt by the UN Conference on Disarmament, based in Geneva.

The Conference on Disarmament

The Conference on Disarmament (CD) was established in 1978, when the UN General Assembly recognized it as the single multilateral disarmament negotiating forum of the international community, in its Tenth Special Session on Disarmament (SSOD-I).[20] It comprises 65 Member States, including the five nuclear-weapon States according to the Treaty on the Non-Proliferation of Nuclear Weapons (China, Russia, the United Kingdom, France, and the U.S.) and 60 other States of key military significance. In its history, the CD and its predecessors have negotiated many key international disarmament and arms control agreements, such as the Treaty on the Non-Proliferation of Nuclear Weapons (NPT), and Comprehensive Nuclear-Test-Ban Treaty (CTBT).[21] It has been significantly less successful in reaching arms control agreements specifically focused on the space domain, although several attempts have been made throughout the years.[22]

Treaty to prevent an arms race in outer space
An attempt to negotiate the Prevention of an Arms Race in Outer Space (PAROS) Treaty emerged during the 10th Special Session of the UN General Assembly on Disarmament, in 1978. In 1985, the CD established an ad hoc committee to examine issues relevant to PAROS. The U.S. objected to the committee engaging in negotiations and, as a result, essentially no progress was made and the committee stopped meeting in 1994.[23] According to the Federation of American Scientists, the U.S. 'argue[d] that PAROS is unnecessary, because there are no weapons – and thus no arms race – in outer space at this time.'[24]

---

[20]   Final Doc. of the Tenth Special Session on Disarmament (SSOD-I), U.N. Doc. A/RES/S-10/2 (1978).

[21]   *Conference on Disarmament*, U.N. Off. Disarmament Aff. https://www.un.org/disarmament/conference-on-disarmament (last visited Nov. 14, 2021).

[22]   See detailed discussion in Chapter 13.

[23]   The CD, like COPUOS, operates by consensus. One member blocking consensus can paralyze progress. Peter Martinez, *The UN COPUOS Guidelines for the Long-Term Sustainability of Outer Space Activities*, Secure World Found. 2 (Nov. 2019), https://swfound.org/media/206891/swf_un_copuos_lts_guidelines_fact_sheet _november-2019-1.pdf.

[24]   *Prevention of an Arms Race in Outer Space: Current Status*, Fed. Am. Sci. (2013), https://fas.org/programs/ssp/nukes/ArmsControl_NEW/nonproliferation/NFZ/ NP-NFZ-PAROS.html.

Treaty to prevent placement of weapons in outer space and the threat or use of force against space objects

In 2008, Russia and China introduced a Draft Treaty on the Prevention of Placement of Weapons in Outer Space and the Threat or Use of Force against Space Objects (PPWT) to the CD. The PPWT failed to receive necessary support. Russia and China returned with a new proposal several years later, in 2014, but it also was met with a lukewarm reception. The U.S. has been the main PPWT critic, stating its belief that it is 'fundamentally flawed'[25] – a sentiment shared by many other States.[26]

Some of the more criticized aspects of the PPWT include the lack of a verification mechanism, the lack of restrictions on the development and stockpiling of ASAT weapons on the ground, and also the fact that while the PPWT bans the placement of weapons in outer space, it does not ban direct-ascent ASATs launched from the ground,[27] nor does it address soft-kill weapons such as lasers that could be employed to permanently or temporarily disable a satellite. Another problematic issue that the PPWT presents is its definition of 'weapon,' which is considered too narrow, as it considers that only objects or components that are 'produced or converted to eliminate, damage or disrupt normal functioning of objects in outer space, on the Earth's surface or in the air, as well as to eliminate population, components of biosphere important to human existence, or to inflict damage to them by using any principles of physics'[28] qualify as weapons. This excludes dual-use technology, which comprises 95% of the existing satellite technology nowadays.[29]

The use of space is an important issue for the international community. The Conference on Disarmament's slow progress does not detract from the important role it plays in facilitating the dialog between nations that furthers global stability.

---

[25]   Ambassador Robert A. Wood, U.S. Permanent Rep. Conference Disarmament, Statement at the Conference on Disarmament Plenary Meeting on Agenda Item Three, 'Prevent of an Arms Race in Outer Space,' (Aug. 14, 2019), https://geneva.usmission.gov/2019/08/14/statement-by-ambassador-wood-the-threats-posed-by-russia-and-china-to-security-of-the-outer-space-environment/.

[26]   *Id.*

[27]   Jeff Foust, *U.S. Dismisses Space Weapons Treaty Proposal As 'Fundamentally Flawed'*, SPACENEWS (Sept. 11, 2014), https://spacenews.com/41842us-dismisses-space-weapons-treaty-proposal-as-fundamentally-flawed/.

[28]   Letter from the Permanent Rep. of the Russ. Fed'n and the Permanent Rep. of China to the Sec.-Gen. of the Conference on Disarmament, CD/1985 (June 12, 2014) (conveying text of the draft Treaty on the Prevention of the Placement of Weapons in Outer Space, the Threat or Use of Force against Outer Space Objects).

[29]   JOAN JOHNSON-FREESE, SPACE AS A STRATEGIC ASSET 30 (2007).

THE RELATIONSHIP BETWEEN SPACE LAW AND INTERNATIONAL LAW

The Link Between Space Law and International Law

The OST drafters wanted to ensure that the exploration and use of outer space comported with international law. Specifically, the OST mentions international law in two separate articles. First, Article I indicates that, '[o]uter space, including the Moon and other celestial bodies, shall be free for exploration and use by all States without discrimination of any kind, on a basis of equality and *in accordance with international law*, and there shall be free access to all areas of celestial bodies.'[30]

The second OST reference to international law is Article III. This is perhaps one of the OST's more significant articles because it incorporates the entire body of international law and applies it to outer space. Article III states:

> States Parties to the Treaty shall carry on activities in the exploration and use of outer space, including the Moon and other celestial bodies, in accordance with international law, including the Charter of the UN, in the interest of maintaining international peace and security and promoting international cooperation and understanding.

The OST drafters prioritized maintaining peace and security in space. To that end, OST Article III reflects and incorporates Article 2(4) of the UN Charter regarding the use of force.[31] The drafters were also deliberate in utilizing broad language to ensure the longevity of the Treaty's terms – in this sense it is akin to a 'constitution' on outer space. The flexibility of the wording in Article III ensures the longevity of the Treaty's terms as well as the continued applicability of international law to the space domain.[32]

Sovereignty Over Space

There is no international consensus as to where airspace ends and outer space begins. That is important because air law and space law are very different legal regimes. International aviation law, also referred to as air law, is based almost entirely on the concept of national sovereignty. The Chicago Convention establishes that all States have 'complete and exclusive sovereignty over the

---

[30] OST, *supra* note 1, at Art. 1 (emphasis added).

[31] 1 COLOGNE COMMENTARY ON SPACE LAW 64–65 (Stephan Hobe, Bernhard Schmidt-Tedd, Kai-Uwe Schrogl eds., 2009).

[32] *Id.* at 69.

airspace above [their] territory.'[33] Generally speaking, one needs specific permission to fly through the airspace of another country.[34] The international civil aviation that we know today is based on States' having negotiated bilateral or multilateral agreements that grant reciprocal, and frequently mutual, traffic rights to airlines of other States.[35]

There is no sovereignty in space. Article II of the OST forbids the national appropriation of space, 'by claim of sovereignty, by means of use or occupation, or by any other means.'[36]

Regarding the question of delimiting outer space from airspace, there are two schools of thought. The 'spatialist' approach suggests that there is a fixed line where airspace ends, and outer space begins. Some scholars, and some U.S. states, but not the federal government, arbitrarily have set 100 kilometers as the limit.[37] Coincidentally, this approximate altitude coincides with what is sometimes called 'the von Kármán line.'[38]

The other primary school of thought in the delimitation debate is known as the 'functionalist' approach in reference to the highest altitude at which an aircraft can fly or 'function,' and the lowest altitude at which a satellite can remain in orbit.[39] The emergence of hybrid aerospace vehicles, such as the U.S. X-37B spaceplane,[40] which can operate in either airspace or outer space and straddle any line established between the two, may compel the legal community to answer this question that has not required an answer for the last 50-plus years.

---

[33] Convention on International Civil Aviation, *done* Dec. 7, 1944, at Art. I, 15 U.N.T.S. 295, T.I.A.S. No. 159.

[34] Dean N. Reinhardt, *The Vertical Limit of State Sovereignty*, 72 J. AIR L. & COM. 65 (2007).

[35] *Id.*

[36] OST, *supra* note 1, at Art. II.

[37] Bhavya Lal & Emily Nightingale, *Where is Space? And Why Does That Matter?*, SPACE TRAFFIC MGMT. CONF. (2014), https://commons.erau.edu/cgi/viewcontent.cgi ?article=1052&context=stm.

[38] Jonathan C. McDowell, *The Edge of Space: Revisiting the Karman Line*, 151 ACTA ASTRONAUTICA 668–677 (2018). For a cogent and compelling argument against using this random altitude to delimit airspace from outer space, *see* Thomas Gangale, The Non Kármán Line: An Urban Legend of the Space Age, 41 J. SPACE L. 151 (2017).

[39] FRANCIS LYALL & PAUL B. LARSEN, SPACE LAW: A TREATISE 453–54 (Routledge 2d ed. 2018); *see* Paul Stephen Dempsey & Maria Manoli, *Suborbital Flights and the Delimitation of Air Space vis-à-vis Outer Space: Functionalism, Spatialism and State Sovereignty*, 42 ANNALS AIR & SPACE L. 209–51 (2018).

[40] *See* Brian Weeden, *X-37B Orbital Test Vehicle Fact Sheet*, SECURE WORLD FOUND. (May 2020), https://swfound.org/media/206982/swf_x-37b_otv_fact_sheet .pdf.

CONNECTION TO DOMESTIC SPACE LAW

Many nations, such as the U.S., apply domestic laws to activities in outer space, in furtherance of their OST Article 6 obligations to authorize and supervise the activities of their nationals. It is essential for a space law practitioner to understand: (1) how the *lex specialis* (special legal structure) of space law is one part of the fabric of public international law (*lex generalis*); as well as (2) the interconnectedness and interwoven structure of international law with domestic law. As space continues to play an increasingly important role in humankind's daily existence, it is critical to understand how international law applies to activities in outer space and how it is reflected in domestic legal systems.

QUESTIONS FOR REVIEW

1. What do you think about customary international law? Do you recall the necessary elements for something to become CIL? Besides the VCLT, the U.S. also follows the U.N. Convention on the Law of the Sea, even though for almost 40 years, the Senate has refused to ratify it.

2. In the 'monist' tradition of international law, as soon as a nation ratifies a treaty, its legal obligations immediately become binding domestically. Even individual citizens can invoke the treaty's provisions, and a judge can apply it in a domestic case. In a 'dualist' legal system, after a treaty is signed, further steps need to be taken domestically to implement that treaty's legal obligations into domestic law. The U.S. generally follows the dualist tradition. Dualism requires the translation of international law into national law. Many states use a combination of both theories. Which approach makes the most sense to you?

3. Do you think there was law in space before Sputnik was launched? Why or why not?

4. Why do you think countries follow international law if there is no penalty for treaty violations?

5. What about those countries that are not party to the Outer Space Treaty? What law governs their conduct in outer space?

3. The Outer Space Treaty

'I have great news, Ruth! You're going to be so excited,' exclaimed the senior partner as he entered Ruth's office. She was immediately skeptical.

'I was invited to speak at one of the local law schools,' he continued. 'Rather than drafting the lecture myself, I think it's a great opportunity for you to practice your writing skills!' In Ruth's experience 'opportunity' usually translated as a weekend in the office.

'I've been asked to talk about the Outer Space Treaty and would like to focus on its key aspects, like the applicability of international law and how States bear responsibility for their nationals' activities. You should also address interesting topics like what types of weapons are allowed in outer space, what is meant by non-appropriation, yadda, yadda, yadda,' he pauses as she just looks at him.

'Ruth – the lecture is next Wednesday night, 5:30, at Georgetown Law. Can you get me my speaking notes by COB Tuesday?'

The senior partner leaves the office and walks down the hall. As he is walking away, she hears him yell back over his shoulder: 'Oh, by the way,... if it turns out that I'm too busy to give the talk myself next week, I'm going to have you do it.'

For the first time in a while, she smiles. She opens her laptop and begins to type. She starts preparing for her very first law school lecture.

INTRODUCTION

On January 27, 1967, representatives of the United States (U.S.), the United Kingdom (U.K.) and the Union of Soviet Socialist Republics (U.S.S.R.), along with 28 other countries, convened in Washington, DC, London, and Moscow, to sign the Outer Space Treaty (OST).[1] As of the date of publication, the OST

---

[1]   Treaty on Principles Governing the Activities of States in the Exploration and Use of Outer Space, Including the Moon and Other Celestial Bodies [hereinafter OST], Jan. 27, 1967, 610 U.N.T.S. 205., T.I.A.S. No. 6347. *Space Treaty 1967*, British Pathe, https://www.britishpathe.com/video/space-treaty/query/wildcard (last visited Nov. 18, 2021).

has been ratified by 110 States and signed by 23 other States.[2] The OST is 'the most important source of space law,'[3] and represents 'one of the key developments in the entire realm of international law.'[4] More than half a century after its signing, the OST 'continues to serve as the foundation of the international legal framework for all space activities.'[5] This chapter examines the OST by providing a brief historical context, followed by a high-level overview of the OST's most relevant articles that focuses on how these articles are incorporated into the practice of space law today.

THE DEVELOPMENT OF THE OST

The OST was drafted in the 1960s during the height of the Cold War. The Treaty was first viewed as an arms control treaty: it was seen by many as the Treaty that banned nuclear weapons from outer space.[6] Drafted in the United Nations (UN), the OST was modeled primarily on previous UN General Assembly (UNGA) Resolutions. In fact, its articles were largely a codification of principles found in prior resolutions that had been thoroughly negotiated, carefully drafted, and unanimously approved by the UNGA years earlier.

The most influential of these documents is the UNGA Resolution, 'Declaration of Legal Principles Governing the Activities of States in the Exploration and Use of Outer Space.'[7] In that unanimously adopted resolution,

---

[2]   *Status of International Agreements Relating to Activities in Outer Space as of 1 JANUARY 2020*, UN Off. for Outer Space Affairs [hereinafter UNOOSA], https://www.unoosa.org/documents/pdf/spacelaw/treatystatus/TreatiesStatus-2020E.pdf) (last visited Nov. 18, 2021). At the time the OST entered into force on Oct. 10, 1967, it had been signed by 109 countries out of the then 123 UN Member States.

[3]   Tanja Masson-Zwaan, *The International Framework for Space Activities*, HANDBOOK FOR NEW ACTORS IN SPACE, Secure World Found., at 5 (2017).

[4]   FRANCIS LYALL AND PAUL LARSEN, *SPACE LAW: A TREATISE*, ROUTLEDGE [HEREINAFTER LYALL/LARSEN], AT 50 N.5 (2018), quoting A.E. GOTTLIEB, *The Impact of Technology on the Development of Contemporary International Law*, 170 Hague Recueil, 1981-1, 115–329, at 311 n.484.

[5]   Christopher Johnson and Ian Christensen, *Letter for the record for the hearing on 'Reopening the American Frontier: Exploring How the Outer Space Treaty Will Impact American Commerce and Settlement in Space'*, S. Comm. on Com. Sci., and Transp., Subcomm. on Space Sci., and Competitiveness (May 23, 2017), S. Hr. 115–219, https://www.govinfo.gov/content/pkg/CHRG-115shrg29998/pdf/CHRG-115shrg29998.pdf.

[6]   Stephen Buono, *Merely a 'Scrap of Paper'? The Outer Space Treaty in Historical Perspective, Diplomacy & Statecraft*, 31 Taylor & Francis Online 350–372 (June 8, 2020).

[7]   The Declaration of Legal Principles Governing the Activities of States in the Exploration and Use of Outer Space, UNGA Res. 1962 (XVIII) 1963, (1964) 3 ILM 157. In this book, 1960s-era treaty references to 'mankind' are intentionally being

UN Member States established that, in the exploration and use of outer space, States should be guided by the following principles:

- The exploration and use of space shall be carried 'for the benefit and in the interests of all [hu]mankind.'
- Outer space and celestial bodies are 'free for exploration and use by all States' ... in accordance with international law.
- Outer space and celestial bodies are 'not subject to national appropriation by claim of sovereignty, by means of use or occupation, or by any other means.'
- That States 'bear international responsibility for national activities in outer space' and that the activities of nongovernmental entities 'shall require authorization and continuing supervision.'
- That States shall be 'guided by the principle of co-operation' and 'shall conduct all their activities in outer space "with due regard for the corresponding interest of other States."'
- That States launching objects shall be 'internationally liable for damage to a foreign State.'
- That States shall regard astronauts as 'envoys of [hu]mankind ... and shall render to them all possible assistance.'

Agreed to in 1963 just years after the launch of Sputnik 1, these nonbinding principles were incorporated into the OST as legally binding obligations almost verbatim to how they were drafted and unanimously approved by the UNGA.

Apart from the UNGA declaration, the OST drafters were also influenced by the Antarctic Treaty of 1959 and the Limited Nuclear Test Ban Treaty of 1963. The Antarctic Treaty was in some respects analogous to outer space insofar as it deals with activities in a remote, inhospitable region.[8] In addition, it preserved Antarctica 'for peaceful purposes only' (Article 1); preserved 'freedom of scientific investigation' (Article II); and prohibited claims of territorial sovereignty (Article IV).[9] Meanwhile, Article 1 of the 1963 Limited Nuclear Test Ban Treaty banned nuclear weapon testing 'in the atmosphere, beyond its limits, including outer space,'[10] a sentiment that, as addressed below, was amplified in Article 4 of the OST.

---

changed to 'humankind' to make them more readable by today's audience, without any changing in the original meaning of the text.

[8]   Lyall/Larsen *supra* note 4, at 51.

[9]   The Antarctic Treaty, Jan. 12, 1959, 402 U.N.T.S. 71, 12 U.S.T. 795. *See generally*, Lyall/Larsen *supra* note 4, at 167–168.

[10]   The Limited Test Ban Treaty prohibited all test detonations of nuclear weapons except for those conducted underground. It was signed by the governments of the

AN EXPLORATION OF THE OUTER SPACE TREATY

The Preamble

Preambles to international agreements do not create rights or legal obligations. However, they do provide context and generally establish the agreement's object and purpose. A Treaty preamble can help with interpreting a treaty's substantive legal obligations.[11] The OST Preamble provides that the States party to this Treaty:

- Recognize the common interest of all [hu]mankind in the progress of the exploration and use of outer space for peaceful purposes;
- Believe that the exploration and use of outer space should be carried on for the benefit of all peoples irrespective of the degree of their economic or scientific development;
- Desire to contribute to broad international cooperation in the scientific as well as the legal aspects of the exploration and use of outer space for peaceful purposes; and
- Believe that such cooperation will contribute to the development of mutual understanding and to the strengthening of friendly relations between States and peoples.

Article I: Freedom of exploration
Article I of the OST establishes the freedom of States to explore and use outer space. Article I provides:

The exploration and use of outer space, including the moon and other celestial bodies, shall be carried out for the benefit and in the interests of all countries, irrespective of their degree of economic or scientific development, and shall be the province of all mankind.
Outer space, including the moon and other celestial bodies, shall be free for exploration and use by all States without discrimination of any kind, on a basis of equality

---

Soviet Union, the United Kingdom, and the United States in Moscow on 5 August 1963 before it was opened for signature by other countries. The Treaty formally went into effect on 10 October 1963. Since then, 123 other states have become party to the Treaty. Treaty Banning Nuclear Weapon Tests in the Atmosphere, in Outer Space, and Under Water with U.S.S.R. and U.K., Aug. 5, 1963, 14 U.S.T. 1313, T.I.A.S. No. 5433.

[11] *See*, Vienna Convention on the Law of Treaties art. 31.2, May 23, 1969, 1155 U.N.T.S. 331.

and in accordance with international law, and there shall be free access to all areas of celestial bodies.

There shall be freedom of scientific investigation in outer space, including the moon and other celestial bodies, and States shall facilitate and encourage international co-operation in such investigation.

As the treaty's lead provision, Article I acknowledges three freedoms related to space: the freedom of exploration and use; the freedom of access; and the freedom of scientific investigation. These freedoms accrue to all States – not just those States that are party to the OST.

Freedom of exploration and use

Article I paragraph 2 provides that all States have the freedom to explore and use outer space. No State needs to request permission to explore or use outer space. As sovereign entities, States may also authorize their nationals to explore and use outer space. As is discussed below, Article VI of the OST requires that a State authorize and supervise the activities of its nationals (whether private individuals or corporations) in outer space.

Freedoms of access and scientific investigation

The specific freedom to access 'the moon and other celestial bodies' in Article I paragraph 2 is complemented by the restriction found in Article II of the OST, which prohibits national appropriation of a celestial body. In other words, since no State may claim sovereignty over a celestial body, there is no legal basis by which to keep others 'out' – hence, the freedom of access.[12] As discussed below in relation to OST Articles VIII and XII, States are responsible for and retain jurisdiction and control over space objects on celestial bodies (such as installations, equipment, and space vehicles), but, per Article XII of the OST, such objects must be open to all on the basis of reciprocity.

Article I paragraph 3 confirms that States have the freedom of scientific investigation in outer space. Moreover, the Treaty encourages States to cooperate internationally in outer space exploration. In fact, the Treaty uses

---

[12]   The U.S. Supreme Court has stated that the right to exclude others from one's private property is 'universally held to be a fundamental element of the property right,' and is 'one of the most essential sticks in the bundle of rights that are commonly characterized as property.' *Kaiser Aetna v. United States*, 444 U.S. 164, at 176, 179–180 (1979). Under the OST, Article XII prohibits this ability to exclude others, providing: 'All stations, installations, equipment and space vehicles on the Moon and other celestial bodies shall be open to representatives of other States Parties to the Treaty on a basis of reciprocity.'

words of a legal obligation: 'States *shall* facilitate and encourage international co-operation' (emphasis supplied).[13]

Province of all [hu]mankind

Article I paragraph 1 provides that 'The exploration and use of outer space, [...] shall be carried out for the benefit and in the interests of all countries, [...] and shall be the province of all [hu]mankind.'[14] Recall that at the time this Treaty was concluded, there were very few countries with the ability to launch objects into orbit; thus, the intention of this provision was to ensure that non-spacefaring countries around the world would also benefit from the discoveries and use of outer space.

Spacefaring nations have been intentional about sharing the benefits of outer space with non-spacefaring countries. Countless examples of this exist, ranging from telecommunications, weather forecasting, agriculture and land use, telemedicine, and the myriad benefits of knowledge-sharing provided by the internet.[15]

In sum, the key takeaways from this first article of the OST are that outer space is free for exploration and use by all States, but those freedoms are not unbridled. The benefits of space exploration are to be shared.

Article II: Non-appropriation principle

Article II of the OST comprises one elegant and unequivocal limitation on outer space – it is not subject to national appropriation. Specifically, Article II states: 'Outer space, including the Moon and other celestial bodies, is not subject to national appropriation by claim of sovereignty, by means of use or occupation, or by any other means.'

This prohibition on national appropriation has been considered 'a fundamental rule regulating the exploration and use of outer space.'[16] Some scholars even claim that this rule has crystallized into customary international law.[17]

---

[13] NASA's program of international cooperation in outer space is addressed in detail in Chapter 6.

[14] OST, *supra* note 1, art. I.

[15] 'Many [UN] delegates noted that the application of space technologies had improved efforts to manage disaster and natural resources, protect the environment, monitor oceans and climate, and eradicate poverty.' *Benefits of Exploration Crucial for Eradicating Poverty, Say Speakers, as Fourth Committee Takes up International Cooperation in Outer Space*, UNGA, GA/SPD/614, Oct. 13, 2016, https://www.un.org/press/en/2016/gaspd614.doc.htm.

[16] 1 COLOGNE COMMENTARY ON SPACE LAW: OUTER SPACE TREATY 45 (STEPHAN HOBE, BERNHARD SCHMIDT-TEDD, KAI-UWE SCHROGL EDS. 2009).

[17] Lyall/Larsen *supra* note 4, at 64. 'We would argue that certain elements of the OST have indeed passed into or now reflect customary international law.'

Nevertheless, scholars and students have spilled a disproportionate amount of ink analyzing this one sentence.

In the last decade this issue has raised a timely, public debate. Some contend that the Moon and neighboring asteroids contain enough natural resources to satiate Earth's needs for energy and wealth for decades to come.[18] There is interest in mining the Moon for its stores of Helium-3[19] and asteroids for platinum and other precious metals.[20] Setting aside the search for rare-Earth (or off-Earth) elements, NASA's Artemis program plans, combined with the exploration plans of other countries, would make the search and recovery of the hundreds of millions of tons of lunar water ice lucrative.[21] Recall that water can be used by astronauts for drinking or processed to make rocket fuel.

Investors are not going to spend incalculable sums to establish off-Earth mining operations if they will not be able to recover their investments. As a result, they have been seeking clarity regarding this legal situation and its impact on resource extraction opportunities.[22]

---

[18]   David Whitehouse, *Moon Map Aids Discovery*, BBC NEWS, Dec. 2, 1998, https://bbc.in/3bNClN7; Fabio Tronchetti, THE EXPLOITATION OF NATURAL RESOURCES OF THE MOON AND OTHER CELESTIAL BODIES: A PROPOSAL FOR A LEGAL REGIME, at 1–2, Martinus Nijhoff Publisher (2009).

[19]   Helium-3 'could provide safer nuclear energy in a fusion reactor, since it is not radioactive and would not produce dangerous waste products.' *Helium-3 mining on the lunar surface*, European Space Agency, https://www.esa.int/Enabling_Support/ Preparing_for_the_Future/Space_for_Earth/Energy/Helium-3_mining_on_the_lunar _surface (last visited Dec. 7, 2021).

[20]   Andrew Dempster, *Space Mining is Closer than You Think, and the Prospects are Great*, DIGG (June 28, 2019), https://digg.com/2015/space-mining-is-getting-closer.

[21]   Alan Boyle, *NASA will send VIPER rover to the moon to track down south pole's water ice*, Geekwire (Oct 25, 2019), https://www.geekwire.com/2019/nasa-plans-send -viper-rover-moon-2022-track-south-poles-ice/.

[22]   'In addition to the technical and financial challenges, considerable regulatory uncertainty surrounds the space mining industry. It remains an unsettled question whether international law allows for private ownership of asteroid resources.' Scot W Anderson, Korey Christensen & Julia LaManna, *The development of natural resources in outer space*, 37 J. of Energy & Nat. Resources Law 2, at 11 (Aug. 27, 2018).

When drafted in the post-colonial period of the 1960s,[23] Article II's prohibition on national appropriation 'by claim of sovereignty' was intended to 'protect outer space from national or exclusive colonization by States.'[24]

If there is any ambiguity in Article II, it concerns a difference in interpretation, regarding appropriation of extraterrestrial 'real estate' (in a layperson's use) versus minerals extracted from that 'real estate.' While some have suggested that Article II's ban on appropriation applies to the resources in outer space,[25] such a restrictive view could also interfere with the freedom to use and explore outer space provided in OST Article I.[26] The authors are aware of no State that has ever suggested that the U.S. violated Article II when it brought back lunar samples.[27] In an effort to explain the issue colloquially, some have framed the question in the context of the oceans: a State cannot own the high seas, but it can extract fish therefrom.[28]

As is its sovereign right, the U.S., for example, has interpreted OST Article II in such a way that it codifies established state practice while stimulating the private sector to explore outer space. Title IV of the 2015 Commercial Space Launch Competitiveness Act (CSLCA) recognizes ownership of space

---

[23] After World War II, many countries around the world were beginning to gain their independence from colonial rule. Just to give a very small sampling of this historical setting, of the post-WWII decolonization era: From France: these countries became independent: Lebanon (1946); Syria (1946); Cambodia (1953); From Malaysia: Singapore (1965); From the U.K.: India (1947); Israel (1948); Cyprus (1960); Kuwait (1960); Singapore (1965); Oman (1970); Bahrain and U.A.E. (1971). For more detailed information on this, *see*, *List of former Trust and Non-Self-Governing Territories*, UN, https://www.un.org/dppa/decolonization/en/history/former-trust-and-nsgts (last visited Dec. 7, 2021).

[24] CoCoSL, *supra* note 16, at 53.

[25] *See*, *e.g.*, STEPHEN GOROVE, STUDIES IN SPACE LAW: THE CHALLENGES AND PROSPECTS (A. W. Sithoff ed., 1977); Report of the 54th Conference of the International Law Association 434 (1970), U.N. Doc. A/AC.105/C.2/L.71; Tronchetti, *supra* note 18, at 220.

[26] Stephan Hobe and Philip de Man, *National Appropriation of Outer Space and State Jurisdiction to Regulate the Exploitation, Exploration and Utilization of Space Resources*, 66 ZEITSCHRIFT FUR LUFT- UND WELTRAUMRECHT 3, 462 (2017); PHILIP DE MAN, EXCLUSIVE USE IN AN INCLUSIVE ENVIRONMENT: THE MEANING OF THE NON-APPROPRIATION PRINCIPLE FOR SPACE RESOURCES EXPLOITATION, SPRINGER 305 (July 30, 2016).

[27] The U.S.S.R. also brought back lunar samples, and Japan has brought back asteroid samples. It appears that we now have established State practice that bringing back these scientific samples is permissible under international law.

[28] D. GOEDHUIS, SOME RECENT TRENDS IN THE INTERPRETATION AND THE IMPLEMENTATION OF THE RULES OF INTERNATIONAL SPACE LAW, 19(2) COLUM. J. TRANSNAT'L L. 213, 219 (1981); CARL Q. CHRISTOL, ARTICLE II OF THE OUTER SPACE TREATY REVISITED, 9 ANN. AIR & SPACE L. 217 (1984).

resources by citizens (and corporations) of the U.S. Luxembourg enacted a similar law in 2017.[29] The CSLCA states that U.S. citizens engaged in commercial recovery of an asteroid resource or a space resource 'shall be entitled to any asteroid resource or space resource obtained, including to possess, own, transport, use and sell the asteroid resource or space resource obtained in accordance with applicable law, including the international obligations of the United States.'[30] In so doing, the U.S. specifically does not assert sovereignty, sovereign or exclusive rights or jurisdiction over, or the ownership of, any celestial body.[31]

It is the view of the U.S. and other countries including Luxembourg, United Arab Emirates[32] and Japan,[33] which have all passed laws that are substantively similar, that States can appropriate the *resources* of the Moon and other celestial bodies, and doing so does not constitute a claim to the territory where such resources are located. These countries maintain the view that such resource appropriation is consistent with Article I's freedom of use and exploration. Moreover, the CSLCA itself specifies that it is to be interpreted and applied 'in accordance with applicable law, including the international obligations of the United States.'[34]

---

[29]   The Luxembourg Chamber of Deputies adopted a law on the exploration of space and the use of space resources on July 13, 2017; the Grand Duke signed the law on July 20, 2017. (Loi du 20 juillet 2017 sur l'exploration et l'utilisation des ressources de l'espace [Law of 20 July 2017 on the Exploration and Use of Space Resources], JOURNAL OFFICIEL DU GRAND-DUCHÉ DE LUXEMBOURG [OFFICIAL GAZETTE OF THE GRAND DUCHY OF LUXEMBOURG], No. 674 (July 28, 2017), LEGILUX; Draft Law on the Exploration and Use of Space Resources, SPACERESOURCES.LU (July 13, 2017).) This development makes Luxembourg the first European country to adopt a legal framework for private companies to extract resources from space.
[30]   Commercial Space Launch Competitiveness Act of 2015, 51 U.S.C. §§ 50901–50923 (2015).
[31]   *Id*, at § 51303.
[32]   Federal Law No. (12) of 2019 (On the Regulation of the Space Sector), Dec. 19, 2019 (Corresponding to 22 Rabi' Al-Akhar 1441H).
[33]   Law Concerning the Promotion of Business Activities Related to the Exploration and Development of Space Resources (Space Resources Act), No. 83 of 2021, art. 1 (Japan). *See also*, Jeff Foust, *Japan Passes Space Resources Law*, SpaceNews, June 17, 2021, https://spacenews.com/japan-passes-space-resources-law/.
[34]   51 U.S.C. § 51303.

Less than a month after the enactment of the CSLCA, the International Institute of Space Law (IISL) adopted, by consensus, a position paper supporting the U.S. view.[35] In relevant part, the IISL stated:

> [In] view of the absence of a clear prohibition of the taking of resources in the Outer Space Treaty one can conclude that the use of space resources is permitted. Viewed from this perspective, the new United States Act is a possible interpretation of the Outer Space Treaty. Whether and to what extent this interpretation is shared by other States remains to be seen. This is independent from the claim of sovereign rights over celestial bodies, which the United States explicitly does not make (Section 403). The purpose of the Act is to entitle its citizens to these resources if 'obtained in accordance with applicable law, including the international obligations of the United States'. The Act thus pays respect to the international legal obligations of the United States and applicable law on which the property rights to space resources will continue to depend.[36]

This issue is different from some of the internet 'entertainment' sites that purport to sell 'lunar real estate' or 'deeds' to Martian lands or asteroids. Unequivocally, those deeds do not have any legal validity. In fact, the IISL passed a resolution of sorts eviscerating any contention that deeds purporting to sell celestial real estate were valid. 'Hence, it is not sufficient for sellers of lunar deeds to point to national law, or the silence of national authorities, to justify their ostensible claims. The sellers of such deeds are unable to acquire legal title to their claims. Accordingly, the deeds they sell have no legal value or significance, and convey no recognized rights whatsoever.'[37]

---

[35] While it is a fundamental tenet of international law that only States (and tribunals) can interpret the treaties to which States are party, the opinion of academic organizations such as the IISL could be reflective of public perception of space-related legal issues.

[36] *Position Paper on Space Resource Mining: Adopted by consensus by the Board of Directors on 20 December 2015*, International Institute of Space Law [hereinafter IISL], https://www.iislweb.org/docs/SpaceResourceMining.pdf (last visited Dec. 7, 2021). *See also*, P.J. BLOUNT, *ONE SMALL STEP: THE IMPACT OF THE U.S. COMMERCIAL SPACE LAUNCH COMPETITIVENESS ACT OF 2015 ON THE EXPLOITATION OF RESOURCES IN OUTER SPACE*, 18 N. CAROLINA J. OF L. & TECH. 160 (2016), https://scholarship.law.unc.edu/cgi/viewcontent.cgi?article=1324&context=ncjolt. ('Although some have said that the CSLCA directly conflicts with Article II of the Outer Space Treaty, the CSLCA should be seen as a valid interpretation of Article II given the numerous ambiguities inherent in the article itself. More importantly, the CSCLA acts as an incremental mechanism in the formation of international space law...').

[37] *Statement by the Board of Directors of the International Institute of Space Law (IISL) On Claims to Property Rights Regarding The Moon and Other Celestial Bodies*, IISL, http://www.iislweb.org/docs/IISL_Outer_Space_Treaty_Statement.pdf (last visited Dec. 7, 2021).

Recall Article II of the OST prohibits 'national appropriation by claim of sovereignty, by means of use or occupation, or *by any other means*' (emphasis supplied). Efforts to interpret the phrase 'any other means' arise periodically in the practice of space law. Setting aside claims of appropriating celestial bodies themselves, the question has arisen in the context of exclusive use of a particular area of a celestial body.

For example, in October 2020, NASA signed the 'Artemis Accords' with eight other nations.[38] The Accords offer 'a practical set of principles, guidelines, and best practices to enhance the governance of the civil exploration and use of outer space.'[39] Section 11 of the Accords, 'Deconfliction of Space Activities,' brings up the concepts of 'safety zones' around spacecraft to prevent the activities of one State from interfering with another.[40] Such safety zones would be reasonable and measured for a particular operation on the lunar surface, and would be limited in duration and size. NASA has stressed that such safety zones are not exclusionary. Pursuant to Article XII of the OST,[41] facilities would remain open to inspection by other States, although NASA and the other Artemis Accords signatories would request advance notice from representatives of other States for safety purposes.[42]

---

[38]   Jeff Foust, *Eight countries sign Artemis Accords*, SPACE NEWS (Oct 13, 2020), https://spacenews.com/eight-countries-sign-artemis-accords/.

[39]   *See*, The Artemis Accords: Principles for Cooperation in the Civil Exploration and Use of the Moon, Mars, Comets, and Asteroids, Section 1, NASA (Oct. 13, 2020), https://www.nasa.gov/specials/artemis-accords/img/Artemis-Accords-signed -13Oct2020.pdf [hereinafter Accords].

[40]   As numerous countries (Russia, China, Japan, India, and the U.S. to name a few) have all expressed interest in operating near the lunar South Pole, it seems quite logical to avoid conflict and have 'due regard' for each other's activities. See discussion of OST Article IX below for more information.

[41]   'All stations, installations, equipment and space vehicles on the Moon and other celestial bodies shall be open to representatives of other States Parties to the Treaty on a basis of reciprocity. Such representatives shall give reasonable advance notice of a projected visit, in order that appropriate consultations may be held and that maximum precautions may be taken to assure safety and to avoid interference with normal operations in the facility to be visited.' OST, *supra* note 1, at art. XII.

[42]   'The Signatories commit to respect reasonable safety zones to avoid harmful interference with operations under these Accords, including by providing prior notification to and coordinating with each other before conducting operations in a safety zone established pursuant to these Accords.' Accords, *supra* note 29, at Section 11, para. 10.

Article III: In accordance with international law

Had there been any doubt previously, Article III makes clear that international law applies in outer space:

> States Parties to the Treaty shall carry on activities in the exploration and use of outer space, including the moon and other celestial bodies, in accordance with international law, including the Charter of the United Nations, in the interest of maintaining international peace and security and promoting international co-operation and understanding.

Article III is significant for several reasons. First, it requires States to maintain 'international peace and security' and promote 'international co-operation and understanding,' two principles found in the UN Charter.[43] Second, it calls on all States to act 'in the interest of maintaining international peace and security and promoting international co-operation and understanding,' which are the two essential principles of the Declaration on Principles of International Law concerning Friendly Relations and Cooperation among States in accordance with the Charter of the United Nations.[44]

The implication of 'international law' applying to the carrying on of 'activities in the exploration and use of outer space' is quite significant. International law is far broader than the treaties that a particular State might sign. International law includes all the rules of customary international law, and general principles including good faith and the doctrine of *pacta sunt servanda*, as well as principles of the UN Charter, such as the sovereign equality of States, the right of self-defense, and the prohibition on the use of force.

Article IV: No nukes in orbit

Recall that when the OST was signed, it was described to Congress and the American public as an arms control treaty. In fact, it was hailed as 'the Treaty banning nuclear weapons from outer space.'[45] In its first paragraph, Article IV works as a disarmament provision and builds on the Limited Nuclear Test Ban Treaty by prohibiting any State Party from placing 'in orbit around the Earth any objects carrying nuclear weapons or any other kinds of weapons of mass destruction.'[46] In its second paragraph, Article IV limits the use of the Moon

---

[43] Paul G. Dembling & Daniel M. Arons, *The Evolution of the Outer Space Treaty*, J. of Air L. & Com. 22 (1967).

[44] G.A. Res. 2625(XXV), Declaration on Principles of International Law concerning Friendly Relations and Cooperation among States in accordance with the Charter of the United Nations (Oct. 24, 1970), https://www.refworld.org/docid/3dda1f104.html (last visited Dec. 7, 2021).

[45] Pathé, *supra* note 1.

[46] OST, *supra* note 1, art. IV.

and other celestial bodies exclusively to peaceful purposes by prohibiting any State from stationing or installing any military fortification or testing any weaponry there.[47] In 1966, President Lyndon B. Johnson stated that Article IV of the OST was 'the most important arms control development since the 1963 treaty banning nuclear testing in the atmosphere, in space and under water.'[48]

It is important to highlight two peculiar features of this article. First, Article IV only explicitly prohibits weapons of mass destruction (WMD) in outer space and thus, by implication, permits other types of weapons.[49] Second, 'the prohibition contained in the first paragraph of Article IV applies to both outer space and celestial bodies, while the prohibition in the second paragraph [...] applies to celestial bodies only.'[50] The exclusion of outer space (the space between the Moon and other celestial bodies) from the second paragraph of Article IV was an acknowledgement of the realities of the Cold War.[51] Additional information about Article IV, WMDs, 'stationing' and 'orbiting' of nuclear weapons, differences between the words, 'peaceful' and 'nonaggressive,' and other aspects of the militarization and weaponization of outer space are discussed in greater detail in Chapter 13 of this book.

Article V: Protection of astronauts

Astronauts frequently spend their entire professional lives training for their missions, putting their very lives on the line to further the cause of scientific inquiry. Article V of the OST accords them special status, referring to them as

---

[47] 'The Moon and other celestial bodies shall be used by all States Parties to the Treaty exclusively for peaceful purposes. The establishment of military bases, installations and fortifications, the testing of any type of weapons and the conduct of military maneuvers on celestial bodies shall be forbidden.' *Id.*

[48] Max Frankel, *President Greets Accord as a Major Step to Peace; Says He Will Ask Quick Senate Action So U.S. Will Be Among First to Ratify – Sees Biggest Gain Since Test Ban PRESIDENT LAUDS ACCORD ON SPACE*, N.Y.T. (Dec. 9, 1966), https://www.nytimes.com/1966/12/09/archives/president-greets-accord-as-a-major -step-to-peace-says-he-will-ask.html.

[49] *See*, MICHEL BOURBONNIERE & RICKY LEE, LEGALITY OF THE DEPLOYMENT OF CONVENTIONAL WEAPONS IN EARTH ORBIT: BALANCING SPACE LAW AND THE LAW OF ARMED CONFLICT, 18 EUROPEAN J. OF INT'L. L. 873 (Nov. 2007), https://doi.org/10 .1093/ejil/chm051 (last visited Dec. 7, 2021).

[50] Dembling, *supra* note 43, at 433.

[51] 'The second paragraph of article IV states that the moon and other celestial bodies shall be used by the parties exclusively for peaceful purposes.... This is not an accidental omission.' STEPHEN GOROVE, ARMS CONTROL PROVISIONS IN THE OUTER SPACE TREATY: A SCRUTINIZING REAPPRAISAL, 3 GA. J. COMP. LAW 114, 117 (1973).

the 'envoys of [hu]mankind.' The two sentences comprising the first paragraph of Article V state that:

> States Parties to the Treaty shall regard astronauts as envoys of mankind in outer space and shall render to them all possible assistance in the event of accident, distress, or emergency landing on the territory of another State Party or on the high seas. When astronauts make such a landing, they shall be safely and promptly returned to the State of registry of their space vehicle.

The emergency situations laid out in paragraph 1 anticipate terrestrial scenarios, where States are required to render to astronauts 'all possible assistance in the event of accident, distress, or emergency landing' on their territory or on the high seas.[52] In such an instance, Article V also requires that a State 'safely and promptly return' the astronauts to their space vehicle's State of registry. While today, this may seem beyond argument, this was quite an issue in the middle of the Cold War. Recall that earlier in the 1960s, American Francis Gary Powers was shot down over the U.S.S.R. for spying in his U-2 aircraft.[53] The U.S. was concerned that if an American astronaut were to land behind the 'Iron Curtain,'[54] they could be arrested for spying and executed. The Soviets shared a reciprocal concern for their cosmonauts that might land in U.S. territory.

Article V's second paragraph simply states: 'In carrying on activities in outer space and on celestial bodies, the astronauts of one State Party shall render all possible assistance to the astronauts of other States Parties.' This obligation was expanded a year later in the 1968 Rescue and Return Agreement, which is elaborated on in the next chapter. Notably, this provision only applies to scenarios in space. It is in this spirit, as well as in furtherance of the 1968 Agreement to rescue astronauts that NASA's recent Artemis Accords contain a section on emergency assistance, where the signatories commit to take 'all reasonable efforts to render necessary assistance to personnel in outer space who are in distress.'[55]

---

[52] OST, *supra* note 1, at art V.1. This seemingly may constitute the first time that a multilateral agreement ever used the term 'astronaut.'

[53] For more on the U-2 program, the political risks it posed, details about Powers' flight and capture, his trial in the U.S.S.R., and his exchange for another Soviet spy held by the U.S. see, *Francis Gary Powers: U-2 Spy Pilot Shot Down by the Soviets*, Freedom of Information Act Electronic Reading Room, Central Intelligence Agency, https://www.cia.gov/readingroom/collection/francis-gary-powers-u-2-spy-pilot-shot-down-soviets (last visited Dec. 7, 2021).

[54] The Iron Curtain was a metaphor during the Cold War for the Soviet Bloc (or Eastern Bloc or Communist Bloc) countries effectively sealing themselves off from Western influence.

[55] Accords, *supra* note 29, at Section 6.

The last paragraph of Article V merely relates to information-sharing about discoveries of hidden dangers to astronauts in space. It provides that 'States Parties to the Treaty shall immediately inform the other States Parties to the Treaty or the Secretary-General of the United Nations of any phenomena they discover in outer space, including the Moon and other celestial bodies, which could constitute a danger to the life or health of astronauts.'

As discussed in the next chapter, while Article V considers astronauts to be the 'envoys of [hu]mankind,' the OST failed to provide any definition of the term.[56] When the OST was drafted, the drafters never contemplated that private, untrained, citizens would go to space on private vehicles, with essentially no government involvement. As a result, there is no legislative history discussing who would or would not be worthy of the title 'astronaut.'

Article VI: International responsibility

Article VI of the OST exemplifies a successful negotiation of the U.S. and U.S.S.R.'s very different perspectives. In the 1960s, the U.S. envisioned that the private sector would become increasingly involved in outer space activities,[57] while all space activities of the U.S.S.R. at that time were performed at the governmental level. The U.S.S.R.'s view from that time is reflected in this explicit sentence: 'All activities of any kind pertaining to the exploration and use of outer space shall be carried out solely and exclusively by States.'[58]

Article VI compels States to 'bear international responsibility for national activities in outer space,' whether they are carried out by governmental agencies or nongovernmental entities. Furthermore, States are responsible for assuring that the activities of their nationals 'are carried out in conformity with the provisions' of the OST.[59]

Article VI of the OST expressly stipulates that anything done by a nongovernmental entity in outer space 'is deemed to be an act imputable to the State as if it were its own act, for which it bears direct responsibility.'[60] Article VI's

---

[56] The standalone agreement written to rescue astronauts only uses that term in its title and not in its operative text.

[57] In fact, shortly after NASA was established in 1958, it began development of the Echo 1 satellite in coordination with AT&T's Bell Labs, which was launched on August 12, 1960.

[58] USSR: Draft Declaration of the Basic Principles Governing the Activities of States Pertaining to the Exploration and Use of Outer Space, U.N. Doc A/AC.105/L.2, pg. 2, para. 6 (Sept. 10, 1962), https://www.unoosa.org/pdf/limited/l/AC105_L002E .pdf; *See also*, International Co-operation in the Peaceful Uses of Outer Space: Report of the COPUOS, UN Doc A/5181 Annex III (Sept. 27, 1962).

[59] OST, *supra* note 1, at art. VI.

[60] BIN CHENG, *ARTICLE VI OF THE 1967 SPACE TREATY REVISITED: 'INTERNATIONAL RESPONSIBILITY', 'NATIONAL ACTIVITIES', AND 'THE APPROPRIATE STATE'*, 26 J. SPACE L. 1, at 15 (1998).

stipulation that a State is responsible for its national activities in outer space was a significant development in public international law.[61] A State could not avoid responsibility by disclaiming responsibility for the acts of its private citizens.[62]

The second sentence of Article VI provides the international legal keystone on which almost all U.S. national space law is built: 'The activities of non-governmental entities in outer space, including the Moon and other celestial bodies, *shall require authorization and continuing supervision* by the appropriate State Party to the Treaty'[63] (emphasis supplied). The Treaty does not tell States how to authorize or supervise the activities of their nationals – it only instructs that they are to be authorized and supervised.

The way most States implement their Article VI responsibilities is through national laws and regulations. Many States have domestic space legislation, including the U.S., U.K., France, Japan, Russia, Finland, Luxembourg, Japan, and Australia, to name a few. Those space laws, at least in the U.S., are detailed even further in hundreds of implementing regulations. The manner in which the U.S. authorizes and supervises the space activities of its nationals is detailed further in Chapters 6–10 of this book.

Article VII: International liability

In the 1960s, many nations were concerned that they could be damaged by space debris falling into their territory. Article VII makes clear that each State

---

[61] Report of the International Law Commission on the work of its fifty-third session, 23 April–1 June and 2 July–10 August 2001, Official Records of the General Assembly, Fifty-sixth session, Supplement No. 10, U.N. Doc. A/56/10 (2001), https://legal.un.org/ilc/documentation/english/reports/a_56_10.pdf (last visited Dec. 7, 2021). There is an entire corpus of international law dedicated to the establishment of what conduct is attributable to a state (e.g., conduct of organs of a state; conduct of persons exercising governmental authority; conduct directed or controlled by a State, etc.) as well as what constitutes the breach of an international obligation, and even responsibility of a state for acts conducted by another state.

[62] Outside of the domain of space law, 'States are internationally responsible for their own conduct only, i.e., for conduct of persons acting in the capacity of organs of a State. As a general rule, the conduct of private persons is not attributable to the State.' *See*, ALEXANDER KEES, RESPONSIBILITY OF STATES FOR PRIVATE ACTORS, MAX PLANCK ENCYCLOPEDIA OF PUB. INT'L. L. (RUDIGER WOLFRUM ED.), 959–964 (2011). *See also*, Jutta Brunneé, INTERNATIONAL LEGAL ACCOUNTABILITY THROUGH THE LENS OF THE LAW OF STATE RESPONSIBILITY, 36 NETHERLANDS YEARBOOK OF INT'L. L., 3–38 (2005).

[63] OST, *supra* note 1, art. VI, emphasis supplied.

that launches a space object is internationally liable for damage caused to another State. Specifically, it provides that:

> Each State Party to the Treaty that launches or procures the launching of an object into outer space, including the Moon and other celestial bodies, and each State Party from whose territory or facility an object is launched, is internationally liable for damage to another State Party to the Treaty or to its natural or juridical persons by such object or its component parts on the Earth, in air space or in outer space, including the Moon and other celestial bodies.

Liability generally means the 'legal obligation "to compensate another [...] for injury" following an event that causes damage.'[64] Launching objects into outer space is an inherently dangerous activity. Thus, strict liability attaches in certain circumstances and only requires the demonstration of causation and damage, without any requirement to prove fault.[65]

Article VII adopts this strict liability regime and imposes an obligation on a launching state to compensate any other State Party that is damaged by the launching State's space activities. To be precise, Article VII establishes that States that *launch* or *procure the launch* of an object (or from whose territory or facility an object is launched) are internationally liable for any damage to another State, its territory, or to the persons for whom that State is responsible. Article VII is only one sentence long. At the time the OST was being drafted, countries were simultaneously drafting more specific details for use in a subsequent treaty solely addressing the topic of international liability for outer space activities, the Convention on International Liability for Damage Caused by Space Objects. Details of that convention are provided in the next chapter.

There is a fundamental, substantive difference between the concept of Article VI (international responsibility) and Article VII (international liability). Article VI creates State responsibility for its actions as well as the actions of private citizens under that State's jurisdiction. Under Article VI, a State has essentially two responsibilities: to authorize and continually supervise the activities of its nationals; and to ensure that the 'national activities are carried out in conformity' with the provisions of the OST. Article VII on the other hand imposes a financial (or pecuniary) obligation to compensate (pay money to) another State for damages caused by its space objects. This strict liability, financial, obligation does not arise in Article VI.

---

[64] JOEL A DENNERLEY, STATE LIABILITY FOR SPACE OBJECT COLLISIONS: THE PROPER INTERPRETATION OF 'FAULT' FOR THE PURPOSES OF INTERNATIONAL SPACE LAW, 29 EUROPEAN J. OF INT'L. L., 281, 287 (Feb. 2018), https://doi.org/10.1093/ejil/chy003.

[65] BIN CHENG, INTERNATIONAL RESPONSIBILITY AND LIABILITY FOR LAUNCH ACTIVITIES, 20 AIR & SPACE L., at 15 (1995).

Article VIII: Registration of spacecraft

Historically speaking, registration was at least conceptually related to liability, but was more driven by a desire to have additional information on space objects. States wanted to have more visibility into what other States were launching into space, where such objects would be, and what their functions were. Article VIII requires launching States to register their space objects with the UN. Article VIII is brief, addressing three fundamental principles and, like the article on liability, supplemented with a specific convention, the Convention on Registration of Objects Launched into Outer Space (Registration Convention).[66]

The first sentence of Article VIII mandates that a State 'on whose registry an object launched into outer space is carried' shall retain jurisdiction and control over the object and its personnel.[67] This sentence allows countries that register space objects to exercise jurisdiction over the spacecraft as well the persons on that spacecraft. Under public international law, the general rule is that States have jurisdiction within their national boundaries. Thus, this article is an explicit recognition of a State's ability to exercise jurisdiction in areas beyond national jurisdiction,[68] even though outer space is 'not subject to national appropriation by claim of sovereignty.'[69] This article is very much in use today, e.g., when NASA or a U.S. commercial company launches foreign nationals on U.S.-registered vehicles, the U.S. can exert jurisdiction over individuals on the spacecraft.

While the Registration Convention is discussed in detail in the next chapter, it is worth noting that under Article VIII, a space object can only be registered by one State, meaning that only one State can have jurisdiction and control over that object. To have 'jurisdiction' over a space object means that a State can legislate and enforce its related laws and regulations, including civil and criminal laws. 'Control' over a spacecraft is different. For example, the International Space Station (ISS) is controlled by mission control centers in both Houston, Texas, and Moscow, Russia.[70] The concepts of jurisdiction

---

[66]   The Registration Convention is addressed in the next chapter.

[67]   OST, *supra* note 1, at art. VIII, emphasis supplied.

[68]   The territoriality principle in public international law enables a state to exercise jurisdiction (the ability to make and enforce laws) over natural and juridical persons in its territory. The famous PCIJ *Lotus* case (1927) concerned territorial jurisdiction (involving Turkish prosecution of a French sailor (the officer on watch) after the French boat collided with, and sunk the Turkish boat, killing ten Turkish mariners.) *See*, S.S. Lotus (Fr. V. Turk.), 1927 P.C.I.J. (ser. A) No. 10 (Sept. 7).

[69]   OST, *supra* note 1, at art. II.

[70]   'Crews aboard the ISS are assisted by mission control centers in Houston and Moscow and a payload control center in Huntsville, Ala. Other international mission control centers support the space station from Japan, Canada and Europe. The ISS can

and control are closely related to Article VI's responsibility to authorize and supervise national space activities, and Article VII's liability for space objects. They all must be read together for a comprehensive understanding of how they interact cohesively. Article VIII plays the important role of linking a State's international obligations under Articles VI and VII.

Article IX: Due regard, harmful interference and harmful contamination

Article IX, the OST's longest article, addressed a global concern that unrestricted space activity could result in contamination of outer space as well as the Earth's surface.[71] From 1961 to 1963, during the escalation of the Cold War, concerns quickly turned to fears as the U.S. and the U.S.S.R. began to increasingly conduct nuclear tests in the high atmosphere and other experiments in outer space of a military nature. The Soviet Union had conducted high-altitude nuclear tests in 1961 and 1962,[72] and the U.S. conducted its infamous 'Starfish Prime' and 'West Ford' experiments in 1962 and 1963.[73]

For this reason, Article IX begins with an exhortation for States 'to be guided by the general principle of cooperation and mutual assistance' followed immediately by the direction to 'conduct all their activities in outer space, including the Moon and other celestial bodies, with due regard to the corresponding

---

also be controlled from mission control centers in Houston or Moscow.' Elizabeth Howell, *International Space Station: Facts, History & Tracking*, Space.com, Oct. 13, 2021, https://www.space.com/16748-international-space-station.html.

[71] Report of the Ad Hoc Committee on the Peaceful Uses of Outer Space, U.N. Doc. A/4141, at 47 (July 14, 1959), https://digitallibrary.un.org/record/840867?ln=en.

[72] Anatoly Zak, THE 'K' PROJECT: Soviet Nuclear Tests in Space, 13 The Nonproliferation Rev. 143–150 (Feb. 18, 2007). To be clear, it was the U.S. that detonated the largest nuclear bomb in space, with its Starfish Prime experiment in 1962. It had the explosive force of 1.4 megatons (the equivalent of 1.4 *million* tons of TNT), and it detonated in space at an altitude of 400 km (240 miles) altitude. To put this into perspective, the bomb dropped on Hiroshima was approximately 1.4 kilotons, making Starfish Prime about 1,000 times more powerful. Reportedly, it turned the night sky bright red for seven minutes across the width of the Pacific Ocean, from Hawaii to Tonga. *See*, Phil Plait, *The 50th Anniversary of Starfish Prime: The Nuke that Shook the World*, Discover Magazine (July 9, 2012), https://www.discovermagazine.com/the-sciences/the-50th-anniversary-of-starfish-prime-the-nuke-that-shook-the-world.

[73] The 'West Ford Experiment,' or 'Project Needles,' as it is sometimes known, was an attempt by the U.S. to create an artificial ionosphere for telecommunications purposes to enable overseas military communications. At the time, international communication was dependent on submarine communication cables. In the event the U.S.S.R. crippled those cables, the military could bounce radio communication off Earth's artificial ionosphere – to do this, the U.S. placed 480 million copper dipole antennas in orbit – many of which remain in space to this day. *See*, Joe Hanson, *The Forgotten Cold War Plan That Put a Ring of Copper Around the Earth*, Wired.com (Aug. 13, 2013), https://www.wired.com/2013/08/project-west-ford/.

interests of all other States Parties.'[74] This obligation to have 'due regard' for the corresponding interests of other States Parties is an explicit limitation on the freedom to use and explore outer space guaranteed by OST Article 1.

The concept of 'due regard' originated from the Chicago Convention on Civil Aviation[75] and imposes an affirmative duty to operate in a manner considerate of other users of that space – e.g., military aircraft must operate with 'due regard' for civil aviation. The concept of 'due regard' is also well documented in the context of the Law of the Sea.[76]

In the context of space law, 'Article IX's due regard principle establishes an obligation upon signatories of the Outer Space Treaty to take the rights of other signatory States into account when exercising their own rights.'[77]

Closely related to the concept of due regard are two subsequent sentences that concern consultations. They provide that if a State believes that its activity or an activity of its nationals would cause 'potentially harmful interference' with the activities of other States Parties, then it shall undertake 'appropriate international consultations' before proceeding with the activity.[78] The obligation to consult is mandatory. Moreover, the Treaty gives potentially affected States the opportunity to request consultations if it has reason to believe that another State's activity could cause potentially harmful interference with its peaceful exploration and use of outer space.[79]

Article IX has not been frequently invoked by States Parties. Specifically, there have been instances where States may have alleged that other States failed to have due regard for their space activities, e.g., India's Mission Shakti ASAT test and resulting debris; China's Fengyun-C ASAT test; even the

---

[74] OST, *supra* note 1, art. IX.

[75] Convention on International Civil Aviation, *signed* Dec. 7, 1944, 61 Stat. 1180, 15 U.N.T.S. 295, at art. 3(d) [hereinafter Chicago Convention] ('The contracting States undertake, when issuing regulations for their state aircraft, that they will have due regard for the safety of navigation of civil aircraft.'); *See,* Michel Bourbonniere et al., Military Aircraft and International Law: Chicago Opus 3, 66 J. AIR L. & COM. 885, 913 (2001) ('The 'due regard' rule remains the principal treaty obligation imposed upon States for the regulation of the flight of military aircraft applicable during times of peace and armed conflict found within the Chicago Convention.').

[76] SHOTARO HAMAMOTO, THE GENESIS OF THE 'DUE REGARD' OBLIGATIONS IN THE UNITED NATIONS CONVENTION ON THE LAW OF THE SEA, 34 THE INT'L. J. OF MARINE AND COASTAL L. 7 (2019); *See,* JULIA GAUNCE, ON THE INTERPRETATION OF THE GENERAL DUTY OF 'DUE REGARD', 32 OCEAN YEARBOOK 27 (2017).

[77] JOHN S. GOEHRING, CAN WE ADDRESS ORBITAL DEBRIS WITH THE INTERNATIONAL LAW WE ALREADY HAVE? AN EXAMINATION OF TREATY INTERPRETATION AND THE DUE REGARD PRINCIPLE, 85 J. AIR L. & COM. 309, 317 (2020), https://scholar.smu.edu/jalc/vol85/iss2/4.

[78] OST, *supra* note 1, art. IX, emphasis supplied.

[79] *Id.*

U.S.'s Operation Burnt Frost.[80] States did make public statements condemning these activities, however no country appears to have presented a claim to the responsible State asserting an Article IX violation.[81]

Apart from having 'due regard' for other States' activities as well as the obligation to undertake or request consultations, the last major takeaway from Article IX is the obligation to avoid harmfully contaminating space. That includes forward and backward contamination. 'Forward' contamination refers to contaminating other planets by Earth microbes,[82] and backward contamination refers to bringing extraterrestrial matter back to planet Earth in a manner that would adversely change Earth's environment with extraterrestrial matter. In relevant part, Article IX provides that:

> States Parties to the Treaty shall pursue studies of outer space, including the Moon and other celestial bodies, and conduct exploration of them so as to avoid their harmful contamination and also adverse changes in the environment of the Earth resulting from the introduction of extraterrestrial matter ...

Article IX has been interpreted in different ways, from the 'policy of protecting pristine celestial environments,'[83] to 'the duty to prevent biological contamination of celestial bodies with potential biological interest, as well as the duty to prevent biological back contamination of the Earth's biosphere as a result of introducing extraterrestrial materials.'[84] Policies to implement Article IX obligations are often referred to as 'planetary protection' policies.

In 2002, the Committee on Space Research (COSPAR) and the International Astronomical Union (IAU) created the first planetary protection plan, which

---

[80]   See Chapter 12 for discussion of all three of these debris-generating events.

[81]   On November 15, 2021, the NASA Administrator condemned harshly the Russian anti-satellite test of earlier that day, calling the action 'irresponsible,' 'destabilizing,' 'unthinkable,' 'reckless,' and 'dangerous.' However, neither he nor U.S. Secretary of State Blinken asserted a violation of OST Article IX. *See*, Marc Etkind & Jackie McGuinness, *NASA Administrator Statement on Russian ASAT Test*, NASA, Nov. 15, 2021, https://www.nasa.gov/press-release/nasa-administrator-statement-on-russian-asat-test.

[82]   The primary reason that the scientific community wishes to protect the space environment from forward contamination is to preserve 'the integrity of the scientific exploration of outer space, including the search for life.' Cheney et al., *Planetary Protection in the New Space Era: Science and Governance,* Front. Astron. Space Sci., Nov. 13, 2020, https://doi.org/10.3389/fspas.2020.589817.

[83]   L. Tennen, *Evolution of the planetary protection policy: conflict of science and jurisprudence?*, 34 Advances in Space Rsch. 2354 (2004), https://www.sciencedirect.com/science/article/abs/pii/S0273117704002935?via%3Dihub.

[84]   Rafael Moro-Aguilar, *Law and Living in the Moon: International Coordination – Role of the UN/COPUOS,* (July 7, 2016), http://www.mat.ucm.es/~aegora/eventos/escorial2016/Instibaerospa%20-%20Rafael%20Moro.pdf.

was updated in July 2020.[85] The plan divides missions and resulting planetary protection levels into five categories. The likelihood of finding biological traces of the origins of life drives the level of requirements.[86] NASA has a dedicated Office of Planetary Protection and numerous internal requirements to preserve the sanctity of its scientific research.[87]

Article XI: Transparency

Article XI of the OST requires States to inform the world about their scientific discoveries. Specifically, Article XI places an obligation on States to inform the UN Secretary-General, the international scientific community, and the public 'of the nature, conduct, locations and results of' their activities in space.[88] Article XI then requires the Secretary-General to 'be prepared to disseminate it immediately and effectively.'[89]

Sharing the nature, conduct, and location of activities fosters greater global participation in space exploration and furthers science. Data-sharing is part of the scientific method and contributes to scientific progress and understanding.[90] It is also one method through which spacefaring nations fulfill one of the central tenets of the first article of the OST – that space activities are carried out 'for the benefit and in the interests of all countries.'[91]

NASA's international agreements always have an article dedicated to distribution of scientific results to the public.[92] In fact, the recent Artemis Accords have two sections devoted to transparency. It states that '[t]he Signatories

---

[85] *COSPAR Policy on Planetary Protection*, Comm. on Space Rsch., Int'l Council for Sci. Unions, June 17, 2020, https://cosparhq.cnes.fr/assets/uploads/2020/07/PPPolicyJune-2020_Final_Web.pdf.

[86] For example, the NASA-ESA Mars Sample Return mission, in which samples of Martian soil will be returned to Earth, NASA and ESA have spent thousands of hours planning and engineering to ensure that they reduce any chance of a Martian microbe contaminating Earth's environment to a less than 1/1,000,000 chance. *See, Mars Sample Return*, Jet Propulsion Lab., NASA, https://www.jpl.nasa.gov/missions/mars-sample-return-msr (last visited Dec. 7, 2021).

[87] *See, Planetary Protection*, Office of Planetary Protection, Office of Safety and Mission Assurance, NASA, https://sma.nasa.gov/sma-disciplines/planetary-protection/ (last visited Dec. 7, 2021).

[88] OST, *supra* note 1, at art. XI.

[89] *Id.*

[90] Carol Tenopir, et al., *Data Sharing by Scientists: Practices and Perceptions*, Nat'l Library of Med., June 29, 2011.

[91] 'The exploration and use of outer space, including the Moon and other celestial bodies, shall be carried out for the benefit and in the interests of all countries, irrespective of their degree of economic or scientific development, and shall be the province of all mankind.' OST, *supra* note 1, art. I.

[92] See Chapter 6 for more about the content of NASA's international agreements.

plan to share scientific information resulting from their activities pursuant to these Accords with the public and the international scientific community on a good-faith basis, and consistent with Article XI of the Outer Space Treaty.'[93] It also provides for the release of scientific data: 'The Signatories are committed to the open sharing of scientific data. The Signatories plan to make the scientific results obtained from cooperative activities under these Accords available to the public and the international scientific community, as appropriate, in a timely manner.'[94] NASA works with space agencies around the globe to encourage them to have similar policies on sharing scientific data publicly and at no cost.[95] Setting aside earth science data, informing the public about a potential impact of an oncoming asteroid is addressed in Chapter 14 of this book.

Final articles

The OST is open to all States, and any State 'may accede to it at any time.'[96] The depositary governments[97] are the U.S.S.R., the United Kingdom, and the United States.[98] States that join the treaty after its entry into force are bound starting 'on the date of the deposit of their instruments of ratification or accession,' which are given to the depositary governments.[99] Any State Party to the OST may withdraw on one year's written notice to the depositary governments.[100] Subsequent articles of the OST provide information about amendments, authentic languages, and other entry into force details that need not be addressed here.

---

[93] Accords, *supra* note 29, at Section 4.

[94] *Id.*, at Section 8.2.

[95] 'NASA's Earth Science Data Systems (ESDS) Program defines open science as a collaborative culture enabled by technology that empowers the open sharing of data, information, and knowledge within the scientific community and the wider public to accelerate scientific research and understanding.' Earth Science Data Systems Program, *Open Science*, Earth Data, NASA, https://earthdata.nasa.gov/esds/open-science (last visited Dec. 7, 2021).

[96] OST, *supra* note 1, at art. XIV.1.

[97] Depositary governments keep original texts of the treaty, facilitate their signatures, and receive instruments relating to the treaties, such as instruments of ratification. *See*, Office of Treaty Affairs, *Treaties for Which the United States is Depositary*, U.S. Department of State, https://www.state.gov/depositary-information/ (last visited Dec. 7, 2021). One advantage of a State being a depositary, as opposed to the UN Secretary General, is that non-UN Member States can become party more easily.

[98] OST, *supra* note 1, at art. XIV. 2.

[99] OST, *supra* note 1, at art. XIV. 3.

[100] Art. XVI provides a mechanism for withdrawal, although no State has withdrawn from the OST.

QUESTIONS FOR REVIEW

1. You learned that outer space exploration is to be carried out for the benefit and in the interests of all countries, and that it is the province of all humankind. Can you explain how non-spacefaring nations benefit from space exploration?

2. Article II of the OST prohibits 'national appropriation' by means of use, sovereignty, or by any other means. If nations cannot appropriate outer space, how can countries like the U.S. (or Japan or Luxembourg) authorize their citizens to be able to extract lunar ice or rare-Earth minerals from the Moon and other celestial bodies? Would your answer change if the extraction is for an astronaut drinking water versus a jeweler desiring platinum?

3. Can you cogently explain the differences between responsibility and liability (OST Articles VI and VII)?

4. Outer space is free for use and exploration by all states. What limitations on those freedoms can be found in the OST?

5. The OST was drafted more than 50 years ago. It doesn't specifically address many of the technological advancements of the last decades. Do you think it is still valuable? Should it be discarded and replaced by a new Treaty?

4. Additional sources of international space law

Last week Ruth lectured on the Outer Space Treaty at Georgetown Law. She thought it went well – once she overcame her nervousness, she really enjoyed the experience. To her delight, many of the students emailed her over the following week seeking advice and asking questions, which she answered with great pleasure.

To Ruth's great surprise and delight, the professor of the Space Law course also followed up and invited her back to give another lecture! 'The students loved your class so much that they asked if you could come back to talk about other treaties and sources of space law beyond the OST.'

She reflects on the questions that some of the students had asked her: What if one satellite collides with another satellite or falls from the sky? Who is liable? If there's no sovereignty in space, what governs behavior on the International Space Station or on the Moon?

A second lecture would be a great opportunity to reply to these questions in some depth. She smiles and readily accepts the invitation.

ELABORATING ON THE OUTER SPACE TREATY

The importance of the Outer Space Treaty (OST) cannot be understated. However, it is not the only space law treaty with which a practitioner needs familiarity. The OST is a treaty of principles that established a foundation upon which four subsequent treaties were built. When the UN Committee on the Peaceful Uses of Outer Space (COPUOS) adopted the OST, it recognized that further treaties would be required to expand upon specific OST principles.[1] This chapter explores the essential aspects of those treaties. In addition, other international organizations and multilateral initiatives also evolved to create international space law. This chapter will explore many of the other international agreements that govern space activities, including the international agreement that governs the design and operation of the International Space Station (ISS).

---

[1] ALBERT K. LAI, THE COLD WAR, THE SPACE RACE, AND LAW OF OUTER SPACE: SPACE FOR PEACE (Routledge eds., 2021).

THE RESCUE AGREEMENT[2]

General Overview

After the OST entered into force, the COPUOS turned its attention to the rescue and return of astronauts. The safety of astronauts became a prime topic in 1967 after two fatal accidents. The first was the Apollo 1 fire on January 27, 1967 – the same day as the signing ceremony for the OST. Gus Grissom, Edward White, and Roger Chaffee perished inside a command module on the ground at Cape Canaveral. A few months later, on April 24, 1967, Soviet cosmonaut Vladimir Komarov died in Soyuz 1 when – after a series of other problems with the spacecraft – the parachute failed to deploy properly after reentry. These accidents highlighted the dangers faced by astronauts and provided the U.S. and the U.S.S.R. at least one topic upon which they could find common ground.

The Agreement on the Rescue of Astronauts, the Return of Astronauts, and the Return of Objects Launched into Outer Space (Rescue Agreement) was considered and negotiated by the Legal Subcommittee from 1962 to 1967. In fact, the U.S. and the U.S.S.R. completed the final draft themselves and presented it to the COPUOS at a special session in December 1967. Their approach incensed non-aligned nations, especially India, which complained that the U.S. and U.S.S.R. were presenting the Rescue Agreement to COPUOS for adoption as a *fait accompli*.[3] Going forward, non-aligned nations would insist on inclusion in the development of outer space law. Indeed, the Rescue Agreement was the last treaty for which either the U.S.S.R. or the U.S. was the principal drafter.[4] Nevertheless, the Agreement entered into force in December 1968 and elaborates on Articles V and VIII of the OST.

---

[2]   Agreement on the Rescue of Astronauts, the Return of Astronauts, and the Return of Objects Launched into Outer Space (1968), 672 U.N.T.S. 119; 19 U.S.T. 7570.

[3]   History repeated itself in the early 2010s, when India accused the Europeans of presenting their 2008 European Code of Conduct (ECOC) to the UN as a *fait accompli*. This accusation sounded the death knell of the ECOC. *See* Zenco, *A Code of Conduct for Outer Space*, COUNCIL ON FOREIGN RELATIONS (Nov. 30, 2011), https://www.cfr .org/report/code-conduct-outer-space. 'Brazil, Russia, India, and China – have indicated that they might not sign the EU code because they were insufficiently consulted in its development...'

[4]   UN COPUOS Legal Sub-Committee, *Draft Agreement on the Rescue of Astronauts, the Return of Astronauts, and the Return of Objects Launched into Outer Space*, U.N. Doc. A/AC.105/C.2/L.28 (Dec. 12, 1967); UN COPUOS, *Verbatim Records*, U.N. Docs. A/AC.105/PV.30 (Nov. 2, 1964), 12 (Brazil), 14 (India), 19 (Lebanon).

Key Principles of the Rescue Agreement

The Rescue Agreement establishes several obligations for States with regard to astronauts and spacecraft, which are briefly explained below.

Duty to notify state of distress or accident (Article 1)

Article V of the OST establishes that States shall render 'all possible assistance [to astronauts] in the event of accident, distress, or emergency landing on the territory of another State Party or on the high seas.' It does not establish an obligation to notify the launching state of any accidents or emergency landings involving humans and/or spacecraft. The Rescue and Return Agreement clarifies the scope of the obligation: if the *'personnel of a spacecraft* (emphasis added) have suffered accident or are experiencing conditions of distress or have made an emergency or unintended landing in territory under its jurisdiction or on the high seas or in any other place not under the jurisdiction of any State' the contracting party that discovers or receives information about such situation of distress shall do two things:

(a)   Notify the launching authority,[5] or if this is not possible, make a public announcement.
(b)   Notify the UN Secretary General, so that they may disseminate the information of the distress-causing event.

The term 'personnel of a spacecraft' is broader than the term astronaut. Note that the word 'astronaut' is not defined in the Treaty: in fact, the only place it appears is in the Treaty's title.[6]

Duty to render assistance (Articles 2 and 3)

Articles 2 and 3 address rendering assistance to astronauts in distress. The U.S. and the U.S.S.R. were legitimately concerned that if their astronauts were to

---

[5]   The term 'launching authority' is defined in art. 6 of the Rescue Agreement as the State or international organization responsible for launching. It is unique to the Rescue Agreement. Both the Liability Convention and the Registration Convention use the term 'launching State' instead, although the definition remains the same. The term 'launching authority' also includes international organizations as long as they have accepted the rights and obligations established by the Rescue Agreement, and the majority of their members are State Parties to it. The Convention on International Liability for Damage Caused by Space Objects (1972), 961 U.N.T.S. 187, 24 U.S.T. 2389 [*hereinafter* LIAB].

[6]   Steven A. Mirmina, Astronauts Redefined: The Commercial Carriage of Humans to Space and the Changing Concepts of Astronauts under International and U.S. Law, 10 FIU L. REV. 669 (2015), https://ecollections.law.fiu.edu/lawreview/vol10/iss2/17.

alight in the other's territory, they might be considered spies and jailed. This concern escalated after the 1960 U-2 incident, in which U.S. pilot Francis Gary Powers was shot down when flying over Soviet territory taking aerial reconnaissance photographs.[7] The Treaty requires States Parties to use 'all possible steps' to rescue personnel of a spacecraft and render them all necessary assistance. Article 3 establishes that a State shall help if in a position to do so. States are not required to go beyond the limit of their capabilities.[8] Article 2 applies if such personnel alight in a State's territory, while Article 3 applies even beyond that, to territories that are not under the jurisdiction of any State, such as the high seas. Personnel who may need assistance in outer space, rather than on Earth, fall within the scope of Article V, para. 2 of the OST.

Duty to return (Article 4)
Once personnel have been found outside of their territory owing to accident, distress, emergency, or unintended landing, they must be returned to representatives of the launching authority. This duty to return is without conditions; as such, this duty remains even if the personnel have allegedly committed a crime or have requested political asylum.

Duty to notify the discovery of a space object and duty to return (Article 5)
As with space personnel, the Rescue Agreement also establishes the duty to notify the discovery of space objects as well as a duty to return them to their launching authority.

The term 'space object' also appears in the OST, Liability Convention and Registration Convention. A space object includes its component parts as well as its launch vehicle and parts thereof, as defined in the Liability and Registration Conventions. As such, this definition includes space debris, if it can be determined to which launching authority it belongs.

If a space object is found in the jurisdiction of a State party to the convention or in a territory beyond the jurisdiction of any State, the finder must notify the launching authority. Unlike personnel of a spacecraft, there is no explicit obligation to recover another State's space objects – it is only at a State's discretion, and only upon the request of (and at the expense of) the launching authority. This Treaty has governed numerous situations when payloads or

---

[7]   For details regarding the Soviet shooting down of the U.S. spy plane overflying its territory, *see*, Francis Gary Powers & Curt Gentry, Operation Overflight: A Memoir of the U-2 Incident (2004).

[8]   Eric R. C. van Bogaert, *Aspects of Space Law,* Kluwer Law and Taxation Publishers 108 (1986).

rocket components splashed down or washed up in another nation's territory.[9] In the U.S., the State Department provides notice and assistance coordinating the recovery of such space objects, as discussed in Chapter 11.

THE LIABILITY CONVENTION

General Overview

Between 1968 and 1971, COPUOS focused almost exclusively on drafting the Convention on International Liability for Damage Caused by Space Objects (Liability Convention).[10] The negotiations were often arduous because of the necessity of precise and technical language for a treaty in which States were agreeing to accept liability.[11]

Several incidents of falling space debris during the period of negotiations highlighted the Convention's necessity. For example, on June 5, 1969, debris from a suspected Soviet launch struck the Japanese freighter *Dai Chi Chinei*, damaging the vessel and injuring five crew members. This is the only recorded incident of falling space objects injuring people.[12] In August 1970, several Soviet space objects ranging from 50 to 200 pounds fell near Pratt, Kansas; Beaver City, Oklahoma; and Adrian, Texas.[13]

The Liability Convention became the first space treaty negotiated principally by States other than the U.S.S.R. or the U.S. Instead, Belgium, Hungary, and India took leading roles. India attempted to shepherd negotiations by hosting an informal conference in New Delhi that helped focus COPUOS on the key issues that had to be resolved, particularly the requirement for binding arbitration of disputes. After years of negotiation, it became clear that the U.S.S.R. would not accept binding arbitration. To resolve this impasse, COPUOS reached a consensus to resolve liability through a Claims

---

[9]   *See* Dan Leone, *SpaceX to Retrieve Fairing that Washed Up in Bahamas*, SPACE NEWS (June 3, 2015), https://spacenews.com/spacex-to-retrieve-fairing-that-washed-up -in-bahamas/.

[10]   LIAB, *supra* note 5.

[11]   Comm. on the Peaceful Uses of Outer Space, Report of the Legal Subcomm. on Its Tenth Session, U.N. Doc. A/AC.105/94 (1971); Comm. on the Peaceful Uses of Outer Space, Rep. of the Legal Subcomm. on Its Seventh Session, U.N. Doc. A/ AC.105/45 (1968).

[12]   U.N. COPUOS, 6th Sess., 15th mtg. at 33–4, 36, 38, U.N. Docs. A/AC.105/PV.15 (Sept. 14, 1962); *Spacecraft Debris Hits Freighter*, 42 PITTSBURGH POST-GAZETTE 291 (July 5, 1969).

[13]   Permanent Rep. of the U.S. to the U.N., Letter dated Sept. 10, 1970, from the Permanent Rep. of the United States address to the Secretary-General, U.N. Doc. A/ AC.105/87 (Sept. 10, 1970).

Commission. On November 29, 1971, the U.N. General Assembly endorsed the Liability Convention for adoption by States.[14]

The only instance in which a claim was presented under the Liability Convention was in 1978, when the U.S.S.R.'s Cosmos 954 nuclear-powered ocean surveillance spacecraft crashed into northern Canada.[15] The Canadian government filed for slightly more than C$6 million in claims against the U.S.S.R. to compensate the Canadian government for environmental damage and clean-up costs.[16] In the end, the U.S.S.R. settled the claim with Canada by making an 'ex gratia' payment of C$3 million,[17] thereby avoiding the establishment of a claims commission under the Liability Convention.[18]

Key Principles of the Liability Convention

Liability

Liability is the compensation of an injured party for damages. The causing of damages is not against international law.[19] However, there is a general duty to compensate an injured party for damages caused.[20] Under the Liability Convention, only States may be held liable for damages.[21] Claims may only be made by States who suffer damage or whose nationals suffer damages, and only for the damages caused by other States. Private citizens have no right of action against their own launching state.[22]

---

[14]   G.A. Res. 2777 (XXVI), Convention on International Liability for Damage Caused by Space Objects (Nov. 29, 1971).

[15]   *See* Joseph Burke, *Convention on International Liability for Damage Caused by Space Objects: Definition and Determination of Damages After the Cosmos 954 Incident*, 8 FORDHAM INT'L L.J. 2 (1984).

[16]   Alexander F. Cohen, *Cosmos 954 and the International Law of Satellite Accidents*, 10 YALE J. INT'L L. 78 (1984).

[17]   Canada: Claim Against the Union of Soviet Socialist Republics for Damage Caused by Soviet Cosmos 954, 18 I.L.M. 899, 907 (1979).

[18]   Settlement of Claim between Canada and the Union of Soviet Socialist Republics for Damage Caused by 'Cosmos 954' (April 2, 1981), available at https://www.jaxa.jp/library/space_law/chapter_3/3-2-2-1_e.html.

[19]   2 COLOGNE COMMENTARY ON SPACE LAW 124 (Stephan Hobe, Bernhard Schmidt-Tedd, Kai-Uwe Schrogl eds., 2009) [*hereinafter* Cologne Commentary].

[20]   In this sense, 'the term "responsibility" should be used only in connection with internationally wrongful acts and that, with reference to the possible injurious consequences arising out of the performance of certain lawful activities, the more suitable term "liability" should be used.' *Summary Records of the 25th Session*, [1973] 1 Y.B. Int'l L. Comm'n 211, U.N. Doc. A/CN.4/SER.A/1973.

[21]   *See* LIAB, *supra* note 5, Art. VII–XI.

[22]   *Id.*

Definitions (Article I)
Article I of the Liability Convention defines the key terms used in its text:

- Damage – is defined to include: (i) loss of life; (ii) physical injury; and (iii) loss of, or damage to, property. This definition does not appear to cover lost profits.[23] Indirect damages are not explicitly within the scope of the definition. While the drafters omitted indirect damages from the definition, the *travaux préparatoires* may indicate otherwise,[24] although Article 32 of the Vienna Convention on the Law of Treaties (VCLT) recommends that reference to a treaty's preparatory text only be made when a treaty's text is unclear or leads to a manifestly absurd result.
- Launching – includes both successful as well as attempted launches, even if a space object does not reach outer space.
- Launching State – can be (i) the State that launches or procures the launch of the space object; or (ii) the State from whose territory or facility the object is launched. Of these potentially four (or more) possible launching States in each launch, there is no hierarchical weight given to one over the other.[25]

Types of liability (Articles II–V)
Under the Liability Convention, a launching State may be liable if it has caused an accident, even if it did everything perfectly:

1. Absolute liability (Article II) – if a space object causes damage to an object 'on the surface of the Earth or to aircraft in flight,' the launching State of that space object shall be absolutely liable. Under this absolute

---

[23] Although some scholars have purported to argue that indirect profits are covered. *See* Tanja L. Zwaan & Walter DeVries, *Liability Aspects of the International Space Station Agreement of 29 September 1988*, 32 COLLOQUIUM L. OUTER SPACE 445, 447 (1989). One tribunal had held that profit would be recoverable as damages unless it 'come[s] under the heading of possible but contingent and indeterminate damage.' Factory at Chorzów (Ger. v. Pol.), Indemnity, 1928 P.C.I.J. (ser. A) No. 17, at 57 (Sept. 13).

[24] Comm. on the Peaceful Uses of Outer Space, Report of the Legal Subcomm. on Its Seventh Session, U.N. Doc. A/AC.l05/C.2/SR.94 (1968). Looking at the object and purpose of the Treaty serves to further corroborate this point: the Liability Convention is a victim-oriented treaty, with a primary aim of compensating individuals for damages caused by spacefaring activities. Armel Kerrest, *Liability for Damage Caused by Space Objects*, in SPACE LAW: CURRENT PROBLEMS & PERSPECTIVES FOR FUTURE REGULATION 92 (Marietta Benkö & Kai-Uwe Schrogl eds., 2005).

[25] *Cologne Commentary*, *supra* note 19, at 109.

standard, a State must compensate a victim State for damages, whether or not the launching State was negligent.[26]

2. Fault-based liability (Article III) – regarding 'damage being caused elsewhere than on the surface of the Earth to a space object of one launching State or to persons or property on board such a space object by a space object of another launching State,' the standard is fault-based liability. To determine the existence of fault, a tribunal (or commission) applying the Convention would assess the specific facts of the case as well as the conduct of the launching State.

A launch may involve multiple launching States, and, according to the Liability Convention, each may be held jointly and severally liable for damage.[27] Specifically, a claimant may pursue its claim against any of the launching States, each of which could be 100% responsible for paying the claim. After the claimant is compensated, any division or proportion of liability among the defendant launching States could be addressed subsequently.

THE REGISTRATION CONVENTION

General Overview

The Convention on Registration of Objects Launched into Outer Space ('Registration Convention') was the fourth COPUOS drafted space treaty to enter into force.[28] Its history is tied to damage caused by space debris that fell in New Zealand between April 3 and May 12, 1972, from a suspected Soviet spacecraft.[29] When New Zealand attempted to return the debris to the U.S.S.R. under the Rescue Agreement, the U.S.S.R. denied responsibility. Although there was no direct damage from the Soviet debris, New Zealand and other members of the COPUOS complained that the incident demonstrated the need for a Registration Convention to allow victim States to identify the

---

[26] There is one minor exception to Article II's absolute liability standard. Article VI of the Convention exonerates a launching State for damage if it can prove that 'the damage has resulted either wholly or partially from gross negligence or from an act or omission done with intent to cause damage on the part of a claimant State or of natural or juridical persons it represents.'

[27] 'Whenever two or more States jointly launch a space object, they shall be jointly and severally liable for any damage caused.' LIAB, *supra* note 5, Art. V.

[28] Convention on Registration of Objects Launched into Outer Space (1975), 28 U.S.T. 695, 1023 U.N.T.S. 15 [*hereinafter* Registration Convention].

[29] *New Light on Mysterious Space Balls* N.Z. Herald (Aug. 23, 2002), https://www.nzherald.co.nz/nz/new-light-on-mysterious-space-balls/VYQ6S2Q IC4QREO55ERXWVIKNSI/.

source of any space object that may harm them. The COPUOS completed the Registration Convention in 1974.[30]

Key Principles of the Registration Convention

Definitions (Article I)
The Registration Convention defines the terms 'launching State' and 'space object' the same as in the Liability Convention. However, the Registration Convention introduces a new term – 'State of registry' – which refers to 'a launching State on whose registry a space object is carried.'

Types of registration and the information to provide
The Registration Convention establishes two different types of space object registers. The first one is maintained by each State, whereas the second one is maintained by the UN Secretary General.

- National Registry (Article II): State Parties are bound to maintain a national register of space objects launched. Joint launching States must determine which of them shall register the object. States must inform the UN Secretary General of the establishment of their registries, but the content of each registry is determined by each State.
- UN Register (Article III): Even though national registries can contain whatever details each State deems necessary, Article IV requires States to submit the following information about their space objects to the UN Secretary General, who shall maintain an open-access register, available to all States:
    - Name of launching State or States;[31]
    - An appropriate designator of the space object or its registration number;
    - Date and territory or location of launch;
    - Basic orbital parameters, including:
        - Nodal period;
        - Inclination;
        - Apogee;
        - Perigee;

---

[30] *Registration Convention, supra* note 28; Paul P. Heller, *Man-Made U.F.O.s – The Problem of Identifying the Launching State of a Space Object*, 7 INT'L LAW. 900 (1973).

[31] This includes States that are not the State of registry, but that are nevertheless launching States.

- General function of the space object.[32]

States are to provide the abovementioned information to the UN 'to the greatest extent feasible and as soon as practicable.'[33] Although the UN has encouraged States to clean up their registration practices,[34] compliance is not uniform. States' compliance with this treaty has waxed and waned over time, with only about 87% of objects being registered with the UN.[35]

Apart from the Registration Convention itself, there is another international registry used by States not party to the Registration Convention. UNGA Resolution 1721B created an international registry for space objects back in 1961.[36] When States register their objects with the UN, they can do so pursuant to either the Registration Convention or the UNGA Resolution.

One final note about the Registration Convention. While its original purpose was to provide a means to identify space objects, it is of less practical use today in space object identification. The data reported in each registry is historic – the objects are not stationary when placed into outer space.[37] More useful information about identifying objects (for either liability purposes or for accident avoidance, i.e., space situational awareness (SSA) or space traffic management (STM)) may be found through publicly available data from either industry consortia or provided by governments such as the U.S. Department of Defense (DOD).[38]

---

[32] This may be described in a very vague and abstract manner, especially for military satellites, some of which merely list 'earth observation,' a moniker for reconnaissance.

[33] *Registration Convention, supra* note 28, Art. IV(3).

[34] *See* G.A. Res. 62/101, Recommendations on Enhancing the Practice of States and International Intergovernmental Organizations in Registering Space Objects (Jan. 10, 2008).

[35] *See* Off. Outer Space Aff., *Space Object Register*, U.N., https://www.unoosa.org/oosa/en/spaceobjectregister/index.html (last updated Oct. 14, 2021).

[36] G.A. Res. 1721 (XVI), International Cooperation in the Peaceful Uses of Outer Space (Dec. 20, 1961).

[37] 'To compound the incompleteness, not all space objects are registered. Indeed, the "timely manner" requirement is often overlooked as satellites are registered months after launch.' Dan St. John, *Is It Time for a More Robust Registration Convention?*, DENV. J. INT'L L. & POL'Y (Mar. 14, 2013), http://djilp.org/is-it-time-for-a-more-robust-registration-convention/.

[38] In addition to Chapter 10, a more fulsome discussion of STM and SSA can be found in Rafael Moro-Aguilar & Steven A. Mirmina, Space Traffic Management and Space Situational Awareness, in ROUTLEDGE HANDBOOK OF SPACE LAW 180–96 (Ram Jakhu & Paul Stephen Dempsey eds., 2017).

THE MOON AGREEMENT

Between 1972 and 1979, COPUOS also focused on the economic exploitation of outer space, particularly mining the Moon and other celestial bodies. In 1972, COPUOS began consideration of what would become known as the Moon Agreement. Most of the agreement reflected what was already contained in the OST.

However, several developing countries insisted on one additional provision that had no analog in the Outer Space Treaty, declaring that natural resources on the moon and other celestial bodies are the 'common heritage' of all humankind, and extraction of those resources would be subject to a future 'international regime,' to be established at the time such resource exploitation would 'become feasible.'[39]

While the verbiage, 'common heritage of mankind,'[40] mirrors wording found in Article 136 of the UN Convention on the Law of the Sea,[41] the two phrases in two different treaties are not synonymous – a fundamental principle of treaty interpretation is that one interprets treaty provisions within the context of the treaty in which they are found.[42] Nevertheless, this phrase has been a reason that the Moon Agreement has so few Parties: many major space-faring nations (i.e., China, India, Japan, Russia, the U.S. and others) have not ratified the Agreement.

Historically, the Carter Administration favored the Moon Agreement, with the State Department recommending that the Moon Agreement be signed by the United States.[43] In July 1980, after the Agreement was submitted to the

---

[39] The Agreement Governing the Activities of States on the Moon and Other Celestial Bodies Art. 11(5) (1979), 1636 U.N.T.S. 3, 18 I.L.M. 1434 [*hereinafter* Moon Agreement].

[40] As a compromise among the delegations, it was actually the U.S. that first formally proposed that the resources found on the lunar surface be considered as the 'common heritage of mankind.'

[41] U.N. Convention on the Law of the Sea (1982), 1833 U.N.T.S. 397.

[42] Vienna Convention on the Law of Treaties Art. 31 (1969) 1155 U.N.T.S. 331 [*hereinafter* VCLT]. Moreover, the Moon Agreement itself, in Article 11, states that the term 'common heritage of mankind' 'finds its expression in the relevant portions of this Agreement and in particular in paragraph 5 of this Article.' It is also noteworthy that it was the U.S. that first officially proposed the term 'common heritage of mankind.' Comm. on the Peaceful Uses of Outer Space, Report of the Legal Subcomm. on Its Eleventh Session, Annex I(15), U.N. Doc. A/AC.105/101 (1972).

[43] State Department Informal Working Paper of October 17, 1979, reprinted in Committee on Commerce, Science and Transportation, Agreement Governing the Activities of States on the Moon and Other Celestial Bodies 363–65 (Comm. Print 1980).

Senate for ratification, the Senate Commerce, Science and Transportation Committee held oversight hearings on the Moon Agreement.[44]

The succession of the Reagan Administration derailed plans for ratification. In reference to the UN Convention on the Law of the Sea (UNCLOS), President Reagan 'criticized the concept of international management,' and viewed UNCLOS as 'being intentionally designed to promote a new world order, a form of global collectivism, that seeks ultimately the redistribution of the world's wealth through a complex system of manipulative central economic planning and bureaucratic coercion.'[45] As a result of the Moon Agreement's lack of widespread acceptance, it is seldom cited, consulted, or applied by space law practitioners in the U.S.[46]

In the future, the Moon Agreement could serve as the basis for increased international cooperation and collaboration for lunar surface activities. It prohibits the use or threat of use of force on the Moon, which is reserved exclusively for peaceful activities.[47] It also forbids the establishment of military bases, installations, and fortifications on the Moon, the testing of weapons, and the conduct of military maneuvers on the Moon.[48] Provisions of the Moon Agreement also appear to be reflected in the U.S.'s expressions to reduce space threats through norms, rules, and principles of responsible behaviors.[49]

Moreover, the Moon Agreement requires States Parties to inform the UN, the public, and the international scientific community, to the greatest extent

---

[44] *The Moon Treaty: Hearings Before the Subcomm. on Sci., Tech. & Space of the S. Comm. on Commerce, Sci. & Transp.*, 96th Cong. 2d Session (1980). During that hearing, State Department Legal Advisor Roberts Owen spoke in favor of the Moon Agreement, emphasizing that: it did not establish a legal moratorium on commercial mineral extraction; it did not obligate the U.S. to become a party to a second resource regime the U.S. finds unsatisfactory; and that the common heritage principle applied to lunar resources under the Moon Agreement would be interpreted independently from the way it was developed in the deep seabed negotiations at the Law of the Sea Conference. See also, Annex D, State Department Informal Working Paper, dated 17 October 1979, at p. 363.

[45] Michelle Hanlon, *What is the Moon Treaty and is it Useful?*, FILLING SPACE (Jan. 17, 2020), https://filling-space.com/2020/01/17/what-is-the-moon-treaty-and-is-it-still-useful/.

[46] Recall, however, for the 18 States Parties to the Moon Agreement, it is valid, legally binding international law, as much as the Outer Space Treaty or any other treaty to which they are parties.

[47] *Moon Agreement, supra* note 39, Art. 3.

[48] *Id.*

[49] G.A. Res. 75/36, Reducing Space threats Through Norms, Rules and Principles of Responsible Behaviors (Dec. 7, 2020); Theresa Hitchens, *In A First, SecDef Pledges DoD To Space Norms*, BREAKING DEFENSE (July 19, 2021), https://breakingdefense.com/2021/07/exclusive-in-a-first-secdef-pledges-dod-to-space-norms/.

feasible and practicable, of their activities concerned with the exploration and use of the Moon.[50] NASA echoed these very sentiments in the Artemis Accords, which has been joined by over a dozen countries as of the date of publication.[51] Sharing information about the time, purposes, locations, orbital parameters, and duration is to be given in respect of each mission to the Moon as soon as possible after launching,[52] would promote transparency for lunar surface activities and potentially decrease safety risks across the lunar surface for current and future missions.

The Moon Agreement has been discussed at COPUOS in recent years. In 2008, some of the State Parties to the Moon Agreement[53] presented a 'Joint statement on the benefits of the adherence to the Agreement Governing the Activities of States on the Moon and Other Celestial Bodies by States parties to the Agreement.'[54] Concerning the Article 11 'common heritage of mankind' principle, these States Parties noted that the 'Agreement does not pre-exclude any modality of exploitation, by public and/or private entities, nor forbids commercial treatment, as long as such exploitation is compatible with the requirements of the Common Heritage of Mankind regime.'[55]

While it has seemed as though the U.S. and most spacefaring nations (save Australia and France) have abandoned the Moon Agreement, the extraction and exploitation of resources on the Moon and other celestial bodies is increasingly becoming a reality.[56] Proponents of the Moon Agreement note that Article 11.5 enables any State Party to participate in the formation of any eventual international regime that would govern exploitation of the Moon's

---

[50]   *Moon Agreement, supra* note 39, Art. 4.

[51]   Artemis Accords: Principles for Cooperation in the Civil Exploration and Use of the Moon, Mars, Comets, and Asteroids for Peaceful Purposes § 11, NASA (Oct. 13, 2021), https://www.nasa.gov/specials/artemis-accords/img/Artemis-Accords-signed -13Oct2020.pdf.

[52]   *Moon Agreement, supra* note 39, Art. 5.

[53]   Austria, Belgium, Chile, Mexico, the Netherlands, Pakistan and the Philippines.

[54]   U.N. Secretariat, Joint Statements on the Benefits of Adherences to the Agreement Governing the Activities of States on the Moon and Other Celestial Bodies by States Parties to the Agreement, Note by the Secretariat, U.N. Doc. A/AC.105/ C.2/L.272 (Apr. 3, 2008).

[55]   Antonella Bini, *The Moon Agreement: Its Effectiveness in the 21st Century*, 14 European Space Pol'y Inst. 1, 6 (Oct. 2008).

[56]   On December 3, 2020, NASA selected four companies to collect lunar regolith and deliver it to NASA on the lunar surface. *See* Stephanie Scheirholz & Josh Finch, *NASA Selects Companies to Collect Lunar Resources for Artemis Demonstrations*, NASA (Dec. 3, 2020), https://www.nasa.gov/press-release/nasa-selects-companies-to -collect-lunar-resources-for-artemis-demonstrations.

natural resources. As a matter of state sovereignty, any State Party not satisfied with the content of that international regime need not agree to it.[57]

After the Moon Agreement was concluded, COPUOS focused on drafting several non-legally binding principles and guidelines.[58]

OTHER MULTILATERAL AGREEMENTS AFFECTING SPACE

In addition to the treaties highlighted in previous sections, the international community has concluded agreements focusing on specific uses of space assets. Some of these treaties are the following:

- International Telecommunications Union Constitution and Convention (1992, as amended) – the International Telecommunications Union (ITU) is the UN specialized agency for information and communication technologies. It was founded in 1865 to facilitate international connectivity in communications networks. To fulfill this objective, ITU allocates global radio spectrum and satellite orbits and develops the technical standards that ensure networks and technologies seamlessly interconnect.[59] The ITU Constitution and Convention are two separate documents that have treaty status. The Constitution establishes the purposes of ITU, highlighted above, in its Article 1, as well as the rights and obligations of member States (Article 3). On the other hand, the Convention focuses on the functioning of the Union.
- Agreement relating to the International Telecommunication Satellite Organization (1971) – the International Telecommunication Satellite Organization (ITSO, previously known as INTELSAT) is an intergovernmental organization with 149 member States that incorporates the principle

---

[57] Based upon review of the U.S. Senate hearings of July 1980, the U.S. and most countries involved in the Moon Agreement negotiations consistently maintained the position that ownership of extracted resources has always been permissible. This has also been echoed by State practice, including by Russia, Japan, and many European countries.

[58] G.A. Res. 62/217, Space Debris Mitigation Guidelines (2007); G.A. Res. 51/122, Declaration on International Cooperation in the Exploration and Use of Outer Space for the Benefit and in the Interest of All States, Taking into Particular Account the Needs of Developing Countries (1996); G.A. Res. 47/68, Principles Relevant to the Use of Nuclear Power Sources in Outer Space (1992); G.A. Res. 41/65, Principles Relating to Remote Sensing of the Earth from Outer Space (1986); G.A. Res. 37/92, Principles Governing the Use by States of Artificial Earth Satellites for International Direct Television Broadcasting (1982).

[59] *See About International Telecommunication Union (ITU)*, ITU (2021), https://www.itu.int/en/about/Pages/default.aspx.

set forth in UNGA Resolution 1721 (XVI), which established that satellite communications should be available to the nations of the world as soon as practicable on a global and non-discriminatory basis.[60] The core principles of ITSO are: (i) maintaining global connectivity and global coverage; (ii) serving lifeline connectivity customers; and (iii) providing non-discriminatory access to Intelsat's system, as established in Article III of the ITSO Agreement.[61]

- Convention on the Establishment of the European Organization for Exploitation of Meteorological Satellites (EUMETSAT) (1983) – EUMETSAT is the European operational satellite agency for monitoring weather, climate, and the environment from space.[62] It has 30 member States, and it operates pursuant to the EUMETSAT Convention. EUMETSAT's functions include monitoring the climate and detecting changes in the global climate.

The treaties described above are space-specific, but there are other treaties and non-binding instruments that, although not focused solely on space, do address the issue of its use. Of note are the instruments detailed below:

- Treaty Banning Nuclear Weapons Test in the Atmosphere, Outer Space and Under Water – the 1963 Limited Nuclear Test Ban Treaty (LTBT) prohibited the testing of nuclear weapons in outer space, underwater, or in the atmosphere.[63]
- Missile Technology Control Regime (MTCR) – the MTCR is an international set of guidelines that seeks to control the exports of missile and rocket technology. It is a non-binding, informal political understanding among States that aims to limit the proliferation of such technology. The MTCR was formed in 1987 by the Group of 7 (G-7) industrialized countries, which include Canada, France, Germany, Italy, Japan, the United Kingdom, and the United States. The MTCR's objective is limiting the risks of proliferation of weapons of mass destruction (WMDs) by controlling exports of goods and technologies that could contribute to delivery

---

[60] *See About Us*, INT'L TELECOOMM. SATELLITE ORG., https://itso.int/about-us/ (last visited Oct. 16, 2021).

[61] Intelsat *was* an international consortium from 1964–2001, then became a U.S. private company, then filed for bankruptcy in 2020.

[62] *See Who We Are*, EUMETSAT, https://www.eumetsat.int/about-us/who-we-are (last visited Oct. 16, 2021).

[63] Treaty Banning Nuclear Weapon Tests in the Atmosphere, in Outer Space and Under Water (1963), 14 U.S.T. 1313, 480 U.N.T.S. 6964.

systems (other than manned aircraft) for such weapons. There are currently 35 countries that are members of the MTCR.[64]

• Wassenaar Arrangement on Export Controls for Conventional Arms and Dual-Use Goods and Technologies – the Wassenaar Arrangement is a multilateral arrangement on export controls for conventional weapons and sensitive dual-use goods and technologies, which received final approval by 33 co-founding countries in July 1996.[65] The Wassenaar Arrangement serves as a non-binding framework through which States agree on which items should be controlled, and aims to promote transparency by calling on States to disclose information regarding their export activities related to weapons and items appearing on the arrangement's two control lists – the List of Dual Use Goods and Technologies and the Munitions List.[66] Space technology is included on the agreed-upon control list, with an emphasis on launch vehicles, which are easily repurposed as intercontinental ballistic missiles (ICBMs).[67]

• Treaty on the Prohibition of Nuclear Weapons (TPNW) – the TPNW entered into force on January 22, 2021. It establishes that States shall under no circumstance '[d]evelop, test, produce, manufacture, otherwise acquire, possess or stockpile nuclear weapons or other nuclear explosive devices,' as well as '[u]se or threaten to use' them.[68] States Parties are also prohibited from encouraging non-parties in any activity prohibited to a State Party under the treaty. This prohibition of encouragement provides an additional layer that limits the use of nuclear weapons in space, but, as with the LTBT, it places no restrictions on conventional weapons.

---

[64] *Frequently Asked Questions (FAQs)*, MISSILE TECH. CONTROL REGIME, https://mtcr.info/frequently-asked-questions-faqs/ (last visited Oct. 16, 2021).

[65] *What is the Wassenaar Arrangement?*, WASSENAAR ARRANGEMENT SECRETARIAT, https://www.wassenaar.org/the-wassenaar-arrangement/ (last visited Oct. 16, 2021).

[66] Daryl Kimball, *The Wassenaar Arrangement at a Glance*, ARMS CONTROL ASS'N (Dec. 2017), https://www.armscontrol.org/factsheets/wassenaar.

[67] Wassenar Arrangement Secretariat, List of Dual-Use Goods and Technologies and Munitions List at 9.A.10 (Dec. 2020), https://www.wassenaar.org/app/uploads/2019/consolidated/WA-DOC-18-PUB-001-Public-Docs-Vol-II-2018-List-of-DU-Goods-and-Technologies-and-Munitions-List-Dec-18.pdf; P.J. Blount, *Space Security Law*, in OXFORD RESEARCH ENCYCLOPEDIA OF PLANETARY SCIENCES (Oxford Univ. Press, 2018).

[68] Treaty on the Prohibition of Nuclear Weapons Art. 1, U.N. Doc. A/CONF.229/2017/8, *opened for signature* Sept. 20, 2017 [*hereinafter* TPNW].

MULTILATERAL, MULTINATIONAL INITIATIVES

The International Space Station

The International Space Station (ISS) is an international partnership comprising 15 nations. The partners include the United States, Russia, Japan, Canada, and 11 European nations acting collectively as the 'European partner.'[69] The principal international agreements that form the legal and programmatic foundation for the ISS include one multilateral intergovernmental agreement (IGA) and four bilateral memoranda of understanding (MOUs) between NASA and each of the other four partners' designated space agencies, collectively 'the ISS Agreements.'[70]

The ISS IGA

The IGA is a government-level agreement that specifies the respective legal rights and obligations of the 15 ISS partner States. In the U.S., the IGA is an executive agreement, not a treaty.[71] Thus, it was not submitted to the Senate for its advice and consent. Rather, it was signed for the U.S. by the Deputy Secretary of State on January 29, 1998. Nevertheless, it is legally binding.[72] All

---

[69]   The 11 European nations are: France, United Kingdom, Belgium, the Netherlands, Denmark, Norway, Spain, Germany, Italy, Sweden, and Switzerland. So, in ISS parlance, there are five IGA partners, even though there are 15 IGA partner States.

[70]   1998 Intergovernmental Agreement; the Agreement among the Government of Canada, Governments of Member States of the European Space Agency, the Government of Japan, the Government of the Russian Federation, and the Government of the United States of America concerning Cooperation on the Civil International Space Station, Washington, done 29 January 1998, entered into force 27 March 2001, 22 T.I.A.S. No. 12927 [*hereinafter* 1998 IGA].

[71]   In the U.S., the power to make international agreements resides in the executive branch, vested in the president's 'foreign affairs' powers. Written agreements between different countries generally fall into two broad categories: treaties and executive agreements. Domestically, the term 'treaty' is a technical characterization applied to those international agreements made by the president with the advice and consent of the Senate. *See* U.S. CONST. art. II, § 2. Alternatively, executive agreements are made by the president pursuant to authority contained in legislation, a treaty, or his independent powers under the Constitution. In contrast, at the international level the term 'treaty' is used to describe international agreements in general, regardless of how they are considered domestically. International law makes no distinction between treaties and executive agreements, having concern only for whether the parties intend their understandings to be legally binding.

[72]   *See* Restatement (Third) of the Foreign Relations Law of the United States §321 (1987). '[E]very international agreement in force is binding upon the parties to it and must be performed by them in good faith.' This section reiterates the international law doctrine on the subject which, according to the official comment following the section,

of the ISS partners regard the IGA as a binding international agreement under international law.

The ISS MOUs

The MOUs are bilateral agreements between NASA (on the one hand), and the four 'cooperating agencies' of the other ISS partners (on the other hand), that provide detailed descriptions of management responsibilities, technical responsibilities for specific elements, and implementing processes.[73] They also establish the governing 'program boards' which control ISS assembly, operation, and integration activities.

In addition, a plethora of lower-level, bilateral implementing arrangements, barter arrangements, and technical understandings provide further program-level definition and specificity to the legal commitments found in the IGA and MOUs.

ISS cooperation

As a general principle of ISS cooperation, there is no exchange of funds among the IGA partners. Each partner has an obligation to fund, design, build, launch, and maintain its own elements and systems, absent an agreement to the contrary.[74] They also must participate in program management and planning and share in common operating costs of the ISS.

Partners generally make two types of contribution:

- Infrastructure (encompassing elements and systems that allow the use and operation of the ISS), including examples such as the power system, life support system, robotic arm, command and data-handling system, or the guidance, navigation, and control system; or
- Accommodations elements (such as laboratories or attach sites for external payloads).

'...lies at the core of the law of international agreements and is perhaps the most important principle of international law.' *Id. Comment (a).* It is also consistent with the 1969 *Vienna Convention on the Law of Treaties,* which the United States has accepted as binding customary international law.

[73] With the one exception involving the Government of Japan (rather than the Japanese Aerospace Exploration Agency (JAXA)). The Japanese Government, represented by its Foreign Ministry, is NASA's MOU 'partner' and retains significant authority and interest in program activities. Other responsibilities are delegated to JAXA.

[74] Partners can arrange for other partners to take on various responsibilities under whatever terms and conditions they may agree upon.

In return for a contribution of infrastructure or accommodations, a partner receives: a share of user accommodations (racks in pressurized labs or external payload sites); a share of utilization resources (power, share of time of on-orbit crew devoted to utilization); and rights to flight opportunities for the partner's astronauts.

Based roughly on the economic value of the contributions, the partners receive corresponding utilization rights. The Russian Space Agency keeps what it brings to the cooperation, and the other four IGA partners divide their share approximately as follows: U.S. 76.6%; Japan 12.8%; Europe 8.3%; and Canada 2.3%.[75]

Inventions on the ISS

On the Earth's surface, generally speaking, inventions are governed by national patent law. Difficulty arises from the fact that patent law is inherently territorial – the rights conferred in patent protection rely on a sovereign to confer and enforce those rights in the face of infringement.[76] This can raise questions about the application of patent law in outer space.

The principle of territorial jurisdiction has been extended to space through the OST and Registration Agreement giving launching States jurisdiction over registered space objects. Building from this principle, in 1990, the U.S. extended national patent protections to 'any invention made, used, or sold in outer space on a space object or competent thereof under the jurisdiction or control of the United States.'[77] Such objects are 'considered to be made, used or sold within the United States for the purposes of [U.S. patent laws.]'[78]

---

[75] This is just an overview and starting point describing the sharing of costs and benefits of ISS cooperation. The partnership has existed for more than 20 years, and in that time, there have been numerous detailed implementation arrangements, barters among the cooperating agencies, and cost offsets that go beyond the scope of this analysis. For example, partners who would normally pay for services (such as a Shuttle launch for their element) have offset the costs by exchanging subsequently agreed additional goods and services.

[76] Theodore U. Ro et al., *Patent Infringement in Outer Space in Light of 35 U.S.C. § 105: Following the White Rabbit down the Rabbit Loophole*, 17 B.U. J. SCI. & TECH. L. 202, 206–07 (2011). There are international regimes for the protection of patents, but application does not become enforceable until accepted by each national jurisdiction in which protection is sought. *Id.*

[77] 35 U.S.C. § 105(a) (2018).

[78] *Id.* It should be noted that there are two exceptions that will remove a space object from U.S. patent jurisdiction. These are if the space object or component is: (1) specifically identified or otherwise provided for by an international agreement to which the U.S. is a party, or (2) carried on the registry of a foreign State in accordance with the Registration Convention. *Id*; *see* Ro et al., *supra* note 72, at 212–13.

As space partnerships evolved, the 1998 IGA elected to further clarify space-based intellectual property rights. Article 21 states that 'an activity occurring in or on a Space Station flight element shall be deemed to have occurred *only* in the territory of the Partner State of that element's registry,' with ESA-registered elements providing territoriality for any European partner State.[79] The IGA further simplifies matters, as the participation of a partner State in an activity 'shall not in and of itself alter or affect the jurisdiction over such activity.'[80]

There are two implications for inventions on the ISS. First, the invention would be seen as domestic to whichever nation had registered the module in which the invention arose. The same applies for any inventions made on vehicles travelling to and from the ISS. Thereby, for creations in the U.S. modules, or made during the flights on a U.S. vehicle, patents could be filed within the U.S.,[81] and a foreign patent application would need to be filed for additional jurisdictions. In a similar vein, even if highly unlikely, if a U.S. astronaut were to conceive of an invention or 'reduce to practice' a patentable invention during the trip to the ISS on a Russian Soyuz vehicle, then Russian intellectual property (IP) law would apply.[82] Second, assuming a patent was obtained, the invention would be protected against activities of patent infringement *in the same national module*, as patents do not afford international protection.

However, it is worth noting that the likelihood of inventions being conceived in the ISS is still remote. When NASA astronauts are in space, their activities are planned on a minute-by-minute basis largely to operational responsibilities, and unplanned or unintended inventive activity during mission operations is relatively unlikely.

ISS crew code of conduct

Article 11 of the IGA and MOUs each required the partners to develop an ISS crew code of conduct (CCOC). The partners developed and approved the CCOC to: establish a clear chain of command on-orbit; establish a clear relationship between ground and on-orbit management; establish a manage-

---

[79] (Emphasis added). 1998 IGA, *supra* note 70, Art. 21(2). However, one must still consider whether a launching State's legal regime permits for the expansion of patent protections to extraterritorial situations, such as space.

[80] *Id.*

[81] For example, when U.S. astronaut Donald Pettit created the first beverage cup for a weightless environment – so he could enjoy the aroma of his coffee along with drinking it – the resultant patent was filed with the U.S. *See* U.S. Patent No. 20110101009A1 (issued May 5, 2011).

[82] While under both U.S. and Russian IP law, title to inventions would vest in the astronauts, under Executive Order 10096, for the U.S. astronaut, the title to the invention would be transferred to the U.S. Government.

ment hierarchy; set forth standards for work and activities in space; establish responsibilities with respect to elements and equipment; set forth disciplinary regulations; establish physical and information security guidelines; and define the ISS commander's authority and responsibility, on behalf of all the partners, to enforce safety procedures, physical and information security procedures, and crew rescue procedures for the ISS.[83]

This CCOC is applicable, and sets forth the standards of conduct, for all ISS crew members during preflight, on-orbit, and postflight activities (including launch and return phases). Crew members must comply with the CCOC. Accordingly, during preflight, on-orbit, and postflight activities, they must follow the ISS commander's orders. In fact, ISS crew members' conduct must contribute to maintaining 'a harmonious and cohesive relationship' among the crew.[84] ISS crew members are subject to various restrictions, including the prohibition against any use of their position that 'is motivated, or has the appearance of being motivated, by private gain, including financial gain, for himself or herself or other persons or entities.' For this reason, there are no ISS astronauts making commercial endorsements of products, such as wrist-watches, tennis shoes, or breakfast cereal.

However, in the highly unlikely event of some inappropriate behavior among the ISS astronauts, IGA Article 22 (Criminal Jurisdiction) provides that each IGA partner may exercise 'criminal jurisdiction over personnel in or on any flight element who are their respective nationals.'[85] That is relatively typical in international law – a State always has jurisdiction over its own nationals. However, for any case of misconduct that either (a) affects the life or safety of a national of another partner State or (b) occurs in or on or causes damage to the flight element of another partner State, the partner State whose national is the alleged perpetrator has an affirmative obligation to consult with the State considering prosecuting the offense. Following that consultation, the affected partner's State may exercise criminal jurisdiction over the alleged perpetrator provided that the partner State whose national is the alleged perpetrator either concurs in such exercise of criminal jurisdiction, or fails to

---

[83]   This code of conduct was implemented in each partner's domestic law as appropriate. *See* 14 CFR § 1214.403 (2021).

[84]   *Id.* at II.B. 'ISS Crewmembers' conduct shall be such as to maintain a harmonious and cohesive relationship among the ISS crewmembers and an appropriate level of mutual confidence and respect through an interactive, participative, and relationship-oriented approach which duly takes into account the international and multicultural nature of the crew and mission.'

[85]   1998 IGA, *supra* note 70, Art. 22(1).

provide assurances that it will submit the case to its competent authorities for the purpose of prosecution.[86]

The European Space Agency

Another example of multilateral cooperation in space is the European Space Agency ('ESA'). ESA is an international organization with 22 member States. ESA seeks to coordinate the financial and intellectual resources of its members, undertaking programs and activities that would otherwise be beyond the scope of any single European country.

Before the ESA took its current form, it had previously been two distinct organizations: the European Launch Development Organisation ('ELDO') and the European Space Research Organisation ('ESRO'), both of which were founded in 1962, with their respective conventions coming into force two years later, in 1964. Ultimately, these two organizations merged in 1975 to create the ESA, with 10 founding member States.[87] These founding States all signed the ESA Convention, which entered into force in 1980, proclaiming the establishment of the Agency, as well as its purpose, which is 'to provide for and to promote, for exclusively peaceful purposes, cooperation among European States in space research and technology and their space applications, with a view to their being used for scientific purposes and for operational space applications systems.'[88]

It should be noted that, although the ESA works closely with the European Union ('EU'), they are different organizations. While the ESA is an intergovernmental organization, the EU is supranational. The two institutions have indeed different ranges of competences, different member States, and are governed by different rules and procedures.[89] Nevertheless, they have worked closely through the years to coordinate their goals for Europe in space, collaborating closely in projects such as the European GNSS Galileo.

QUESTIONS FOR REVIEW

1. Can you name the five primary space law treaties?

---

[86] *Id.* Art. 22(2).

[87] The founding member States of the ESA were Belgium, Germany, Denmark, France, United Kingdom, Italy, the Netherlands, Spain, Sweden and Switzerland.

[88] Convention for the Establishment of European Space Agency Art. II, Paris, *done* May 30, 1975, 14 I.L.M. 864.

[89] *See ESA and the EU*, ESA, https://www.esa.int/About_Us/Corporate_news/ESA _and_the_EU (last visited Oct. 16, 2021).

2.   What does the term 'launching State' mean? Does it matter which treaty you are looking at? Can a space object have more than one launching State?

3.   Can a State demand reimbursement for rescuing another State's astronauts? What about recovering another State's space object?

4.   Why does it matter if a space object causes damage on Earth versus in outer space? What is the liability regime for collisions in space?

5.   Who is liable for damages produced by space debris?

6.   What if a criminal space tourist from State A visits the ISS and kills an astronaut from State B? What if State A is not a party to the IGA? Who would have jurisdiction over the criminal?

PART III

Space agencies and laws of the United States

5. Domestic law primer

Ruth is ecstatic to be leaving the office while it is still light outside. She managed to leave earlier than usual today to participate in a 'young space professionals' career panel organized by the Georgetown Space Law Society. She was invited by the Space Law Society President, who attended her lectures in the previous weeks. After checking with her senior partner, who loved the idea and visibility it provides the firm, Ruth had happily accepted. As she walks to the law campus, she marvels at D.C.'s beauty when bathed in the sunset's golden glow.

In inviting Ruth, the Space Law Society President suggested that she share class recommendations for aspiring space lawyers. Ruth reflected fondly on her conversation with her cousin Ramzi at her dad's birthday about the importance of international law for space lawyers. She still stood by that recommendation, but looked forward to also highlighting the benefits of administrative law. Ruth had learned that administrative law was essential to navigating domestic space law issues.

INTRODUCTION

The U.S. enacts domestic laws and regulations to govern the activities of its agencies and citizens and to implement its international treaty obligations. The U.S. governs domestic space activities and fulfills its many OST and other treaty obligations through a combination of federal statutes published in the U.S. Code and executive agency-enacted regulations published in the Code of Federal Regulations (CFR). In accordance with the U.S. Constitution, Congress adopts legislation that empowers executive agencies to issue regulations interpreting and implementing the authorities granted by statute. Together, statutes and regulations governing space activities form the landscape of U.S. space law.

This chapter focuses on the specific processes that Congress and the executive agencies use to enact laws and regulations. Understanding how laws and regulations are created is critical to the practice of U.S. space law and efforts to influence the interpretation and implementation of commercial space regulations.

BRIEF BACKGROUND ON THE U.S. CONSTITUTION

When drafting the U.S. Constitution, the framers wanted to avoid the 'accumulation of all powers'[1] of a future government from falling into the hands of few and, therefore, 'sought to guard against it by dispersing federal power to three interdependent branches of Government.'[2] The Constitution divides the federal government's power among the legislative, executive, and judicial branches. The powers of the federal government are limited to those enumerated in the Constitution.[3]

CONGRESS'S POWERS

Congress's powers, processes, and limitations are defined in Article I of the Constitution. Article I, Section 8 contains 18 clauses enumerating the specific powers granted to Congress.[4] Importantly, the last clause of that section enables Congress to 'make all laws which shall be necessary and proper for carrying into execution' a functioning central government.[5]

The 'necessary and proper' clause touches space law in two ways. First, it is the mechanism through which Congress enacts legislation to implement U.S. treaty obligations. Only the president has the authority to make treaties under Article II, Section 2, Clause 2, but congressional action is required to codify treaty obligations into law. Second, this clause contributes to Congress's power to create and empower federal agencies.[6]

The Organization of Congress

The Constitution grants legislative powers to a bicameral congress comprising two chambers: a Senate and a House of Representatives. The Senate comprises 100 senators serving six-year terms;[7] each state elects two senators. The House

---

[1]   The Federalist No. 47 (James Madison) (Clinton Rossiter ed., 1999).

[2]   *Thomas v. Union Carbide Agric. Prods. Co.*, 473 U.S. 568, 594 (1985) (Brennan, J., concurring).

[3]   *See, Zivotofsky v. Kerry*, 135 S. CT. 2076, 2098 (2015) (Thomas, J., concurring in part and dissenting in part).

[4]   U.S. Const., art. I, § 8, cl. 1–18.

[5]   U.S. Const., art I., § 8, cl. 18.

[6]   Todd Gravey and Daniel J. Sheffner, *Congress's Authority to Influence and Control Executive Branch Agencies*, Cong. Rsch. Serv. at 1, R45442 (updated May 12, 2021).

[7]   Terms are overlapping. In practice, this means that one-third of Senate seats are up for election in any election cycle. U.S. Const., art. I.

of Representatives is composed of 435 members who serve two-year terms and represent one of the 435 population-based districts.[8]

Some congressional powers are reserved for a specific chamber of commerce. For instance, the Senate is the only chamber that may confirm presidential nominations and approve treaties, while the House is the only chamber where revenue legislation may originate.[9] However, the legislative, oversight, and administrative tasks of both chambers are organized similarly and are divided among more than 200 committees and subcommittees.[10]

Congressional committees

Committees are essentially 'little legislatures' with specific subject matter jurisdiction that 'monitor on-going governmental operations, identify issues suitable for legislative review, gather and evaluate information, and recommend courses of action to their parent body.'[11]

Committees are of three types: standing, select or special, and joint. Standing committees are permanent panels designated by Senate or House rules.[12] These committees have legislative jurisdiction and consider bills, conduct oversight of agencies or programs within their jurisdiction, and recommend measures for their respective members to consider.[13] Typically, standing committees have subcommittees with similar powers focused on particular issue areas.[14]

Select or special committees are created for a specific purpose, such as conducting investigations and studies on certain issues, and are typically only temporary, but may be permanent.[15] Joint committees comprise members from both chambers and are focused more on conducting studies or performing housekeeping tasks.[16]

Committee members

Committees are populated with members of Congress in varying numbers. All committees have a chair, who chairs the committee, is a member of the

---

[8] *Id.*

[9] *Id.*

[10] The framework for committees and subcommittees was set by the 1948 Legislative Reorganization Act. Valerie Heitshusen, *Committee Types and Roles*, Cong. Rsch. Serv. at 1, (98-241) (May 2, 2017).

[11] United States Senate, *Senate Committees; Chapter 1: Why Committees?* (last accessed Dec. 5, 2021), https://www.senate.gov/artandhistory/history/common/briefing/Committees.htm.

[12] Heitshusen, *supra* note 10, at 1.

[13] *Id.*

[14] *Id.* at 2.

[15] *Id.*

[16] *Id.* at 3.

majority party, and hires the majority committee staff. Committees also have a ranking member, who leads the minority party on the committee and hires the minority committee staff.[17] The division of committee seats between the party members reflects the overall partisan ratio in the given chamber.[18]

Depending on their expertise, seniority, and interests, members will serve on multiple committees where they will develop and assess legislation, lead investigations, and hold hearings. Often, members will serve on the same committees for years, making them especially knowledgeable in that committee's policy area.[19]

How Laws Are Made

Legislation may only be introduced by a member of the House or Senate.[20] Prior to introducing a bill, members and their staff will consult the chamber's nonpartisan legislative counsel office, who help to translate policy proposals into actual legislative language.[21] Bill sponsors may also gather support for the bill by asking other members to sign on as original co-sponsors prior to introducing or 'dropping' the bill.[22]

Once the bill is introduced, it will receive a designation based on the chamber and a number. In the House, the speaker of the House will refer a bill to all the committees that have jurisdiction over the bill's provisions. When a bill is referred to multiple committees, each committee will only work on the portions of the bill that are under its jurisdiction.[23] In the Senate, a similar process is followed, but bills are almost always referred to the one committee with jurisdiction over the issues most prevalent in the bill.[24]

---

[17]   *Id.*

[18]   *Id.*

[19]   Valerie Heitshusen, *Introduction to the Legislative Process in the U.S. Congress,* Cong. Rsch. Serv. Rep. R42843 at 5 (updated Nov. 24, 2020).

[20]   *Id.* at 3. *See,* John V. Sullivan, *How Our Laws Are Made,* U.S. House of Representatives (House Document 110-49) (July 2007), https://www.govinfo.gov/content/pkg/CDOC-110hdoc49/pdf/CDOC-110hdoc49.pdf.

[21]   *Id.*

[22]   In the House, a bill is introduced when it is dropped in the hopper, which is a wooden box on the House floor. In the Senate, the bill is submitted to the clerks on the Senate floor. *Id. See, e.g.,* Mark J. Oleszek, *Sponsorship and Cosponsorship of Senate Bills,* Cong. Rsch. Serv. (98-279) (updated Feb. 5, 2021); and Mark J. Oleszek, *Sponsorship and Cosponsorship of House Bills,* Cong. Rsch. Serv. Rep. RS22477 (updated Oct. 7, 2019).

[23]   Heitshusen, *supra* note 19, at 3.

[24]   *Id.*

Committee chairs have the authority to set the committee's agenda and identify which bills will receive the committee's formal consideration during the two-year Congress.[25] Committees can consider bills by conducting public hearings and by engaging with involved stakeholders or a federal agency to review a bill's strengths and weaknesses.[26] When the committee wants to formally proceed with the bill's consideration, it will hold a markup on the bill to vote on any proposed amendments. A markup concludes when a majority of the members vote to report the bill to the corresponding full chamber.[27]

PRACTICE TIP

To successfully lobby Congress on behalf of your client, you must be aware of the relevant committees with jurisdiction over your space law issue. That information is critical to initiate a targeted engagement campaign with members and their staff.

Space-relevant committees

The most relevant congressional committees with jurisdiction over space-related issues are presented in Table 5.1.

EXECUTIVE POWERS

The Constitution vests all executive power with the president, who is elected for a term of four years.[28] The president is the commander in chief of the armed forces, and nominates for Senate approval all cabinet members, including agency secretaries, as well as ambassadors, federal judges, and all officers of the U.S. 'whose Appointments … shall be established by Law[.]'[29] The president has the power to enter into treaties, but treaties must be ratified by two-thirds of the Senate.[30]

The primary responsibility of the president and the executive branch agencies is to 'take Care that the Laws be faithfully executed[.]'[31] During the

---

[25]   *Id.* at 2.

[26]   *Id.* at 4. *See,* Valerie Heitshusen, *Types of Committee Hearings*, Cong. Rsch. Serv. Rep. 98-317 (updated Nov. 15, 2018).

[27]   *Id.*

[28]   U.S. Const., art. II.

[29]   *Id.*

[30]   A discussion of the differences between treaties and 'executive agreements' is found in Chapter 4 above.

[31]   *Supra* note 28.

Table 5.1   U.S. *congressional committees with jurisdiction over space policy*

Chamber	Committee	Subcommittee	Jurisdiction	Subject agency
Senate	Commerce, Science, and Transportation	Aviation, Operations, and Innovation[28]	Civil aviation, including safety, security, technology, engineering, manufacturing, infrastructure, consumer protection, research and development, airspace, and international aviation matters	FAA, Transportation Security Administration (TSA), National Transportation Safety Board (NTSB), and aviation programs of the Department of Transportation (DOT)
		Communications, Media, and Broadband[29]	All sectors of communications, including wired and wireless telephony, the Internet, commercial and noncommercial television, cable, satellite broadcast, satellite communications, wireline and wireless broadband, radio, spectrum and associated consumer electronic equipment, and public safety communications	Federal Communications Commission (FCC), the Corporation for Public Broadcasting, the National Telecommunications and Information Administration

Chamber	Committee	Subcommittee	Jurisdiction	Subject agency
		Space and Science[30]	National and civil space policy, legislation and oversight of science, technology, engineering, and math research, development, and policy, and standards and measurements	NASA, FAA's Office of Commercial Space Transportation, Department of Commerce's (DOC) Office of Space Commerce, National Institute of Standards and Technology (NIST), the National Space Council, the National Science Foundation, the White House Office of Science and Technology Policy (OSTP), and the US Arctic Research Commission
Senate	Armed Services	Emerging Threats and Capabilities[31]	Policies and programs related to science and technology, special operations, intelligence, countering weapons of mass destruction, and homeland defense	U.S. Special Operations Command, Defense Advanced Research Projects Agency, Defense Security Cooperation Agency, National Security Agency, Defense Intelligence Agency, National Reconnaissance Office, and National Geospatial-Intelligence Agency
		Strategic Forces[32]	Nuclear and strategic forces, arms control and nonproliferation programs, space programs, Department of Energy defense nuclear, and ballistic missile defense	U.S. Strategic Command, U.S. Space Command, U.S. Space Force, Space Development Agency, Missile Defense Agency, National Nuclear Security Administration, and Defense Threat Reduction Agency

Chamber	Committee	Subcommittee	Jurisdiction	Subject agency
Senate	Appropriations[33]	Commerce, Justice, Science, and Related Agencies[34]	All three subcommittees are tasked with drafting legislation to allocate funds to government agencies within their jurisdictions	DOC, including NIST, National Oceanic and Atmospheric Administration (NOAA), National Science Foundation, NASA, and OSTP
		Defense[35]		Department of Defense, including Air Force, Army, Marine Corps, Defense Advanced Research Projects Agency, Missile Defense Agency, National Geospatial and Intelligence Agency, National Security Agency, Defense Intelligence Agency, National Reconnaissance Office
		Transportation, Housing and Urban Development, and Related Agencies[36]		Department of Transportation, FAA, National Transportation Safety Board
House of Representatives	Transportation and Infrastructure	Aviation[37]	All aspects of civil aviation, including safety, infrastructure, labor and international issues. Select issues include air traffic control modernization, air traffic management, aviation safety, and commercial space transportation and tourism	FAA and NTSB

Chamber	Committee	Subcommittee	Jurisdiction	Subject agency
	Science, Space and Technology	Space and Aeronautics[38]	All matters relating to astronautical and aeronautical research and development, national space policy, including access to space, suborbital access and application, space commercialization, exploration and use of outer space, international space cooperation, space communications, Earth remote sensing policy, and space law	Commercial space activities relating to the Department of Transportation and DOC, NASA, National Space Council, and the FAA's demonstration programs
	Appropriations[39]	Commerce, Justice, Science, and Related Agencies	DOC, NASA, National Science Foundation, OSTP	

Chamber	Committee	Subcommittee	Jurisdiction	Subject agency
		Defense	Departments of Army, Navy (including Marine Corps), Air Force, and Defense Agencies, Central Intelligence Agency, and the Office of the Director of National Intelligence (jurisdiction excludes DOD-related accounts and programs that are under other subcommittees)	
		Transportation, and Housing and Urban Development, and Related Agencies	Department of Transportation, National Transportation Safety Board	

Notes: [28] *Aviation Safety, Operations, and Innovation*, U.S. Senate Comm. On Com., Science, & Transp., https://www.commerce.senate.gov/aviation-safety-operations-and-innovation -subcommittee (last accessed Dec. 5, 2021). [29] *Communications, Media, and Broadband*, U.S. Senate Comm. On Com., Science, & Transp., https://www.commerce.senate.gov/ communications-media-and-broadband-subcommittee (last accessed Dec. 5, 2021). [30] *Space and Science*, U.S. Senate Comm. On Com., Science, & Transp., https://www.commerce.senate .gov/space-and-science-subcommittee (last accessed Dec. 5, 2021). [31] *Subcommittees*, U.S. Senate Comm. On Armed Serv., https://www.armed-services.senate.gov/about/subcommittees (last accessed Dec. 5, 2021). [32] *Id.* [33] The Senate Appropriations Committee is the largest committee in the Senate and 'writes the legislation that allocates federal funds to numerous government agencies, departments, and organizations on an annual basis,' as required by art. 1, § 9 of the U.S. Constitution, which states that 'No money shall be drawn from the Treasury, but in consequence of Appropriations made by law.' *Committee Jurisdiction*, U.S. S. Comm. On Appropriations, https://www.appropriations.senate.gov/about/jurisdiction (last visited Dec. 5, 2021). [34] *Commerce, Justice, Science, and Related Agencies*, U.S. Senate Comm. On Appropriations, https://www.appropriations.senate.gov/subcommittees/commerce-justice -science-and-related-agencies (last visited Dec. 21, 2021). [35] *Defense*, U.S. Senate Comm. On Appropriations, https://www.appropriations.senate.gov/subcommittees/defense (last visited Dec. 21, 2021). [36] *Transportation, Housing and Urban Development, and Related Agencies*, U.S. Senate Comm. On Appropriations, https://www.appropriations.senate.gov/subcommittees/ transportation-housing-and-urban-development-and-related-agencies (last visited Dec. 21, 2021). [37] *Aviation*, U.S. House Comm. On Transp. & Infrastructure, https://transportation.house.gov/ subcommittees/aviation-116th-congress (last visited Dec. 21, 2021). [38] *Space and Aeronautics (117th Congress): Subcommittee Jurisdiction*, U.S. House Comm. On Sci., Space, & Tech., https://science.house.gov/subcommittees/space-117th-congress (last visited Dec. 21, 2021). [39]

Subcommittees, U.S. House Comm. On Appropriations, https://appropriations.house.gov/ (last visited Dec. 21, 2021).

First Congress, the earliest members of the U.S. Congress recognized that the Constitution permitted the establishment of 'departments of an executive nature' to assist the president in executing the laws enacted by Congress.[32]

Congress's Substantive Control of Executive Agencies

Congress controls an agency's jurisdiction and authority in two ways: in its organic statute and in its annual appropriations. For example, NASA's authorizing statute is a separate piece of legislation, subject to the jurisdiction of a different committee than NASA's funding bill. Congress may give an 'agency the authority to issue legislative rules, enforce violations of law, or adjudicate claims made to the agency.'[33] The regulation of launch and reentry represents authorities granted to an agency that were then implemented and enforced through rules (regulations). Similarly, as discussed in this book, the Federal Communications Commission (FCC) has regulatory authority, but Congress uniquely created it as an independent agency, responsible directly to Congress. The more detailed Congress is in its grant of authority to an agency, the agency is given less discretion in executing its delegated authority.[34] Congress can enlarge, narrow, or alter an agency's authority at any time.[35]

There are several reasons why Congress gives executive branch agencies rulemaking authority. Agencies typically have more subject matter expertise and are better informed on how to implement a particular policy and where it should fit in the existing regulatory framework. Agencies are also better positioned to receive input from the stakeholders they regulate when creating new regulations. It is also generally easier to amend or repeal an agency's rule(s) than it is to amend or repeal a statute.

The study of the specific rules and procedures that federal agencies are required to follow is commonly known as 'administrative law,' and is discussed further below. In practicing U.S. space law, which continues to be dynamic in response to ongoing innovation, it is important to understand how to interpret as well as engage in modifying and developing the statutes and regulations that govern U.S. space activities.

---

[32] Gravey, *supra* note 6, at 5 (citing statement of Rep. Elias Boudinot, 1 Annals of Cong. 383 (1789)).

[33] *Id.* at 9.

[34] Jack M. Beermann, *Congressional Administration*, 43 San Diego L. Rev. 61, at 77 (2006).

[35] Garvey, *supra* note 6, at 9 (citing Ctr. For Biological Diversity v. Zinke, 313 F. Supp. 3d 976, 989 (D. Alaska 2018)).

ADMINISTRATIVE LAW BACKGROUND

Administrative law is law that governs how federal agencies exercise their regulatory functions. In administrative law parlance, the terms 'regulations' and 'rules' are used synonymously. They are issued by an agency, board, or commission and have the weight and effect of law.[36] The process that federal agencies use to develop, amend, or repeal rules (or regulations) is called 'rulemaking' and is '[the] crucial intermediate process [that] stands between the enactment of a law by Congress and the realization of the goals that both Congress and the people it represents seek to achieve by that law.'[37] Throughout the other chapters on domestic space law, numerous references are made to regulations and key regulatory reform efforts. Those regulations and efforts are governed by the laws and processes discussed here.

Administrative Procedure Act

The 'most long-standing and broadly applicable federal rulemaking require-ments are in' the Administrative Procedure Act (APA).[38] The APA 'governs the process by which federal agencies propose and establish new regulations,' and is 'written to bring regularity and predictability to agency decision-making.'[39] The APA 'applies to all executive branch and independent agencies, prescribes procedures for agency rulemakings and adjudications, as well as standards for judicial review of final agency actions.'[40]

Relevant definitions

The APA defines rulemaking as the 'agency[41] process for formulating, amend-ing, or repealing a rule.'[42] A 'rule' is defined broadly to include 'any agency statement of general or particular applicability and future effect designed to implement, interpret, or prescribe law or policy or describing the organization, procedure, or practice requirement of an agency.'[43] In order for rules to have

---

[36] Maeve P. Carey, *The Federal Rulemaking Process: An Overview*, Cong. Rsch. Serv. RL32240, at 1 (June 17, 2013).

[37] Cornelius M. Kerwin and Scott R. Furlong, *Rulemaking: How Government Agencies Write Law and Make Public Policy*, CQ Press (4th ed. 2011), at p. 2.

[38] Carey, *supra* note 36, at 5.

[39] *Id.*

[40] Todd Garvey, *A Brief Overview of Rulemaking and Judicial Review*, Cong. Rsch. Serv. R41546 (Mar. 27, 20217).

[41] The APA defines 'agency' as 'each of authority of the Government of the United States,' exempting 'Congress' and the 'courts of the United States.' 5 U.S.C. § 551(1).

[42] 5 U.S.C. § 551(5).

[43] 5 U.S.C. § 551(4).

the force and effect of law, they must be 'issued in compliance with certain legal requirements' and 'fall within the scope of authority delegated to the agency by Congress.'[44] These are often referred to as legislative rules and are different from non-legislative rules, which are generally interpretive rules and policy statements that do not have the force and effect of law.[45]

Formal and informal rulemaking

Generally, there are two types of rulemaking that an agency can engage in under the APA: formal and informal rulemaking. Formal rulemaking is mostly used in ratemaking proceedings and 'when rules are required by statute to be made "on the record" after an opportunity for a trial-type agency hearing.'[46] The requirements for formal rulemaking are provided in §§ 556 and 557 of the APA. However, agencies do not typically engage in formal rulemaking because there are few statutes that require on-the-record hearings.[47] None of the regulatory authorities related to space discussed in this book resulted from formal rulemaking.

Instead, when an agency promulgates legislative rules (rules made pursuant to congressionally delegated authority), the informal rulemaking procedures of 5 U.S.C. § 553 govern. Section 553 is informally referred to as 'notice and comment' rulemaking because it requires that the public be provided with 'adequate notice' and 'a meaningful opportunity to comment' on the proposed regulation's content. The requirements are designed 'to ensure public participation in the informal rulemaking process.'[48] This is the process by which domestic space regulations over commercial launch and reentry, remote sensing, and communications have been adopted.

Adequate notice

When an agency embarks on a rulemaking, Section 553(b) of the APA requires that the agency publish a notice of proposed rulemaking (NPRM) in the Federal Register[49] to provide the public with adequate notice.[50] Further, the APA requires NPRMs to include '(1) the time, place, and nature of public

---

[44]   Garvey, *supra* note 40, at 1 (citing Appalachian Power Co. v. EPA, 208 F.3d 1015, 1020 (D.C. Cir. 2000) and Nat'l Mining Ass'n v. McCarthy, 758 F.3d 243, 250 (D.C. Cir. 2014)).

[45]   *Id.*

[46]   Carey, *supra* note 36, at 5.

[47]   *Id.*

[48]   Garvey, *supra* note 40, at 2.

[49]   *Federal Register*, National Archives, https://www.federalregister.gov/ (last accessed Dec. 5, 2021).

[50]   5 U.S.C. § 553(b).

rulemaking proceedings; (2) reference to the legal authority under which the rule is proposed; and (3) either the terms or substance of the proposed rule or a description of the subjects and issues involved.'[51] The § 553 notice requirement is generally satisfied when an agency 'affords interested person a reasonable and meaningful opportunity to participate in the rulemaking process.'[52]

PRACTICE TIP

Monitoring the Federal Register for notices of import to your client is key to effective representation. You will want to track rulemakings that affect your client's interests. The Federal Register is available online and allows anyone to register for updates on agency actions.

Meaningful opportunity to comment

When adequate notice is provided to the public, the agency must then allow the public a meaningful opportunity to comment on a proposed rule through the submission of 'written data, views, or arguments with or without opportunity for oral presentation.'[53] Even though the APA does not provide a minimum period of time for agencies to accept public comments on a proposed rule, 'most federal agencies accept comments on documents within a defined timeframe, known as the open comment period.'[54] It is typical for agencies to allow the comment period to be open for 30 to 60 days.[55] If the comment period is short, a request for an extension may be submitted before the comment period closes. For example, when the FAA requested comments on its rulemaking to update launch and reentry licensing, many members of industry filed and were successful in obtaining an extension to the comment period. Finally, any public comments and their supporting materials are placed in a rulemaking 'docket' and become available for public inspection.[56]

---

[51] *Id.*

[52] Forester v. CPSC, 559 F.2d 774, 787 (D.C. Cir. 1977).

[53] 5 U.S.C. § 553(c).

[54] *Frequently Asked Questions: General Information: Commenting: When can I comment?*, Regulations.gov, https://www.regulations.gov/faq (last accessed Dec. 5, 2021).

[55] *A Guide to the Rulemaking Process*, Office of the Federal Register, https://www.federalregister.gov/uploads/2011/01/the_rulemaking_process.pdf (last accessed Dec. 5, 2021).

[56] *See, Frequently Asked Questions: General Information: Commenting: How do I view comments on a document?*, Regulations.gov, https://www.regulations.gov/faq (last accessed Dec. 5, 2021).

THE RULEMAKING PROCESS

The rulemaking process can generally be broken down into three stages: the pre-rule stage, the proposed rule stage, and the final rule stage.[57]

Pre-rule Stage

The pre-rule stage includes the time before a proposed rule is published. During this time, individuals and entities can submit requests and recommendations for rulemaking and regulatory reform efforts. Prior to engaging in a rulemaking, an agency must confirm that it has the statutory authority to regulate on the proposed subject. Typically, agencies engage in the rulemaking process after considering several factors, including but not limited to:

- New technologies or new data on existing issues;
- Concerns arising from accidents or various problems affecting society;
- Recommendations from Congressional committees or federal advisory committees;
- Petitions from interest groups, corporations, and members of the public;
- Lawsuits filed by interest groups, corporations, States, and members of the public;
- Presidential directives;
- Requests from other agencies; or
- Studies and recommendations of agency staff.[58]

PRACTICE TIP

To find the source of an agency's rulemaking authority in a proposed or final rule, look at the 'Summary' or 'Supplementary Information' section of their published rule.

Once a year, agencies are required to publish a 'Regulatory Plan' and an 'Agenda of Regulatory and Deregulatory Actions' in the spring and fall, respectively.[59] Together, these two publications are referred to as the Unified Agenda and list the regulatory actions that an agency is planning to take in the future. The Unified Agenda signals to the public the future rulemaking

---

[57] *See, The Reg Map: Informal Rulemaking*, ICF.com (2020), https://www.reginfo.gov/public/reginfo/Regmap/REG_MAP_2020.pdf.

[58] Office of Federal Register, *supra* note 55, at 2.

[59] *About the Unified Agenda*, Executive Office of the President, https://www.reginfo.gov/public/jsp/eAgenda/UA_About.myjsp (last accessed Dec. 6, 2021).

activities the agency plans to engage in and updates the public on pending and completed regulatory actions.[60]

Public petitions and advance notices of rulemaking

There are multiple ways for the public to influence an agency's decision to start the rulemaking process. Members of the public (i.e., individuals, groups, trade associations, and/or companies) may submit a 'Petition for Rulemaking'[61] requesting rulemaking on a single or multiple matters. Once an agency receives a Petition for Rulemaking from the public, it may publish the petition on the Federal Register and accept public comments on it. Space law advocates have petitioned various agencies for rulemaking when faced with rules they deemed outdated or inappropriate to their operations.

Conversely, before an agency begins drafting a rule, it can formally invite the public to provide their input on what shape a rule should take by publishing an advance notice of proposed rulemaking (ANPRM) in the Federal Register.[62] An ANPRM announces to the public that 'an agency is considering a regulatory action,' and gives the public an opportunity to provide their input on whether the agency should initiate a rulemaking on the proposed topic.[63] Interested parties 'may then respond to the ANPRM by submitting comments aimed at developing and improving the draft proposal or by recommendation against issuing a rule.'[64]

ANPRMs are used by commercial space regulatory agencies. For instance, NOAA's rule on Licensing Private Remote Sensing Space Systems, which is discussed in detail in Chapter 8, was initially published as an ANPRM.[65]

---

[60] *Id.*

[61] These petitions are referred to as 553(e) petitions and are named after § 553(e) of the APA, which gives 'an interested person the right to petition [an agency] for the issuance, amendment, or repeal of a rule.' 5 USC §553(e). *See,* Maeve P. Carey, *Petitions for Rulemaking: An Overview,* Cong. Rsch. Serv. (Jan. 23, 2020), https://fas.org/sgp/crs/misc/R46190.pdf.

[62] *Abbreviations,* Executive Office of the President, https://www.reginfo.gov/public/jsp/eAgenda/Abbrevs.myjsp (last accessed Dec. 6, 2021).

[63] *Id.*

[64] Office of Federal Register, *supra* note 55, at 3.

[65] *Request for Comments on Remote Sensing Regulatory Reform,* Office of Space Commerce (June 29, 2018), https://www.space.commerce.gov/request-for-comments-on-remote-sensing-regulatory-reform/.

Negotiated Rulemaking Act and the Federal Advisory Committee Act

To develop regulations, agencies may create negotiated rulemaking committees or federal advisory committees to seek the input of the involved public.[66] The Negotiated Rulemaking Act gives agencies the authority to 'establish a negotiated rulemaking committee to negotiate and develop a proposed rule, if the head of the agency determines that the use of the procedure is in the public interest.'[67] Negotiated rulemaking offers a supplement to traditional informal rulemaking procedures with the goal of reaching a consensus on the contents of a proposed rule.[68] Agencies use negotiated rulemaking to 'increase administrative efficiency and decrease subsequent opposition' to a rule by working with outside groups who have 'significant interest' in the rule's subject matter.[69]

When a negotiated rulemaking committee is established, the agency must publish notice in the Federal Register as well as other appropriate trade publications that includes a description of the subject and scope of the rule; the interests that may be significantly impacted by the rule; and the persons proposed to represent such interests.[70] A negotiated rulemaking committee may have a maximum of 25 members, unless the agency determines more members are necessary, with one person representing the agency.[71] The agency may set a timeframe for the negotiated rulemaking committee or allow the members to work to reach an agreement on the proposed rule's contents. The agency may then issue the agreement as a proposed rule but is not bound by the agreement.[72]

An agency establishing a negotiated rulemaking committee is subject to the Federal Advisory Committee Act (FACA) of 1972 to ensure that agencies are receiving impartial and relevant expertise, unless otherwise stated.[73] However,

---

[66]   Maeve P. Carey, *Negotiated Rulemaking: In Brief*, Cong. Rsch. Serv. R46756 at 4 (Apr. 12, 2021); Wendy Ginsberg and Casey Burgat, *Federal Advisory Committees: An Introduction and Overview*, Cong. Rsch. Serv. R44253 at 2 (Oct. 27, 2016). Negotiated rulemaking committees can be created by Congress or an agency head, while federal advisory committees can be created by Congress, the president, or agency head.

[67]   5 U.S.C. § 563(a). 'Interest' means, 'with respect to an issue or matter, multiple parties which have a similar point of view or which are likely to be affect in a similar manner.' 5 U.S.C. § 562(5).

[68]   Carey, *supra* note 36, at 22; Carey, *supra* note 66, at 5.

[69]   *Id. See*, Laura I. Langebein and Cornelius M. Kerwin, *Regulatory Negotiation versus Conventional Rulemaking: Claims, Counterclaims, and Empirical Evidence*, 10 J. of Pub. Admin. Rsch. & Theory 599 (2000).

[70]   5 U.S.C. § 564 (a)(1)–(8).

[71]   5 U.S.C. § 565 (b).

[72]   Carey, *supra* note 36, at 22.

[73]   *Id.* at 24; 5 U.S.C. § 565(a)(1).

in some instances, Congress may exempt a rulemaking committee from being subject to FACA, which requires committee meetings and record to be available to the public, in order to facilitate a more frank discussion.[74] For example, the FAA's Office of Commercial Space Transportation may use an Aerospace Rulemaking Committee, known as a SpARC, to begin developing occupant safety regulations for its Part 460, although it is prohibited by statute from issuing such regulations.[75]

Federal advisory committees are similar to negotiated rulemaking committees in the sense that the expertise of the involved public is sought and utilized by an agency to develop regulations or policy. The difference between the two is that a federal advisory committee is not asked to develop a rule, but to advise on a specific topic or task asked of by an agency. Advisory committees[76] typically consist of experts in the relevant field, including representatives of interest groups that may be impacted by the rule, and representatives from the relevant federal or state agencies.[77] The FAA's Commercial Space Transportation Advisory Committee (COMSTAC), which is discussed in more detail in Chapter 7, and the Advisory Committee on Commercial Remote Sensing, discussed in Chapter 8, are two active commercial space FACAs.[78]

The president's role in developing a proposed rule

The Office of Information and Regulatory Affairs (OIRA, pronounced 'oh-eye-ruh') within the Executive Office of the President is typically charged with analyzing an agency's draft regulations before it is published in the Federal Register.[79] In addition to making sure that the regulation is in line

---

[74] 5a U.S.C. § 10(a)–11(a); *See*, Ginsberg, *supra* note 66, at 2.

[75] *Commercial Space Transportation Advisory Committee (COMSTAC): November 2021*, Federal Aviation Administration (FAA), https://www.faa.gov/space/additional _information/comstac/presentations/ (last accessed Dec. 6, 2021).

[76] The Federal Advisory Committee Act (FACA) of 1972 defines 'advisory committee' as 'any committee, board, commission, council, conference, panel, task force, or other similar group, or any subcommittee or other subgroup thereof, which is established or utilized by statute, the President or by one or more agencies.' 5 U.S.C. §3(2).

[77] Carey, *supra* note 36, at 21.

[78] *Advisory and Rulemaking Committees: Commercial Space Transportation Advisory Committee (COMSTAC)*, FAA, https://www.faa.gov/regulations_policies/ rulemaking/committees/documents/index.cfm/committee/browse/committeeID/78.

[79] OIRA is 'the United States Government's central authority for the review of Executive Branch regulations.' OIRA only reviews significant rules and does not review any rules submitted by independent regulatory agencies. *Information and Regulatory Affairs*, Office of Management and Budget, https://www.whitehouse.gov/ omb/information-regulatory-affairs/ (last accessed Dec. 6, 2021); *Regulations and the Rulemaking Process*, Executive Office of the President, https://www.reginfo.gov/ public/jsp/Utilities/faq.jsp#oira (last accessed Dec. 6, 2021).

with the president's policy and agenda, OIRA also analyzes rules to determine whether they are 'significant' due to a rule's economic impact or because they raise important policy issues.[80] If OIRA approves the publication of an agency's rule in the Federal Register, the rule enters the proposed rule stage.

The Proposed Rule Stage

The proposed rule stage begins when a notice of proposed rulemaking (NPRM) is published on the Federal Register. Publication provides official notice to all interested parties of the agency's intent on amending, repealing, or issuing a new rule, and allows the public to provide their comments on the proposed rule. Due to the APA's broad definition of 'person,'[81] anyone has the right to submit public comments on Federal Register notices or proposed and final rules. After the public comments are received, the agency reviews those comments as well as the rule in light of the comments received.[82] In some instances, after a comment period is closed, an agency will open a second comment period to allow the public to reply to the comments the agency received, creating a more informed public dialogue.[83]

When the comment period is officially closed, the agency may amend its proposed rule to incorporate public input, or it may reject the public's comments. Regardless, the agency must respond to every substantive comment and explain why it chose to ignore or incorporate the input.

Structure of a proposed rule

Every proposed rule begins with a preamble that contains the rule's summary, publication date, contact information, and supplementary information.[84] The preamble can be key to interpreting the rule for practice purposes. Commercial space regulations' preambles often provide key explanations of how the agency intends its regulations to work that may be key to advocacy efforts before the agency.

The rule's summary explains the issues, the proposed actions being considered, and why the rule is necessary. The rule then provides dates and directions

---

[80]   Office of Federal Register, *supra* note 55, at 3. 'For significant rules, the agency must estimate the costs and benefits of the rule and consider alternate solutions.'

[81]   A 'person' is defined to include 'an individual, partnership, corporation, association, or public or private organization other than an agency.' 5 U.S.C. § 551 (2).

[82]   Office of Federal Register, *supra* note 55, at 8.

[83]   Having multiple periods to comment publicly is also typical when an agency issues an ANPRM.

[84]   Office of Federal Register, *supra* note 55, at 8.

for submitting comments.[85] After the preamble, the explanatory and regulatory text is published in full. In preparing comments to a proposed rule, it is important to closely compare the explanatory text with the actual regulatory text that will be adopted. Any disagreements or ambiguities between the two are important to include in comments for clarification in the final rule.

The Final Rule Stage

Before publishing the final rule, the agency must base its reasoning and conclusions on all of the comments, scientific data, expert opinions, and facts accumulated in the rulemaking record.[86] After reviewing the record, the agency may either move forward with a final rule, if it finds that the proposed rule will accomplish its goals, or it may terminate the rulemaking considering the public comments.

After ensuring that the agency properly followed the mandated procedural processes, OIRA publishes the final rule in the Federal Register. Once published, significant rules may not take effect for 60 days, while non-significant rules are effective no less than 30 days after publication.[87] This delay provides interested stakeholders time to legally challenge the rule.

Judicial Review of Agency Rulemaking

Arbitrary and capricious

Under U.S. federal law, there is a 'strong presumption that Congress intends judicial review of administrative action,'[88] as it is embodied in the APA, which states that 'final agency action for which there is no other adequate remedy in a court [is] subject to judicial review.'[89]

---

[85] *Id.*

[86] *Id.*

[87] *Id.*

[88] Garvey, *supra* note 6, at 13 (citing Bowen v. Mich. Acad. Of Family Phys. 476 U.S. 667, 670 (1986)).

[89] 5 U.S.C. §§ 702, 704. Note that a statute may specifically exclude judicial review. 5 U.S.C. § 701(a).

When a federal court does review a final agency action, there are six circumstances wherein the APA allows a court to set it aside, including agency actions, findings, and conclusion found to be –

(A)   Arbitrary, capricious, an abuse of discretion, or otherwise not in accordance with law;

(B)   Contrary to constitutional right, power, privilege, or immunity;

(C)   In excess of statutory jurisdiction, authority, or limitations, or short of statutory right;

(D)   Without observance of procedure required by law;

(E)   Unsupported by substantial evidence in a case subject to sections 556 and 557 of this title or otherwise reviewed on the record of an agency hearing provided by statute; or

(F)   Unwarranted by the facts to the extent that the facts are subject to trial de novo by the reviewing court.[90]

The arbitrary and capricious standard is the most common standard of review that courts apply when reviewing legal challenges of agency actions.[91] This fact-based and situation-specific standard applies to all factual determinations an agency makes in an informal rulemaking proceeding, including notice-and-comment rulemakings as well as many other discretionary determinations.[92]

At its simplest, the arbitrary and capricious standard of review instructs a court to not 'substitute its judgments for that of the agency.'[93] Instead, agency determinations should only be invalidated by a court if they fail to 'examine the relevant data and articulate a satisfactory explanation for [the] action including a "rational connection between the facts found and the choices made."'[94] Judicial precedent has added that courts must 'consider whether the decision was based on a consideration of the relevant factors and whether there has been a clear error of judgment.'[95]

---

[90]   5 U.S.C. § 706(2).

[91]   Garvey, *supra* note 6, at 14.

[92]   *See*, Assoc. of Data Processing Serv. Orgs., Inc. v. Bd. of Govs. of the Fed. Res. Sys., 745 F.2d 677, 684 (D.C. Cir. 1984); and Troy Corp. v. Browner, 120 F.3d 277, 284 (D.C. Cir. 1997).

[93]   *Motor Vehicle Manufacturers Association v. State Farm Auto Mutual Insurance Co.*, 463 U.S. 29, 42–44 (1983).

[94]   *Id.*

[95]   *Id.* at 43.

As the Supreme Court clearly said, an agency action or decision is arbitrary or capricious:

> if the agency has relied on factors which Congress has not intended it to consider, entirely failed to consider an important aspect of the problem, offered an explanation for its decision that runs counter to the evidence before the agency, or is so implausible that it could not be ascribed to a difference in view or the product of agency expertise.[96]

In the rulemaking context, the arbitrary and capricious standard of review is intended to ensure that agencies are not exceeding their authority and are making reasoned decisions when it comes to creating regulations that have the weight and effect of law.

Chevron deference

When reviewing whether an agency has appropriately implemented a statute that Congress has charged it with administering, courts will apply the standard of review established in the *Chevron U.S.A. Inc. v. National Resources Defense Council, Inc.* case. In that case, the Supreme Court established a 'two-step analysis for determining the appropriate level of deference to an agency's interpretation of the statutes it administers.'[97]

The first step 'is the question whether Congress has directly spoken to the precise question at issue. If the intent of Congress is clear, that is the end of the matter; for the court as well as the agency, must give effect to the unambiguously expressed intent of Congress.'[98] The second step is 'if the statute is silent or ambiguous with respect to the specific issue, the question for the court is whether the agency's answer is based on a permissible construction of the statute.'[99]

Here, the Supreme Court introduced the principle of deference to administrative interpretations of statutes that are silent on the issue, resulting in the standard of reviewing becoming referred to as the Chevron deference.[100] Thus, Chevron deference refers to the 'concept that executive agencies are entitled to deference in interpreting their authorizing legislation and their regulations

---

[96] *Id.*

[97] David K. Tochen, *The National Transportation Safety Board's Authority to Investigate Commercial Space Launch Accidents*, National Transportation Safety Board at 2 (July 1, 2015).

[98] *Chevron U.S.A. Inc. v. National Resources Defense Council, Inc.*, 467 U.S. 837, at 842 (1984).

[99] *Id.* at 843.

[100] Tochen, *supra* note 97, at 3.

based on such legislation.'[101] In short, 'courts defer to agencies' expertise on their areas of authorized responsibility.'[102]

QUESTIONS FOR REVIEW

1. If you were representing a client, how would you go about getting Congress to change a law or pass a new one?
2. How does Congress exercise its 'power of the purse' in respect to the executive branch?
3. What is the main purpose of administrative law? What are the primary purposes of the Administrative Procedure Act?
4. Why are rulemakings with the opportunity to hear, and respond to, public comment important?
5. What is the purpose of judicial review of agency action? How does this compare with the system of checks and balances in U.S. constitutional law?
6. Your client walks into your office and wants to pay you to change an agency's rule. Where do you start? How long do you think it might take?

---

[101] *Id.*
[102] *Id.*

6. The National Aeronautics and Space Administration

Ruth is thrilled – she has tickets to see Hamilton *at the Kennedy Center! She's looking forward to walking through the Hall of States and then sipping a glass of champagne on the patio overlooking the Potomac River. Her reverie is broken as she reaches for her jacket – at that very moment, her senior partner walks in and plops down in her office guest chair.*

'Great news! One of our international clients just called. They need our help submitting a response to a NASA request for proposals,' he explains. 'NASA is looking for a company to scoop up some lunar regolith and deliver it to them. The client is looking for us to tell them where to start.'

Abandoning all hopes of making it to Hamilton, *Ruth picks up a pen and notepad and starts peppering the senior partner with questions. 'There is so much that we need to figure out: who is our client? Is it a domestic entity or a foreign space agency? Is NASA looking for an international cooperation or a commercial services contract? What kind of contract? Cost-plus or firm fixed price? We need to answer some questions before we determine what legal instrument is the correct one ... '*

The senior partner replies, 'Those are all good questions, Ruth. I'll forward you the information I have so far.'

After the senior partner leaves, Ruth sighs deeply and extracts the two Opera House tickets from her purse. She walks over to the paralegal and drops them on her desk. 'Have fun!' Ruth tells her. 'It's going to be a late night for me.'

THE NATIONAL AERONAUTICS AND SPACE ADMINISTRATION

In response to the launch of Sputnik 1, Congress created the National Aeronautics and Space Administration (NASA) in 1958 as a civilian agency to 'exercise[e] control over aeronautical and space activities sponsored by the United States.'[1] NASA's high-profile role in human spaceflight, deep space exploration, and international partnerships may lead some to assume that it is

---

[1]   National Aeronautics and Space Act of 1958, PUB. L. 85-568, 72 STAT. 426 (July 29, 1958) [*hereinafter* NASA Act 1958].

responsible for all U.S. space activities, but it is just one of many executive branch agencies involved in U.S. space activities. In fact, in the grand scheme of federal spending, NASA's budget is small. NASA gets less than one half of one penny of every tax dollar collected – making its budget about 0.49% of federal spending. In 2021, Congress gave NASA a budget of $23.3 billion, out of a $4.8 trillion budget.[2] This chapter will examine NASA's history, as well as the legal structures within which it administers its international and commercial partnerships.

NASA'S LEGISLATIVE AUTHORITY

NASA was created by the National Aeronautics and Space Act of 1958, 'to provide for research into problems of flight within and outside the earth's atmosphere, and for other purposes.'[3] It is under the aegis of that one simple proviso that humankind first walked on the Moon.

The 1958 Act has been amended over time but has largely stayed consistent with its 1958 original text. Section 102 of the Act, codified today at 51 U.S.C. § 20102, continues to lay out the agency's purpose and responsibilities. It is in that section that Congress declared that 'the general welfare and security of the United States require that adequate provision be made for aeronautical and space activities.' The declaration that the general welfare and security of the U.S. required that provision be made for aeronautical and space activities reflects the reaction of the U.S. to the Soviet launch of Sputnik 1.[4]

Congress put control of aeronautical and space activities in the hands of a civilian agency,[5] with the explicit exception that 'activities peculiar to or primarily associated with the development of weapons systems, military operations, or the defense of the United States (including the research and devel-

---

[2]   NASA, FY 2021 Budget Estimates (Feb. 10, 2020), https://www.nasa.gov/sites/default/files/atoms/files/fy_2021_budget_book_508.pdf. For comparison, the Department of Defense got about $715 billion, more than 30 times NASA's budget.

[3]   NASA Act 1958, *supra* note 1, at Preamble.

[4]   ALBERT K. LAI, THE COLD WAR, THE SPACE RACE, AND LAW OF OUTER SPACE: SPACE FOR PEACE 48: 'In October 1958, the United States established NASA to create a coherent space program in response to the launch of *Sputnik* the previous year.' (Routledge eds., 2021).

[5]   'Aeronautical and space activities' is actually a defined term under the statute. 51 U.S.C. § 20103(1) (2018). 'The term "aeronautical and space activities" means: (A) research into, and the solution of, problems of flight within and outside the Earth's atmosphere; (B) the development, construction, testing, and operation for research purposes of aeronautical and space vehicles; (C) the operation of a space transportation system including the space shuttle, upper stages, space platforms, and related equipment; and (D) such other activities as may be required for the exploration of space.'

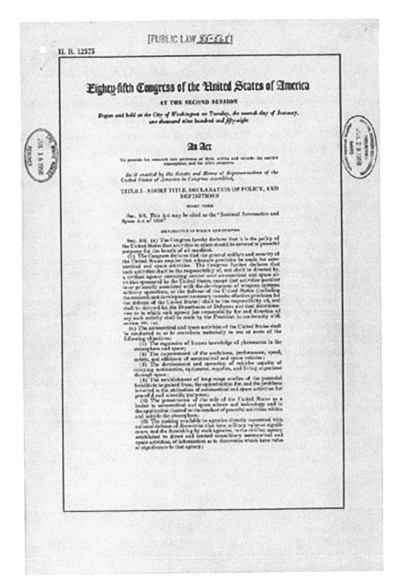

Figure 6.1   Public Law of 1958

This is a copy of the Public Law of 1958 that created NASA. Section 102(a) is particularly noteworthy, where it is called out explicitly that: 'The Congress hereby declares that it is the policy of the United States that activities in space should be devoted to peaceful purposes for the benefit of all mankind.'

opment necessary to make effective provision for the defense of the United States) shall be the responsibility of, and shall be directed by, the Department of Defense.'[6]

In the very next section of its foundational statute, Congress also declared that the general welfare of the U.S. requires that NASA 'seek and encourage, to the maximum extent possible, the fullest commercial use of space.' NASA has cited this direction for a multitude of its commercialization activities, including its opening up of the ISS for commercial activities.[7]

NASA's organic statute then instructs that the 'aeronautical and space activities' of the U.S. shall contribute to the following objectives:

(1)   The expansion of human knowledge of the Earth and of phenomena in the atmosphere and space.

(2)   The improvement of the usefulness, performance, speed, safety, and efficiency of aeronautical and space vehicles.

(3)   The development and operation of vehicles capable of carrying instruments, equipment, supplies, and living organisms through space.

(4)   The establishment of long-range studies of the potential benefits to be gained from, the opportunities for, and the problems involved in the utilization of aeronautical and space activities for peaceful and scientific purposes.

(5)   The preservation of the role of the United States as a leader in aeronautical and space science and technology and in the application thereof to the conduct of peaceful activities within and outside the atmosphere.

(6)   The making available to agencies directly concerned with national defense of discoveries that have military value or significance, and the furnishing by such agencies, to the civilian agency established to direct and control nonmilitary aeronautical and space activities, of information as to discoveries which have value or significance to that agency.

(7)   *Cooperation by the United States with other nations and groups of nations* in work done pursuant to this chapter and in the peaceful application of the results thereof.

(8)   The most effective utilization of the scientific and engineering resources of the United States, with close cooperation among all interested agencies of the

---

[6]   *Id.* § 20102(b).

[7]   See Section IV.B.5, *infra.* In June 2019, NASA opened the ISS to private tourists for visits of up to 30 days and invited U.S. commercial companies to use the ISS for commercial and marketing activities. *See* Karen Northon, *NASA Opens International Space Station to New Commercial Opportunities, Private Astronauts*, NASA (Jan. 7, 2019), https://www.nasa.gov/press-release/nasa-opens-international-space-station-to -new-commercial-opportunities-private. Shortly thereafter, there were rumors about Tom Cruise flying to the ISS to make a movie. Loren Grush, *Tom Cruise Will Work with NASA on First Movie Filmed in Space, NASA Says*, VERGE (May 6, 2020), https:// www.theverge.com/2020/5/5/21248460/nasa-tom-cruise-movie-international-space -station. Those plans were moved to the right in light of the COVID-19 pandemic.

United States in order to avoid unnecessary duplication of effort, facilities, and equipment.

(9)   The preservation of the United States preeminent position in aeronautics and space through research and technology development related to associated manufacturing processes.

(10) The search for life's origin, evolution, distribution, and future in the universe.[8]

INTERNATIONAL COOPERATION

When Congress created NASA in 1958, the Space Act compelled NASA to pursue cooperation 'with other nations and groups of nations.'[9] This principle of international cooperation has been a guiding philosophy for NASA, and it is as important now as it was at NASA's creation. Working cooperatively with other countries is critical to addressing the inherently global and interrelated scientific challenges (like climate change) that we encounter; expanding human knowledge through answering profound questions about the Earth and the universe in which we live; resolving engineering issues related to managing air traffic; making aviation safer for everyone; and pushing the boundaries of innovation.

The Space Act authorizes NASA to engage in a program of international cooperation to fulfill its mission: under the foreign policy guidance of the president, NASA 'may engage in a program of international cooperation in work done pursuant to this Act, and in the peaceful application of the results thereof, pursuant to agreements made by the President with the advice and consent of the Senate.'[10]

An accompanying signing statement by President Eisenhower on July 29, 1958, underscored NASA's authority to conclude international executive agreements on behalf of the United States: 'I regard this section merely as recognizing that international treaties may be made in this field, and as not precluding, in appropriate cases, less formal arrangements for cooperation. To construe the section otherwise would raise substantial constitutional questions.' Since NASA's founding 60 years ago, NASA has consistently interpreted this provision to require 'legally binding agreements.'[11] President

---

[8]   51 U.S.C. § 20202 (d) (2018) (*emphasis added*).

[9]   NASA Act 1958, *supra* note 1, § 102(c)(7).

[10] 51 U.S.C. § 20115 (2018).

[11] Parallel NASA authority to conduct activities with U.S. entities through binding agreements under U.S. law; in the performance of its functions, NASA is authorized: 'to enter into and perform such contracts, leases, cooperative agreements, or other transactions as may be necessary in the conduct of its work and on such terms as it may deem appropriate, with any agency or instrumentality of the United States, or with any

Eisenhower's reference to 'less formal arrangements for cooperation' refers to international arrangements less formal than treaties requiring the advice and consent of the Senate, yet which are, nevertheless, legally binding agreements.[12] In U.S. parlance, these 'less formal arrangements for cooperation' are known as 'executive agreements,'[13] and under the Case-Zablocki Act, executive agreements must be notified to the Congress within 60 days of their entry into force.[14]

NASA's International Partners

NASA's foreign partners can be government agencies, space agencies, universities, or international organizations. Some of these entities have the legal capacity to enter into binding agreements under international law. Where a foreign agency is authorized to make commitments binding under international law on behalf of its respective government, or an international organization has authority to make such binding commitments, NASA will normally conclude an international agreement with that entity to cooperate on a space-related project.

If a foreign governmental entity lacks the legal capacity to execute agreements binding under international law, an exchange of diplomatic notes with the party's government may be required to conclude the agreement (see discussion, *infra*), or the international agreement may be signed at the appropriate government level (e.g., foreign ministries). Alternatively, the agreement can be signed pursuant to U.S. federal law (more on that below).

Additionally, the U.S. Government has concluded 'framework agreements' (discussed below) with several foreign governments, which include the legal provisions necessary for NASA to initiate project-specific cooperative agreements, called implementing arrangements. Pursuant to a framework agreement, implementing arrangements with foreign agency counterparts provide the purpose, specific responsibilities, and other terms necessary for the cooperation.

State Territory, or possession, or with any political subdivision thereof, or with any person, firm, association, corporation, or educational institution.' *Id.* § 20113(a).

[12]   Youngstown Sheet & Tube Co. v. Sawyer, 343 U.S. 579 (1952) (concurring opinion of Frankfurter, J.).

[13]   For a discussion of U.S. practice with executive agreements, *see* ANTHONY AUST, MODERN TREATY LAW AND PRACTICE 157–8 (1st ed., Cambridge Univ. Press 2002).

[14]   *See generally* 22 U.S.C. § 2656d (2018); Case-Zablocki Act, PUB. L. 92-403, 1 U.S.C. §§ 112a, 112b (2018); 22 C.F.R. Part 181 (2021) (regulations implementing the Case Act).

NASA's Coordination with the State Department

NASA's international agreements must comply with the procedural guidelines provided in the Case-Zablocki Act (1 U.S.C. § 112(b)) and its implementing regulations (22 C.F.R. § 181).[15] Before negotiating and executing an international agreement under international law, NASA submits the draft agreement to the State Department to determine whether the Circular 175 (or 'C-175') process would apply to a particular agreement.[16] Following this intra-governmental review through this C-175 process, the State Department typically gives NASA authorization to negotiate and conclude the draft agreement, subject to final approval of the State Department, which would review and approve any changes to the draft agreement that occur during negotiations. Some agreements may only receive authority to *negotiate* and must be submitted for a second C-175 review for authority to *conclude* an agreement (this was seen in relation to the Gateway MOUs that NASA concluded in 2020). After final approvals are received, the agreement may be signed.

As discussed in the next section, when U.S. federal law is selected as the governing law in an agreement, the agreement would not typically require formal coordination with the State Department.[17]

Addressing Conflict of Laws

NASA agreements that are governed by international law contain no choice of law clause – there's a general drafting presumption that agreements between foreign countries are governed by international law.[18] However, for those instances when a foreign party lacks the legal capacity to conclude a legally binding agreement under international law, NASA will propose that U.S. federal law govern the agreement. This is a longstanding NASA practice used to make the agreement legally binding.[19] This also ensures that both foreign

---

[15] The Case-Zablocki Act requires that the State Department report significant international commitments of the U.S. to the Foreign Relations Committees of the U.S. Senate and House of Representatives. 1 U.S.C. § 112b(a) (2018).

[16] *See* U.S. Dep't State, 11 FOREIGN AFF. MANUAL § 724.4(b) (2006).

[17] State Department's C-175 regulations only apply to agreements that are made legally binding under international law. 22 C.F.R. § 181.2(a)(1) (2021).

[18] 'In the absence of any provision in the arrangement with respect to governing law, it will be presumed to be governed by international law.' 22 C.F.R. § 181.2(a)(1) (2021).

[19] While all the provisions of an international agreement are important, there are certain provisions for which NASA must secure a legally binding commitment from the partner due to potential legal ramifications. Some of those include: transfer of goods and technical data; intellectual property rights; liability and risk of loss; and con-

and domestic commercial entities are treated alike by NASA.[20] Regardless of the choice of law, however, NASA's performance of its responsibilities under any agreement is subject to applicable U.S. laws. Similarly, the other party's performance of its responsibilities under a NASA agreement is subject to its applicable laws.

Exchange of Diplomatic Notes

If a foreign entity lacks the legal capacity to conclude an international agreement binding under international law in its own name (such as is the case with the Italian Space Agency, ASI (Agenzia Spaziale Italiana)), an international agreement may require additional steps before it enters into force, such as the exchange of diplomatic notes.[21] This occurs either because the other country requires this added step or because the other party does not have the authority to enter into an international agreement binding under international law. The final provisions clause will define the requirements for the international agreement to enter into force.[22]

NASA'S FRAMEWORK AGREEMENTS FOR INTERNATIONAL COOPERATION

Over the last 25–30 years, NASA has developed a practice of concluding bilateral framework agreements to establish the parameters for the conduct of cooperative space missions with space agencies of other countries. These framework agreements are both useful and, in some cases, necessary. NASA's framework agreements generally contain a core set of legal clauses governing activities under those agreements, including topics such as liability, intellectual property rights, and the transfer of goods and technical data. Successful conclusion of legal framework agreements in advance of international cooper-

---

sultation and dispute resolution. *See* Steven A. Mirmina, *International Framework Agreements Governing Civil Uses of Outer Space*, 22 AIR & SPACE LAW. 9 (2009).

[20] All of NASA's international agreements with foreign commercial entities must include a choice of law clause to specify that U.S. federal law is the governing law. Off. Gen. Counsel, NASA Advisory Implementing Instruction 1050-1C, Space Act Agreements Guide § 3.3.2.17 (Feb. 25, 2013) [*hereinafter* NAII 1050-1C].

[21] When exchange of diplomatic notes (dip notes) is necessary, NASA works closely with the Department of State to ensure that this additional procedural step occurs. Otherwise, without the exchange of both dip notes, the international agreement may not legally be in force. Mirmina, *supra* note 19, at 10.

[22] Sometimes, even further procedural steps are required, such as an additional exchange of dip notes to confirm that all domestic processes required to bring the agreement into force have occurred. NAII 1050-1C, *supra* note 20, at § 4.6.25.

ation facilitates the resolution of legal issues and makes scientific and technical cooperation between the parties proceed more smoothly.

As of this book's publication date, NASA currently has 14 active framework agreements. Eleven of those are State-to-State and three are agency-to-agency. There are State-to-State agreements with Argentina, Brazil, Canada, France, Italy, Japan, the Republic of Korea, Norway, Russia,. Sweden and the United Arab Emirates. Other agreements are pending in various stages of drafting and negotiation, including with: Australia, Luxembourg, New Zealand, Spain, and Vietnam. Additionally, NASA also has three active agency-to-agency framework agreements with: DLR (Germany Space Agency), ISRO (Indian Space Research Organisation), and ISA (Israel Space Agency).

When a foreign space agency does not have the authority to conclude agreements that are legally binding under international law, the space cooperation agreement generally must be concluded by the foreign ministry of the other country. The U.S. Government can accomplish this in two basic ways. One way is for NASA to request that the State Department conclude the legal framework agreement on a government-to-government level. The other option involves NASA requesting the State Department to exchange diplomatic notes with the corresponding ministry of foreign affairs (or other appropriate ministry) of the other country authorizing the cooperation described in the underlying agency-to-agency agreement. In this circumstance, the international agreement is not the underlying space cooperation instrument itself, but rather is found in the exchange of diplomatic notes.

CONTENTS OF NASA'S INTERNATIONAL FRAMEWORK AGREEMENTS

1.   Preamble

Most framework arrangements for civil cooperation in outer space are structured similarly. They often start with a preamble, in which the countries or the space agencies recall successful cooperation that they have shared in the past. For example:

> Recognizing a mutual interest in the exploration and use of outer space for peaceful purposes; Considering the desirability of enhanced cooperation between the Parties

in human space flight, space science and exploration, Earth science, civil aeronautics research and other activities; ... [and]
Recalling their long and fruitful cooperation since 19XX in the exploration and peaceful use of outer space, through the successful implementation of cooperative activities in a broad range of space science and applications areas; ...[23]

The preamble is then followed by an operative sentence stating something like: 'the Parties have agreed as follows...' (then setting forth the substance of the agreement).

2. Purpose and Scope

The preamble is often followed by a 'purpose' article explaining that the Parties wish to establish a legal framework to govern the terms and conditions for their future cooperation. After the purpose, when needed, agreements contain an article with any necessary definitions of specific terms for the agreement. Following that, one finds the scope article explaining the broad range of activities covered by the agreement.

3. Implementing Agencies

When the agreement is a government-to-government agreement, it usually contains an article explaining that NASA would be the 'implementing agency' on behalf of the U.S., and the foreign country's space agency would be the implementing agency for that country. Generally, the implementing arrangements refer to and are subject to the legal framework agreement, and should there be any inconsistency between the implementing arrangements and the framework agreement, the framework agreement prevails.

4. Financial Arrangements

NASA's legal framework agreements customarily contain a clause on financial arrangements generally stating that the obligations of the parties (or implementing agencies in the case of a government-to-government agreement) are subject to the availability of appropriated funds, and that if one party should encounter budgetary difficulties that may affect its performance under the agreement, it would consult with the other as soon as possible.

---

[23] *See* Framework Agreement Between the Government of the United States of America and the Government of Canada for Cooperation in the Exploration and Use of Outer Space for Peaceful Purposes (2009), T.I.A.S. No. 10-511.2.

5.   Customs Duties and Taxes

NASA has legal authority to exempt from customs duties and taxes articles that are used in international space cooperative activities.[24] Thus, legal framework agreements routinely contain a clause obliging the other party to waive customs duties and taxes if they have authority to do so, or to pay those duties or taxes should they be imposed.

6.   Intellectual Property

Intellectual property (IP) rights are also typically addressed in a legal framework agreement. Generally, any IP created by one party before or outside the scope of the agreement belongs to that party; and allocation of any IP rights solely created by one party or its contractors during the implementation of the agreement is determined by that party's national laws. For any IP jointly created during performance of the agreement (which is relatively unusual), the parties would be obliged to consult to determine any IP rights resulting from such a joint invention.

7.   Transfer of Goods and Technical Data

NASA follows applicable export control laws and regulations, including the Export Administration Regulations (EAR) and the International Traffic in Arms Regulations (ITAR). For this reason, NASA's legal framework agreements contain a clause concerning the transfer of goods and technical data. While the specific clause is very detailed, it essentially states a few fundamental principles: that only those technical data and export-controlled goods necessary to fulfill the agreement are transferred; and that, in performance of the agreement, the Parties will follow all applicable laws and regulations, particularly those concerning export control and control of classified information. Additionally, the clauses provide that if export-controlled goods or data are transferred, they must be marked appropriately, and that such goods and data are to be used solely for purposes of fulfilling that Party's responsibilities under the agreement, and then either returned or destroyed.

---

[24] The U.S. Harmonized Trade Schedule provides that imports of articles for NASA's use and articles imported to implement NASA's international programs would be eligible for duty-free customs entry. Int'l Trade Comm'n, 98 H.T.S. § 9808.00.80 (rev. 8, 2021) (enacted at 19 U.S.C. § 1202).

8.   Cross-waiver of Liability

NASA's liability provisions are complex, and they contain precise definitions. Nevertheless, they are well recognized over decades of practice as the standard of risk allocation for cooperative space activities throughout the globe. Succinctly stated, the fundamental principle of NASA's liability article states that each Party assumes its own risks inherent in the cooperative activity. The article contains a mutual promise by both Parties not to sue each other for losses caused by any of the activities that take place under the agreement, subject to a few exceptions. The article also requires that each Party flow this cross-waiver of claims down to any 'related entities' to ensure that they also waive claims against the other Party and the other Party's related entities. With each entity assuming its own risks under the agreement, the clause functions to encourage the collaborative exploration of outer space by lowering the costs of cooperation by reducing the risk of exposure to liability. Since NASA's waiver of claims includes waiving claims of other U.S. Government agencies, NASA looks to its partner space agencies (or their governments) to ensure that the scope of their waiver is reciprocal.[25]

9.   Consultations and Settlement of Disputes

NASA's agreements typically contain provisions on dispute settlement that state unequivocally that the parties will resolve disputes through negotiations and consultations. NASA aims to resolve disputes at the lowest possible technical level – for example at the level of the program managers. Failing that, disputes can be resolved at a higher managerial level. Only in rare cases would a dispute be elevated as high as the NASA Administrator or their designee for joint resolution.

10.   Final Clauses

NASA's legal framework agreements conclude with relatively standard final clauses, generally comprising the procedures for amendments, entry into force, duration, and termination of the agreement.[26]

---

[25]   *See generally* Steve Mirmina, *Cross-Waivers of Liability in Agreements to Explore Outer Space: What They Are and How They Work,* 9 SciTech Law. 1 (2012) (providing a more detailed explanation of cross-waivers in outer space exploration).

[26]   Final clauses 'owe their designation as *final clauses* not merely to the fact that they are normally placed at the end of a treaty but to the fact that they cannot be negotiated until work on the substantive provisions of the treaty itself is essentially com-

11.   Conclusion

Each of NASA's framework agreements has varying levels of detail and the scope can sometimes vary.[27] Nevertheless, successful conclusion of a framework agreement establishing the legal regime for potential cooperation between space agencies has proven to facilitate scientific and technical cooperation in a variety of areas, often on an expedited basis. By resolving legal questions in advance, NASA and its partner space agencies around the globe can focus their attention on what they do best: pioneering the future in space exploration, scientific discovery, and aeronautics research.

NASA AND SPACE COMMERCIALIZATION

Brief History

While many people exhort the benefits of 'new space,' it would be a mistake to say that the commercialization of outer space is a new endeavor. From the beginning of space exploration, private industry has been involved in space activities. In 1962, Bell Telephone Laboratories created the first U.S. communications satellite. Bell owned and operated the Telstar satellite, the first orbital satellite to transmit television and telephone signals from outer space, and the first satellite to broadcast the opening ceremony of the Olympics (Tokyo, 1964).[28]

Even earlier, in 1961, commercial industry was very involved with the Apollo program. North American Aviation – now part of Boeing – began developing various subsystems and ground support equipment for the Apollo spacecraft. It also designed and built the Apollo command and service

---

pleted.' Shabtai Rosenne, *When is a Final Clause Not a Final Clause*, 98 AM. J. INT'L L. 546 (2004).

[27]   For example, the U.S. concluded an agreement with Japan in 1995 solely in the area of cross-waiver of liability. *See* Agreement Between the Government of the United States of America and the Government of Japan Concerning Cross-Waiver of Liability for Cooperation in the Exploration and Use of Space for Peaceful Purposes, U.S.-Japan, Apr. 24, 1995, T.I.A.S. No. 12638 (1995) (including Exchange of Notes).

[28]   While the Olympics has been televised since 1936, it was only to a local audience and on tape delay for other countries. The 1964 'TV Olympics' were the first ones to be broadcast in the U.S. by NBC. However, coverage was still limited. What was not shown live was supplemented with taped events that had to be flown across the Pacific (by airplane) and then aired later in the U.S. *See* Todd Kortemeier, *How the 1964 Games Brought Live Olympic Sports to the United States for the First Time*, TEAM USA (Jan. 8, 2019), https://www.teamusa.org/News/2019/January/08/How-The-1964 -Games-Brought-Live-Olympic-Sports-To-The-United-States-For-The-First-Time.

modules, while the lunar module, the vehicle that landed the first humans on the Moon, was built by Grumman Aviation – now Northrop Grumman.[29] Rocketdyne built the Saturn V's rocket engines.[30]

Boeing built the lunar orbiter, which was the first U.S. vehicle to orbit the Moon. The orbiter had the mission of photographing the surface of the Moon to search for ideal landing sites for the Apollo missions.[31] Boeing also built the lunar roving vehicles (also known as the moon buggies), which were used on Apollo missions 15, 16 and 17. These vehicles allowed astronauts to extend their scientific research by driving miles from where they landed.[32]

Boeing was also involved in the U.S. Space Shuttle program. In July 1972, North American Rockwell (which became Rockwell International in 1973 and would eventually be acquired by Boeing) won a $2.6 billion contract to build the Space Shuttle orbiter, designated OV-101 (orbiter vehicle 101).[33] The orbiter is what most people picture when they hear the term 'Space Shuttle,' but the space transportation system (STS) included the orbiter, the SRBs, the external tank, and, of course, the engines. The first test shuttle, the Enterprise, named after Captain Kirk's vessel in the *Star Trek* TV show,[34] started flight testing activities in 1977 (although never actually flew in space). After the success of the Enterprise, Boeing also built the subsequent shuttles: Columbia in 1981; Challenger in 1982; Discovery in 1983; Atlantis in 1985; and Endeavour in 1992.[35]

In 1996, Boeing and Lockheed Martin created a joint venture called United Space Alliance (USA) to provide day-to-day management of the Space Shuttles. Boeing was also selected by NASA in 1993 as the prime contractor

---

[29]   *Space Legacy*, NORTHROP GRUMMAN (2021), https://www.northropgrumman.com/space/space-legacy/.

[30]   *See Apollo Lunar Spacecraft: Historical Snapshot*, BOEING (2021), https://www.boeing.com/history/products/apollo-lunar-spacecraft.page; *see also* Michael Lombardi & Erik Simonsen, *The High and the Mighty*, 8 BOEING FRONTIERS 54, 56 (Dec. 2009– Jan. 2010).

[31]   This spacecraft also took the first picture of the Earth taken from the vantage point of the Moon. Apollo Lunar Spacecraft, *supra* note 30.

[32]   All three moon buggies remain on the Moon today.

[33]   While Rockwell built the orbiter, other commercial industry also played critical roles. Rocketdyne made the engines; Thiokol made the solid rocket boosters (SRBs); and Martin Marietta built the external tank.

[34]   Many people don't know that NASA originally called the first Space Shuttle the 'Constitution.' It was only after the U.S. public had a 'write-in' campaign that NASA changed the name to honor the sci-fi TV show *Star Trek*. John Uri, *50 Years of NASA and Star Trek Connections*, NASA (June 3, 2019), https://www.nasa.gov/feature/50-years-of-nasa-and-star-trek-connections/.

[35]   *Space Shuttle Orbiter: Historical Snapshot*, BOEING (2021), https://www.boeing.com/history/products/space-shuttle-orbiter.page.

for the ISS. It was tasked with the design, development, construction, and operations of the ISS.[36] Boeing was the company that built all the major U.S. elements, and as the prime contractor for NASA it oversaw the activities of thousands of subcontractors,[37] such as Lockheed Martin, which constructed the ISS's solar arrays.[38]

Commercialization Initiatives from 2004–Present

While an entire textbook by itself could be written about NASA's commercialization efforts over the last two decades, below is a short chronological synopsis of how NASA got to the point that private companies are transporting astronauts to the ISS.

Since 2004, there have been four major NASA initiatives that created the market for commercial services and human spaceflight that exists today. They are addressed in order below, and they are as follows:

1. Commercial Orbital Transportation Services (COTS);
2. Commercial Resupply Services (CRS);
3. Commercial Crew Program (CCP); and
4. Commercial Lunar Payload Services (CLPS).

NASA's attorneys were intimately involved in every step of creating and implementing this deliberate acquisition strategy.[39]

Commercial Orbital Transportation Services (COTS)
The COTS program grew out of the 2004 U.S. Space Exploration Policy, established by President George W. Bush, which directed the retirement of the Space Shuttle by 2010, after the construction of the ISS was finished. In 2005, Administrator Michael Griffin challenged U.S. industry to develop cargo (and eventually crew) transportation to the ISS. NASA offered up to $500 million

---

[36] *International Space Station: Historical Snapshot*, BOEING (2021), https://www.boeing.com/history/products/international-space-station.page.

[37] *Id.*

[38] PRNewswire, *Massive Lockheed Martin Solar Arrays To Be Launched To International Space Station*, LOCKHEED MARTIN (Aug. 21, 2006), https://news.lockheedmartin.com/2006-08-21-Massive-Lockheed-Martin-Solar-Arrays-to-Be-Launched-to-International-Space-Station.

[39] This is not an exhaustive list – besides these four exemplary initiatives discussed, NASA had *numerous* commercialization initiatives, including: CCDEV (commercial crew development); CCDEV-2; CCiCAP (commercial crew integrated capability); CCtCAP (commercial crew transportation capability) CRS-2; HLS (human landing systems), and many more. A detailed legal analysis of all of these initiatives is beyond the scope of this book.

to develop and demonstrate commercial capabilities. NASA's goal was to support the growth of an industry from which it could eventually become a customer. NASA first entered into public–private partnerships with industry using Space Act Agreements[40] – that program was referred to as COTS – a play on another government contracting phrase, 'commercial-off-the-self.'

In May 2012, the SpaceX Dragon became the first commercial vehicle to demonstrate that it could transport cargo to the ISS.[41] A bit more than a year later, Orbital Sciences (now part of Northrop Grumman) launched its Cygnus cargo ship to resupply the ISS.[42]

Commercial Resupply Services (CRS)

Recall that when the Space Shuttle flew its last flight in 2011, the U.S. had no way to transport its astronauts or cargo (water, food, clothes, science experiments) up to the ISS, without reliance on foreign partners. Some of that reliance came at quite a cost as well – both in national prestige as well as in U.S. taxpayer dollars.[43] The CRS program built on the success of the COTS program, but was structured differently. CRS involved legally binding contracts for performance of a commercial service – the transportation of cargo to the ISS. Under the CRS program, NASA awarded two contracts at a combined value of $3.5 billion to two companies on the condition that they each deliver at least 20 metric tons of cargo to the ISS: $1.9 billion to Orbital Sciences (for

---

[40] Erin Kisliuk, *COTS: Program Approach*, NASA (Aug. 3, 2017), https://www.nasa.gov/content/cots-program-approach.

[41] *See* Trent J. Perretto & Josh Byerly, *SpaceX Dragon Capsule Returns To Earth After First Commercial Flight To Space Station*, NASA (May 31, 2012), https://www.nasa.gov/home/hqnews/2012/may/HQ_12-179_SpaceX_Splashdown.html.

[42] Interestingly, Orbital Sciences was not originally selected by NASA to participate in the COTS program. NASA had selected a different company called Rocketplane Kistler (RpK) in October 2007. However, after RpK failed to raise enough private equity to stay in business and pay their workforce, NASA selected Orbital to succeed RpK. In October 2013, Orbital then became the second private company in history to resupply cargo to the ISS. *See* Jeff Foust, *Commercial Cargo: The Next Generation*, SPACENEWS (Oct. 28, 2019), https://spacenews.com/commercial-cargo-the-next-generation/.

[43] It is difficult to say precisely how much NASA paid the Russian Space Agency (Roscosmos) for transporting U.S. astronauts into space, as the contract also includes numerous ancillary and support services; however, NASA's watchdog Office of Inspector General (OIG) estimated that number to be, on average, about $55 million per seat, and as much as $86 million as recently as 2019. In the OIG report, the OIG estimated that NASA was paying $90 million to fly with Boeing – and just $55 million to fly with SpaceX. Off. Inspector General, NASA, Rep. No. IG-20-005, NASA's Management of Crew Transportation to the International Space Station (Nov. 14, 2019). 'Overall, NASA paid an average cost per seat of $55.4 million for the 70 completed and planned missions from 2006 through 2020 with prices ranging from approximately $21.3 million to $86 million for each round trip.'

eight flights) and $1.6 billion to SpaceX (for 12 flights).[44] The CRS program supported a new industry in low Earth orbit (LEO), where there had been none previously, while maintaining the supremacy of the U.S. commercial space industry; it also enabled the agency to focus on those endeavors (e.g., lunar or Martian exploration) that only NASA can do.

Commercial Crew Program (CCP)

As a direct outgrowth of the COTS and CRS successes, and to break the reliance on the Russian space agency for ISS transportation, NASA once again entered into Space Act Agreements followed by services contracts for human spaceflight services to the ISS. In 2020, the SpaceX Demo-2 test flight became the first flight with crew to launch from the U.S. since the Space Shuttle's retirement in 2011. In mid-November 2020, NASA certified the SpaceX crew Dragon capsule, and the Crew-1 mission became the first of six crewed missions commercially contracted by NASA for ISS delivery under NASA's Commercial Crew Program (CCP).

The CCP demonstrated a new way of doing business; it was the first time NASA contracted with a private company to transport humans to outer space under a firm, fixed-price services contract. Under the CCP, NASA established requirements that had to be satisfied, but did not dictate hardware design. Importantly, the companies own all the hardware as well as all the intellectual property (IP) they developed to service the NASA customer. NASA is, in effect, buying a service for its astronaut crews.[45]

Commercial Lunar Payload Services (CLPS)

NASA's Commercial Lunar Payload Services (CLPS) initiative was enabled by the previous three programs described above. The idea behind the CLPS is to permit rapid acquisition of lunar delivery services by U.S. industry.[46] NASA

---

[44] John Yembrick & Josh Byerly, *NASA Awards Space Station Commercial Resupply Services* Contracts, NASA (Dec. 23, 2008), https://www.nasa.gov/offices/c3po/home/CRS-Announcement-Dec-08.html. Experienced procurement attorneys will note that these were 'indefinite delivery/indefinite quantity' (ID/IQ) contracts. NASA and other government agencies use an ID/IQ contract when the government knows it needs a service, but it is unknown how much of that service will be required.

[45] *See* Steven A. Mirmina, Astronauts Redefined: The Commercial Carriage of Humans to Space and the Changing Concepts of Astronauts under International and U.S. Law, 10 FIU L. REV. 669 (2015).

[46] The actual CLPS request for proposals (RFP) was worded as follows: 'The principal purpose of this requirement is to acquire end-to-end commercial payload services between the Earth and the lunar surface for NASA Headquarters' Science, Human Exploration and Operations, and Space Technology Mission Directorates (SMD, HEOMD, and STMD). The contractor shall provide all activities neces-

wants private companies to provide a *service* – delivery to the lunar surface. In short, with only limited exceptions, NASA generally does not care *how* the contractor delivers the payload – only *that* the contractor delivers the payload. It is the contractor's responsibility to design their own launch vehicles, landers, rovers, etc. As of January 2021, NASA sorted through the proposals of 30 different countries and then selected 14 providers under the CLPS program.[47] To provide further economic incentives, NASA is permitting U.S. industry to transport additional commercial payloads simultaneously in addition to the NASA payloads. NASA will pay about $1 million per kilogram of payload delivered (although that figure may be adjusted upward when actual costs are known). According to a recent report, 'it is not clear yet that this target price is viable.'[48]

Other recent NASA commercialization initiatives

ISS commercialization policy
In June 2019, NASA issued a policy permitting use of the ISS for commercial and marketing activities, citing NASA's strategic objective to 'maintain a constant human presence in low-Earth orbit (LEO) to be enabled by a commercial market.'[49] To develop the LEO economy, NASA is using the ISS to stimulate

---

sary to safely integrate, accommodate, transport, and operate NASA payloads using contractor-provided assets, including launch vehicles, lunar lander spacecraft, lunar surface systems, Earth re-entry vehicles, and associated resources.... The contracts will be performed offsite.' The last sentence was too good not to include. Office Procurement, NASA, Notice No. 80HQTR18R0011R (Sept. 6, 2018), https://beta.sam .gov/opp/5d1f3be4ae92255828a07e2936d98719/view.

[47] Astrobotic Technology; Blue Origin; Ceres Robotics; Deep Space Systems; Draper; Firefly Aerospace; Intuitive Machines; Lockheed Martin Space; Masten Space Systems; Moon Express; Orbit Beyond; Sierra Nevada Corporation; SpaceX; and Tyvak Nano-Satellite Systems. *See* Gary Daines, *Commercial Lunar Payload Services: Providers,* NASA (Oct. 1, 2020), https://www.nasa.gov/content/commercial -lunar-payload-services. These contracts have a combined maximum contract value of $2.6 billion. NASA hopes to have at least two deliveries to the lunar surface every year through the end of the decade.

[48] COMM. ASTROBIOLOGY & PLANETARY SCI., REVIEW OF THE COMMERCIAL ASPECTS OF NASA SMD'S LUNAR SCIENCE AND EXPLORATION INITIATIVE 15-6 (Nat'l Acad. Press 2019).

[49] *See* Memorandum from William H. Gerstenmaier, Assoc. Adm'r. Human Expl. & Operations Mission Dir. to Officials-In-Charge of Headquarters Offices & Dir. NASA Centers, NASA Interim Directive 8600.121 (June 6, 201) [*hereinafter* NID 8600].

a marketplace of supply and demand in which NASA becomes one of numerous customers.[50] This June 2019 policy expressly permits:

- Manufacturing, production, transportation, or marketing of commercial resources and goods, including products intended for commercial sale on Earth;
- Inclusion of private astronauts on U.S. Government (USG) or commercial missions to the ISS and associated on-orbit activities; and
- Provision of resources available for use on the ISS for commercial and marketing activities and associated pricing.[51]

Some of these commercial activities may intersect with U.S. Government ethics regulations. There are certain ethics requirements and prohibitions that apply to NASA astronauts (like all federal civil servants). For example, under U.S. Government ethics regulations, astronauts generally cannot endorse commercial products, services, or enterprises.[52] That is the primary reason why we see athletes rather than astronauts on the covers of cereal boxes.[53] In order to be approved, any astronaut support of marketing activity must occur 'behind the scenes' without being able to recognize or identify the astronaut.[54] All NASA and international partner astronauts that fly to the ISS under the IGA are also bound by the Code of Conduct for the ISS Crew.[55] This code of conduct provides that: 'ISS crewmembers shall refrain from any use of the position of ISS crewmember that is motivated, or has the appearance of being motivated, by private gain, including financial gain, for himself or herself or

---

[50]   Over the last century, there are numerous instances in which the government has affirmatively transitioned its role over to the private sector: railroads; commercial aviation; telecommunications; space launch, to name a few.

[51]   NID 8600, *supra* note 50.

[52]   'An employee shall not use his public office for his own private gain, for the endorsement of any product, service or enterprise, or for the private gain of friends, relatives, or persons with whom the employee is affiliated in a nongovernmental capacity, including nonprofit organizations of which the employee is an officer or member, and persons with whom the employee has or seeks employment or business relations.' 5 C.F.R. § 2535.702 (2021).

[53]   *See* Mike Wall, *Astronauts on Cereal Boxes, Logos on Spaceships? NASA Chief Says It Could Happen*, SPACE.COM (Aug. 30, 2018), https://www.space.com/41668 -nasa-space-commercialization-options-committee.html.

[54]   Estée Lauder made a deal to pay $128,000 to NASA for a 4.5-hour photo shoot inside the ISS. *See* Grace Dean, Estée Lauder and NASA Partner for a Skincare Serum Photoshoot on the International Space Station, BUSINESS INSIDER (Sept. 28, 2020), https://www.businessinsider.com/estee-lauder-pays-nasa-skincare-serum-photoshoot -in-space-2020-9#:~:text=Beauty%20giant%20Est%C3%A9e%20Lauder%20is ,Station%20%E2%80%93%20but%20the%20cosmos%20will.

[55]   14 C.F.R. § 1214.403 (2021).

other persons or entities. Performance of ISS duties shall not be considered to be motivated by private gain.' NASA therefore concluded that, commercial and marketing activities supported under an authorized written agreement with NASA, and coordinated and scheduled through established crew assignment processes, are not – for purposes of the Code of Conduct for the International Space Station Crew – considered motivated by private gain. Private astronauts not employed by the U.S. Government would not, of course, be subject to the U.S. Government ethics regulations; however, all ISS crew members (including private astronauts) would be subject to the ISS Crew Code of Conduct.[56]

Private astronaut missions (PAMs)

Under the new ISS commercialization policy, NASA expects having as many as two private astronaut missions (PAMs) per year. According to NASA, a PAM is a 'privately-funded, dedicated commercial flight to the International Space Station (ISS) whereby approved commercial activities can be conducted by private astronauts on the space station.'[57] These private missions must use U.S. transportation vehicles and will normally be of short duration, less than 30 days. Visiting crew must meet NASA's medical standards as well as any FAA regulatory requirements, such as the liability waivers discussed in Chapter 7. Private citizens wanting to visit the ISS can make their own independent arrangements with a company that has an agreement with NASA to conduct private astronaut missions.[58]

---

[56]   For more information on the ISS Crew Code of Conduct, *see* A. Farand, The Code of Conduct for International Space Station Crews, 105 ESA BULLETIN 64 (Feb. 2001).

[57]   Ana Guzman, Private Astronaut Missions, NASA (Apr. 29, 2021), https://www.nasa.gov/leo-economy/private-astronaut-missions.

[58]   For example, one company made a deal with SpaceX to send four tourists to the ISS by the end of 2021. *See* Marcia Smith, *Axiom and SpaceX Agree to Send Four Private Astronauts to ISS Next Year,* SpacePolicyOnline (Mar. 5, 2020), https://spacepolicyonline.com/news/axiom-and-spacex-agree-to-send-four-private-astronauts-to-iss-next-year/. This SpaceX mission is to carry the Inspiration 4 mission, the first all-civilian mission to orbit, which raffled off one ticket to space to raise awareness (and donations) for the St. Jude Children's Research Hospital. *The Mission,* INSPIRATI4N, https://inspiration4.com/mission (last visited Nov. 14, 2021).

Future Areas for Commercial Involvement

The possibilities for commercial activity in outer space are as broad as the imagination. Just a short list of the possible future areas for potential cooperation between the commercial sector and NASA include:

- Active debris removal (removing debris from orbit);
- Satellite servicing (refueling; repositioning; harvesting);
- Mining activities;[59]
- Optical space communications to relay data over long distances;
- Manufacturing in micro-gravity;
- Wireless power generation; and
- Delivery of crew and cargo beyond LEO.[60]

Challenges Facing NASA

NASA's biggest challenge may be that it is an executive agency reporting to the president. Every four years, there is a potential for the agency to change direction. NASA's history is littered with projects that have been started, stopped, and shelved.[61] The Constellation program is but one example of a NASA project ending due to a change in the space policy of a new presidential administration. In early 2004, President George W. Bush asked NASA to develop a proposal to 'establish an extended human presence on the Moon' to 'vastly reduce the costs of further space exploration.'[62] President Bush's request became known as the Vision for Space Exploration (VSE).[63]

In response to President Bush's request, NASA developed the Constellation program in 2005. The goals of the program were to complete the construction of the ISS, replace the Space Shuttle, 'return to the Moon no later than 2020,'

---

[59] On September 20, 2020, NASA issued a solicitation seeking offers from companies to deliver to it Moon rocks and Moon dust. Shared Serv. Center, NASA, Notice No. 80NSSC20737332Q (Oct. 9, 2020), https://sam.gov/opp/e8ae04fbe2a44 5d49c0c67135637c0dd/view.

[60] *See generally,* Off. Strategy Formulation, *Public-Private Partnerships for Space Capability Development: Driving Economic Growth and NASA's Mission,* NASA (July 30, 2013), https://www.nasa.gov/sites/default/files/files/CSC_PotentialMarkets _July2013_TAGGED.pdf.

[61] *See, e.g.,* John F. Connolly, *Constellation Program Overview,* NASA (Oct. 2006), https://www.nasa.gov/pdf/163092main_constellation_program_overview.pdf.

[62] President George W. Bush, Address at NASA Headquarters: New Vision for Space Exploration Program (Jan. 14, 2004), https://history.nasa.gov/Bush%20SEP .htm.

[63] *See* NASA, THE VISION FOR SPACE EXPLORATION (Feb. 2004).

as well as to 'develop a sustained presence on the Moon.'[64] To transport supplies and crew to the Moon or Mars, the Constellation program developed the Ares I and Ares V booster rockets.[65]

However, only four years into the program, the Augustine Commission, a group of experts convened by NASA to review the progress of human spaceflight programs, found that the program was over budget and behind schedule.[66] Specifically, the committee found that the Ares V rocket would not be available until the late 2020s and even questioned whether there would be sufficient funds to develop a lunar lander. As a result, President Barack Obama removed the Constellation program from the 2010 budget and effectively canceled the program shortly after he took office.[67]

Another example of NASA's changing political climate can be seen in NASA's Asteroid Redirect Mission (ARM), which was intended to advance technologies required for a human mission to Mars. The ARM would have been the 'first-ever robotic mission to visit a large near-Earth asteroid, collect a multi-ton boulder from its surface, and redirect it into a stable orbit around the moon.'[68] However, as President Obama canceled the NASA mission the previous administration had been planning, in 2017, the subsequent presidential administration canceled President Obama's asteroid mission.[69] This abrupt cancellation irritated some of NASA's international partner space agencies, who had started spending money to join with NASA in this exciting mission.

The Constellation program and the ARM are but two examples of how the vicissitudes of changing presidential administrations can quickly end programs in which billions of dollars and thousands of hours have already been invested.

DOING BUSINESS WITH NASA

While a detailed discussion of NASA's contracting practices is outside the scope of this book (it could fill a book in itself), it is worthwhile having

---

[64] Connolly, *supra* note 61, at 2.

[65] The name Ares (the god of war in Greek mythology) was chosen for the booster rockets as a reference to the Constellation program's ultimate goal of landing on Mars (the god of war in Roman mythology).

[66] U.S. HUMAN SPACEFLIGHT COMM., SEEKING A HUMAN SPACEFLIGHT PROGRAM WORTHY OF A GREAT NATION 57–9 (Oct. 8, 2009).

[67] John Matson, *Phased Out: Obama's NASA Budget Would Cancel Constellation Moon Program, Privatize Manned Launches*, SCI. AM. (Feb. 1, 2010), https://www.scientificamerican.com/article/nasa-budget-constellation-cancel/.

[68] Jim Wilson, *What is NASA's Asteroid Redirect Mission*, NASA (Aug. 13, 2018), https://www.nasa.gov/content/what-is-nasa-s-asteroid-redirect-mission.

[69] Jeff Foust, *NASA Closing Out Asteroid Redirect Mission*, SPACENEWS (June 14, 2017), https://spacenews.com/nasa-closing-out-asteroid-redirect-mission/.

a brief discussion of how one goes about doing business with NASA. NASA frequently takes on partners to help it achieve its goals or fill gaps in NASA's own abilities. NASA's partners can be domestic or foreign; local and state governments; universities; museums; and space agencies all over the world.

For U.S. companies, a very common way to partner with NASA is in response to a public announcement: NASA uses various types of public announcements to communicate information about available opportunities, including announcements for proposals (AFPs), requests for information (RFIs), and notices of availability (NOAs).[70]

NASA utilizes a broad toolbox of instruments to transact with industry and advance its mission to support research in science and technology, including: (1) broad agency announcements, (2) government procurement contracts, and (3) Space Act Agreements (SAAs) pursuant to its 'other transactions' authority. Each of these instruments is discussed in more detail below.

Broad Agency Announcements

To kickstart a new relationship, NASA may issue a broad agency announcement (BAA).[71] A BAA is a competitive procedure that agencies use to solicit scientific study and experimentation, and may only be used when 'meaningful proposals with varying technical/scientific approaches can be reasonably anticipated.'[72] A BAA is broad in scope and will identify research areas of interest to the agency.[73] BAAs may set out criteria for the award of contracts, grants, or 'other transactional authority,'[74] and submitted proposals are subject to peer or scientific review prior to an award.[75] However, proposals are *not* evaluated against one another;[76] rather, the agency evaluates proposals consid-

---

[70]　These opportunities are found on the Contract Opportunities website (https://sam .gov/content/home), and the NASA Acquisition Internet Service website (https://prod .nais.nasa.gov/cgibin/nais/index.cgi).

[71]　A broad agency announcement is defined as a 'general announcement of an agency's research interests including criteria for selecting proposals and soliciting the participation of all offerors capable of satisfying the government's needs.' 48 C.F.R. § 2.101 (2021). Foreign participation is allowed in response to a BAA. *See* 48 C.F.R. § 1835.016-70(a)(1) (2021).

[72]　48 C.F.R. § 6.102(d)(2), § 35.016 (2021).

[73]　*Id.* § 6.102(d)(2).

[74]　Tina Reynolds & Victoria Dalcourt Angle, *Acquisition Disruption – Innovative Concepts in Government Contracting*, MORRISON & FOERSTER (Feb. 21, 2018), https://govcon.mofo.com/compliance/acquisition-disruption-innovative-concepts-in -government-contracting/.

[75]　48 C.F.R. § 6.102(d)(2)(ii) (2021).

[76]　*Id.* § 35.016(d).

ering technical capabilities, importance to agency programs, and fund availability, with realism and reasonableness considered 'to the extent appropriate.'[77]

NASA's Use of Procurement Contracts

Generally speaking, all USG agencies contract for the provision of commercial goods or services to the government.[78] NASA is statutorily authorized to contract for 'transactions as may be necessary in the conduct of its work and on such terms as it may deem appropriate.'[79] The government must use a procurement contract when: (1) the principle purpose of the instrument is to acquire property or services for the direct benefits or use of the government; or (2) the agency decides in a specific instance that the use of a procurement contract is appropriate.[80]

While general government contracting is regulated by the Federal Acquisition Regulations (FAR),[81] NASA supplements the FAR through its own regulations, the NASA FAR Supplement (NFS).[82] It is NASA policy to forecast to the public expected contract opportunities for the year to come.[83] NASA must additionally release a public announcement for contracts that have an expected value of $5 million or more.[84] Full and open competition is the norm in government contracting.[85]

---

[77] *Id.* § 35.016(e).

[78] *See, e.g.,* Office Mgmt. & Budget, *Circular No. A-76 Revised* (May 29, 2003) ('The longstanding policy of the federal government has been to rely on the private sector for needed commercial services.').

[79] 51 U.S.C. § 20113(e) (2018). An agency is only allowed to spend public funds when authorized by Congress. 'The established rule is that the expenditure of public funds is proper only when authorized by Congress, not that public funds may be expended unless prohibited by Congress.' United States v. MacCollom, 426 U.S. 317 (1976).

[80] 31 U.S.C. § 6303 (2018).

[81] 48 C.F.R. Chapter 1 (2021). Pursuant to 41 U.S.C. section 1302 and FAR 1.103(b), the FAR is jointly prepared, issued, and maintained by the Secretary of Defense, the Administrator of General Services, and the Administrator, National Aeronautics and Space Administration, under their several statutory authorities.

[82] *Id.* at Chapter 18.

[83] *Id.* § 1807.7200.

[84] *Id.* § 1805.303.

[85] *Id.* § 6.101. NASA is granted several specific statutory exceptions to full and open competition, such as if there is only one responsible source and no other suppliers can satisfy NASA's requirements. An additional exception NASA uses as a 'justification for other than free and open competition' (known as a JOFOC) is when an international agreement or treaty specifically limits the acquisition in support of the treaty to less than full and open competition. *Id.* § 1806.302-4. Other JOFOCs generally include those in the 'public interest,' NASA direction to 'sole source' an acquisition, and

Various Forms of NASA Contracts

Generally, there are several varieties of government contracts[86] that NASA may utilize and even combinations of the various contract types. Numerous factors go into the selection of the right contract type, and the type of contract and the pricing go hand in hand. Some examples of contract types include:

1. **Fixed-price contracts.** A firm fixed-price contract sets a specific cost to the government for the acquisition of supplies or services, with no adjustment made based on costs to the contractor for performance or production.[87] These are useful when the cost of production and performance are known. If a contractor does not perform efficiently, they may suffer a loss using this form of contract.

2. **Cost-reimbursement contracts.** Under a cost-reimbursement contract, the government will provide payment for allowable costs incurred by the contractor during contract performance.[88] This form of contract is sought by the contractor for activities never performed previously, like building a new spaceship or creating a new technology. The government pays the contractor's allowable, allocable, and reasonable incurred costs. This kind of contract shifts the risks of development costs to the government.

3. **Incentive contracts.** Incentive contracts are used to acquire supplies or services at a lower cost than fixed-price contracts by correlating payment to the contractor with the contractor's performance. Incentive contracts provide the opportunity for the contractor to realize increased profit for attaining cost, performance, and/or schedule criteria.[89]

4. **Indefinite delivery/indefinite quantity (ID/IQ) contracts.** An ID/IQ contract is used to acquire supplies or services when the exact times and quantities of deliverables are unknown at the time of contracting. These contracts are common for repeat acquisitions by the government, such as for office supplies.[90] Under these contracts, usually the government orders an agreed minimum. For example, NASA awarded two ID/IQ contracts to two companies (Virgin Galactic and Masten Space Systems) to integrate and fly technology payloads on platforms that provide high

---

'unusual and compelling urgency.' Federal procurement law provides additional exceptions as well.

[86]   A general overview of the flavors of government contracting, and the appropriate selection of a specific contract type, can be found at 48 C.F.R. Part 16 (2021).

[87]   48 C.F.R. Subpart 16.2 (2021).

[88]   *Id.* Subpart 16.3.

[89]   *Id.* Subpart 16.4.

[90]   *Id.* Subpart 16.5.

altitude, reduced gravity, or other relevant environments required to test and advance NASA technologies.[91]

NASA's 'Other Transaction' Authority, and Space Act Agreements

Completely separate from contracting, NASA also has what is called 'other transaction authority' (OTA). Statutorily created for the first time during the space race against the USSR,[92] the 1958 Space Act gave NASA the flexibility 'to enter into and perform such contracts, leases, cooperative agreements, or *other transactions* as may be necessary in the conduct of its work....'[93] While OTA is not precisely defined via statute, OTA permits an agency to tailor terms and conditions of an agreement to meet a specific situation.[94]

Agreements concluded under NASA's OTA tend to be more flexible than a standard procurement contract and NASA has used this authority liberally for activities beyond R&D and prototypes.[95] Additionally, NASA has relatively unfettered OTA, with no statutory limitations or requirements on the types of projects or research that fall under this designation.[96]

NASA exercises its OTA through Space Act Agreements (SAAs). SAAs comprise legally enforceable promises between NASA and an SAA partner for commitments of resources – including personnel, funding, services, equip-

---

[91] Clare Skelly & Leslie Williams, *NASA Awards Contract for Flight and Integration Services,* NASA (Nov. 30, 2020), https://www.nasa.gov/press-release/nasa -awards-contract-for-flight-and-integration-services.

[92] NASA was the first USG agency to receive other transactions authority. Surya Gablin Gunasekara, *'Other Transaction' Authority: NASA's Dynamic Acquisition Instrument for the Commercialization of Manned Spaceflight or Cold War Relic?*, 40 Pub. Contract L. J. 893, 894 (2011).

[93] Emphasis added. National and Commercial Space Programs, 51 U.S.C. et seq (2018); 51 U.S.C. § 20113 (2018).

[94] U.S. Gov't Accountability Office, GAO-16-209, Federal Acquisitions: Use of 'Other Transaction' Agreements Limited and Mostly for Research and Development Activities 4 (2016); Gunasekara, *supra* note 92, at 894.

[95] In 2014, NASA concluded 2,220 agreements under OTA, compared with an average of 75 or fewer for other agencies with similar statutory authority. U.S. Gov't Accountability Office, *supra* note 95, at Overview.

[96] Of 11 agencies that have OTA, four – NASA, ARPA-E, FAA, and TSA – do not have statutory limitations on its use. *Id.* at 10.

ment, expertise, information, or facilities – to accomplish stated objectives of a joint undertaking.[97] There are generally four types of SAA:

- **Non-reimbursable SAA.** Under these cooperative arrangements, each party assumes responsibility for its own risks and costs; these are utilized when NASA and its partner(s) are collaboratively performing activities to which each is particularly suited, and for which the result is of common interest.
- **Reimbursable SAA.** NASA sometimes provide services to the commercial sector. Under these agreements, a partner reimburses NASA for its costs and assumes any risks under the agreement. To do this, the activity must be: (1) consistent with NASA's mission; and (2) not reasonably available on the commercial market from another source.
- **Funded SAA.** Under very unusual circumstances, NASA may provide funding to a partner to accomplish a goal consistent with the SAA's mission. These are never used to fulfill any NASA requirements (if a NASA 'need' is being filled, NASA must use a procurement contract).
- **International SAA.** NASA has concluded thousands of international SAAs with public and private entities around the world. Currently, NASA has about 600 active international agreements in force.

Differences Between Procurement Contracts and SAAs

While procurement contracts are required when the principal purpose of the transaction is to acquire property or services for the direct benefit or use the of government, SAAs are generally used to: (1) support the needs of the external partner where the partner reimburses government expenses; or (2) achieve a mutual goal when working collaboratively on a project.

Perhaps the most impactful difference between contracts and SAAs involves the rights of the contractor or partner to contest awards. When using a procurement contract, NASA must comply with various procurement laws and regulations, including the Competition in Contracting Act (CICA)[98] and the Federal Acquisition Regulation (FAR). Doing so provides NASA contractors with the

---

[97]   NASA, NAII 1050-1C, NASA ADVISORY IMPLEMENTING INSTRUCTION: SPACE ACT AGREEMENTS GUIDE 2 (2014 eds.).

[98]   The Competition in Contracting Act (CICA) was passed into law in 1984 as the basis for the Federal Acquisition Regulation (FAR) in order to foster competition and reduce costs. The theory was that more competition would reduce costs and allow more small businesses to win federal government contracts. Under CICA, procurements must be competed as full and open, subject to a very few exceptions. 41 U.S.C. § 3301, *et seq.* (2018).

opportunity to seek judicial review of NASA action during the contractual relationship – from solicitation to award to performance. NASA contractors are entitled to seek recourse through Government Accountability Office (GAO) review,[99] in the Court of Federal Claims,[100] or through the agency itself.[101] This can include a stay award under the CICA stopping or delaying contract performance. In contrast, SAAs are *only* reviewed by the GAO for misuse of a non-procurement instrument,[102] and there is no CICA jurisdiction for stay provisions to apply. Additionally, the Court of Federal Claims[103] jurisdiction to hear bid protests under the Tucker Act refers *exclusively* to procurement solicitations and contracts.[104] This very brief explanation is not exhaustive: when doing business with NASA, selection of the appropriate instrument (SAA or procurement contract) is fundamental.[105]

Bidding for NASA Work

To be selected, companies proposing to do work for NASA must convince NASA of their qualifications.[106] Some typical information a bidder might offer to the agency for consideration includes:

(a)   **Innovation.** A good proposal describes the uniqueness and benefits of the proposed research, technology, or new approach that the agency might wish to purchase. A proposer should provide a basic description of the potential benefit to the public, such as development of future prod-ucts and services contributing to U.S. industrial capacity and economic growth or improving STEM education.

(b)   **Expected results.** Bidders may need to give NASA a short description of the outcome, products, or process that may be expected at the end of the project.

---

[99]   31 U.S.C. § 3552 (2018); 4 C.F.R. § 21.0 (2021) (defining 'interested parties').

[100]   28 U.S.C. § 1491 (2018).

[101]   48 C.F.R. § 33.103 (2021).

[102]   Rocketplane Kistler, B-310741 (Comp. Gen. Jan. 28, 2008).

[103]   As established by Congress in 1855, the purpose of the Court of Federal Claims is to allow citizens to file claims for money against the federal government. *United States Court of Federal Claims: The People's Court*, FED. CL., http://www.uscfc.uscourts .gov/sites/default/files/uscfc_court_history_brochure_20210325.pdf (last visited Nov. 14, 2021).

[104]   *Hymas v. U.S.*, 810 F.3d 1312 (Fed. Cir. 2016).

[105]   *See* Andrew Strauss, *Failure to Launch: Why NASA's Unchecked Use of OTA Power May One Day Doom the Agency*, 40 DAYTON L. REV. 131 (2015).

[106]   For a general checklist of information that an agency will include in a solicitation document, *see* CONTRACT & FISCAL LAW DEP'T, JUDGE ADVOCATE GEN. LEGAL CTR. & SCH., 2020 CONTRACT ATTORNEYS DESKBOOK 2-11 to 2-19 (2020).

(c) **Technical rationale.** Offerors may wish to describe how their proposal benefits NASA's mission capabilities, efficiency, or effectiveness.

(d) **Technical approach.** A strong proposal explains the technical approach and plan to realize and accomplish the technical goals in support of claims and deliverables.

(e) **Experience.** Well-counseled bidders would provide a short general discussion of other research by their team members in this technical area. Why should NASA choose this bidder over others? How does NASA know that the offer can do what's promised?

Bidders must provide a great deal of other information as well, ranging from detailed proposal information, to cost and pricing information, to other requirements for government contracts. A strong bid provides all required information for the specific type of contract sought.

QUESTIONS FOR REVIEW

1. How does NASA engage with foreign space agencies?
2. What are the key components of NASA's international agreements?
3. How does NASA engage with private space entities? What are the different types of agreements and contracts that NASA can use and what are their benefits?
4. Should NASA let Hollywood actors film movies on the ISS? What legal restrictions are in place for private visitors to the ISS?

7. U.S. commercial space launch, reentry and spaceports

'Ok, Ruth, explain it to me again,' said Christian. Ruth turns to look at her friend, who has been barraging her with questions about the oversight of commercial space launch companies. 'The Federal Aviation *Administration regulates space activities? How does that make any sense?'*

Ruth is picnicking on the National Mall with friends. The sun is already setting, and the 4th of July fireworks will be starting soon. Talk about fireworks has evolved into talk about rockets and launches. She's pleased to be in the company of a bunch of space nerds.

'Isn't that what NASA does?' Christian continues.

'It's actually the FAA,' replies Laura, who is sitting beside Ruth. Laura actually interned at the FAA during one of the summers during law school.

Christian regards her quizzically. 'So, the FAA is the go-to authority for all space-related stuff in the U.S.?'

'Well, no. They have authority to regulate launch and reentry in order to protect public safety as well as spaceports,' Laura explains.

Christian isn't satisfied. 'If the FAA regulates rockets on the way up, and on the way back, what about all that time in the middle, when they're in space?' Ruth smiles, as she reaches for the cooler. 'Let me explain...'

FEDERAL AVIATION ADMINISTRATION OFFICE OF COMMERCIAL SPACE TRANSPORTATION

The Federal Aviation Administration's Office of Commercial Space Transportation (FAA AST) within the U.S. Department of Transportation (DOT) licenses commercial launch and reentry activities, as well as spaceports. A license is required for a person or entity subject to the FAA AST's jurisdiction 'to launch a launch vehicle or to operate a launch site or reentry site, or to reenter a reentry vehicle, in the United States.'[1] A license is also required for a 'citizen of the United States'[2] when they are operating a launch, reentry or

---

[1] 51 U.S.C. § 50904(a)(1).

[2] The definition for who is a 'citizen of the United States' is uniquely defined by 51 U.S.C. § 50902(1)(A)–(C) as: '(A) an individual who is a citizen of the United States;

launch/reentry site outside the United States.[3] Launch and reentry sites are also referred to as spaceports. This chapter will examine the FAA AST, its history, and the licensing of commercial launch, reentry and spaceports, including issues related to liability, human spaceflight, and airspace integration.

HISTORY

In 1984, Executive Order (EO) 12465 designated the Department of Transportation (DOT) 'as the lead agency within the Federal government for encouraging and facilitating commercial [expendable launch vehicle] activities by the United States private sector.'[4] That EO was preceded by National Security Decision Directive 42 (NSDD-42) following a comprehensive space policy review.[5] NSDD-42 reflected the White House's support for space commerce: 'The United States Government will provide a climate conducive to expanded private sector investment and involvement in civil space activities, with due regard to public safety and national security. Private sector space activities will be authorized and supervised or regulated by the government to the extent required by treaty and national security.'[6] EO 12465 was also influenced by the September 9, 1982, launch of Conestoga I, the first privately developed commercial rocket.[7] Before Conestoga I could be launched, the company confronted a morass of legal and regulatory requirements involving 22 different U.S. statutes and 18 federal agencies, including the FAA, Federal Communications Commission (FCC), NASA, U.S. State Department, and the Bureau of Alcohol, Tobacco and Firearms.[8]

To relieve some of the administrative and bureaucratic morass encountered with gaining U.S. Government (USG) approval for the Conestoga I launch,

---

(B) an entity organized or existing under the laws of the United States or a State; or (C) an entity organized or existing under the laws of a foreign country if the controlling interest (as defined by the Secretary of Transportation) is held by an individual or entity described in subclause (A) or (B) of this clause.'

[3]   51 U.S.C. § 50904(a).

[4]   Commercial expendable launch vehicle activities, Exec. Order No. 12465, 49 Fed. Reg. 7099 (Feb. 24, 1984), https://www.archives.gov/federal-register/codification/executive-order/12465.html.

[5]   This directive replaced NSDD-8 and the three Carter Administration space policy statements, NSDD-37, 42, and 54.

[6]   National Security Decision Directive No. 42 (NSDD-42), *National Space Policy*, The White House (July 4, 1982), https://irp.fas.org/offdocs/nsdd/nsdd-42.pdf.

[7]   Conestoga I was launched by Space Services Incorporated of America from a private launch facility on Matagorda Island, Texas; *See*, Nicolas Giacomin, *The History of the Conestoga Rocket*, Space Legal Issues (June 6, 2021), https://www.spacelegalissues.com/the-history-of-the-conestoga-rocket/.

[8]   130 Cong. Rec. S1388 (Feb 1. 1984).

Congress passed the Commercial Space Launch Act of 1984 (CSLA) establishing the Office of Commercial Space Transportation within the DOT.[9] Congress granted DOT the authority to license commercial launches and spaceports based on the finding that 'private applications of space technology have achieved a significant level of commercial and economic activity and offer the potential for growth in the future, particularly in the United States.'[10] The CSLA was amended in 1988 to add an indemnification regime to limit exposure to third-party liability claims. The first licensed commercial launches occurred in 1989.[11]

In November 1995 during an agency reorganization, the Office of Commercial Space Transportation (FAA AST) was transferred from the Secretary of Transportation's office to the Federal Aviation Administration (FAA) as the FAA's only space-focused line of business.[12] Significant amendments to the CSLA followed in 1998,[13] 2004[14] and 2015,[15] to address reusable launch vehicles and reentry licensing, private human spaceflight, and resource utilization, respectively.

REGULATION OF COMMERCIAL SPACEFLIGHT ACTIVITIES

Commercial launches, reentries and spaceports may only be regulated, 'to the extent necessary [...] to ensure compliance with international obligations of the United States and to protect the public health and safety, safety of property, and national security and foreign policy interests of the United States.'[16] That means launches, reentries and spaceports *are not regulated to protect the*

---

[9]   *About the Office of Commercial Space Transportation*, Federal Aviation Administration [hereinafter FAA], https://www.faa.gov/about/office_org/headquarters_offices/ast/ (last visited Oct. 19, 2021); *See*, 51 U.S.C. § 50901–50923; Pub. L. No. 98-575; H.R. 3942, Commercial Space Launch Act, (Oct. 30, 1984) https://www.congress.gov/bill/98th-congress/house-bill/3942.

[10]   The 'Findings' of Pub. L. No. 98-575 note that the 1984 CSLA only authorized licensing expendable launch vehicles. The authority to license reusable launch vehicles and reentries was added in 1998. The CSLA was further amended in 1988 to add an indemnification regime and limit third-party liability claims.

[11]   *Origins of the Commercial Space Industry*, FAA, https://www.faa.gov/about/history/milestones/media/commercial_space_industry.pdf (last visited Oct. 19, 2021).

[12]   AST is one of five lines of business within the FAA. The other four are the Office of Aviation Safety; the Office of Airports; the Air Traffic Organization; and the Office of Security and Hazardous Materials Safety.

[13]   Pub. L. 105-303.

[14]   Pub. L. 108-492.

[15]   Pub. L. 114-90.

[16]   51 U.S.C. § 50901(a)(7).

entities or people involved with the operations – the statute states that the FAA AST is not responsible for regulating to ensure mission success or to protect those people who are not defined as public.[17] FAA AST does not have statutory authority to regulate activities conducted on orbit.[18]

Unlike the rest of FAA, which is authorized under Title 49, 'Transportation,' of the United States Code, authority for FAA AST is located in Title 51, 'National and Commercial Space Programs.' Notably, the FAA AST is the only office within the FAA that has a 'dual mandate' to regulate as well as promote, encourage and facilitate the industry and activities within its jurisdiction,[19] an authority that may be modified in the future.[20]

Activities Requiring an FAA AST License

In assessing AST's role in licensing a launch, reentry or site, one must determine whether the activity is subject to AST's jurisdiction. If the activity is a 'launch,'[21] of a 'launch vehicle,'[22] the operation of a 'launch site'[23] or 'reentry site'[24] or the 'reentry'[25] of a 'reentry vehicle'[26] (collectively referred to in this chapter as 'spaceflight activities') in the United States, then it requires a license from AST.[27] Those activities may also require a license if they are conducted outside the U.S. by a person or entity who is a 'citizen of the United States.'[28]

Entities 'organized or existing under the laws of a foreign country'[29] that fall within the FAA AST's definition for a citizen are required to have a license

---

[17] The FAA defined 'public' in § 401.5 of 14 C.F.R. 450, to mean 'for a particular licensed or permitted launch or reentry, people that are not involved in supporting the launch or reentry and includes those people who may be located within the launch or reentry site, such as visitors, individuals providing goods or services not related to launch or reentry processing or flight, and any other operator and its personnel.'

[18] H. Rept. 108-492, Commercial Space Launch Amendments Act of 2004; *See*, 150 Cong. Rec. H703, 2004.

[19] 51 U.S.C. § 50901(b).

[20] *Chairs DeFazio, Larsen Statements from Hearing on the FAA's Role in the Future of Spaceflight*, U.S. House of Representatives Transportation and Infrastructure Committee (June 16, 2021), https://transportation.house.gov/news/press-releases/chairs-defazio-larsen-statements-from-hearing-on-the-faas-role-in-the-future-of-spaceflght.

[21] 51 U.S.C. § 50902(7); *See*, 14 C.F.R. § 450.3(b).

[22] 51 U.S.C. § 50902(11); *See*, 14 C.F.R. § 401.5.

[23] 51 U.S.C. § 50902(10); *Id.*

[24] 51 U.S.C. § 50902(18); *See*, 14 C.F.R. § 450.3(c).

[25] 51 U.S.C. § 50902(16); *See*, 14 C.F.R. § 401.5.

[26] 51 U.S.C. § 50902(19); *Id.*

[27] 51 U.S.C. § 50904(a).

[28] *Supra* note 2.

[29] 51 U.S.C. § 50902(1)(C).

for spaceflight activities occurring 'outside the United States and outside the territory of a foreign country unless there is an agreement between the United States Government and the government of the foreign country providing that the government of the foreign country has jurisdiction over the launch or operation or reentry.'[30] Additionally, those entities require a license if they are conducting spaceflight activities in a foreign country's territory if that country has a bilateral agreement with the U.S. 'providing that the United States Government has jurisdiction over the launch or operation or reentry.'[31] 14 C.F.R. Section 413.13 adds additional detail regarding AST's jurisdiction.

If the spaceflight activity requires a license under Section 50904, the second jurisdictional question is whether the activity is one that 'the Government carries out for the Government.'[32] In 1990, the Department of Transportation requested a ruling from the U.S. Attorney General on 'whether the [CSLA] licensing authority extends to private firm launches of United States Government payloads.'[33] The launch at issue was conducted by General Dynamics Corporation carrying NASA's Combined Release and Radiation Effects Satellite ('CRRES') and a U.S. Air Force (USAF) payload. The DOT asserted that, 'its licensing authority extends to all launches in which operation of the launch vehicle is conducted by a non-Government entity;' NASA and the USAF disagreed.[34]

Citing Section 50919(g)(1),[35] the DOJ concluded that the DOT did not have authority to license missions such as the CRRES mission, 'in which an agency of the United States is so substantially involved that it is effectively directing or controlling the launch.'[36] In discussing its conclusion regarding the Section 50919 exemption, the DOJ noted that, 'the purpose of the CSLA was to ensure supervision of private, commercial launches, not to require licensure of essentially governmental launches.'[37]

---

[30] 51 U.S.C. § 50904(a)(3).

[31] 51 U.S.C. § 50904(a)(4).

[32] 51 U.S.C. § 50919(g)(1).

[33] Memorandum for Edward A. Frankle, Office of the Assistant Attorney General, US Department of Justice (Nov. 15, 1990), at 1.

[34] *Id.,* at 2.

[35] Previously, 49 U.S.C. § 2620(c)(1).

[36] *Supra* note 33, at 2.

[37] 'At bottom, DOT's construction of CSLA inadequately recognized that the purpose of the CSLA was to ensure supervision of private, commercial launches, not to require licensure of essentially governmental launches.' *Supra* note 33, at 7.

Spaceflight operators conducting launch and/or reentry missions for a USG customer (as was the case for CRRES mission) will look to the contract for licensing requirements.[38]

Launch and Reentry Licenses

It was Congress's intent to create a single licensing regime for launch and reentry.[39] That is true in some sense – only the FAA AST has the authority to license launch and the reentry activities.[40] Other aspects of the spaceflight activity will require approvals from other U.S. Government regulators.[41]

The FAA will issue a license within 180 days of accepting the application, if it is deemed 'consistent with the public health and safety, safety of property, and national security and foreign policy interests' of the U.S.[42] The procedures for submitting an application or renewing a license are detailed in Part 413 of the FAA's regulations, 'License Application Procedures.' Applicants may request confidential treatment of their application materials.[43]

When a license is issued, it 'authorizes a licensee to conduct launches or reentries, in accordance with the representations contained in the licensee's application, […], and subject to the licensee's compliance with terms and conditions contained in license orders accompanying the license, including financial responsibility requirements.'[44] A licensee is responsible for compliance with all documentation submitted to the AST as part of its license application materials, which should encourage applicants to refrain from submitting materials that exceed the AST requirements.

The requirements for receiving a launch or reentry license are detailed in Part 450, 'Launch and Reentry License Requirement.'[45] Part 450 is divided into four subparts – A through D – and includes requirements for the documen-

---

[38] For example, the NASA contracts for cargo delivery services (CRS) to the International Space Station include a requirement for FAA licensing.

[39] 51 U.S.C. § 50904(d).

[40] 14 C.F.R. § 450.

[41] For example, radio communications between the ground and the vehicle will required a license from the Federal Communications Commission (FCC). Remote sensing of the Earth will require a license from NOAA. *See*, Chapters 8 and 9 for more information on the FCC's and NOAA's roles in licensing space activities.

[42] 51 U.S.C. § 50905(a)(1); *See*, 14 C.F.R. § 413.11.

[43] 14 C.F.R. § 413.9.

[44] AST-issued licenses are publicly available on the FAA AST website. *See*, *Commercial Space Transportation: Operational Information*, FAA, www.faa.gov/space (last visited Oct. 19, 2021).

[45] 14 C.F.R. §450.

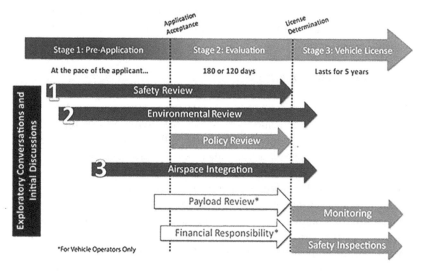

Figure 7.1   Process for issuing launch and reentry licenses[1]

---

[1]   *Getting Started with Licensing*, FAA , https://www.faa.gov/space/streamlined _licensing_process/licensing_process/ (last visited July 14, 2021).

tation that licensees must submit in their applications and what licensees must do to achieve the required level of safety.

The scope of a launch or reentry license is determined in accordance with 14 C.F.R.§ 450.3. A license for launch from a U.S. launch site covers preflight, flight and postflight activities;[46] however, if the launch is at a non-U.S. site, it 'begins at ignition or at the first movement that initiates flight.'[47] A reentry license covers activities 'conducted in Earth orbit or outer space to determine reentry readiness' as well as 'activities necessary to return the reentry vehicle, or vehicle component, to a safe condition on the ground after impact or landing.'[48] A license may be granted for up to five years.[49] The FAA AST publishes the licenses it issues on its website; however, the highly technical

---

[46]   The applicant can propose the preflight activity or operation that would define the beginning of the licensed launch activity at a U.S. launch site. Establishing the license scope is a key milestone in an applicant's pre-application discussions with the FAA AST. The regulation provides examples of hazardous preflight activities for which a license would need to be in place. 14 C.F.R. § 450.3(b)(1).

[47]   14 C.F.R. § 450.3 (b).

[48]   14 C.F.R. § 450.3 (c).

[49]   14 C.F.R. § 450.5.

and often proprietary materials that applicants submit may be protected from disclosure.[50]

Standard of Review/Level of Safety/Protecting the Public

The FAA's regulations are largely focused on protecting the public.[51] The primary focus of the licensing regulations and review is public safety. The FAA AST does not regulate to ensure mission success. In other words, so long as the level of acceptable public risk is not violated, the regulations do not evaluate whether the launch vehicle can deliver its payload to the intended orbit or whether it can launch without significant damage to the launch or landing site. That is significantly different from the FAA's regulation of aviation activities, which are regulated to protect the public as well as everyone involved in the flight, particularly paying passengers.[52]

The Section 450.101 safety criteria include four categories: individual risk, collective risk, aircraft risk, and risk to critical assets. For example, the risk associated with launch or reentry to an individual member of the public must be less than one in one million ($Ec \leq 1 \times 10\text{–}6$). Applicants must demonstrate how they will ensure that the public is excluded from the hazard area for the FAA to grant the license.

Launch and reentry hazard areas are determined based on the applicant's and the FAA's analysis of the information required by Part 450, such as information regarding the vehicle's design, materials, fuel, operations, safety systems, reliability, and operating area to determine compliance with the flight safety regulations.

The FAA protects the public on the ground, in the air or at sea, utilizing a three-dimensional approach to the safety zone from which the public must be excluded. Launch and reentry operations almost always require closing airspace.[53] Launch and reentry operations along the coast or at sea, such as a reentry involving an ocean splashdown, require issuing a notice to mariners to avoid certain areas of the ocean. Air and sea coordination requirements are discussed further below.

---

[50]   14 C.F.R. § 413.9.

[51]   *Supra* note 18.

[52]   *See, e.g.*, 49 U.S.C. § 106(g).

[53]   A license must have an agreement in place with the FAA or foreign air navigation service providers (ANSP) to issue notice to airmen (NOTAMs) and with the U.S. Coast Guard (USCG) for issuing notice to mariners (NOTMARs). 14 C.F.R. § 450.147.

Payload Review

A payload is 'an object that a person undertakes to place in outer space by means of a launch vehicle, including components of the vehicle specifically designed or adapted for that object.'[54] The payload review process is an inter-agency review to determine:

(1) 'whether a license applicant or payload owner or operator has obtained all required licenses, authorization, and permits,'[55] or is exempt from review;[56] and

(2) 'whether launch of a proposed payload would present any issues affecting public health and safety, safety of property, U.S. national security or foreign policy interests, or international obligations of the United States.'[57]

After consulting other federal agencies and concluding its review, the FAA AST will issue a favorable payload determination unless it determines that the payload's launch 'would jeopardize public health and safety, safety of property, national security or foreign policy interests, or international obligations of the United States.'[58]

The FAA AST conducts a payload review as part of a launch or reentry authorization.[59] In those cases, the launch or reentry licensee is responsible for submitting the payload information. Payload reviews may also 'be requested by a payload owner or operator in advance or apart from a license application.'[60]

Traditional commercial space activities (i.e., telecommunications and remote sensing satellites) have fallen under the jurisdiction of a USG agency

---

[54] 'Payload' is defined as 'an object that a person undertakes to place in outer space by means of a launch vehicle, including components of the vehicle specifically designed or adapted for that object.' 14 C.F.R. § 401.5.

[55] 14 C.F.R. § 415.51.

[56] Per 14 C.F.R. § 415.53, 'The FAA does not review payloads that are (a) Subject to regulation by the Federal Communications Commission (FCC) or the Department of Commerce, National Oceanic and Atmospheric Administration (NOAA); or (b) owned or operated by the U.S. Government.'

[57] The FAA AST will consult with the Department of Defense and Department of State to determine whether a payload launch would present any issues affecting U.S. national security or international obligations, respectively. *See*, 14 C.F.R. § 415.57 (b).

[58] 14 C.F.R. § 415.61 (a).

[59] Payload Reviews, FAA (Jan. 28, 2020), https://www.faa.gov/space/licenses/payload_reviews/#:~:text=If%20not%20otherwise%20exempt%2C%20Commercial,obligations%20of%20the%20United%20States.

[60] 14 C.F.R. § 415.17(a).

and are exempt from the FAA's payload review.[61] However, there has been a proliferation of planned activities in space or on celestial bodies, such as on-orbit servicing, resource extraction and commercial human exploration, that do not fall within another USG agency's authority.[62] These novel space activities have leveraged the FAA AST payload review process as a means to receive USG review and assurances that their planned spaceflight activities are authorized. For example, Moon Express received a favorable payload determination for its MX-1E spacecraft, which was intended to land on the lunar surface and perform post-landing propulsive 'hops.'[63] Moon Express's CEO characterized the approval as overcoming a significant barrier to their mission by being granted a 'license to leave Earth orbit.'[64] Despite the granting of a handful of FAA AST payload approvals, the process has been ad hoc and the subject of discussion in the executive and legislative branches over which agency – Commerce or Transportation – should have 'mission authority' oversight.[65]

Experimental Permits

License applicants may apply for an experimental permit instead of a license for an unlimited number of experimental flights for a particular vehicle design under 14 C.F.R. Part 437.[66] The experimental permit option was created by the 2004 Commercial Space Launch Amendments Act (CSLAA)[67] to '[make] it easier for the industry to test new types of reusable suborbital rockets by allow-

---

[61] *Supra* note 41.

[62] Mark J. Sundahl, *Regulating Non-Traditional Space Activities in the United States in the Wake of the Commercial Space Launch Competitiveness Act*, 42 Air and Space L. 29 (2017), https://kluwerlawonline.com/journalarticle/Air+and+Space+Law/42.1/AILA2017003.

[63] *Fact Sheet – Moon Express Payload Review Determination*, FAA (Aug. 2, 2015), https://www.faa.gov/news/fact_sheets/news_story.cfm?newsId=20595.

[64] Jeff Foust, *Moon Express wins U.S. government approval for lunar lander mission*, SPACE NEWS (Aug. 3, 2016), https://spacenews.com/moon-express-wins-u-s-government-approval-for-lunar-lander-mission/.

[65] *See, Memorandum on The National Space Policy*, White House (Dec. 9, 2020), https://trumpwhitehouse.archives.gov/presidential-actions/memorandum-national-space-policy/; *See also,*
Reopening the American Frontier: Exploring How the Outer Space Treaty Will Impact American Commerce and Settlement in Space, U.S. Senate Committee on Commerce, Science and Transportation (May 23, 2017), https://www.commerce.senate.gov/2017/5/reopening-the-american-frontier-exploring-how-the-outer-space-treaty-will-impact-american-commerce-and-settlement-in-space.

[66] 51 U.S.C. § 50906; *See*, 14 C.F.R. § 437.

[67] Pub. L. 108-492.

ing AST to issue experimental permits that can be granted more quickly and with fewer requirements than licenses.'[68] The House Committee on Science, Space and Technology, in passing the CSLAA, stated its belief that 'permits are necessary to enable the development of new and innovative launch vehicle designs and to allow for crew training on experimental vehicles.'

Experimental permits are an option for reusable 'suborbital rockets'[69] or 'reusable launch vehicles'[70] and to launches of those vehicles into a 'suborbital trajectory' or reentries[71] solely for:

(1)   research and development to test design concepts, equipment, or operating techniques;

(2)   showing compliance with requirements as part of the process for obtaining a license under this chapter; or

(3)   crew training for a launch or reentry using the design of the rocket or vehicle for which the permit would be issued.

An experimental permit holder is required to carry insurance to cover third-party and/or U.S. Government claims, as calculated by the FAA,[72] but

---

[68]   H.R. Rep. No. 109-429.

[69]   'Suborbital rocket means a vehicle, rocket-propelled in whole or in part, intended for flight on a suborbital trajectory, and the thrust of which is greater than its lift for the majority of the rocket-powered portion of its ascent.' 14 C.F.R. 401.5.

[70]   'Reusable launch vehicle (RLV) means a launch vehicle that is designed to return to Earth substantially intact and therefore may be launched more than one time or that contains vehicle stages that may be recovered by a launch operator for future use in the operation of a substantially similar launch vehicle.' 14 C.F.R. 401.7. The ability to obtain an experimental permit for a reusable launch vehicle was added in 2015 by Pub. L. 114-90, § 104.

[71]   'For most suborbital launches, whether the flight entails a reentry [does] not matter from a regulatory perspective. The FAA will authorize the flight under a single license or permit, implementing safety requirements suitable to the safety issues involved. Recognizing suborbital reentry matters for two reasons. First, if a suborbital rocket is flown from a foreign country by a foreign entity into the United States, that entity may require a reentry license or permit from the FAA, depending on whether the planned trajectory of the rocket includes flight in outer space. Second, a permanent site that supports the landing of suborbital rockets may now be considered a reentry site depending, once again, on whether the planned trajectory reaches outer space.' Experimental Permits for Reusable Suborbital Rockets, 72 Fed. Reg. 17001 (Apr. 6, 2007), https://www.faa.gov/about/office_org/headquarters_offices/ast/licenses _permits/sub_orbital_rockets/newregs/media/EP_FR.pdf.

[72]   'The FAA requires financial responsibility [i.e., insurance] for losses to the U.S. government and third parties resulting from a permitted activity based on a maximum probable loss (MPL) analysis. Maximum probable loss is the greatest dollar amount of loss for bodily injury or property damage that is reasonably expected to result from a permitted activity.' *Experimental Permit Program Report to COMSTAC*, FAA

is not eligible for U.S. Government indemnification, discussed later in this chapter, above the insured amount. Despite those limitations, the benefits of an experimental permit may be significant, based upon the expedited procedures and reduced requirements for issuance under 14 C.F.R. 437, including the time for the FAA's review, which is 120 days for a permit[73] versus 180 days for a license.[74] The experimental permit application procedures are outlined in 14 C.F.R. Part 413. A quick comparison between the regulations governing permits in Part 437 and licenses in Part 450 reveals a significant difference in the magnitude of the requirements.

The key components of the FAA's review for an experimental permit are the three elements of their safety strategy: (1) a hazard analysis;[75] (2) operating area containment;[76] and (3) abiding by operating requirements.[77]

The criteria for public risk are established in 14 C.F.R. §437.55(3)(i), which states that '[a]ny hazardous condition that may cause death or serious injury to the public must be extremely unlikely.'

Examples of launch activities that were conducted under an experimental license include Virgin Galactic's test flights of its hybrid vehicle with crew; SpaceX's 'Grasshopper' program to test reusability aspects of the Falcon 9 vehicle; and Blue Origin's New Shepard test flights.

Hybrid Vehicles

Hybrid vehicles have characteristics and components from aircraft and launch or reentry vehicles to optimize space operations. The determination whether the vehicle is subject to the FAA's aviation regulations under the Office of Aviation Safety (FAA AVS) or the FAA AST's rules has turned on the intent

---

Office of Commercial Space Transportation (May 2008), https://www.faa.gov/about/office_org/headquarters_offices/ast/licenses_permits/sub_orbital_rockets/media/EP%20Report%20to%20COMSTAC.pdf.

[73]   51 U.S.C. § 50906(a).

[74]   51 U.S.C. § 50905(a).

[75]   The FAA issued guidance for the hazard analysis in an advisory circular, AC 437.55-1, Hazard Analysis for the Launch or Reentry of a Reusable Suborbital Rocket Under an Experimental Permit.

[76]   'The FAA requires an applicant to demonstrate, at a minimum, either that there are physical limits on the ability of the reusable suborbital rocket to leave the operating area, or that the operator will use abort procedures and other safety measures derived from a system safety engineering process to contain the instantaneous impact point (IIP).' *Supra* note 75.

[77]   *Id.*

Table 7.1   Statutory differences between a license and an experimental permit[1]

	Experimental permit	License
Review period	The FAA has a maximum of 120 days to review an accepted permit application	The FAA has a maximum of 180 days to review an accepted license application
Compensation or hire (i.e., paying customer)	Carrying any property or human being for compensation or hire is prohibited under a permit	Revenue-generating launches are allowed under a license
Indemnification	Permitted launches are not eligible for indemnification	Licensed launches are eligible for government indemnification for third-party liability greater than the required financial responsibility (i.e., insurance)
Transferability	Permits are not transferable	Licenses are transferable

[1]   *Supra* note 76, at 1.

of the flight.[78] If the vehicle's flight is initiated to conduct a launch operation, it is a space operation and subject to the same FAA AST regulations as traditional vertical launch vehicles. However, if the intent is traditional aviation activities, it will be subject to aviation regulations.[79] As a result, an aircraft may be subject to FAA AST one day and then FAA AVS the next day.[80] Notably, the jurisdiction does not change mid-flight.

Virgin Galactic's SpaceShipTwo spaceflight system is an example of a hybrid system. It uses a custom-built carrier aircraft, Mothership, to carry SpaceShipTwo to an altitude of approximately 50,000 feet. Once released,

[78]   *See, e.g.,* Memorandum to Kelvin B. Coleman from Lorelei Peter, Assistant Chief Counsel for Regulations, FAA (July 23, 2018), https://www.faa.gov/about/office_org/headquarters_offices/agc/practice_areas/regulations/interpretations/data/interps/2018/coleman-ast-1%20-%20(2018)%20legal%20interpretation.pdf;   Legal Interpretation to Laura Montgomery from Lorelei Peter, Assistant Chief Counsel for Regulations, FAA (Dec. 10, 2019), https://www.faa.gov/about/office_org/headquarters_offices/agc/practice_areas/regulations/interpretations/Data/interps/2019/Montgomery-Ground%20Based%20Space%20Matters%20-%202019%20Legal%20Interpretation.pdf.

[79]   *Id.*

[80]   *See, Report to Congress: DOT/FAA Approach to Enabling Non-Launch Flight Operations of Space Support Vehicles Related to Commercial Space Transportation,* FAA (June 29, 2017), https://www.faa.gov/about/plans_reports/congress/media/Sect_105_Report_on_Enabling_Space_Support_Vehicles.pdf.

SpaceShipTwo ignites its rocket motor, which propels it to speeds approaching three and a half times the speed of sound to reach space for a suborbital flight.[81]

Spaceport Licenses

Part 420 of Title 14 of the Code of Federal Regulations governs launch site operator licenses (LSOL) and Part 433 governs reentry site operator licenses (RSOL). A spaceport operator can obtain an LSOL and an RSOL for the same spaceport. A license to operate a launch and/or reentry site authorizes the licensee to offer its site to multiple operators. It does not include the license to perform the launch or the reentry. The operator seeking to conduct either of those activities must apply and receive a separate license under Part 450.

A Part 420 LSOL applicant must provide the FAA AST with a description of the launch site, including information on its location, boundaries, ownership, planned operational date and the types of launch vehicles that the site plans to support.[82] An applicant for an LSOL or RSOL must conduct an environmental review as described later in this chapter. The environmental review is the only aspect of the spaceport license process subject to public comment.[83]

The RSOL regulations in Part 433 are brief. When an RSOL is granted, the licensee is authorized 'to offer use of the site to support reentry of a reentry vehicle for which the three-sigma footprint of the vehicle upon reentry is wholly contained within the site.'[84]

As with the launch and reentry license, a spaceport applicant (LSOL and RSOL) must enter into agreements, as appropriate to the site, with the FAA and U.S. Coast Guard for issuing notice to airmen and notice to mariners, respectively.

Environmental Review

An environmental review is a required step in the application review process for launch, reentry and spaceports.[85] An applicant's proposed activity and loca-

---

[81]   *Welcome to the world of Virgin Galactic*, Virgin Galactic Holdings, Inc., https://www.virgingalactic.com/learn/ (last visited Oct. 19, 2021).

[82]   14 C.F.R. § 420.15.

[83]   John Aguilar, *Rural resident on Colorado's Eastern Plains wary of launch issues related to planned spaceport at Front Range Airport*, The Denver Post (June 4, 2018), https://www.denverpost.com/2018/06/04/spaceport-colorado-concerns-eastern-plains/.

[84]   14 C.F.R. § 433.5.

[85]   Applicants must meet the requirements of the National Environmental Policy Act (42 U.S.C. § 4321 et seq.), the Council on Environmental Quality Regulations (40 C.F.R. Parts 1500 to 1508), and FAA Order 1050.1F in order to receive a license.

tion will determine the type of environmental review that will be required. An environmental assessment (EA) will be required to determine if the applicant's activities will have a significant human impact. It will describe the project's 'proposed action,' including its purpose, scope and analysis of potential impacts and alternatives. An applicant must demonstrate compliance with environmental laws and include any mitigation measures that are necessary to avoid, eliminate, or reduce anticipated impacts. The EA process concludes if the FAA AST issues a finding of no significant impact (FONSI), which must occur before a license can be granted.

An environmental impact statement (EIS) is required when the FAA AST determines that the proposed activity may have significant environmental impacts. The EIS is a much more detailed analysis of the environmental consequences of the applicant's proposed action than the EA. It provides the FAA and public with an opportunity to review the proposed activity's cumulative impacts, planned mitigation actions and alternatives to the proposed action. An EIS concludes with a record of decision (ROD).

Financial Responsibility and Indemnification

The Commercial Space Launch Act (CSLA) of 1984 included a requirement for licensees to carry liability insurance in an amount 'necessary for the launch or operation, considering the international obligations of the United States.'[86] In the 1994 CSLA updates, the insurance requirements were expanded and an indemnification regime was added.[87] That bill clarified the license requirement for obtaining insurance to cover third-party and certain U.S. Government claims arising from the licensed activities as codified in 51 U.S.C. 50914, 'Liability Insurance and Financial Responsibility.' The required insurance is for claims by third parties – the uninvolved public – and for damage to United States Government property. There is no requirement for a policy to cover damages incurred by the licensee or its customers, including spaceflight participants.

To satisfy the FAA insurance requirement, the licensee has the option of obtaining a liability insurance policy or demonstrating financial responsibility[88] in the amount dictated by the FAA AST. The insurance policy or method

---

[86]   Pub. L. 98-575, § 16.

[87]   Pub. L. 103-272, § 70112.

[88]   *See*, Streamlined Launch and Reentry License Requirements, 85 Fed. Reg. 79719, at 79566 (Dec. 10, 2020) (Effective March 10, 2021), https://www.govinfo .gov/content/pkg/FR-2020-12-10/pdf/2020-22042.pdf#page=154; 14 C.F.R. § 440.9(f) regarding options for demonstrating financial responsibility instead of obtaining an insurance policy; Legal Interpretation to Caryn Schenewerk from Lorelei Peter, Assistant Chief Counsel for Regulations (Aug. 4, 2016), https://www.faa.gov/about/

of compliance[89] must conform to requirements in Part 440 of the FAA AST's regulations and be submitted for the FAA AST's approval.[90]

The FAA AST determines the required insurance amount by calculating the maximum probable loss (MPL) based on information the license applicant provides. The insurance requirement cannot exceed the amounts established in the CSLA:

- No more than $500,000,000[91] to cover claims by 'a third party for death, bodily injury, or property damage';[92] and
- No more than $100,000,000[93] to cover claims by the United States Government 'for damage or loss to Government property resulting from an activity carried out under the license.'[94]

The 1994 CSLA established an indemnification regime to cover claims by third parties or the USG that exceed the insurance amount dictated by an FAA AST-issued license.[95] There are three tiers to the regime, as illustrated in Figure 7.2. The first is the MPL-based insurance that the licensee must purchase. The second is the amount the USG will indemnify exceeding insurance up to approximately $3 billion.[96] Any amount above the cap on USG indemnification is the responsibility of the licensee. The USG waives claims for its losses if those exceed the required insurance.

A licensee must include the USG as an additional insured and conclude all litigation related to the third-party claims to initiate the process for obtaining reimbursement from the USG for settlements or judgments in excess of insurance. The indemnification process then requires a recommendation from the DOT Secretary to the President. If the president concurs, the White House will submit a request to Congress, which must pass a joint resolution supporting the payment and appropriate the funds necessary.[97]

As of the date of this publication, there have been very few third-party claims against the FAA AST-required policies, and none exceeded the insured amount. There have been no instances to date that triggered indemnification.

---

office_org/headquarters_offices/agc/practice_areas/regulations/interpretations/Data/interps/2016/Schenewerk%20-%20(2016)%20Legal%20Interpretation.pdf.

[89]   *Id.* The FAA has accepted, for example, a captive insurance company established by an applicant for purposes of providing third-party liability insurance.

[90]   *See,* 14 C.F.R. Part 440 for compliance requirements.

[91]   51 U.S.C. § 50914(a)(3)(A)(i).

[92]   51 U.S.C. § 50914(a)(1)(A).

[93]   51 U.S.C. § 50914(a)(3(A)(ii).

[94]   51 U.S.C. § 50914(a)(1)(B).

[95]   51 U.S.C. § 50915.

[96]   Pub. L. 103-272 established the cap on indemnification at $1.5 billion but included an inflation adjustment. 51 U.S.C. § 50915(a)(1)(B).

[97]   51 U.S.C. § 50915.

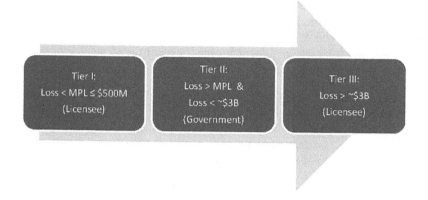

Figure 7.2   Indemnification tiers

Since its establishment in 1994, the indemnification has consistently been subject to a sunset clause. Multiple extensions have been granted. The last extension was passed in 2015; it extended the expiration date until September 30, 2025.[98]

The indemnification regime applies only to licensed activities; it does not apply to experimental permits. The Committee Report accompanying the 2004 CSLA (H.R. 3752) explained that Congress anticipated lighter regulations and higher risk related to experimental permits; therefore, no indemnification was granted.[99] Additionally, the limited activities authorized by an experimental permit decrease the likelihood of claims exceeding the MPL or having international implications under the Liability Convention.

While the licensee must procure third-party liability insurance, there are no FAA AST licensing requirements for first-party insurance to cover the licensee's or its customer's losses. Instead, the 2004 CSLA included a requirement for 'reciprocal waivers of claims' between the 'applicable parties' involved in the licensed activity and the USG.[100] The waiver of claims is intended to prevent litigation between the entities involved in the licensed activity.[101]

---

[98]   Pub. L. 114-90; *See*, 51 U.S.C. § 50915(f).

[99]   *Supra* note 18.

[100]   Applicable parties, 'means (i) contractors, subcontractors, and customers of the licensee or transferee; (ii) contractors and subcontractors of the customers; and (iii) space flight participants.' The clause including spaceflight participants expires September 30, 2025, unless it is extended. 51 U.S.C. § 50914(b).

[101]   *See*, H.R. Rep. No. 108-429, https://www.congress.gov/congressional-report/108th-congress/house-report/429/1?overview=closed.

> **First and second parties** are those involved in the spaceflight activity.
> **Third parties** are everyone else, i.e., the uninvolved public.
> The **insurance and indemnification regime** is for third-party claims.
> **Cross-waivers** are among those involved in the spaceflight activity.

The parties to the licensed activity agree 'to be responsible for personal injury to, death of, or property damage or loss' they or their employees suffer from the licensed activity.[102] Those parties also waive all claims against the USG. The USG waives claims only to the extent that the claims exceed the amount of insurance or demonstration of financial responsibility.[103] The required text of the waivers is included in the appendices to Part 440.[104]

AIRSPACE INTEGRATION

An applicant for a launch, reentry or spaceport license must complete a letter of agreement (LOA) with the FAA Air Traffic Control (ATC) office having jurisdiction over the airspace through which the proposed operations will occur.[105] The LOA establishes procedures for coordinating the spaceflight activities, including issuing notice to airmen (NOTAM) or temporary flight restrictions (TFRs) that result in closing air routes and other measures the FAA ATC deems necessary to protect public health and safety. For example, the LOA may require giving the FAA ATC access to real-time verbal updates and trajectory data from the licensee. The LOA often includes coordination activities that are initiated in the event of a mishap. A draft LOA must be submitted to the FAA AST as part of the application process. A final, signed LOA is required before licensed operation commences.

In accordance with the LOA, blocks of airspace are designated as hazard areas and closed to protect the flying public when a licensed launch or reentry occurs.[106] During those closures, air traffic is directed around, not through, the

---

[102]   51 U.S.C. § 50914(b)(1)(A).

[103]   51 U.S.C. § 50914 (b)(2).

[104]   The licensee is responsible for submitting a fully executed waiver to the FAA AST 'at least thirty days before the start of any licensed or permitted activity involving a customer, crew members, or space flight participant.' 14 C.F.R. § 440.15.

[105]   14 C.F.R. § 420.31 (launch site operator license), § 450.XXX (launch and reentry licenses), and § 437.35 (experimental permits).

[106]   Hazard areas are also referred to as 'blast danger areas,' 'safety zones,' 'aircraft hazard areas,' and 'ship hazard areas,' depending on the context. They are all areas from which members of the public must be excluded to achieve the level of safety required by the FAA AST regulations and comply with an issued license.

closed airspace. Spaceflight activities are carefully segregated from aviation activities.

HUMAN SPACEFLIGHT

In 1996, the X Prize Foundation offered $10 million for the first nongovernment organization to launch a reusable crewed spacecraft into space twice within two weeks. In 2004, Scaled Composites won the X Prize by being the first to finance privately, build, and launch a vehicle able to carry three people to an altitude of 100 kilometers (62 statute miles).[107] In light of the interest in human spaceflight generated by the X Prize, as well as the successful demonstration by Scaled Composites, Congress passed the 2004 CSLAA.[108] The CSLAA required that the FAA issue regulations relating to crew, spaceflight participants, and permits for launch or reentry of reusable suborbital rockets. Additionally, the CSLAA introduced the concept of the 'learning period' or 'moratorium,' discussed in more detail below.

In accordance with the CSLAA, the FAA developed 14 C.F.R. Part 460, which prescribes the human spaceflight requirements an operator must follow if a launch or reentry will occur with people on board the launch or reentry vehicle. Part 460 is divided into two subparts: subpart A for launch and reentry with crew[109] and subpart B for launch and reentry with spaceflight participants (SFPs).[110]

For launch and reentry with crew, crew members must complete training in nominal and off-nominal conditions on how to carry out their role on board or on the ground so that the vehicle will not harm the public, demonstrate certain abilities during spaceflight and meet medical requirements.[111] In addi-

---

[107] *Launching A New Space Industry*, X Prize (last visited Apr. 3, 2021), https://www.xprize.org/prizes/ansari.

[108] For a discussion of the law and political landscape surrounding the 2004 Space Act, *see*, Timothy Robert Hughes & Esta Rosenberg, *Space Travel Law (and Politics): The Evolution of the Commercial Space Launch Amendments Act of 2004*, 31 J. Space L. 1 (2005).

[109] 'Crew' is defined as 'any employee or independent contractor of a licensee, transferee, or permittee, or of a contractor or subcontractor of a licensee, transferee, or permittee, who performs activities in the course of that employment or contract directly relating to the launch, reentry, or other operation of or in a launch vehicle or reentry vehicle that carries human beings. A crew consists of flight crew and any remote operator.' 14 C.F.R. § 401.5.

[110] A spaceflight participant is an individual who is neither crew nor a government astronaut carried within a launch or reentry vehicle. 51 U.S.C. § 50902(20).

[111] 14 C.F.R. § 460.5(a), (b) & (e).

tion to training, an operator[112] must inform in writing any individual serving as crew that the USG has not certified the launch vehicle and any reentry vehicle as safe for carrying flight crew or spaceflight participants.[113] Crew must also execute a reciprocal waiver of claims with the FAA in accordance with Part 440.[114] Finally, an operator is required to provide environmental control and life support systems adequate to sustain life and consciousness for all inhabited areas within a vehicle.[115]

Pilots and remote operators must satisfy certain additional requirements. A pilot is a flight crew member who has the ability to control, in real time, a launch or reentry vehicle's flight path.[116] A remote operator is a crew member who: (1) has the ability to control, in real time, a launch or reentry vehicle's flight path, and (2) is not on board the controlled vehicle.[117] These additional requirements for pilots and remote operators focus on an understanding of the vehicle and an understanding of operating safely in the national airspace system (NAS).

For launch and reentry with SFPs, an operator must train each SFP before flight on how to respond to emergency situations, including smoke, fire, loss of cabin pressure, and emergency exit.[118] An operator must also implement security requirements to prevent any SFP from jeopardizing the safety of the flight crew or the public. An SFP may not carry on board any explosives, firearms, knives, or other weapons.[119] Before receiving compensation or making an agreement to fly an SFP, an operator must inform the SFP in writing about the risks of launch and reentry, including the safety record of the launch or reentry vehicle type.[120] The operator must also provide the SFP an opportunity to ask questions orally to better understand the risks and hazards of the mission.[121] The SFP must provide consent in writing.[122] Finally, an SFP must execute

---

[112] 'Operator' is defined as 'a holder of a license or permit under 51 U.S.C. Subtitle V, Chapter 509.' 14 C.F.R. § 401.5.

[113] 14 C.F.R. § 460.9.

[114] 14 C.F.R. § 460.19.

[115] 14 C.F.R. § 460.11.

[116] 14 C.F.R. § 401.5.

[117] *Id.*

[118] 14 C.F.R. § 460.51.

[119] 14 C.F.R. § 460.53.

[120] 14 C.F.R. § 460.45(a).

[121] 14 C.F.R. § 460.45(f).

[122] 14 C.F.R. § 460.45(f).

a reciprocal waiver of claims with the FAA and the licensee in accordance with Part 440[123] and 51 U.S.C. 50914.[124]

Although the CSLAA granted the FAA authority over the safety of launch vehicles designed to carry humans, it limited the FAA's ability to propose requirements governing the design or operation of a launch vehicle to protect the health and safety of people on board for eight years from the date of enactment. Specifically, 51 U.S.C. 50904(b)(2)(D) authorizes the FAA to prescribe 'additional license requirements, for a launch vehicle carrying a human being for compensation or hire, necessary to protect the health and safety of crew, government astronauts, or space flight participants, only if such requirements are imposed pursuant to final regulations issued in accordance with subsection (c).'

Subsection (c) establishes what has been referred to as the 'learning period' or 'moratorium' that prevents the FAA from proposing any regulations governing the design or operation of a launch vehicle for the purpose of protecting the health and safety of crew, government astronauts, and spaceflight participants. The FAA may only restrict or prohibit design features or operating practices that (1) have resulted in a serious or fatal injury to persons on board during a licensed or permitted launch or reentry; or (2) contributed to an unplanned event or series of events during a licensed or permitted commercial human spaceflight that posed a high risk of causing a serious or fatal injury to persons on board.[125] Most recently, this period was extended to October 1, 2023.[126]

Finally, in 2015 Congress passed the Commercial Space Launch Competitiveness Act (CSLCA), which created a separate category of people on board a launch or reentry vehicle called government astronauts. The CSLCA defines a government astronaut as an individual who is designated by the National Aeronautics and Space Administration; is carried within a launch vehicle or reentry vehicle in the course of his or her employment, which may include performance of activities directly relating to the launch, reentry, or other operation of the launch vehicle or reentry vehicle; and is either an employee of the United States Government, including the uniformed services,

---

[123]   14 C.F.R. § 460.49.

[124]   As part of the Commercial Space Launch Competitiveness Act passed in 2015, Congress added SFPs as applicable parties with whom a licensee must make a reciprocal waiver of claims. The FAA has not yet updated its regulations to reflect this addition.

[125]   51 U.S.C. § 50905(c)(2)(C).

[126]   51 U.S.C. § 50905(c)(9).

engaged in the performance of a federal function under authority of law or an executive act; or an international partner astronaut.[127]

The AST's Commercial Space Astronaut Wings

For decades, the FAA, NASA, and the US military have awarded astronaut badges or wings to civilians and members of the military who fly 50 miles (80km) above the Earth.[128] The FAA first issued commercial astronaut wings in 2004 to the pilots of a FAA-licensed suborbital commercial launch vehicle.[129]

However, on July 20, 2021, the same day that Blue Origin flew Jeff Bezos and three others well above the 80km mark, the FAA issued an order that 'provides guidelines, eligibility, and criteria for the administration of the FAA Commercial Space Astronaut Wings Program.'[130] The FAA described the policy change as necessary to 'maintain the prestige of the Commercial Space Astronaut Wings,' adding that flight crew must also 'demonstrate activities during flight that were essential to public safety, or contributed to human spaceflight safety.'[131]

---

[127] 51 U.S.C. § 50902(4). *See*, Steven A. Mirmina, Astronauts Redefined: The Commercial Carriage of Humans to Space and the Changing Concepts of Astronauts under International and U.S. Law, 10 FIU L. Rev. 669 (2015).

[128] While NASA, the FAA, and the US military all recognize 50 miles as where space begins for human spaceflight, the US does not have an official position internationally on where space starts. *See*, Louis de Guoyon Mtignon, *Why Does the FAA Use 50 Miles for Defining Space?*, Space Legal Issues (Nov. 24, 2019), https://www.spacelegalissues.com/why-does-the-faa-uses-50-miles-for-defining-outer-space/ . There is not an agreed definition for where space starts. The Karman Line is recognized internationally as the start of space at 100km above Earth. However, scholars have recently argued that the Karman Line is actually closer to 80km instead of 100km. *See*, Jonathan C. McDowell, *The edge of space: Revisiting the Karman Line*, Harvard-Smithsonian Center for Astrophysics, (2018), https://planet4589.org/space/papers/Edge.pdf.

[129] Mike Melvill was the first recipient of the FAA's commercial astronaut wings. 'Like U.S. military and NASA astronauts, the FAA now has its own way to recognize those who reach space in the United States through private endeavors.' *See*, Patricia Grace Smith, *Presentation of FAA Commercial Astronaut Wings to SpaceshipOne Pilot Mike Melvill*, FAA (June 21, 2004), https://www.faa.gov/about/office_org/headquarters_offices/ast/media/PGS_Melvill_wings_2004-06-21.pdf.

[130] *FAA Commercial Space Astronaut Wings Program*, FAA (July 20, 2021), https://www.faa.gov/documentLibrary/media/Order/FAA_Order_8800.2.pdf.

[131] The FAA AST associate administrator is the final authority who will determine whether a commercial crew member is eligible for the wings. Notably, the order included an honorary award provision that would give the associate administrator 'total discretion' to bestow wings 'to individuals who demonstrated extraordinary contribution or beneficial service to the commercial human space flight industry.' *Id.*

INVESTIGATION OF SPACEFLIGHT ACCIDENTS AND MISHAPS

Title 51 U.S.C. § 50917 gives the FAA AST the authority to conduct mishap investigations for all FAA-licensed or permitted launch activities.[132] In the event of a mishap or accident, the FAA AST requires operators to have investigation plans that contain procedures for reporting, responding to, and investigating mishaps or accident that occur during such activities. Those plans must contain procedures to identify and adopt preventive measures to avoid a future recurrence of the event.

In the event of a spaceflight accident, the National Transportation Safety Board (NTSB) – not the FAA AST – is in charge of the investigation. Since 1979, the NTSB and the FAA AST have signed multiple memoranda of understanding (MOU) outlining their roles and responsibilities in the event of a commercial spaceflight accident.[133] In each of the MOUs, both agencies have agreed that:

NTSB will investigate all commercial space launch accidents resulting in:
a. Known impact of a commercial launch vehicle, its payload or any component thereof outside the impact limit lines designated by the launch range facility; or
b. A fatality or serious injury (as defined in 49 C.F.R. 830.2) to any person who is not associated with commercial space launch activities and who is not located on the launch range facility; or
c. Any damage estimated to exceed $25,000 to property which is not associated with commercial space launch activities and which is not located on the launch range facility.[134]

---

[132] 'Mishap' is defined to mean 'a launch or reentry accident, launch or reentry incident, launch site accident, failure to complete a launch or reentry as planned, or an unplanned event or series of events resulting in a fatality or serious injury (as defined in 49 C.F.R. 830.2), or resulting in greater than $250,000 worth of damage to a payload, a launch or reentry vehicle, a launch or reentry support facility or government property located on the launch or reentry site.' 14 C.F.R. § 401.5.

[133] *See, e.g., Reimbursable Memorandum of Agreement Between Department of Transportation and National Transportation Safety Board* (May 5, 1975), https://www.phmsa.dot.gov/sites/phmsa.dot.gov/files/docs/1975_DOT_NTSB.pdf; *Memorandum of Understanding Between the National Transportation Board, Department of the Air Force, and Federal Aviation Administration Regarding Space Launch Accidents,* (Aug. 3, 2004) https://www.faa.gov/space/legislation_regulation_guidance/media/mou_space_launch_accidents.pdf; FAA Order 8020.11D (May 10, 2018), https://www.faa.gov/documentlibrary/media/order/faa_order_8020.11d.pdf.

[134] *Aerospace Accident Report: In flight Breakup During Test Flight Scaled Composites SpaceShipTwo, N339SS, Near Koehn Dry Lake, California Oct. 31, 2014,* National Transportation Safety Board (July 28, 2015), https://www.ntsb.gov/investigations/AccidentReports/Reports/AAR1502.pdf, at A-15.

In its Aerospace Accident Report on the in-flight breakup of Scaled Composites' SpaceShipTwo, the NTSB interpreted 49 U.S.C. § 1131(a)(1)(F) using its *Chevron* deference as providing it with the 'authority to investigate commercial space accidents.'[135] Specifically, that statute states:

(a)   General. – (1) The National Transportation Safety Board shall investigate or have investigated (in detail the Board prescribes) and establish the facts, circumstances, and cause or probable cause of...

      (F)   any other accident related to the transportation of individuals or property when the Board decides –

          (i)   the accident is catastrophic;
          (ii)   the accident involves problems of a recurring character; or
          (iii) the investigation of the accident would carry out this chapter.[136]

In 2018, the FAA issued an order elaborating on each agency's role in the event of air or spaceflight accident.[137] The order reiterated the NTSB's role as defined above and explained that the FAA AST authority to conduct independent investigations parallel to an NTSB one includes: '(1) Accidents not investigated by the NTSB; (2) Incidents or other identified mishaps; (3) Flight safety systems malfunctions; (4) Failure of a safety organization or safety process associated with or related to commercial space activities; (5) Suspected regulatory violations or violations of an FAA license or experimental permit and associated orders.'[138]

COMMERCIAL SPACE TRANSPORTATION ADVISORY COMMITTEE

The Commercial Space Transportation Advisory Committee (COMSTAC) is the one space-related committee that provides 'information, advice and recommendations' to the FAA administrator under the Federal Advisory Committee Act.[139] COMSTAC membership includes executives from various aspects of the commercial space transportation industry as well as representatives from academia, industry associations, and advocacy organizations.

---

[135]   *Id.* at 73.

[136]   49 U.S.C. § 1131(a)(1)(F).

[137]   *Aircraft Accident and Incident Notification, Investigation, and Report*, FAA Order (May 10, 2018), https://www.faa.gov/documentlibrary/media/order/faa_order_8020.11d.pdf.

[138]   *Id.* at 58.

[139]   *Commercial Space Transportation Advisory Committee (COMSTAC)*, FAA (last visited Oct. 19, 2021) https://www.faa.gov/space/additional_information/comstac/.

QUESTIONS FOR REVIEW

1. How is the FAA AST's oversight of commercial spaceflight different from the FAA's oversight of aviation activities? What are the statutory and regulatory roots of that difference?

2. High-profile USG space missions, including astronaut flights to the ISS, are FAA-licensed. With that in mind, do you think the CRRES decision would have a different outcome today?

3. How is public interest served by the FAA's insurance and indemnification regime? What is the interplay with the USG's obligations under the Liability Convention?

4. What is the FAA's role in meeting the USG's OST Article VI obligations to provide 'authorization and continuing supervision' for the activities of its nationals?

5. You learned that the FAA has authority to regulate launch and reentry activities, but not on-orbit activities. How has that limitation affected applicants seeking USG approval for in-space or in-situ activities? How might granting 'mission authority' to the FAA versus the Commerce Department affect the level of regulation applied to non-traditional space activities?

6. What is the basis for the statutory limitation on FAA issuing regulations specific to human occupant safety and is that justification still valid?

8. Commercial remote sensing, space commerce and space weather

'Ruth, we just got a new client for a space-related matter. This one is U.S.-based, so it'll be an exciting chance for you to expand your U.S. space law knowledge,' her senior partners says as he drops a thick file on her desk. 'The client is investing in a company that provides space-based imagery, and they have questions regarding the licensing of remote-sensing systems.'

'She nods while taking notes. 'Sure, I can prepare a memo to answer their questions,' she says.

'Great, I told them we would have the answers for them first thing on Monday.' Then he points to the binder and adds, 'This should be a good start for understanding the company and its operations.'

'Ruth looks at the binder and thinks, 'It's still Thursday, but based on the size of that file, bye, bye weekend.' She grabs the file and also bids farewell to worrying about meeting her billable hour requirement when her yearly performance evaluation comes up.

The Department of Commerce (DOC) is home to U.S. Government space operations, including utilizing space assets for weather prediction and gathering environmental science data. The DOC also leads efforts to promote the U.S. space industry, regulate private remote-sensing regulations, and coordinate federal spectrum use. This chapter will largely focus on the National Oceanic and Atmospheric Administration (NOAA) within the DOC. It will also discuss proposals to expand the DOC's role to include the provision of space situational awareness (SSA) data and approval of space activities not specifically regulated by another U.S. Government agency.

NATIONAL OCEANIC AND ATMOSPHERIC ADMINISTRATION

NOAA is responsible for environmental sciences, including atmospheric research and remote sensing, as well as the licensing of commercial remote-sensing space systems. It is 'the Nation's authoritative environmental intelligence agency,' with a mission that covers climate change as well as conservation and management of coastal and marine ecosystems.[1] NOAA has broad statutory authority across many different activities,[2] but most relevant here is NOAA's role in commercial remote sensing and space weather.

NOAA History

In 1966, Congress authorized the creation of the Commission on Marine Science, Engineering, and Resources to study oceanic resources and recommend a national oceanic plan.[3] Following that report, in 1970, NOAA and the Environmental Protection Agency (EPA) were created in a consolidation of agencies and programs designed to address or oversee specific environmental issues.[4]

LANDSAT

The Landsat program is the ongoing U.S. Government program dedicated to collecting spectral information of the Earth's surface. The Landsat program has provided images of the Earth's surface for over 40 years.[5] The Landsat program, since its inception, was subject to continual agency juris-

---

[1]   Nat'l Envtl. Satellite Data & Info. Serv., *Strategic Plan*, NOAA 5 (2016), https://www.nesdis.noaa.gov/s3/2021-09/NESDIS_Strategic_Plan_2016_1.pdf.

[2]   'NOAA currently operates under nearly 200 separate legislative authorities to conduct its business.' Tim Hall & Mary Kicza, *An Organic Act for NOAA to Formalize Its Purpose and Authorities*, AEROSPACE 1 (Aug. 2018), https://aerospace.org/sites/default/files/2018-08/Hall-Kicza_Organic%20Act_08082018.pdf.

[3]   The agency was created by the Marine Resources and Engineering Development Act of 1966. Nat'l Oceanic and Atmospheric Admin., *NOAA Legal History*, NOAA, https://www.gc.noaa.gov/gcil_history.html (last visited Nov. 10, 2021).

[4]   Reorganization Plan No. 3 of 1970, 35 Fed. Reg. 15623 (Dec. 2, 1970); Reorganization Plan No. 4 of 1970, 35 Fed. Reg. 15627 (Oct. 3, 1970); EILEEN L. SHEA, A HISTORY OF NOAA: BEING A COMPILATION OF FACTS AND FIGURES REGARDING THE LIFE AND TIMES OF THE ORIGINAL WHOLE EARTH AGENCY ix (1987). The space-related aspects of NOAA evolved from the previous Environmental Science Services Administration. The ESSA was placed under DOC for effective management, and also because the activities would produce 'two types' of 'economies': (1) cost-sharing for large technical investments like satellites, (2) cost reduction through consolidation of offices. Reorganization Plan No. 2 of 1965, 30 Fed. Reg. 8815, 8819-20 (July 14, 1965) (message from the President of the United States, Transmitting Reorganization Plan No. 2 of 1965, Providing for the Reorganization of Two Major Agencies of the Department of Commerce: the Weather Bureau and the Coast and Geodetic Survey).

[5]   Landsat Science, *About*, NASA (Oct. 8, 2020), https://landsat.gsfc.nasa.gov/about/.

dictional battles.[6] President Carter, after review of civil and military space policies, transferred control of the Landsat program to the Department of Commerce, and specifically to NOAA.[7] Management of Landsat, which equated to management of U.S. civil operational land remote-sensing activities, was seen to correlate with NOAA's ongoing atmospheric and oceanic responsibilities.[8] One goal of President Carter's 1979 reorganization was transferring civil remote-sensing operations (i.e., the Landsat program) to the private sector.

The Land Remote-Sensing Commercialization Act of 1984 (Commercialization Act) did three important things: (1) codified nondiscriminatory data access and created a national data archive; (2) addressed the licensing of private remote-sensing systems; and (3) began the formal commercialization of the Landsat program.[9]

NOAA was created to improve and oversee the use of sea resources; consolidate programs to achieve a better understanding of oceanic and atmospheric phenomena; and 'facilitate the cooperation between public and private interests that can best serve the interests of all.'[10] NOAA space authorities arise from various statutes, including the Coast and Geodetic Survey Act,[11] the Land Remote-Sensing Policy Act of 1992,[12] and the Space Weather Authority.[13] NOAA's statutory authority over commercial remote sensing derives from

---

[6]   Donald T. Lauer et al., *The Landsat Program: Its Origins, Evolution, and Impacts*, 63 PHOTOGRAMMETRIC ENG'G & REMOTE SENSING 831, 835 (1997).

[7]   However, NOAA was not meant to go it alone; Landsat was to be run by a program board, which included coordination with, and involvement of, other federal organizations. *Civil Operational Remote Sensing*, Presidential Directive NSC-54 § 2 (Nov. 16, 1979). This Presidential Directive was classified and has only been released in part. *See*, John Pike & Steven Aftergood, *Presidential Directives (PD): Carter Administration, 1977–81*, FED'N AM. SCIENTISTS (Sept. 18, 2020), https://fas.org/irp/offdocs/pd/index.html; *infra* note 13.

[8]   Pike & Aftergood, *supra* note 7.

[9]   *Land Remote-Sensing Commercialization*, 15 U.S.C. Chap. 68 (repealed, 1992); Joanne Irene Gabrynowicz, *The Perils of Landsat from Grassroots to Globalization: A Comprehensive Review of US Remote Sensing Law with a Few Thoughts for the Future*, 6 Chi. J. Int'l L. 45, 53-4 (2005).

[10]   Reorganization Plan No. 3 of 1970, *supra* note 4, at Appendix; William J. Merrell et al., *The Stratton Commission: The Model for a Sea Change in National Marine Policy*, 14 OCEANOGRAPHY 11, 15-6 (2001).

[11]   33 U.S.C. § 883j (2018) (directing the NOAA administrator to ensure availability of ocean satellite data for the maritime community).

[12]   51 U.S.C. §§ 60101-60162 (2018).

[13]   15 U.S.C. § 1532 (2018).

the Land Remote-Sensing Policy Act of 1992 (Policy Act).[14] The Policy Act resulted from a U.S. Government initiative – the Landsat program.[15]

NOAA has six offices responsible for specific missions: the Office of Marine and Aviation Operations; the National Marine Fisheries Service; the National Ocean Service; the Office of Oceanic and Atmospheric Research; the National Weather Service; and the National Environmental Satellite, Data, and Information Service.[16] The NOAA administrator is appointed by the president and confirmed by the Senate.[17]

National Environmental Satellite, Data, and Information Service

The National Environmental Satellite, Data, and Information Service (NESDIS) is responsible for providing operational satellite services for NOAA and the U.S. at large. Additionally, NESDIS runs the National Centers for Environmental Information, which provides global environmental data from satellites and other sources according to a schedule of fees.[18] The Office of Space Commerce and the Commercial Remote-Sensing Regulatory Affairs Office are within NESDIS.[19]

The Office of Space Commerce

The Office of Space Commerce (OSC) integrates space policy and space commerce issues.[20] This includes coordinating space policy for the DOC and

---

[14] 51 U.S.C. §§ 60101-60506 (2018).

[15] *See, e.g.*, Gabrynowicz, *supra* note 9, at 48 (estimating that the amount of the U.S. population that is aware of the Landsat programs numbers in the thousands or low tens of thousands).

[16] Nat'l Oceanic and Atmospheric Admin., *NOAA Corporate Finance and Administrative Services Offices: NOAA Line Offices*, NOAA, https://www .corporateservices.noaa.gov/public/lineoffices.html (last visited Nov. 15, 2021).

[17] Reorganization Plan No. 4, *supra* note 4, at § 4(b).

[18] *See, e.g., Schedule of Fees for Access to NOAA Environmental Information, and Related Products and Services*, 84 F.R. 3101 (2019). However, it is increasingly unusual for NOAA data to be provided for a fee. Data is made available at no fee, straight from the spacecraft, and through cloud partnerships such as the NOAA Big Data Program. *See generally Comprehensive Large Array-Data Stewardship System (CLASS)*, NOAA, https://www.avl.class.noaa.gov/saa/products/welcome;jsessionid= 5CF4169F3FC6E8E81664236E87BB3B6C (last visited Nov. 15, 2021).

[19] *See* NESDIS, *Commercial Remote Sensing Regulatory Affairs*, NOAA, https:// www.nesdis.noaa.gov/about/our-offices/commercial-remote-sensing-regulatory -affairs (last visited Dec. 22, 2021).

[20] Office of Space Comm., *Department of Commerce Accomplishments: Space and Space Commerce*, Dep't Comm. (Jan. 20, 2021), https://www.space.commerce.gov/ report-on-doc-accomplishments-in-space-commerce/.

representing the DOC in international discussions.[21] The OSC's mandate is to 'foster the conditions for the economic growth and technological advancement of the U.S. commercial space industry.'[22] The OSC also supports NOAA in the acquisition of commercial weather satellite data and development of remote-sensing regulations.[23]

In 2018, Space Policy Directive 3 (SPD-3), National Space Traffic Management Policy, proposed giving the DOC responsibility for publicly releasable space situational awareness (SSA) data, stating that: 'To facilitate this enhanced data sharing, and in recognition of the need for DoD to focus on maintaining access to and freedom of action in space, a civil agency should, consistent with applicable law, be responsible for the publicly releasable portion of the DoD catalog and for administering an open architecture data repository.'[24] The Administration also requested congressional approval for elevating OSC from within NOAA to a new Bureau of Space Commerce that would report directly to the Commerce Secretary.[25]

In response, Congress mandated a National Academy of Public Administration (NAPA) study. The NAPA study recommended that OSC 'be selected to conduct the SSA/STM mission,' and that 'OSC be elevated to the Office of Secretary of Commerce.'[26] However, further congressional action necessary for codifying authority over SSA/STM and the move from DOD to Commerce was not taken before the end of the Administration.[27]

---

[21]   51 U.S.C. § 50702 (2018).

[22]   Office of Space Comm., *Mission*, Dep't Comm., https://www.space.commerce .gov/about/mission/#:~:text=The%20Office%20of%20Space%20Commerce,the%20U .S.%20commercial%20space%20industry (last visited Nov. 15, 2021).

[23]   *Id.*

[24]   Space Policy Directive 3: National Space Traffic Management Policy, 83 Fed. Reg. 28969 (June 18, 2018).

[25]   Marcia Smith, *Senate Committee Approves Space Act, But Without A Bureau of Space Commerce*, Spacepolicyonline.com (Nov. 18, 2020), https://spacepolicyonline .com/news/senate-committee-approves-space-act-but-without-a-bureau-of-space -commerce/.

[26]   *Space Traffic Management: Assessment of the Feasibility, Expected Effectiveness, and Funding Implications of a Transfer of Space Traffic Management Functions*, Nat't Academy of Pub. Admin. (Aug. 2020), https://napawash.org/academy-studies/united -states-department-of-commerce-office-of-space-commerce.

[27]   Justification for the transfer was summarized as follows in testimony to the Senate: 'Three core ideas underpin the request for the Office of Space Commerce: as a signal of the importance of the U.S. commercial space industry to our nation's economic and national security future; as a way of leveraging the many different Commerce bureaus and organizations to support U.S. space commerce; and as a way of ensuring that economic and commercial views have equal representation in high-level Executive Branch discussions.' *The Emerging Space Environment: Operational, Technical, and Policy Challenges*, Hearing Before the Subcomm. on Aviation and

Additionally, the 2020 National Space Policy as well as industry represent-atives and congressional legislation have supported granting OSC authority to approve U.S. commercial in-space and in-situ operations, referred to as novel or nontraditional activities.[28] The proposed authority over novel activ-ities is meant to capture those that are not primarily overseen by the Federal Communications Commission, Federal Aviation Authority, or NOAA. Should such authority be codified, an application, review and approval process would have to be implemented.

Office of Commercial Remote-Sensing Regulatory Affairs[29]

The Office of Commercial Remote-Sensing Regulatory Affairs' (CRSRA) mission is 'to regulate the operation of private Earth remote sensing space systems,[30] subject to the jurisdiction or control of the United States, while preserving essential national security interests, foreign policy and international obligations.'[31] CRSRA oversees remote-sensing licensing and compliance and monitoring activity.[32]

CRSRA will consult with private organizations prior to their application submission to help ensure the completeness of their application.[33] CRSRA conducts compliance and monitoring activities over licensees to ensure com-

---

Space, Senate Committee on Commerce, Science & Transportation, 116 Cong. (May 14, 2019) (Statement of Kevin M. O'Connell), https://www.commerce.senate.gov/services/files/E80EF6E9-38DA-4ACF-8838-7089139F2933.

[28] The National Space Policy, 85 Fed. Reg. 81755 § 5.3.a (Dec. 9, 2020); *Reopening the American Frontier: Exploring How the Outer Space Treaty Will Impact American Commerce and Settlement in Space,* U.S. Senate Committee on Commerce, Science and Transportation (May 23, 2017) https://www.commerce.senate.gov/2017/5/reopening-the-american-frontier-exploring-how-the-outer-space-treaty-will-impact-american-commerce-and-settlement-in-space; American Space Commerce Free Enterprise Act, H. R. 2809, 115 Cong. § 3 (2017).

[29] Commercial Remote Sensing Regulatory Affairs [hereinafter CRSRA], CRSRA Organizational Chart, NOAA, https://www.nesdis.noaa.gov/CRSRA/files/CRSRA_at_NOAA.pdf (last visited Nov. 15, 2021).

[30] The definition of a 'remote-sensing space system' is scoped to include the imaging instrumentality, unenhanced data receipt systems, and data preprocessing. In essence, the system includes the remote-sensing instrument and components that support the instrument.15 C.F.R. § 960.4 (2020); *Licensing of Private Remote Sensing Space Systems,* 85 Fed. Reg. 30790, 30796 (May 20, 2020) (codified at 15 C.F.R. Part 960).

[31] CRSRA, *About Commercial Remote Sensing Regulatory Affairs,* NOAA, https://www.nesdis.noaa.gov/CRSRA/index.html (last visited Nov. 15, 2021).

[32] *Id.*

[33] CRSRA, *License Application Process,* NOAA, https://www.nesdis.noaa.gov/CRSRA/generalApplication.html (last visited Nov. 15, 2021).

pliance with U.S. laws, regulations, and policies.[34] CRSRA also oversees the NOAA Advisory Committee on Commercial Remote Sensing (ACCRES), discussed later in this chapter.[35]

COMMERCIAL REMOTE-SENSING LICENSING

The 1984 Commercialization Act authorized the Commerce Secretary to license private companies to develop and market commercial remote-sensing capabilities.[36] Applicants were required to certify that they would operate in a manner to preserve U.S. national security, notify the secretary of any foreign agreements, and grant the government inspection rights to facilities, equipment, and financial records.[37] Additionally, the Commercialization Act mandated nondiscriminatory access to remote-sensing data, which required unenhanced data[38] be offered without any barriers to any class of buyer.[39] This statutory requirement applied to civil and commercial operators alike and dealt a large blow to the nascent private remote-sensing data market.[40] Nondiscriminatory access prevented potential commercial providers from offering attractive pricing benefits to particular customers,[41] and is blamed for disincentivizing nascent private remote-sensing development within the U.S.[42]

The Land Remote Sensing Policy Act of 1992 (Policy Act) replaced the Commercialization Act.[43] The Policy Act is divided into six subchapters: (1)

---

[34] For more information on the licensing process, see below. CRSRA, *About Commercial Remote Sensing Compliance & Monitoring*, NOAA, https://www.nesdis .noaa.gov/CRSRA/complianceHome.html (last visited Nov. 15, 2021).

[35] For information on ACCRES, see below. Nat'l Envtl. Satellite Data & Info. Serv. *Commercial Remote Sensing Regulatory Affairs*, NOAA, https://www.nesdis.noaa .gov/CRSRA/ (last visited Nov. 15, 2021).

[36] *Land Remote-Sensing Commercialization*, 98th Cong., 98 Stat. 451 § 101(5) (1984).

[37] *Id.*

[38] Unenhanced data is data which has not undergone processing, or only minimal processing, of signals or film products. *Id.*

[39] However, there was an exception or carve-out to this policy for national security concerns. *Id.* at § 104(4).

[40] David P. Radzanowski, *U.S. Civil Earth Observation Programs: Landsat, Mission to Planet Earth, and the Weather Satellites*, CRS Rep. IB 92-082 at 3 (May 5, 1992).

[41] *Id.* at 13.

[42] *See, e.g.,* KEVIN M. O'CONNELL ET AL., RAND NAT'L SEC. RES. DIV., U.S. COMMERCIAL REMOTE SENSING SATELLITE INDUSTRY: AN ANALYSIS OF RISKS 67 (2001); *The Regulation of Commercial Remote-sensing systems: Hearing Before the Comm. on Sci., Space & Tech.* 4-5 (Mar. 1994) (statement of Scott Pace), https://www.rand.org/ content/dam/rand/pubs/testimonies/2006/CT112.pdf.

[43] 51 U.S.C. Chapter 601 (2010).

general, (2) Landsat, (3) licensing of private remote-sensing space systems, (4) research, development, and demonstration, (5) general provisions, and (6) prohibition of commercialization of weather satellites. The Policy Act has remained largely the same since its passage.[44]

The Policy Act diverged from the Commercialization Act by removing the nondiscriminatory access requirement,[45] thereby allowing private companies to charge different prices for different customers. The statutory evolution supported commercial creations while also ensuring a government catalogue would survive. The Policy Act maintained the secretary's power to archive government-generated remote-sensing data (i.e., Landsat data) and acquire remote-sensing data from private operators.[46] Thus, the government continues to curate and act as steward to a national remote-sensing archive.[47]

The Policy Act defines land remote sensing as the 'collection of data which can be processed into imagery of surface features of the Earth from...satellite or satellites.'[48] Under the Policy Act, the Commerce Secretary is granted the authority to license and promulgate regulations for the licensing of private

---

[44] The Policy Act has been amended twice. Once in the 1998 Commercial Space Act, which changed the requirement that commercial sensing licensees notify the Secretary of Commerce of 'any agreement entered into with foreign entities' to 'any significant or substantial agreement intended to be entered into with a foreign entity.' (Interestingly, this Act also required NASA to acquire remote-sensing data from a commercial provider where appropriate.) The Policy Act was again amended in 2010, but this amendment did not alter any legal obligations – it moved the Policy Act's location within the U.S.C. and restated the bill as 'positive law.' Commercial Space Act of 1998, H.R. 1702, 105th Cong., 112 Stat. 2854 §§ 107(a),(f) (1984); Enactment of Title 51 – National and Commercial Space Programs, H.R. 3237, 111th Cong., 124 Stat. 3328 (2010); Rob Sukol, *Positive Law Codification: Title 51, United States Code*, OFF. L. REVISION COUNS. U.S.C. (last visited 10/24/2020), https://uscode.house.gov/codification/t51/index.html.

[45] While the Policy Act does not require commercial operators to follow the policy of nondiscriminatory data access, it does still require them to provide unenhanced remote-sensing data to the government of sensed states. This data must be provided as soon as it is available and on reasonable terms and conditions. 51 U.S.C. § 60122(2) (2018).

[46] Private operators would own the data that they generated, and could market such data; however, the secretary was permitted to demand access to any unenhanced data. Any such privately generated data would be *stored* in the archive by the USG during a protective period – of no more than ten years – after which, the government could release the data for cost. *Land Remote-Sensing Commercialization, supra* note 36, at §§ 602(d)–(f).

[47] The archive is controlled and overseen by the Secretary of the Interior. 51 U.S.C. § 60142 (2018).

[48] *Id.* § 60101(4).

remote-sensing space systems.[49] This licensing power is delegated to NOAA's Assistant Administrator for Satellite and Information Services and carried out by the CRSRA office.[50]

In 2020, NOAA's private remote-sensing regulations were significantly reformed.[51] That effort was supported by Space Policy Directive 2 (SPD-2), which directed the DOC to examine and reform commercial remote-sensing regulations to align with the policy of promoting private industry and encouraging American leadership in space commerce.[52]

The NOAA remote-sensing regulations apply to the operation of private (commercial) remote-sensing systems within the U.S. or by a U.S. person.[53] Any remote-sensing activity conducted within the U.S. must be licensed by NOAA, and any person who is eligible may apply for a license.[54] Further, NOAA authority is exercised over any remote-sensing activity by U.S. persons, no matter where they operate a system.[55]

NOAA's regulations define 'remote sensing' as 'the collection of unenhanced data by an instrument in orbit of the Earth which can be processed into imagery of surface features of Earth.'[56] Importantly, the 2020 regulations excluded from NOAA's licensing regime instruments primarily used for mission assurance or other technical purposes, such as navigation, attitude control, monitoring spacecraft health, separation events, and technologies related to payload deployment, including traditional star trackers, sun sensors, and horizon sensors.[57] A 'remote-sensing space system' is scoped to include the imaging instrumentality, unenhanced data receipt systems, and data preprocessing. In essence, the system includes the remote-sensing instrument and components that support the instrument.

---

[49] If a commercial space system is used for purposes beyond remote sensing, the secretary's power is limited to licensing the remote-sensing applications. *Id.* § 60121(a), (a)(2). The power to license also includes the power to issue regulations to carry out provisions of the Policy Act. *Id.* § 60124.

[50] *Supra* note 43.

[51] *Id.*

[52] Space Policy Directive 2: Streamlining Regulations on Commercial Use of Space, 83 Fed. Reg. 24901 (May 24, 2018).

[53] 15 C.F.R. § 960.2(a) (2020).

[54] *Id.* § 960.4 (2020); *supra* note 43.

[55] 'Persons' includes citizens, lawful residents, and entities organized or existing under U.S. laws. For example, entity organizations can be corporations, partnerships, and more. 15 C.F.R. § 960.4 (2020); *supra* note 43, at 30795.

[56] *Id.*

[57] 15 C.F.R. § 960.2(b) (2020); *Id.*

A licensee may own and manage the entire remote-sensing system or have legal arrangements with third parties regarding ownership and management.[58] In instances where there are multiple parties engaged in the remote-sensing system's operations, the entity with the 'ultimate ability to decide what unenhanced data to collect with the instrument and to execute that decision' is the operator.[59] The entity with ultimate imaging authority remains the vested 'operator' even though a third party may control implementing the commands.[60]

Private remote-sensing systems are those not owned by a U.S. Government agency or instrumentality. It should be noted that a private entity is allowed to apply for a license for a private system hosted on a government satellite or launch vehicle.[61] In the spirit of public–private partnerships, the Policy Act allows the secretary to assist private sector entities in finding opportunities to utilize USG assets.[62]

Licensing Process

The licensing process for an applicant can be divided into four stages.[63] A first, optional step is pre-application consultation. Prior to submitting a commercial remote-sensing system license application, an applicant may informally consult with CRSRA. These informal consultations may cover matters in the application, including whether an application for a license is necessary.[64] Second, an applicant formally submits their application and CRSRA determines whether it is complete. Third, CRSRA reviews the application and conducts an interagency review during which more information may be requested. Fourth, and finally, a decision is made whether to grant a license and, if so, with what conditions.

License application

An application for a privately operated remote-sensing license must include three main categories of information.[65] Every fact required for a complete

---

[58]   *Id.*

[59]   To 'operate' a private remote-sensing system 'means to have decision making authority over the functioning of a remote sensing instrument.' *Id.*

[60]   *Id.*

[61]   51 U.S.C. § 60125(a) (2018).

[62]   *Id.* at § 60125(b).

[63]   *License Application Process, supra* note 47.

[64]   15 C.F.R. § 960.5(a).

[65]   Application information required is found in Appendix A to the regulations, and the specific instructions for submitting an application are found in Appendix B. *Id.* at § 960.5(b).

application is considered a 'material fact,' or facts upon which NOAA will rely in issuing a license.[66] The first category of submitted information is a description of the applicant, or operator, including their corporate ownership and any subsidiaries and affiliates that are integrated in the project, including a description of their role.[67] The second category of information for a license application is a description of the remote-sensing system and the mission[68] as well as technical specifications, including information such as sensor type,[69] imaging or frame rate,[70] special resolution in meters,[71] spectral range,[72] collective volume in area per unit time per spacecraft,[73] and ability of imaging instrumentality to move off-axis.[74] The applicant must also provide information on the spacecraft hosting the remote-sensing instrument, including launch and orbital information.[75] If an entity other than the applicant will have power over the remote-sensing instrument, this must be disclosed.[76]

The third category of information to complete a private remote-sensing application is any requests to waive or adjust the standard license conditions.[77] For a waiver or adjustment request, the applicant must identify the applicable standard, and then select one of three reasons for a waiver or adjustment: (1) the requirement is not applicable to the applicant or system, (2) the goal will be achieved in a different manner, or (3) good cause.[78]

Application consideration

License applications are considered on a tier-based system delineated by the availability of unenhanced data from other sources.[79] Licensing constraints are based upon 'the degree to which the unenhanced data to be generated by their proposed system [is] already available.'[80] In this manner, the 2020 regulatory updates sought to balance national security concerns against the realities of a competitive commercial marketplace.

---

[66]   15 C.F.R. § 960.4 (2020).
[67]   *Id.* Appendix A, Part A.
[68]   *Id.* Appendix A, Part B(1).
[69]   *Id.* Appendix A, Part B(2)(a).
[70]   *Id.* Appendix A, Part B(2)(b).
[71]   *Id.* Appendix A, Part B(2)(c).
[72]   *Id.* Appendix A, Part B(2)(d).
[73]   *Id.* Appendix A, Part B(2)(e).
[74]   *Id.* Appendix A, Part B(2)(f).
[75]   *Id.* Appendix A, Part B(4).
[76]   *Id.* Appendix A, Part B(3).
[77]   *Id.* Appendix A, Part C.
[78]   *Id.* Appendix A, Part C(1)–(3).
[79]   *Licensing of Private Remote Sensing Space Systems, supra* note 29, at 30792.
[80]   *Id.*

Following the application's submission, NOAA has seven days to consult with the DOD and the Department of State ('State') to determine whether the application is complete.[81] If it is not deemed complete, the applicant will have the opportunity to submit additional information or correct any previously incorrect submissions.[82] Depending on the substantiveness of new information, the revision may constitute a new application.[83]

Within seven days of confirming that the application is complete, a determination is made by NOAA in consultation with the DOD and State, regarding the system's tier. All applicants must follow the general conditions of Tier 1, with possible additional constraints added in Tier 2 and Tier 3. The tiers are as follows:

- Tier 1 – A system with capability to collect unenhanced data *substantially the same*[84] as that available from entities/individuals not licensed under Part 960 (i.e., foreign entities).[85] License conditions for Tier 1 are outlined in 15 C.F.R. § 960.8.
- Tier 2 – A system with capability to collect unenhanced data *substantially the same* as enhanced data from systems licensed under Part 960.[86] Tier 2 systems must comply with all Tier 1 license conditions and additional conditions under 15 C.F.R. § 960.9.
- Tier 3 – A system with capability to collect unenhanced data **not substantially the same** as data already available from any domestic or foreign entities.[87] Tier 3 systems must comply with all Tier 1 and 2 license conditions and additional conditions under 15 C.F.R. § 960.10.

If a proposed system is categorized as Tier 3, NOAA, in consultation with the DOD and State, will determine any temporary license restrictions necessary to address national security concerns or international obligations.[88] Any crafted limitations expire one year after either of the following two conditions is met: (1) the licensee first delivers unenhanced data suitable for evaluating the

---

[81]   For more discussion of the policy surrounding this consultation, see the 'Policy Tensions in Remote Sensing' section below.

[82]   15 C.F.R. § 960.5(d) (2020).

[83]   *Id.*

[84]   'Substantially the same' is defined as 'one item is a market substitute for another, taking into account all applicable factors.' These factors for consideration include the data's spatial resolution, spectral bandwidth, number of imaging bands, temporal resolution, persistence of imaging, local time of imaging, geographic or other restrictions, and all technical factors listed in the application in Appendix A. *Id.* § 960.4.

[85]   *Id.* § 960.6(a)(1).

[86]   *Id.* § 960.6(a)(2).

[87]   *Id.* § 960.6(3).

[88]   *Id.* § 960.10(b).

system's capabilities, or (2) when the DOD or State first obtains comparably suitable data from another source.[89]

When an additional license condition is required, CRSRA will construct the least restrictive condition(s) possible.[90] Six factors are considered when crafting the restriction(s): (1) risk addressed by the condition; (2) effectiveness of condition against the risk; (3) condition's impact is limited to unavailable data; (4) mitigation of risk to the USG absent the condition; (5) less restrictive means to limit the risk to the U.S. Government; and (6) alternative actions the applicant could take to limit the risk.[91]

The tiered system was intended to create flexibility in the categorization process that may respond adeptly to swift advances in technology. It is therefore possible for a system to move between tiers. For example, if a foreign system produces unenhanced data substantially the same as previously only a U.S. licensee could produce, the licensee may transit from a higher tier to a lower tier.[92] The dynamic tier system only works to reduce burdens; if a foreign system that gave rise to lowering a system's tier ceases operations, the U.S. system remains in the lower tier.[93] However, modifications to a licensee's system could result in a recharacterization of the system's tier. If a modification would recategorize a Tier 1 system to Tier 2, the secretary will notify the licensee of the potential reclassification and give the licensee an opportunity to withdraw or revise the modification request.[94] If a Tier 1 or 2 licensee requests a modification that would potentially reclassify them as a Tier 3 system, CRSRA will consult with the DOD and State Department the necessity of additional conditions, then notify the licensee and give them an opportunity to withdraw or revise their modification plans.[95]

License issuance

After confirming that an application is complete, the agency has 60 days to determine whether the applicant will comply with the requirements of the

---

[89]   However, the license condition may be extended if there is an ongoing need for the temporary condition; the secretary may extend the condition for a maximum of one year, and there is a limit of two extensions for a condition. Additional extensions beyond three years may *only* be requested by either the Secretary of Defense or State themselves. *Id.* § 960.10(b),(e).

[90]   *Id.* § 960.10(c).

[91]   *Id.* § 960.10(c)(1)–(6).

[92]   'Systems will automatically move to lower-numbered tiers as the unenhanced data they are capable of producing become available.' *Licensing of Private Remote Sensing Space Systems, supra* note 30, at 30798.

[93]   *Id.*

[94]   15 C.F.R. § 960.13(a) (2020).

[95]   *Id.* § 960.13(c).

Policy Act, Part 960 regulations, and the license.[96] CRSRA must determine that the applicant will act to preserve U.S. national security, uphold U.S. international obligations, and comply with applicable regulations.[97] Compliance is presumed without contrary specific, credible evidence, and a license is accordingly granted.[98]

If a license is granted, a licensee has several obligations. First, they must continue to act to preserve U.S. national security and uphold U.S. international obligations.[99] Second, a licensee must furnish orbital and data characteristics of the systems to the secretary; this obligation includes a requirement to inform the secretary immediately of any deviation from the listed characteristics.[100] Finally, the licensee must dispose of space assets in an approved manner upon termination of licensed operations.[101]

License conditions, enforcement, and appeals

NOAA has broad discretion to grant, condition, or transfer licenses granted to private remote-sensing licensees.[102] An example of a license condition is requiring the licensee to provide unenhanced data to the government.[103] This and other such requirements are levied following CRSRA consultation with other U.S. Government agencies,[104] and attaches under two specific scenarios: (1) the system is substantially or completely funded by the U.S. Government;[105] or (2) a determination considering the impact on the licensee when weighed against the importance of promoting widespread access to remote-sensing data.[106] License condition, such as providing the USG with unenhanced data, may not be inconsistent with any contract or other arrangement between the U.S. Government and the licensee.[107]

---

[96]   *Id.* § 960.7(b). The regulatory timeline is condensed as compared with the timeline mandated by the statute. Under the Policy Act, a final decision on an application is to be made within 120 days; if a decision is not made within 120 days, the applicant must be informed of any ongoing issues, and steps necessary to resolve them. 51 U.S.C. § 60121(b),(c) (2018).

[97]   51 U.S.C. § 60121(b) (2018).

[98]   15 C.F.R § 960.7(a) (2020).

[99]   51 U.S.C. § 60122(b)(1) (2018).

[100]   *Id.* § 60122(b)(5).

[101]   *Id.* § 60122(b)(4).

[102]   *Id.* § 60123(a)(1).

[103]   *Id.* § 60122(b)(3). This unenhanced data may be made available to the USG and affiliated users at a reduced cost for noncommercial uses and is under a nondiscriminatory access obligation. *Id.* § 60141(a),(b).

[104]   *Id.* § 60121(e)(1).

[105]   *Id.* § 60121(e)(2)(A).

[106]   *Id.* § 60121(e)(2)(B).

[107]   *Id.* § 60121(e)(3).

If NOAA determines that a licensee has failed to comply with the Policy Act, any license restrictions, or any international obligations or national security concerns of the U.S. Government, the agency may seek an order and injunction in federal court to terminate, modify, or suspend a license.[108] In response, an applicant or licensee may request review and will be entitled to adjudication by the Secretary of Commerce, on the record, after the opportunity for an agency hearing.[109] Final action of the secretary is subject to judicial review.[110]

POLICY TENSIONS IN REMOTE SENSING

The United States' approach to licensing remote-sensing systems has, at times, been criticized for driving capabilities out of the U.S.[111] A key motivation for the U.S. licensing regime has been national security, which has created tension with commercial interests. This section will examine national security concerns and remote sensing, touching on 'consultation' as required in the regulations, and the exercise of shutter control by U.S. national security organizations. Finally, this section will close with an examination of the Kyl-Bingaman Amendment and its limitation on remote-sensing data.

National Security and Remote Sensing

The ability to remotely sense from satellites opened a door to the ability to surveil anywhere, anytime. Entering the twenty-first century, policymakers had to balance several tensions. First, remote sensing enables important civilian capabilities such as tracking weather patterns, agricultural yields and damage; observing ice cover and monitoring glacial growth; and providing natural disaster assistance.[112] Additionally, the ability to remote-sense impli-

---

[108] *Id.* § 60123(a)(2).
[109] Specifically, adverse action to: (1) grant, condition, or transfer licenses, (2) provide penalties for noncompliance, (3) issue subpoenas for the purpose of conducting a hearing, or (4) seize items pursuant to a warrant. *See Id.* § 60123(b) (specifying review of adverse action under subsections (a)(1), (3), (5), and (6)).
[110] *Id.* § 60123(b).
[111] Jeff Foust, *House Panel Criticizes Commercial Remote Sensing Licensing*, Space News (Sept. 8, 2016) https://spacenews.com/house-panel-criticizes-commercial -remote-sensing-licensing/.
[112] This list is not meant to be exhaustive. *See, e.g.*, Nat'l Envtl. Satellite Data & Info. Serv., *Strategic Plan*, NOAA 5 (2016), https://www.nesdis.noaa.gov/sites/ default/files/asset/document/the_nesdis_strategic_plan_2016.pdf.

cates civil rights, such as the First Amendment's freedom of speech and the press, as well as an individual's right to privacy.[113]

Remote-sensing images can also reveal sensitive national information, such as troop deployment, weapons capabilities, and strategic national sites such as industrial zones.[114] Indeed, space-based imaging capabilities have been characterized as 'more advantageous' than aerial remote sensing, including the ability to image 'denied' areas[115] without violating airspace sovereignty, and the ability to provide continuous coverage of the Earth.[116]

When Congress moved to commercialize the remote-sensing industry, it recognized the tension between commercialization and national security. 'It is clearly inappropriate for the United States government to permit its citizens to engage in activities that amount to intelligence gathering as a commercial enterprise.'[117] However, commercialization of remote-sensing capabilities was not opposed by the national security apparatus; rather, the concern was how to control the flow of data.[118]

To resolve tensions, the government instrumentalized three main means of control over commercial remote-sensing activities: interagency consultation, shutter control, and export laws.[119]

---

[113] *See* Office Tech. Assessment, *Science, Technology, and the First Amendment: Special Report*, U.S. CONG. OTA-CIT-396 (Jan. 1988), https://ota.fas.org/reports/8835 .pdf.

[114] *See, e.g.*, Capt. Michael R. Hoversten, *U.S. National Security and Government Regulation of Commercial Remote Sensing from Outer Space*, 50 A.F. L. REV. 253, 265–66 (2001).

[115] O'CONNELL ET AL., *supra* note 42.

[116] *See, e.g.*, Norman Kerle & Clive Oppenheimer, *Satellite Remote Sensing as a Tool in Lahar Disaster Management*, 26 DISASTERS 140 (2002) (discussing the possible use of continuous-coverage unclassified satellite remote sensing to mitigate natural disasters).

[117] H. R. Rep. 98-647, at 7 (1984).

[118] Additionally, the DOD was faced with a declining defense budget. Entities that had been DOD contractors began looking for ways to commercialize their remote-sensing capabilities; there was worry that unless commercialization was allowed, the U.S. primacy in this technology would begin to atrophy. Brian Dailey & Edward McGaffigan, *U.S. Commercial Satellite Export Control Policy: A Debate* in FIGHTING PROLIFERATION: NEW CONCERNS FOR THE NINETIES (Henry Sokolski eds., 1996).

[119] The licensing and regulation process were further supplemented in 1994 by President Clinton's PDD-23, which discusses the sale (or export) of commercial remote-sensing assets. H. R. Rep. 98-647, at 23 (1984); EXEC. OFFICE OF THE PRESIDENT, PRESIDENTIAL DECISION DIRECTIVE/NSC-23: U.S. POLICY ON FOREIGN ACCESS TO REMOTE SENSING SPACE CAPABILITIES (Mar. 9, 1994), available at https://fas .org/irp/offdocs/pdd/pdd-23.pdf.

Interagency consultation

The Policy Act authorized broad power to place restrictions on licenses.[120] That authority introduced the opportunity to require constraints in the name of national security that arose out of consultations with the DOD. The interagency consultation process was historically lengthy and identified as burdensome.[121] In 2017, pursuant to the Policy Act, NSPD-27,[122] and PPD-4,[123] the Departments of Commerce, State, Defense, the Interior, and the Office of the Director of National Intelligence signed an MOU 'Concerning the Licensing and Operations of Private Remote Sensing Satellite Systems.' That MOU was the governing document for interagency review of commercial remote-sensing licensing applications until it was superseded by the 2020 updates to Part 960.[124] Today, the MOU only applies to the extent that it does not conflict with the 2020 regulations – namely, sections describing dispute resolution and the process for imposing shutter control.

Limited-operation directives, 'shutter control'

In coordination with the interagency application review, NOAA has struck a balance between national security and commercial operation through a mechanism colloquially known as 'shutter control.' This condition on licensing, as

---

[120] 51 U.S.C. § 60123(a)(1) (2018).

[121] *See* S. REP. NO. 104-81, at 4 (1995) ('These delays undoubtedly had an adverse impact on the affected applicants, and, perhaps more importantly, the uncertainties regarding the length and structure of the process – particularly as to the DOD and State Department license review – may have discouraged other potential applicants from seeking DOC approval for their proposed remote sensing ventures.').

[122] NSPD-27 is the U.S. Commercial Remote Sensing Policy passed under President George W. Bush in 2003. It remains a highly significant presidential directive for national policy on commercial remote-sensing systems. EXEC. OFFICE OF THE PRESIDENT, U.S. COMMERCIAL REMOTE SENSING POLICY § IV, NSPD-27 (Apr. 25, 2003); *see generally* James A. Vedda, *Updating National Policy On Commercial Remote Sensing*, AEROSPACE CORP. (Mar. 2017), https://aerospace.org/sites/default/files/2018-05/CommercialRemoteSensing_0.pdf.

[123] U.S. National Space Policy (PPD-4) was issued by President Obama in 2010. PPD-4 broadly supports a competitive commercial sector, use of space to mitigate disasters, expanded international cooperation, and strengthened U.S. leadership. EXEC. OFFICE OF THE PRESIDENT, NATIONAL SPACE POLICY OF THE UNITED STATES OF AMERICA, PPD-4 (June 28, 2010).

[124] Text of the MOU can be found in Appendix D of the current regulation on remote sensing. Appendix D to Part 960 – Memorandum of Understanding, 85 Fed. Reg. 30813 (May 20, 2020).

permitted under the Policy Act,[125] is detailed in the remote-sensing regulations promulgated by NOAA, and was referenced in the 2003 NSPD-27.[126]

> U.S. companies are encouraged to build and operate commercial remote sensing space systems whose operational capabilities, products, and services are superior to any current or planned foreign commercial systems. […] In such cases, the United States Government may restrict operations of the commercial systems in order to limit collection and/or dissemination of certain data and products, e.g., best resolution, most timely delivery, to the United States Government, or United States Government approved recipients.[127]

The Secretaries of State and Defense, to comply with international obligations or foreign policy interests or at times of increased national security concerns, may create a *limited-operation directive*.[128] A limited-operation directive requires licensees to temporarily limit data collection and/or dissemination. Limited-operation directives are imposed for the smallest area possible, and for the shortest time period necessary.[129] Before resorting to a prohibition on collection or distribution, the agencies must investigate whether a lesser degree of 'modified operations' is sufficient. These modified operations can include delaying or restricting the transmission or distribution of data, restricting a field of view or obfuscation, restricting quality of the data disseminated, or data control such as encryption.[130]

Limited-operation directives cannot be imposed without reason or justification and, under the 2020 regulations, apply only to Tier 2 and Tier 3 systems.[131] If time permits, interagency consultation must occur and result in an agreement on an appropriate action in response to a DOD or State-raised concern.[132] In situations of urgency, the Secretary of State or Defense shall determine condi-

---

[125] As stated above, the Policy Act gives the Secretary of Commerce broad power to condition any license granted for commercial remote sensing. 51 U.S.C. § 60123(a)(1) (2018).

[126] Appendix D to Part 960 – Memorandum of Understanding §IV(D)(2)-(6), 85 Fed. Reg. 30813, 30815 (May 20, 2020); EXEC. OFFICE OF THE PRESIDENT, U.S. COMMERCIAL REMOTE SENSING POLICY § IV, NSPD-27 (Apr. 25, 2003).

[127] U.S. COMMERCIAL REMOTE SENSING POLICY, *supra* note 126, at § IV.

[128] These directives are created pursuant to Section IV(D) of the MOU between the Secretaries of State and Defense, signed on April 25, 2017. Appendix D to Part 960 – Memorandum of Understanding §IV(D), 85 Fed. Reg. 30813, 30815 (May 20, 2020).

[129] *Id.*

[130] *Id.*

[131] This is included in licenses for Parts 960.9 and 960.10 as a standard condition. 15 C.F.R. § 960.9-10 (2020).

[132] *Licensing of Private Remote Sensing Space Systems*, *supra* note 29, at 30815 (Appendix D).

tions of operation; this decision cannot be delegated to anyone below the rank of secretary (or acting secretary).[133]

The Secretary of State or Defense will communicate to the Secretary of Commerce a condition to be imposed upon a licensee, and the Secretary of Commerce will notify the operator.[134] However, if the Secretary of Commerce believes an imposed condition is improper, together with notification to the licensee, the secretary may notify the Secretary of State or Defense of the disagreement, and further elevate the disagreement to an assistant to the president.[135] If a principals-level consensus is not reached, the issue may be elevated to the president for resolution.[136]

'Checkbook' shutter control

As indicated above, the government may limit the taking of images, as well as their dissemination. In some instances, the U.S. Government has not banned the collection of data, instead limiting downstream dissemination in what is known as 'checkbook' shutter control. Exemplified by the U.S. purchasing satellite imagery of Afghanistan in 2001,[137] 'checkbook' shutter control is an arrangement whereby the U.S. Government purchases exclusive rights to commercial satellite imagery, preventing it from entering the commercial market.

The perceived effectiveness of checkbook shutter control has been decreasing.[138] The proliferation of remote-sensing capabilities and commercial products means it is unlikely that the U.S. Government would buy exclusive rights to all imagery, of all sensitive areas, for an indefinite duration.

The Kyl-Bingaman Amendment

The Kyl-Bingaman Amendment (KBA) was adopted during congressional consideration of the Fiscal Year 1997 Defense Appropriation Act.[139] It was the result of lobbying by pro-Israel interests and the only example of U.S.

---

[133] *Id.*

[134] *Id.*

[135] This is either the Assistant to the President for National Security Affairs or the Assistant to the President for Science and Technology. *Id.*

[136] *Id.*

[137] Sarah Scoles, *How the Government Controls Sensitive Satellite Data*, WIRED (Feb. 8, 2018), https://www.wired.com/story/how-the-government-controls-sensitive -satellite-data/.

[138] James A. Vedda, *Updating National Policy on Commercial Remote Sensing*, AEROSPACE CORP. (Mar. 2017), https://aerospace.org/sites/default/files/2018-05/Com mercialRemoteSensing_0.pdf.

[139] 1997 National Defense Authorization Act, 104 P. L. 201 § 1064 (1997).

censorship of imagery enshrined in statutory law.[140] The KBA disallowed imagery that was more detailed or precise than images available from non-U.S. commercial sources.

The amendment is a Cold War relic, indicative of effective congressional lobbying from commercial sources. Due to U.S. dominance of early commercial remote sensing, no alternative non-U.S. commercial sources existed, creating a de facto ban against observations of Israel.[141] As a result, the Israeli occupation of Palestine was largely unwatched for over 20 years.[142]

In 2020, the DOC published an update to the Kyl-Bingaman Amendment based on a finding that 'satellite imagery of Israel is readily and consistently available from non-U.S. commercial sources.'[143] The limit on the resolution of images was adjusted to 0.4 meters ground sample distance (GSD)[144] from 2.0 meters GSD.[145]

NOAA WEATHER ACTIVITIES

The U.S. Government's efforts in weather observations and research, including the U.S. Weather Bureau,[146] predate NOAA's formation in 1970. Today, NOAA is the main government agency that observes and forecasts terrestrial and space-based weather. NOAA weather activities are conducted primarily through the National Weather Services (NWS), with supplement space-based observations critical to weather forecasting from the National Environmental Satellite, Data, and Information Service (NESDIS).

---

[140] *See, e.g.,* Andrea Zerbini & Michael Fradley, *Higher Resolution Satellite Imagery of Israel and Palestine: Reassessing the Kyl-Bingaman Amendment*, 44–45 Space P. 14, 15–17 (2018).

[141] Zena Agha, *Israel Can't Hide Evidence of Its Occupation Anymore*, Foreign Policy (Aug. 3, 2020), https://foreignpolicy.com/2020/08/03/israel-cant-hide-evidence -of-its-occupation-anymore/.

[142] *Id.*

[143] *Notice of Findings Regarding Commercial Availability of Non-U.S. Satellite Imagery with Respect to Israel*, 85 F.R. 44059 (July 21, 2020).

[144] The distance between pixel centers measured on the ground.

[145] *Notice of Findings Regarding Commercial Availability of Non-U.S. Satellite Imagery with Respect to Israel, supra* note 143.

[146] The U.S. Weather Bureau was formed in 1870, but U.S. meteorology can trace its roots all the way back to the observations of Thomas Jefferson and James Madison in 1778. Robert M. White, *The Making of NOAA, 1963-2005*, Address before the National Air and Space Museum Smithsonian Institution (Dec. 1, 2005).

NOAA's History in Weather

NOAA and NASA have a history of enjoying comingled responsibilities in weather observations. NASA is normally in charge of developing experimental research systems; if and when these transition to operational systems, they enter NOAA jurisdiction.[147] The nation's weather satellite programs trace their early history to the 1950s. Development and testing for national weather satellites began in the Weather Bureau. The first polar-orbiting weather satellite, Television Infra-Red Observation Satellite 1 (TIROS 1), was launched by NASA in April 1960.[148] The success of this mission helped to usher in a new age of meteorology.

Current Weather Activities

Broadly speaking, the Secretary of Commerce is charged with responsibility for forecasting the weather, issuing storm warnings, distributing meteorological information in the interests of agriculture and commerce, and otherwise taking meteorological observations as necessary to record climatic conditions within the U.S.[149] NOAA currently oversees nine satellites in multiple orbits for those purposes.[150] Those capabilities and their operational information[151] are crucial to safety and the U.S.'s economic vitality. For example, the agricultural industry contributes $136.1 billion to the national GDP, and is heavily reliant on weather predictions.[152] NOAA issues 1.5 million forecasts

---

[147] 51 U.S.C. § 20301 (2018); Exec. Order No. 13744 § 4(f), 81 FR 71573 (Oct. 13, 2016); Radzanowski, *supra* note 40, at 9.

[148] EILEEN L. SHEA, A HISTORY OF NOAA: BEING A COMPILATION OF FACTS AND FIGURES REGARDING THE LIFE AND TIMES OF THE ORIGINAL WHOLE EARTH AGENCY 11 (1987). The TIROS-1 bus hosted two TV cameras and two video recorders and provided the first views of cloud formations developing above, and transiting across, the surface of the Earth. Gary Davis, *History of the NOAA Satellite Program*, 1 J. APPLIED REMOTE SENSING 1, 4 (2017).

[149] 15 U.S.C. § 313 (2018).

[150] Nat'l Envtl. Satellite Data & Info. Serv., *Currently Flying*, NOAA, https://www .nesdis.noaa.gov/content/currently-flying (last visited Nov. 17, 2021).

[151] 'Operational information,' in contrast to research information, is information which can be acted upon; good operational information informs decision-making on a timely basis, allowing accurate predictions, and engenders positive perceptions by users. Off. of Chief Fin. Officer, *NOAA by the Numbers: NOAA's Value to the Nation*, NOAA 6-7 (June, 2018), https://www.performance.noaa.gov/wp-content/uploads/ NOAA-by-the-Numbers-Accessible-Version-Corrected-17-JUL-18.pdf.

[152] Kathleen Kassal & Rosanna Mentzer Morrison, *Ag and Food Sectors and the Economy*, USDA (Nov. 6, 2020), https://www.ers.usda.gov/data-products/ag-and -food-statistics-charting-the-essentials/ag-and-food-sectors-and-the-economy/#:~:

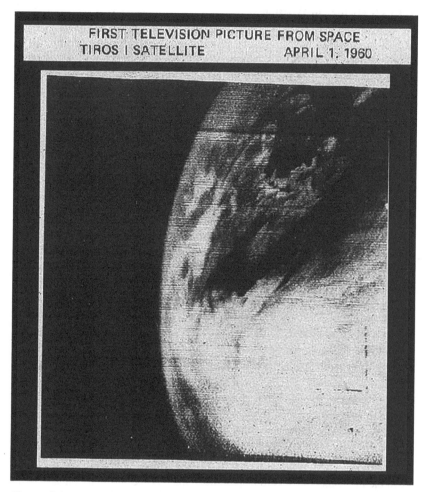

Figure 8.1   First image from a weather satellite, taken by TIROS-1

Image credit: NASA

and 50,000 weather warnings per year. For extreme weather events such as

---

text=Agriculture%2C%20food%2C%20and%20related%20industries,about%200.6%20percent%20of%20GDP.

hurricanes, the GOES-series satellites can capture and transmit high-definition images once a minute, aiding forecasters and emergency responders.[153]

More Than Weather: The Joint Polar Fleet and COSPAS-SARSAT

Operational environmental satellites have also been vessels for international cooperation. Countries have learned to share the burden of gathering meteorological information and have also taken advantage of polar orbit to host additional payloads on satellite buses.

The Joint Polar Program

Meteorological data from polar orbit is extremely valuable: polar-orbiting (and similarly, sun-synchronous-orbiting) satellites generally complete 14 orbits per day, equating to full global coverage twice a day.[154] The timeliness of data increases accuracy of weather forecasts, enabling advanced severe-weather alerts.

In 1998, NOAA and the European Organization for the Exploitation of Meteorological Satellites (EUMETSAT)[155] signed an international agreement to integrate their polar-orbiting fleets and share meteorological data.[156] NOAA and EUMETSAT cooperation has continued into the twenty-first century, and NOAA has also entered into a mutually beneficial exchange of climate data with EUMETSAT, the French Space Agency (Centre National d'Etudes Spatiales (CNES)), and NASA.[157]

---

[153] *NOAA at 50: By the Numbers*, NOAA (Oct. 23, 2020), https://www.noaa.gov/stories/noaa-at-50-by-numbers.

[154] Most satellites will complete 14 orbits per day, viewing the entire Earth's surface twice. U.S. Gov't Accountability Office, GAO-12-604, Polar-Orbiting Environmental Satellites: Changing Requirements, Technical Issues, and Looming Data Gaps Require Focused Attention 3 (2012).

[155] EUMETSAT is an intergovernmental organization created through an international agreement with 30 member States. 'EUMETSAT is the European operational satellite agency for monitoring weather, climate and the environment from space.' *Who We Are*, EUMETSAT (Nov. 16, 2020), https://www.eumetsat.int/about-us/who-we-are.

[156] The overall intent of the treaty was to 'provide long-term continuity of observations from polar orbit...' Agreement Between the United States National Oceanic and Atmospheric Administration and the European Organization for the Exploitation of Meteorological Satellites on an Initial Polar-Orbiting Operational Satellite System, U.S.-EUMETSAT, Nov. 19, 1998, 2909 U.N.T.S. I-50697 [*hereinafter* Initial Polar-Orbiting Agreement].

[157] NOAA is responsible for the operation of Jason-3, as well as launch services and some technical components. *What is Jason-3?*, NOAA (Sept. 17, 2018), https://www.nesdis.noaa.gov/jason-3/mission.html. While NOAA remains involved in Sentinal-6A

COSPAS-SARSAT

NOAA's meteorological work has worldwide safety benefits, as does its operation of a global search and rescue satellite-aided tracking (SARSAT) program.[158] In the mid-1970s, the U.S., Canada, and France collectively tested technology that would enable the location of emergency beacons from satellites.[159] Russia also had a growing interest in search and rescue satellite-aided tracking, driven by the practicalities of protecting a global fishing fleet as well as a desire to demonstrate humanitarian applications of their space technology.[160]

With the 1975 Apollo-Soyuz 'handshake in space' paving the way for international diplomacy, the Western partners and Russia entered into discussions to build compatible systems.[161] In 1979, a memorandum of understanding was signed, with the U.S.S.R. agreeing to build and launch two low-Earth orbit (LEO) satellites with COSPAS[162] payloads, and Canada and France building a SARSAT payload to launch on a NOAA polar weather satellite.[163] Distress

---

Michael Freilich, the partnership is to a lesser extent. JPL, *Jason-CS (Sentinel-6)*, NASA, https://sealevel.jpl.nasa.gov/missions/jason-cs-sentinel-6/summary/ (last visited June 28, 2021).

[158] For why the scope of a weather agency was expanded to include search and rescue, *see* Richard J. H. Barnes & Jennifer Clapp, *Cospas-Sarsat: A Quiet Success Story*, 11 SPACE P. 261, 267 (1995); Search & Rescue Satellite Aided Tracking, *Frequently Asked Questions,* NOAA, https://www.sarsat.noaa.gov/faq%202.html (last visited Nov. 17, 2021).

[159] 'The ability of satellites to detect signals from an emergency beacon on a downed aircraft was first demonstrated in 1975 in Canada [...] Early tests led to agreement among Canada, France and the USA [...] to carry out a systematic demonstration and evaluation. The space platform selected was the US polar orbiting weather satellite to which were added a transponder/repeater unit provided by Canada and a multifrequency processor provided by France. Line of sight signals detected from beacons on downed aircraft or vessels in distress are relayed by the satellite to ground receivers...' *Id.* For more details on the early tests, including frequency information, *see* Daniel Levesque, *Cospas-Sarsat 1979-2009: A 30-year Success Story*, 22 COSPAS-SARSAT INFO. BULLETIN ENCLOSURE 1, 2 (2010), https://vnmcc.vishipel.vn/images/uploads/attach/IB22.PDF.

[160] Richard J. H. Barnes & Jennifer Clapp, *Cospas-Sarsat: A Quiet Success Story*, 11 SPACE P. 261, 262 (1995).

[161] *Id.*

[162] COSPAS is an acronym for 'Space System for the Search of Vessels in Distress,' (Космическая Система Поиска Аварийных Судов). *International Cospas-Sarsat Programme*, Int'l Cospas-Sarsat Programme (2014), https://cospas-sarsat.int/en/about-us/about-the-programme.

[163] Cooperation in a Joint Experimental Satellite-Aided Search and Rescue Project, Nov. 23, 1979, KAV 2392; Barnes & Clapp, *supra* note 160, at 263; Herbert J. Kramer, *COSPAS-SARSAT (International Satellite System for Search and Rescue Services)*,

beacon transmissions would be bounced to all satellites and receiving ground stations, anywhere in the world.[164]

In the following years, testing and implementation of satellite search-and-rescue burgeoned. The cost of the new satellite search-and-rescue system was minimal, as equipment was flown as a secondary payload on polar-orbiting weather satellites.[165] The first COSPAS payload was launched in 1982, and in 1983, another COSPAS payload as well as a SARSAT payload were launched.[166] The system was officially declared operational in 1985,[167] and by 1987 the nascent system had been used to complete 847 saves.[168] In 1988, the original MOU was transitioned to a formal international agreement.[169] Since it was first launched in 1982, the COSPAS-SARSAT system has supported more than 48,000 rescues, approximately 9,400 of those being in the U.S. or its surrounding waters, and more than 300 in 2020 alone.[170]

> Recognizing that it is therefore desirable to operate the COSPAS-SARSAT system, in accordance with international law, so as to endeavor to provide long term alert and location services in support of search and rescue and access to the System to all States on a non-discriminatory basis, and free of charge for the end user in distress.[171]

ESA (2021), https://directory.eoportal.org/web/eoportal/satellite-missions/c-missions/cospas-sarsat.

[164] The transmissions were specifically at the frequencies 121.5 MHz or 406 MHz. Levesque, *supra* note 159, at 2.

[165] Search and rescue by satellite also offers increased coverage for less cost as compared with aerial search and rescue missions. Barnes & Clapp, *supra* note 160, at 263.

[166] Kramer, *supra* note 163.

[167] A second MOU was signed on October 5, 1984, to update the positions of each of the partners, and the system was formally declared operation in 1985 at the first meeting of a newly established Steering Committee. Levesque, *supra* note 159, at 3.

[168] Barnes & Clapp, *supra* note 160, at 263.

[169] '…[T]he Cospas-Sarsat partners concluded that an intergovernmental agreement that preserved cooperation among independent national technical agencies could provide the international community greater assurance of continuity of the system, without affecting cost or control issues.' *Id.* at 265 (1995). The treaty served to define a management structure for the international program, creating a Council and administrative body, the Secretariat. The four parties to the MOU were NOAA for the U.S, CNESCNES, Canada's Department of National Defense, and the Ministry of Merchant Marine of the U.S.S.R. The International COSPAS-SARSAT Programme Agreement, July 1, 1988, 1518 U.N.T.S. 210.

[170] *NOAA satellites helped save 304 lives in 2020*, NOAA (Jan. 28, 2021), https://www.noaa.gov/media-release/noaa-satellites-helped-save-304-lives-in-2020.

[171] The International COSPAS-SARSAT Program Agreement, *supra* note 169.

As time passed, the maturation of the program demanded a reexamination of the fleet that COSPAS-SARSAT receivers were carried on. The polar-orbiting fleet did provide global coverage twice a day; however, regulator-users that mandated use of emergency position-indicating radio beacons (EPIRB)[172] on vessels desired as close to real-time alerting as possible.[173] With increased demand, alternatives to the limited LEO fleet were pursued in the 1990s.

GEOSAR

The convenience of GEO reception for space-based search and rescue faced skepticism; the emergency beacons aboard vessels were designed to power signals to 850-kilometer LEO satellites, not GEO satellites 36,000 kilometers away. Additionally, GEO satellites do not create the Doppler effect that LEO satellites can use to help locate beacons.[174]

In 1995, NOAA's GOES-8, GOES-9, and India's INSAT-2A were flying with new technologies and an updated communication network to assess GEO search and rescue capabilities. The Geostationary Orbiting Search and Rescue (GEOSAR) satellite program underwent demonstration and evaluation in 1996 and 1997. GEOSAR data provided a significant time advantage in rescues, and GEOSAR data could actually be combined with LEO data to enhance Doppler location capabilities.[175] GEOSAR was officially incorporated into the COSPAS-SARSAT system in 1998.

Medium-Earth orbit (MEO) satellite search and rescue coverage provides the best parts of GEO and LEO: near-instantaneous notification, global coverage, and independent beacon location.[176] The COSPAS-SARSAT Council signed a first MEO search and rescue (MEOSAR) implementation plan in 2004.[177] The MEOSAR fleet continues to be built, with a total of 72 MEOSAR satellites planned.

The COSPAS-SARSAT program continues to this day and is credited with helping save more than 33,000 lives – worldwide – in the first 30 years

---

[172] For example, in 1993, it became mandatory for all ships subject to the International Convention for the Safety of Life at Sea (SOLAS) to carry EPIRBs. Levesque, *supra* note 159, at 6.

[173] *Id.* at 7.

[174] *Id.*

[175] *Id.*

[176] *MEOSAR*, INT'L COSPAS-SARSAT PROGRAMME (2014), http://www.cospas-sarsat.int/en/2-uncategorised/177-meosar-system.

[177] Daniel Levesque, Int'l Astronautical Fed., *The History and Experience of the International COSPAS-SARSAT Programme for Search and* Rescue, MEOSAR, INT'L COSPAS-SARSAT PROGRAMME at 7-7 (2014), http://www.cospas-sarsat.int/en/2-uncategorised/177-meosar-system.

of operation.[178] As of 2020, 45 different countries and organizations participate in COSPAS-SARSAT. As human spaceflight operations expand, the COSPAS-SARSAT capabilities may be increasingly used to locate astronauts, commercial or otherwise.[179]

NOAA and Space Weather

The Secretary of Commerce is authorized to investigate the impact of electromagnetic radiation on the propagation of radio waves, relay conditions and issue warnings of disturbances, and generally conduct research into telecommunications sciences.[180] In late 2020, Congress passed the Promoting Research and Observations of Space Weather to Improve the Forecasting of Tomorrow (PROSWIFT) Act, significantly updating NOAA's space weather responsibilities.[181]

The secretary's statutory space weather authority is further specified by two executive orders. Executive Order (EO) 13744 succinctly directed the secretary to 'provide timely and accurate operational space weather forecasts, watches, warnings, alerts, and real time space weather monitoring for the government, civilian, and commercial sectors...'[182] In the same EO, the secretary was directed to develop partnerships with academia and the private sector to facilitate development of research and operational space weather systems.[183] Three years later, EO 13865 directed the secretary to observe, analyze, and forecast natural electromagnetic pulses (EMPs).[184]

The secretary has assigned space weather responsibilities to NOAA. Within NOAA, NESDIS maintains NOAA's space weather data and develops and

---

[178] James V. King, M. Eng. & P. Eng, *Overview of the Cospas-Sarsat Satellite System for Search and Rescue*, 85 Proceedings Radio Club Am. 8, 9 (2013).

[179] In 2018, NASA used MEISAR to find astronauts after a launch-abort Soyuz mission. The distress signal was relayed using one Galileo and one GPS satellite. Rajesh Uppal, *MEOSAR, the Global Search and Rescue (SAR) Service Has Become Reality, Could Avoid Accidents in Sea, Land, Air and Now in Space*, Int'l Def., Sec. & Tech. (June 3, 2020), https://idstch.com/space/meosar-the-global-search-and-rescue-sar-service-has-become-reality-could-avoid-accidents-in-sealand-air-and-now-in-space/.

[180] 15 U.S.C. § 1532 (2018).

[181] Promoting Research and Observations of Space Weather to Improve the Forecasting of Tomorrow, Pub. L. No. 116-181, 134 Stat. 882 (2020).

[182] *Coordinating Efforts to Prepare the Nation for Space Weather Events*, Exec. Order 13744, 81 Fed. Reg. 71573 (Oct. 18, 2016).

[183] *Id.*

[184] *Coordinating National Resilience to Electromagnetic Pulses*, Exec. Order 13865, 84 Fed. Reg. 12043 (Mar. 29, 2019).

manages satellite programs that collect space weather data.[185] The NWS supports forecasting of space weather through monitoring and modeling, incorporating data generated by NWS operation of ground-based observatories.[186]

NOAA SPACE-RELATED FEDERAL ADVISORY COMMITTEES

NOAA has three space-related committees that support it under the Federal Advisory Committee Act. Colloquially, these types of committees are known as 'FACAs.' They provide a means for the government to receive 'expert advice, ideas, and diverse opinions' from nongovernmental entities and individuals.[187] FACA's objectives and scope of activities are contained in their charters.

NOAA Science Advisory Board

The NOAA Science Advisory Board (SAB) advises the NOAA administrator on 'strategies for research, education, and application of science to operations and information services, so as to better understand and predict changes in Earth's environment and conserve and manage coastal and marine resources to meet the Nation's economic, social, and environmental needs.'[188] The board is composed of 15 members appointed by the Under Secretary of Commerce for Oceans and Atmosphere and the NOAA administrator.[189]

NOAA Advisory Committee on Commercial Remote Sensing

The Advisory Committee on Commercial Remote Sensing (ACCRES) is charged with evaluating 'economic, technological, and institutional developments relating to commercial remote sensing' and assisting NOAA in obtaining 'information and advice from a knowledgeable, and independent

---

[185] Eric Lipiec & Brian E. Humphreys, *Space Weather: An Overview of Policy and Select U.S. Government Roles and Responsibilities*, CRS Rep. R 46049 at 7 (Jan. 6, 2020).

[186] NWS operates the National Solar Observatory Global Oscillation Network Group, ground-based observatories. *Id.*

[187] 5 U.S.C. APPENDIX – FEDERAL ADVISORY COMMITTEE ACT Sec. 2 (01/02/01).

[188] *NOAA Science Advisory Board Charter*, NOAA (June 26, 2021), https://sab .noaa.gov/wp-content/uploads/2021/08/2203-DOC-2021-NOAASAB-CharterRenewal -6.26.2021.pdf.

[189] *Science Advisory Board*, NOAA, https://www.sab.noaa.gov/ (last visited Nov. 17, 2021).

perspective.'[190] ACCRES members, the majority of whom represent the commercial space sector, provide recommendations for remote-sensing policies and programs to the administrator (or their designated representative).[191] ACCRES is also responsible for providing advice to NOAA in carrying out responsibilities for the Land Remote-Sensing Policy Act.[192]

NOAA Space Weather Advisory Group

The Space Weather Advisory Group (SWAG) was established in 2020 by the PROSWIFT Act to advise the Space Weather Interagency Working Group.[193] The SWAG is tasked with receiving advice from the academic community, the commercial space weather sector, and nongovernmental space weather end users and then applying those inputs to advise the working group. It is also charged with conducting a 'comprehensive survey of the needs of space weather products users to identify the space weather research, observations, forecasting, prediction, and modeling advances required to improve space weather products, as required by 51 U.S.C. 60601(d)(3).'[194]

QUESTIONS FOR REVIEW

1. What is the role of the Office of Space Commerce and what aspects of its role have been proposed for change or expansion?
2. Why was the Policy Act's change to the Commercialization Act's nondiscriminatory access requirement impactful for commercial remote-sensing operators?
3. What is the significance of the tier categorization approach that was implemented in the 2020 commercial remote-sensing regulations?
4. Why has there been a tension between U.S. national security interests and commercial remote-sensing operations?
5. What role might NOAA play in human spaceflight?

---

[190] *See* CRSRA, *Advisory Committee on Commercial Remote Sensing*, NOAA (Sept. 30, 2020), https://www.nesdis.noaa.gov/CRSRA/accresHome.html; NOAA ACCRES, *Charter*, §4 US Dept. of Com. (Mar. 6, 2020), https://www.nesdis.noaa.gov/CRSRA/pdf/NOAA_ACCRES_Charter_signed_3_5_2020.pdf.

[191] *Charter*, *supra* note 190.

[192] *Id.*

[193] Pub. Law No: 116-181 (2020).

[194] *Establishment of the Space Weather Advisory Group and Solicitation of Nominations for Membership*, 86 Fed. Reg. 24390 (May 6, 2021).

9. U.S. commercial space communications

Ruth and her friends are celebrating Marty's birthday in Shenandoah National Park over the Labor Day holiday. Night has fallen and they are gathered around the firepit, roasting marshmallows and telling stories.

Ruth raises her eyes to the sky and smiles. It is a clear night and she can see the stars. It's always a treat to get away from the city lights and marvel at the magnificence of the stars.

Following her gaze, Marty asks, 'How do you know which are planets and which are stars? What about satellites? Can those be seen from here too? Especially since there are so many now, don't they get in the way of seeing the stars?'

'Well, to the naked eye, it all looks very similar, I guess. But you actually raise a really important point. There are a lot more satellites being launched to Earth's orbit. They offer really exciting benefits, like space-based broadband, but there are also concerns about the impact on astronomy,' Ruth replies.

Commercial satellite communications are regulated by the Federal Communication Commission (FCC), an independent federal agency.[1] The FCC also licenses the spectrum launch and reentry vehicles use for telemetry, tracking, and command operations between those vehicles and ground stations during space launch and reentry operations. If commercial users are requesting use of federal bands, the National Telecommunications and Information Administration (NTIA) within the Department of Commerce is involved in the licensing process. This chapter will examine the history of U.S. telecommunications law, the FCC's licensing regulations and processes as well as the NTIA's role.

---

[1] *See, Satellite*, FED. COMMC'N COMM'N, https://www.fcc.gov/general/satellite (last visited Nov. 25, 2021); *Significant Satellite Rulemakings*, FED. COMMC'N COMM'N (Jan. 27, 2016), https://www.fcc.gov/significant-satellite-rulemakings (searchable webpage of significant satellite rulemakings at the FCC).

THE FEDERAL COMMUNICATIONS COMMISSION

History of the FCC and General Authority

On April 15, 1912, the RMS Titanic hit an iceberg. Within hours, the ship sank, killing most of the over 2,000 people on board. In the immediate aftermath of the tragedy, news of the sinking was muddled, including some messages indicating that all passengers had been saved. Blame for the Titanic's failure to reach a would-be rescuer was placed partly on the lack of consistent radio procedures for distress calls and partly on the poor radio skills of those on board the ship.[2] Within months, Congress passed the Radio Act of 1912 to better oversee the use of radio-frequency communications.[3] The new law gave direction about how radio frequencies could be used, including requirements that users of this spectrum limit transmissions to designated frequencies[4] and to give priority to distress calls from ships.[5]

The Radio Act of 1912 was superseded by the Radio Act of 1927,[6] which set up the Federal Radio Commission[7] and first set forth the guiding principle for radio regulations – that policies must further the nebulous 'public interest.' This Act was itself overtaken by the Communications Act of 1934.[8] The 1934 Act established the Federal Communications Commission, which oversees communications to this day.[9] President Franklin D. Roosevelt recommended the creation of a 'Federal Communications Commission'[10] after an extensive study of the nation's communications.[11] The FCC has been responsible for licensing access to radio spectrum since its inception.

---

[2]   For an in-depth recounting of the radio communications on board the Titanic that fateful night, *see* Daniel D. Hoolihan, *Titanic, Marconi's 'Wireless Telegraphers' and the U.S. Radio Act of 1912*, 5 INST. ELEC. & ELECS. ENG'R 35 (2016).

[3]   An Act to Regulate Radio Communication, Pub. L No. 62-364, 37 Stat. 302 (1912).

[4]   *Id.* § 4.

[5]   *Id.* § 4.9 ('Right of way' for distress signals).

[6]   Radio Act of 1927, Pub. L No. 69-632, 44 Stat. 1162 (1927).

[7]   *Id.* § 3.

[8]   Communications Act of 1934, Pub. L. 73-416, 48 Stat. 1064 (1934).

[9]   *Id.* § 1.

[10]   The new Commission would have authority that was, at that point, vested in the Radio Commission and Interstate Commerce Commission. FRANKLIN D. ROOSEVELT, MESSAGE FROM THE PRESIDENT OF THE UNITED STATE RECOMMENDING THAT CONGRESS CREATE A NEW AGENCY TO BE KNOWN AS THE FEDERAL COMMUNICATIONS COMMISSION, S. DOC. No. 73-144 (2d. Sess. 1934).

[11]   *See, A Bill to Provide for the Regulation of Interstate and Foreign Communication by Wire or Radio, and for Other Purposes: Hearing on H.R. 8301 Before the H. Comm.*

After 62 years, Congress updated the Communication Act with the Telecommunications Act of 1996 (the 1996 Act).[12] This Act was the first to address telecommunications since the invention of the Internet. The legislative design broadly directed the FCC to enable communications by reducing outdated regulatory silos, control predatory practices, and respond to social interests:[13] through the various statutory iterations, the flexible 'public interest' standard endures.[14]

Federal Communications Commission Structure

Motivated by the technical nature of the FCC's decisions, Congress created the FCC as an independent federal regulatory agency that is responsible directly to the U.S. Congress.[15] The FCC's structure reflects the intent to maintain independence from the executive. Unlike other executive branch agencies, such as NASA, the FAA, and NOAA, the FCC is not run by a single secretary or administrator in a chain of command with the president. The FCC is overseen by a board of five presidentially appointed, Senate-confirmed, commissioners. No more than three commissioners can be from the president's political party, and the commissioners' five-year terms are staggered so that a different commissioner's term expires each year.[16] The president designates one of the commissioners as the chair. The chair controls the FCC's agenda by determining which issues will be considered and when it will make determinations on those issues. While independent of the executive in its policy process, the FCC is overseen by the Senate Commerce, Science and Transportation Committee and the House Energy and Commerce Committee.

---

on Interstate and Foreign Commerce, 73d Cong. 1-3 (1934) (statement of Daniel C. Roper, Sec'y of Commerce).

[12]   Telecommunications Act of 1996, Pub. L. 104-104., 110 Stat. 56 (1996).

[13]   Thomas G. Krattenmaker, *The Telecommunications Act of 1996*, 49 FED. COMM. L. J. 1, 9 (1996).

[14]   Telecommunications Act of 1996, *supra* note 12, at § 42 ('The Commission shall repeal or modify any regulation it determines to be no longer necessary in the public interest.'); Communications Act of 1934, *supra* note 8, at § 309(a) ('If upon examination of any application for a station license…the Commission shall determine that public interest, convenience, or necessity would be served by granting thereof…'); Radio Act of 1927, *supra* note 6, at § 11 ('If upon examination of any application for a station license…the licensing authority shall determine the public interest, convenience, or necessity would be served by the granting thereof…').

[15]   '[A] fundamental…policy choice that underlies U.S. regulation of telecommunications markets: Congress decided, in 1927 and again in 1934 to regulate these markets through an industry-specific federal commission. No other medium of communication in this country is regulated in this fashion;…' Krattenmaker, *supra* note 13 at 4.

[16]   47 U.S.C. § 154 (2018).

Bureaus and offices

The FCC staff is divided into seven main policymaking bureaus and eleven offices. The bureaus were structured in 2002 around the industries they regulate:

- Consumer and Government Affairs Bureau (CGB);
- Enforcement Bureau (EB);
- International Bureau (IB);
- Media Bureau (MB);
- Public Safety and Homeland Security Bureau (PSHSB);
- Wireless Telecommunications Bureau (WTB);
- Wireline Competition Bureau (WCB).

These bureaus are organized into divisions, each with a particular area of expertise. Each bureau has a role in space-based communications issues based on the specific issue and how it arose. Because space is inherently a global environment, most space-related issues are considered by the Satellite Division within the International Bureau.

FCC divisions are tasked with becoming the Commission's experts on certain industries. As its name implies, the Satellite Division is responsible for understanding the satellite and related industries. This division is responsible for engaging with interested stakeholders, including satellite companies, industry associations, other interested agencies like NASA, and even experts from the public. Armed with this knowledge, the division's primary actions involve authorizing satellites and developing policies that encourage the efficient use of radio frequencies by satellite operators. The Satellite Division also considers how to best use orbital resources.[17]

Consideration of space-related issues is not limited entirely to the Satellite Division. In fact, every bureau and office within the FCC can oversee aspects of certain space-based activities. For instance, nearly all radio frequencies are shared among multiple services. Depending on the other users of the spectrum bands, rules for use of the band could also be considered in other bureaus, such as the Wireless Telecommunications Bureau. Similarly, to the extent that satellite systems are used to deliver consumer broadband services, they could also be regulated through the Wireline Competition Bureau. Additionally, any time

---

[17] *See International Bureau Satellite Division*, FED. COMMC'N COMM'N, https://www.fcc.gov/general/international-bureau-satellite-division (last visited July 30, 2021). 'Orbital resources' refers to the orbits and orbital 'slots' available for use. Different mission types require different orbital parameters and must be coordinated with other systems in their orbital neighborhood. Orbital resources, like spectrum, are finite natural resources.

satellite services are provided to consumers, they could be overseen by the Consumer and Government Affairs Bureau. Even less intuitively, the FCC's Office of Engineering and Technology is responsible for authorizing use of the radio-frequency spectrum for every commercial space launch and reentry.

Decision-making process

All decisions made by the FCC must adhere to the processes set out in the Administrative Procedures Act (APA).[18] Specifically, major actions must be made available for public comment.[19] The FCC cannot act without having first considered the input it receives as part of the APA notice and comment period. So long as the FCC follows the proper procedures set out in the APA, the courts will consider the FCC to be an expert agency on topics within its authority and give those decisions deference.[20]

The FCC can initiate the notice and comment procedure in two ways, depending on the maturity of the issues being considered. For policy questions that are in their early stages, the FCC could issue a notice of inquiry (NOI), which largely asks questions about how technology or markets are developing and whether additional policy steps are necessary to protect the public interest. Based on the information it receives and its own analysis, the FCC will next issue a notice of proposed rulemaking (NPRM). These NPRMs can set out the factual basis for FCC action and propose new regulations.[21] Depending on how developed the Commission's policy proposals are, NPRMs may even include tentative conclusions, indicating clearly how new rules are likely to turn out. Although the FCC can still reevaluate these tentative conclusions based on public input and other changes, tentative conclusions and specific proposals usually indicate how the Commission is prepared to act.

The internal process for generating these NOIs, NPRMs, and even final orders can be convoluted and circuitous as the policies make their way through the various organs of the FCC. As a simple example, consider the flowchart in Figure 9.1. In this case, we can assume that existing rules for sharing spectrum

---

[18] 5 U.S.C. § 551(1); *See*, Chapter 5 for discussion on the APA.

[19] *See*, 5 U.S.C. § 553 (2018).

[20] 5 U.S.C. § 706 (2018) (specifying that 'arbitrary and capricious' agency actions will be held unlawful); *see Motor Vehicle Mfrs. Ass'n v. State Farm Mut. Auto. Ins. Co.*, 463 U.S. 29, 42–3 (1983) (determining that review under the arbitrary and capricious standard 'is narrow, and a court is not to substitute its judgment for that of the agency. Nevertheless, the agency must examine the relevant data and articulate a satisfactory explanation for its action including a rational connection between the facts found and the choice made.'). *See, also, Chevron U.S.A. Inc. v. National Resources Defense Council, Inc.*467 U.S. 837, at 842 (1984).

[21] *Rulemaking Process*, FED. COMMC'N COMM'N, https://www.fcc.gov/about-fcc/rulemaking-process (last visited July 30, 2021).

for satellite operations have become outdated as technology has evolved. Stakeholders with an interest in the well-being of the satellite industry have petitioned for new rules.

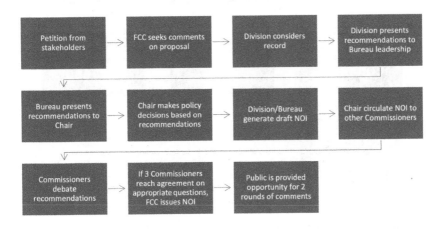

Figure 9.1   FCC NOI process

At the conclusion of this notice and comment cycle, the division reviews the comments and makes recommendations to the bureau leadership. The process at this point is largely the same as that for initiating an NOI, but now the FCC may have a sufficient record to determine whether to propose new rules for notice and comment. Overall, the process from petition to final rules is as depicted in Figure 9.2.

This idealized chart (Figure 9.2) shows the FCC's steps prior to issuing final rules, but in practice, the FCC has many options to either circumvent or expand steps depending on the situation and the record. For instance, the FCC is always free to issue its own NPRM *sua sponte* without an initial petition from stakeholders. The FCC could also skip an NOI if the commissioners believe they understand an issue sufficiently to go straight to the NPRM phase. The one step that cannot be eliminated, however, is that the FCC must always give the public sufficient notice and opportunity to comment through an NPRM before it issues an order with a major action.[22] FCC actions are rarely overturned by the courts, but in the unusual cases when they are, failing to provide adequate notice or opportunity to comment is one of the most likely culprits.

---

[22]   5 U.S.C. § 553 (2018).

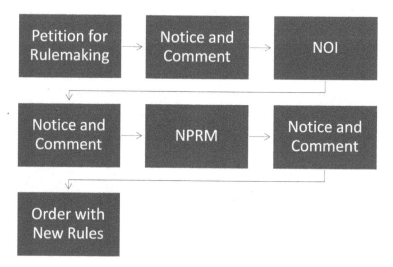

Figure 9.2   FCC rulemaking process

The FCC oversees a high volume of industries and individual actions such that it would effectively grind to a halt if the commissioners were required to vote on each action. For instance, just with regard to space, the FCC must approve each individual earth antenna in many spectrum bands, it must license each satellite, and it must approve every launch and reentry spectrum use. For these lower-profile actions, the Commission has delegated authority to the bureaus and offices to take certain actions on their own.[23] In fact, most actions taken by the FCC are taken by the staff on delegated authority. Only when the relevant stakeholders disagree with these decisions are they appealed for reconsideration by the full Commission. Even then, the Commission rarely overturns decisions by the staff.

Statutory Authority and Commercial Satellites

The Communications Act of 1934 did not contemplate satellite communications. However, by the early 1960s, the space race was under way in earnest after the Soviet Union launched the first man-made satellite, Sputnik, in 1957.[24] The U.S. Congress, keen to develop a space communications network, passed the Communications Satellite Act of 1962, delegating regulatory authority

---

[23]   47 C.F.R. §§ 0.201-0.392 (2021).
[24]   Garrett Shea, *Sputnik and the Dawn of the Space Age*, NASA, https://history.nasa .gov/sputnik.html (last visited Nov. 25, 2021).

over commercial satellites to the FCC.[25] The Act empowers the Commission to promulgate regulations to (1) ensure effective competition in the procurement of satellite equipment; (2) ensure all authorized carriers had nondiscriminatory access to the satellite communications network; (3) regulate satellite connections with foreign communications networks; (4) ensure that satellite communications are technically compatible with existing infrastructure; (5) ensure that any economies made possible by satellites are reflected in public communication rates; (6) approve technical characteristics of satellite systems; (7) grant authorizations for the operation of earth stations *in the public interest*; and (8) ensure no substantial modifications are made to satellite systems unless they are *in the public interest*.[26] This broad grant of authority allows the FCC to regulate commercial satellites and their terrestrial components similarly to other radio transmitters and receivers.

The Communications Satellite Act also established a publicly traded, government-regulated corporation with the purpose of establishing a satellite communication network.[27] The resulting COMSAT corporation was the U.S. signatory to the major international communications satellite organizations, INTELSAT and INMARSAT.[28] At first, the only commercial satellite operators were these governmental and international organizations. Questions were raised about the FCC's authority to license nongovernmental entities to provide satellite services. These were answered in a 1970 proceeding in which the Commission, with the support of the White House,[29] laid out its position in a detailed memorandum of law.[30] Here, the FCC gave its justifications for licensing domestic satellite operators and asserted its consistency with the various international agreements that governed the international satellite organizations.[31] The FCC reasoned that satellites were radio stations within the meaning of the Act, that, considering the FCC's mandate to encourage new uses of radio in the public interest, their location in space was immaterial to the Commission's jurisdiction over them, and that the public interest standard was broad, allowing wide discretion in its application and interpretation.[32]

---

[25] Communications Satellite Act of 1962, Pub. L. 87-624, § 201(c), 76 Stat. 419, (1962).

[26] *Id.* (emphasis added).

[27] *Id.* Title III.

[28] David M. Lieve, *Essential Features of INTELSAT,* 9 J. SPACE L. 47 (1981).

[29] *Establishment of Domestic Communication-Satellite Facilities by Nongovernmental Entities*, 22 F.C.C.2d 86, app. B, ¶ 67 (Memorandum from Peter Flanigan, Asst. to the President of the U.S., to Dean Burch, Chairman, Fed. Commc'n Comm'n) (1970).

[30] *Id.* at app. C.

[31] *Id.* at 86, ¶ 3 & app. C.

[32] *Id.* at app. C, ¶ 3–5.

By the turn of the century, Congress believed that the sector was sufficiently advanced to introduce more competition into commercial space telecommunications. The legislature enacted the ORBIT Act in 2000, which led to the privatization of the satellite corporations INTELSAT and INMARSAT.[33] Consequently, the sections of the Communications Satellite Act that dealt with the government-funded corporation were repealed.

RADIO SPECTRUM AND ITS REGULATION

'Spectrum' refers to electromagnetic waves that, with technology, can be used to transmit data, voice, video, or other communications wirelessly.[34] There are a host of important, modern, terrestrial applications that use spectrum, from cell phones, mobile internet, and 'over-the-air' media broadcasting, to space communications including GPS navigation and timing, remote weather sensing, and satellite command and control.[35]

At its most basic, wireless communication happens when a transmitter generates a radio wave that is subsequently detected by a receiver. Transmitters and receivers that operate as a system are designed to use the same spectrum frequency, 'talking' and 'listening' in the same wavelength.[36] Spectrum is finite in any one place because two systems cannot use the same frequency at the same time. If two systems transmit on the same channel within range of one another, their signals interfere with each other, and receivers are not able to make sense of the message. Multiple systems may work properly and be used in tandem only because of the careful regulation of spectrum users by international and domestic regulatory agencies. Spectrum is managed along the dimensions of geography (where the transmission occurs), power (how 'loud' the signal is, which affects its range), time (who can transmit when), and frequency (which part of the spectrum is used).[37]

Anyone who has driven a significant distance while listening to the radio can observe this management in action. Driving from city to city while tuned to a particular radio frequency, one can observe the degradation of the signal as the receiver in their vehicle moves farther away from the transmitter's

---

[33] Open-market Reorganization for the Betterment of International Telecommunications Act, Pub. L 106-180, 114 Stat. 48 (2000).

[34] LINDA K. MOORE, CONG. RESEARCH SERV., CRS R44433, FRAMING SPECTRUM POLICY: LEGISLATIVE INITIATIVES 1 (2016).

[35] NASA, SPECTRUM 101: AN INTRODUCTION TO NATIONAL AERONAUTICS AND SPACE ADMINISTRATION SPECTRUM MANAGEMENT 6 (2016), https://www.nasa.gov/sites/default/files/atoms/files/spectrum_101_0.pdf.

[36] *Id.* at 6–7.

[37] *Id.* at 7.

location. This is the limitation on transmitter power – the receiver finds it increasingly difficult to 'hear' the transmitter at its licensed 'volume' as the radio waves attenuate over distance. As the original station fades, one can tune the receiver to a different, closer station, and hear the music with perfect clarity. This demonstrates that while the two stations may have overlapping range, their differing frequency ensures they will not interfere with one another. Driving a bit farther and tuning in to the original frequency may allow you to hear a completely different station from a different, now closer location. This demonstrates regulation by geography – broadcast licenses may be issued for the same frequency ('reused' or 'shared') provided that the transmitters' ranges, operating at their licensed power, do not overlap.

This complicated and technical management process is necessary for every wireless device to function properly, from a Predator drone to a car's key fob. It is not difficult to imagine that this management process becomes significantly more complicated when the transmitter being licensed is not a static radio tower, but an antenna hurtling through the void of outer space at 7.8 kilometers per second,[38] crossing international boundaries, and passing above, below, and across the orbits of many other satellites using the same radio spectrum to communicate with each other and receivers on the planet.

Allocation and Assignment

Spectrum management consists of two primary activities: allocation and assignment. Allocation consists of designating a certain 'band' of frequencies for a common use. Returning to the road trip example, the frequencies between 88 and 108 MHz are recognizable as the numbers of FM radio stations. This band has been 'allocated' for nongovernmental broadcast radio.[39] The FCC, as the agency responsible for commercial radio licensing in the U.S., has authority to 'assign' specific frequency channels within the FM band to particular operators, in this case, the radio stations. These entities hold a license to use this spectrum free from interference.

Because all nations utilize the same radio spectrum and a satellite's orbit often takes it over numerous international borders, international coordination is a necessity to avoid harmful interference. The International Telecommunications Union (ITU), a treaty-based, specialized organ of the UN

---

[38] *Types of Orbits*, ESA (Mar. 30, 2020), https://www.esa.int/Enabling_Support/Space_Transportation/Types_of_orbits.

[39] *FM Radio,* FED. COMMC'N COMM'N, https://www.fcc.gov/general/fm-radio (last visited July 30, 2021).

with 193 member States, is the international spectrum management agency.[40] Each member of the ITU – practically every nation on earth – is obligated to abide by ITU coordination procedures before operating any new radio stations in space.[41]

The ITU first sets allocations for different types of radio services for different regions. Services are allocated in a radio band on a primary or secondary basis. Secondary services may operate in the same radio band but may not interfere with nor claim protection from a primary service.[42] States applying to use a certain satellite frequency allocated to the region to which it will provide service must notify the ITU of its requested spectrum and orbital position. The ITU examines the application on a first-come, first-served basis for conformity with its Radio Regulations (RR), and if there is no issue, enters it into the Master International Frequency Register. The State is thus 'protected' from interference by other States' operations, meaning that subsequent systems operating in the same frequency range must ensure they do not interfere with the original authorization.[43] The ITU process is discussed further in the licensing section, below.

It then falls to the national spectrum managers to promulgate allocation rules that are (mostly)[44] consistent with ITU regulations, and to assign licenses to specific operators in accordance with those allocations. In the U.S., regulatory responsibility for the nation's spectrum resources is split between the National Telecommunications and Information Administration (NTIA), responsible for federal government users, and the FCC, which manages commercial, state, local, and amateur users.[45] These agencies coordinate radio users by use of the Table of Frequency Allocations, published in the Federal Register and codified at 47 C.F.R. § 2.106.[46] Allocations for space services are fragmented

---

[40]   *List of ITU Member States*, INT'L TELECOMM. UNION, https://www.itu.int/en/ITU-R/terrestrial/fmd/Pages/administrations_members.aspx (last visited July 30, 2021).

[41]   ITU, RADIO REG. Art. 9 (2021).

[42]   *ITU Regulatory Framework for Space Services*, ITU 2–3, https://www.itu.int/en/ITU-R/space/snl/Documents/ITU-Space_reg.pdf (last visited July 30, 2021) [*hereinafter ITU Space Regulatory Framework*]; ITU, RADIO REG. Art. 5.23–5.33 (2021) [*hereinafter* RR].

[43]   *ITU Space Regulatory Framework*, *supra* note 42, at 1–2.

[44]   *Article 5: Frequency Allocations*, ITU (Jan. 17, 2017), https://life.itu.int/radioclub/rr/art05.htm (sub-regional jurisdictions may utilize bands that do not conform to the master ITU table. These are referred to as additional and alternative allocations).

[45]   *Radio Spectrum Allocation*, FED. COMMC'N COMM'N, https://www.fcc.gov/engineering-technology/policy-and-rules-division/general/radio-spectrum-allocation (last visited July 30, 2021).

[46]   Online version accessible at https://transition.fcc.gov/oet/spectrum/table/fcctable.pdf.

and wide-ranging, and cover service types such as fixed satellite service (FSS, satellite to static receivers), mobile satellite service (MSS, satellite to mobile receivers), Earth exploration satellite service (EESS, which studies Earth from space), radionavigation satellite service (RNSS, like GPS), radio astronomy, space research, and more. Similar to ITU allocations, services in each band are allocated on a primary or secondary basis. The FCC then assigns frequencies to operators through the relevant licensing process.

Processing Rounds

At the ITU level, if a coordination agreement cannot be reached between systems requesting the same spectrum and orbital location, the system that filed first is 'protected' from harmful interference from later entrants: any later applicants must not cause harmful interference to incumbents.[47] What this means in practice is that if two satellites using the same frequency are in a position to interfere with one another's transmissions, the first system to be approved by the ITU can maintain service, while the other must suspend service until it moves far enough away to be able to transmit without causing interference.

The FCC, however, has adopted a different approach for coordinating satellite operators' spectrum use to allow more flexibility in its licensing procedures. The FCC has implemented a system of 'processing rounds' in which applicants are considered in phases.[48] In geostationary orbit (GSO),[49] new applicants are considered in the order that they file, and generally must protect incumbents much like the ITU process. In the case that two or more new GSO systems that use the same spectral or orbital resources are granted authorizations at the same time, these systems are considered part of the same round, and they must split the available spectrum equally.[50] In non-geostationary orbit

---

[47] *ITU Space Regulatory Framework, supra* note 42, at 4.

[48] *See, e.g.,* 47 C.F.R. § 25.157(c) (2021) (processing rounds for NGSO-like constellations).

[49] Geostationary orbit is a high orbit where satellites move at the same speed as the rotation of the Earth, staying stationary relative to the Earth's surface. This allows a satellite to provide constant coverage to a particular geographic area, making these orbital positions highly sought after for communications satellites. Non-geostationary orbits encompass all other orbit types, where a satellite moves relative to the Earth's surface. *See Types of Orbits,* ESA (Mar. 30, 2020), https://www.esa.int/Enabling_Support/Space_Transportation/Types_of_orbits.

[50] 47 C.F.R. § 25.158 (2021).

(NGSO), operators in the same round can coordinate with equal spectrum rights, increasing their ability to share and reuse frequencies.[51]

The fact that co-equal spectrum rights in NGSO only apply to members of the same processing round is critical. Applicants in subsequent rounds are approved on a case-by-case basis 'based on the situation at the time and considering both the need to protect existing expectations and investments and provide for additional entry.'[52] This means new entrants in subsequent rounds must protect earlier operators from interference, rather than sharing spectrum with them. The FCC initiates a processing round when it designates an application a 'lead' for that round. It sets a deadline for filing for that round, and every bona fide applicant that files by that date is a 'competing' application and member of the same round. This process repeats after the close of each round.[53]

In 2019, the Commission adopted an alternative licensing process for qualifying 'small satellite' (small sat) systems, covered in more detail below.[54] The small sat authorization process, which applies to satellites often designed with much shorter operational lifetimes than those subject to the standard process, are exempt from processing rounds. Small sat operators must demonstrate that they will not materially constrain the current and future operations of other systems in its band.[55] In general, they hold the same spectrum rights as others in their service (i.e., primary or secondary allocation), but must not interfere with systems in their own service licensed under the standard Part 25 process.[56]

Milestones and Surety Bonds

Spectrum 'warehousing' occurs when a licensee 'holds exclusive authorization or priority for spectrum use or an orbital position but is unable or unwilling to deploy its authorized satellite system in a timely manner. Such warehousing can hinder the availability of services to the public by deterring entry by another party committed and able to proceed.'[57] To combat warehousing of spectrum and orbital positions, the Commission adopted a deployment mile-

---

[51] *Update to Parts 2 and 25 Concerning Non-Geostationary, Fixed-Satellite Service Systems and Related Matters*, Report & Order and Further Notice of Proposed Rulemaking, 32 FCC Rcd. 7809, 7823 (2017) [*hereinafter* NGSO Order].

[52] *Id.* at 7829.

[53] 47 C.F.R. § 25.157 (2021).

[54] *Streamlining Licensing Procedures for Small Satellites*, Report and Order, 34 FCC Rcd 13077 (2019) [*hereinafter* Small Sat Order].

[55] *Id.* at 13107–8.

[56] *Id.* at 13108.

[57] *NGSO Order, supra* note 51, at fn. 135.

stone system designed to cancel satellite authorizations which are not deployed in a timely manner.[58]

Under the current rules, GSO operators must deploy a licensed system within five years of its authorization. NGSO operators must deploy at least half of their system within six years, with an additional three years to complete the system.[59] If an operator does not meet the deployment milestone, it forfeits the required surety bond it provides to the government,[60] and the system's authorization is canceled or reduced to the number of satellites currently in operation.[61] The Commission stated that its rationale for this rule was to 'discourage applicants from seeking authorizations for oversized, unrealistic constellations, even if those applicants eventually provide substantial service to the public.'[62] By creating the milestone system, the Commission sought both to guard against companies that would attempt to squeeze out competition by laying unrealistic claims to spectral and orbital resources, and to ensure that those that failed to utilize these valuable resources would have to surrender unused spectrum to new applicants.[63]

Spectrum Sharing and NGSOs

Unlike the licenses issued for many terrestrial wireless services like 5G, NGSOs do not receive license for exclusive rights to specific frequencies. Instead, NGSOs generally operate using shared spectrum bands. These spectrum bands may be shared by more than just NGSO systems. The frequencies may also be home to GSOs, scientific exploration like radio astronomy, government satellites, government terrestrial systems, and even terrestrial wireless services. The FCC and other countries design elaborate sharing structures to ensure that all these disparate technologies can work together harmoniously. NGSOs must therefore design their operations to ensure they can not only operate alongside all other NGSOs but can accommodate the other technologies as well. For instance, NGSOs must operate with strict power limits and

---

[58]   *Id.* at 7829.

[59]   47 C.F.R. § 25.164 (2021). Direct Broadcast Satellite systems in GSO and Satellite Digital Audio Radio Service systems in GSO or NGSO are exempt from this requirement.

[60]   47 C.F.R. § 25.165 (2021).

[61]   If no space station has been placed in authorized orbit, the license is canceled. If some satellites are operational, but less than the milestone amount, the license is reduced to the currently operating stations. 47 C.F.R. § 25.161(a) (2021).

[62]   *NGSO Order, supra* note 51, at 7830.

[63]   Edmund Andrews, *Tiny Tonga Seeks Satellite Empire in Space,* N.Y. Times (Aug. 28, 1990), https://www.nytimes.com/1990/08/28/business/tiny-tonga-seeks -satellite-empire-in-space.html.

may even have large swaths of geographic territory where they cannot transmit in some frequencies.

The rules for sharing spectrum between NGSOs can be complex. Operators are expected to attempt to reach coordination agreements to avoid interference with one another in good faith, but in case no agreement is reached, a default sharing mechanism serves as a backstop.[64] Operators may utilize the entire licensed spectrum band unless an 'in-line interference' event occurs. This is when a satellite of one system passes between a satellite and an earth station of another, blocking the line of sight between transmitter and receiver[65] and causing a specified amount of interference.[66]

In-line interference events trigger splitting of the licensed frequency band, with each system limited to operating with half of its bandwidth, its assigned 'home' spectrum.[67] Priority for choosing home spectrum is based on the first operator to launch its system and begin serving customers.[68] Spectrum splitting incentivizes coordination between NGSO operators because the decrease in bandwidth under the default splitting rule would result in degraded quality of service for noncoordinating systems. While avoiding interference with one another, splitting the licensed spectrum effectively halves the data transmission rate of both systems during the in-line event, causing noticeable disruptions to data-heavy applications such as voice or video calls.[69] Accordingly, operators seek to avoid spectrum splitting. As discussed above, these sharing rules only apply to members of the same processing round, and later entrants must protect systems from earlier rounds.

PROCESSING OF SATELLITE LICENSES

Under the Outer Space Treaty, private space activities are subject to 'authorization and continuing supervision' by the *appropriate* State Party.[70] The

---

[64]   *Id.* at 7825.

[65]   Shree Krishna Sharma et al., *Inline Interference Mitigation Techniques for Spectral Coexistence of GEO and NGEO Satellites*, Am. Inst. of Aeronautics & Astronautics 1 (Oct. 11. 2013).

[66]   47 CFR 25.261 (2021); *NGSO Order, supra* note 52, at 7825 ('We will require band splitting when the $\Delta T/T$ [interference temperature] for an interfered link exceeds 6 percent.').

[67]   *Id.* at 7823–25.

[68]   47 C.F.R. 25.261(c)(1) (2021).

[69]   *See* Comments of the Boeing Company, IB Docket No. 16-408 at 14 (Feb. 27, 2017).

[70]   Treaty on Principles Governing the Activities of States in the Exploration and Use of Outer Space, Including the Moon and Other Celestial Bodies art. VI, *opened for signature* Jan. 27, 1967, 610 U.N.T.S. 205., T.I.A.S. No. 6347.

appropriate State is normally the country from which the satellite was launched or another country that authorized the satellite for launch. The ITU maintains a registry of all telecommunications satellites. Satellite registrations must meet certain requirements regarding how they will use spectrum before they can be approved by the ITU.[71] The ITU maintains a lengthy set of rules documenting how satellites may operate and how they can share frequencies. For instance, the ITU's regulations dictate certain power levels for transmissions that help facilitate use of shared frequencies and set which types of satellites or satellite operators have more or fewer rights than others.[72] The ITU also requires that satellite operators must coordinate their operations with each other.[73] The ITU's requirements then become the stage for these discussions.

The ITU's regulations therefore are a backdrop for satellite operations for most of the world. Predictably, the rules are intensely negotiated and do not change without thorough debate. Rules are set and modified at an international event called the World Radiocommunication Conference (WRC), held every three to four years.[74] The WRC is technically a conference of the world's regulators, but many delegations comprise industry representatives, public interest groups, and other interested stakeholders. These different parties have varying degrees of influence within the group.

The agendas for each WRC are set years in advance, and countries take the intervening time to carefully prepare their positions on each agenda item.[75] During the interim, all interested stakeholders study changes in technology, prepare position papers, debate policies, negotiate agreements, and generally position themselves for the big event at the WRC. When the WRC finally arrives, the countries debate intensively any proposed changes in the rules with the support of their delegation. As a result, rule changes can take years or even more than a decade to finally be put in place, and only after significant discussion and compromise.

For as important a coordinating role the ITU has, it remains only as powerful as its member States allow it to be. The ITU has minimal enforcement power on its own and instead relies on its member States to honor the ITU's decisions. ITU decisions are the basis for part or all of some countries' national rules on the ITU's regulations. Countries can also condition their own national authorizations on receiving favorable rulings from the ITU.

---

[71] *ITU Space Regulatory Framework, supra* note 43, at 2–3.
[72] *See, e.g.*, RR, *supra* note 43, at Art. 22.
[73] *Id.* Art. 9.
[74] *World Radiotelecommunication Conferences*, ITU, https://www.itu.int/en/ITU-R/conferences/wrc/Pages/default.aspx (last visited July 30, 2021).
[75] Constitution and Convention of the ITU, with Annexes, Art. 7.2.2, Oct. 14, 1994.

Licensing in the United States

The first step for licensing a satellite system in the U.S. is for an operator to request that the FCC submit an application on its behalf to the ITU. Generally, the satellite operator will prepare the technical documentation that the FCC submits to the ITU.[76] Subsequently, the prospective satellite operator must then apply for an official license from the FCC itself. The FCC issues satellite licenses under three licensing regimes. Most commercial satellites are authorized under the normal Part 25 process,[77] but qualifying small satellites may be licensed under the streamlined process within Part 25.[78] Additionally, experimental and proof-of-concept satellites that are not meant to provide commercial service may be licensed under Part 5 of the Commission's rules.[79]

The FCC derives its authority to issue these licenses from the power Congress delegated to it to manage the public's airwaves in the public interest.[80] Therefore, applicants must persuade the FCC that granting a license is in the public interest. This public interest requirement is somewhat ephemeral, as the FCC has never set out a firm declaration of how it determines whether issuing a license would be in the public interest. As a result, public interest statements tend to be more general, explaining how the satellite will be used and how that use can serve the public. These benefits can range from providing earth observation service to offering broadband to underserved communities. The application must also include two more specific showings: technical details about how the satellite will use spectrum and an orbital debris mitigation plan.[81] For the spectrum showing, the application should explain how the system can comply with existing rules for transmitting and receiving signals. For the debris mitigation plan, the application must detail how the satellites can avoid collision, limit the creation of debris in orbit, and the plan for their disposal at the end of their operational lifetime.[82] Earth stations that transmit to space are also authorized through Part 25.[83] These include not only the command and control stations for satellites, but also 'Earth stations in motion'

---

[76]	47 C.F.R. § 25.111 (2021).

[77]	47 C.F.R. pt. 25, subpt. B (2021).

[78]	*Id.*; *see* 47 C.F.R. §§ 25.122–25.123 (2021).

[79]	47 C.F.R. pt. 25, subpt. B (2021); 47 C.F.R. § 5.64 (2021) (containing special satellite licensing provisions). The FCC also permits amateur satellites under Part 97 of its rules, but these are exceedingly rare, considering the technical requirements. *See* 47 C.F.R. § 97.207 (2021).

[80]	47 U.S.C. § 309(a) (2018).

[81]	47 C.F.R. § 25.114 (2021).

[82]	*Id.* § 25.114(d)(14).

[83]	*Id.* § 25.115.

(ESIMs) that enable high-speed satellite communications and navigation for aircraft, ships, and other vehicles.[84]

As mentioned above, small satellites may be authorized outside of the default service rules or normal processing round format if they meet the FCC qualifications, including a maximum mass, a minimum dimension of 10 cm on any axis, an orbital lifetime of less than six years, a unique signal that will allow it to be tracked and identified, and additional certifications regarding limiting the probability of the satellite becoming a source of debris.[85] The small sat process only applies to NGSO and satellites meant to operate beyond Earth's orbit.

Experimental satellite licenses are issued pursuant to Part 5 of the FCC's rules but are still subject to the orbital debris disclosures applicable to other satellite applications.[86] These limited licenses, issued only for testing purposes, are not subject to ITU filing requirements.

Licensing of Foreign Satellites

Non-U.S. satellites may serve the U.S. market and communicate with U.S. earth stations if authorized by the FCC under the DISCO II framework established in 1997 to implement American commitments to open the U.S. satellite market.[87] This procedure was revised and refined in 1999, allowing foreign satellite operators to request 'market access' from the FCC.[88] Before approving a foreign operator, the DISCO II analysis considers the effect on competition in the U.S., spectrum availability, technical requirements, along with national security, law enforcement, foreign policy, and trade reciprocity concerns.[89]

Foreign satellites may obtain market access in one of two ways. First, a non-U.S. satellite system may apply under one of the processing round processes for GSO and NGSO systems, and its application, if it passes DISCO II

---

[84] *See e.g., Amendment of Parts 2 and 25 of the Commission's Rules to Facilitate the Use of Earth Stations in Motion Communicating with Geostationary Orbit Space Stations in Frequency Bands Allocated to the Fixed Satellite Service*, Report and Order, 35 FCC Rcd 5137, 5138 (2020).

[85] 47 C.F.R. §§ 25.122–25.123 (2021); *Small Sat Order, supra* note 54, at 13107–08.

[86] 47 C.F.R. § 5.64 (2021).

[87] *Amendment of the Commission's Regulatory Policies to Allow Non-U.S. Licensed Satellites Providing Domestic and International Service in the United States*, Report and Order, 12 FCC Rcd 24094, 24174 (1997) [hereinafter *DISCO II Order*].

[88] *Amendment of the Commission's Regulatory Policies to Allow Non-U.S.-Licensed Space Stations to Provide Domestic and International Satellite Service in the United States*, First Order on Reconsideration, 15 FCC Rcd 7207, 7209–10 (1999).

[89] *See generally DISCO II Order, supra* note 87.

review, would be considered along with U.S. systems. Second, satellites can be authorized as points of communication for U.S. earth stations.[90]

License Modifications

Earth and space station licenses must be modified to reflect any material change to their operation. Changes that affect the parameters of a system's operations or its license terms and conditions, including utilizing different or additional spectrum, updates to the technical specifications of a system, or a revision of its orbital debris plan, all require filing a modification application at the FCC.[91] Exceptions to this rule exist for earth stations, as long as adding new points of communication do not contravene any of the station's licensing conditions.[92] Likewise, GSO and NGSO space stations may be relocated within an operator's current licensed orbital positions without prior FCC authorization, as long as the operators maintain service to all of their customers during the move.[93] Operators must notify the FCC at least 30 (GSO) or 10 (NGSO) days prior to repositioning assets in this manner. This 'fleet management' process is most often used to replace satellites within a system as older fleet elements are retired or if a station suffers a technical issue.

Orbital Debris Mitigation

For decades after the first spaceflight, national space programs gave little thought to the disposal of rocket bodies or satellites at the end of the operational lifetime. In 1996, the first accidental collision between two space objects occurred when a French Cerise military satellite was struck by a fragmented rocket body previously launched by the European Space Agency (ESA).[94] Although this event was relatively undramatic, it disabled the satellite and drew the attention of the international space community. Far more dramatic was the wholesale destruction of an Iridium communications satellite in a conjunction with a derelict Russian spacecraft in 2009, which resulted in a loss of service to Iridium's customers.[95]

---

[90] 47 C.F.R. § 25.137 (2021).

[91] *Id.* § 25.117.

[92] *Id.* § 25.118.

[93] *Id.*

[94] NASA, History of On-Orbit Satellite Fragmentations 368 (14th ed., 2008).

[95] Becky Iannotta, *U.S. Satellite Destroyed in Space Collision*, Space.com (Feb. 11, 2009) https://www.space.com/5542-satellite-destroyed-space-collision.html.

The problem of space debris has long been considered in managing U.S. space activities. As far back as 1988, the executive branch made it national policy that both the public and private space industries seek to minimize the creation of debris.[96] In 1995, NASA and the Department of Defense debuted a set of guidelines for building future spacecraft that minimized debris creation. The FCC used these guidelines as the baseline for its first orbital debris proceeding.[97] Although the FCC had adopted orbital debris rules previously for different types of service, it extended the disclosure requirements to all space station applicants in 2004, requiring a narrative description of the applicant's plan to minimize debris generation and safely dispose of its spacecraft along with a casualty risk assessment for spacecraft parts that may survive reentry of the atmosphere.[98] The FCC roots its debris assessment requirements in its authority to regulate radio stations in the public interest. The Commission reasons that a calculation of debris production could be relevant to its determination of whether each individual satellite system is in the public interest.[99] Further, the radio links necessary to operate satellites are licensed by the FCC, providing a nexus between the FCC's authority to license spectrum and the physical operations of a space station.[100]

The FCC published an update to its orbital debris rules in 2020, consistent with the overhaul of the government-wide Orbital Debris Mitigation Standard Practices (ODMSP) the previous year.[101] The new rules require a more detailed and comprehensive set of disclosures, including: (1) a statement regarding any debris the satellite will generate as part of its operations; (2) a collision risk assessment using NASA's debris assessment software; (3) a statement that the operator has limited the probability of accidental explosions during a satellite's operation and disposal; (4) any steps taken to coordinate with other operators' systems; (5) the accuracy with which the spacecraft will maintain orbital position; (6) a certification that the operator will take all steps to assess and avoid collisions if it receives a conjunction warning; (7) disposal plans, whether through reentry (NGSO), raising the satellite to 'graveyard orbit'

---

[96] Presidential Directive on National Space Policy (Feb. 11, 1988), *unclassified summary available at* https://www.hq.nasa.gov/office/pao/History/policy88.html.

[97] *Amendment of the Commission's Space Station Licensing Rules and Policies; Mitigation of Orbital Debris*, First Report and Order, 18 FCC Rcd 10760, 10785 (2003).

[98] *Mitigation of Orbital Debris*, Second Report and Order, 19 FCC Rcd 11567, 11568 (2004).

[99] *Id.* at 11575.

[100] *Id.*

[101] *Mitigation of Orbital Debris in the New Space Age*, Report and Order and Further Notice of Proposed Rulemaking, 35 FCC Rcd 4156, 4160 (2020) [*hereinafter* New Space ODM Order].

(GSO), or direct retrieval of the satellite, including the quantity of fuel that will be reserved for disposal maneuvers; and (8) the probability of successful disposal.[102] For non-U.S.-licensed satellites requesting market access, the orbital debris plan requirement may be satisfied by demonstrating the system is subject to 'direct and effective regulatory oversight' by its home national licensing authority.[103]

The FCC has continued to develop the record on several debris issues. Outstanding issues include how to calculate the probability of accidental explosions on-orbit, developing a metric for understanding the aggregate risk of collision between large objects and an entire complex satellite constellation, whether propulsion should be required on satellites above a certain altitude in low-Earth orbit to enable collision avoidance maneuvers, whether the FCC should reduce the orbital lifetime of space stations from the current 25-year standard, modifications to the casualty risk assessment, incorporating an indemnification regime into the licensing process, and implementing a performance bond system (similar to the spectrum milestone regime described above) for successful post-mission disposal.[104]

Launch Licensing and Spectrum

Licenses for the actual launch and reentry of space vehicles are issued by the FAA,[105] but these launches could not be controlled without wireless radio spectrum use. Space launch activities were the exclusive domain of the U.S. Government for many years.[106] Consequently, the spectrum frequency bands used for space vehicle tracking, telemetry and control, and potential abort signals ended up allocated to federal use, rather than non-federal, commercial use. As a result, the federal spectrum used for commercial space launches and reentries is not wholly controlled by the FCC, but is substantially overseen by the National Telecommunications and Information Administration (NTIA), which manages the use of federal spectrum and is discussed below.

---

[102] 47 C.F.R. § 25.114(d)(14) (2021).

[103] *Id.* § 25.114(d)(14)(viii).

[104] *New Space ODM Order, supra* note 101, at 4226–49.

[105] Commercial Space Launch Act of 1984, Pub. L. 98-575, 98 Stat. 3055 (codified as amended at 51 U.S.C. §§ 50901–50923).

[106] *Amendment of Part 2 of the Commission's Rules for Federal Earth Stations Communicating with Non-Federal Fixed Satellite Service Space Stations; Federal Space Station Use of the 399.9-400.05 MHz Band; and Allocation of Spectrum for Non-Federal Space Launch Operations,* Notice of Proposed Rulemaking, 28 FCC Rcd 6698, 6723–24 (2013).

The FCC is responsible for processing licenses for spectrum use for launch and reentry. As commercial launch and reentry activities began occurring with greater frequency using federal spectrum, the FCC began granting special temporary authority (STA) for use of the relevant parts of the federal spectrum through its Part 5 experimental radio rules. This required the FCC to coordinate and get the approval of the NTIA for each launch on a case-by-case basis, and the process was fraught with uncertainty.[107] By 2013, commercial space operators were asking for a solution. After an initial NPRM, the Commission took no further action until 2021, adopting rules which would add a non-federal allocation in the 2200–2290 MHz band on a secondary basis. Because this band is used extensively by federal spectrum users, the FCC still requires coordination with the NTIA for each launch, but the routine licensure of launches under the new rules may make the coordination process easier and more streamlined.[108]

This dedicated allocation is the first step towards providing FCC licenses for commercial launch spectrum. Until service-specific rules are adopted, however, the STA process will continue on a case-by case-basis.[109] Among the issues to be addressed in the future are non-federal allocations for commercial space launch operations in a diverse set of bands and accompanying licensing and technical rules for each band.[110] In a significant departure from the previous STA process, the FCC is considering a ten-year license term[111] for space launch operations. The FCC has also indicated an interest in revising the licensing and operating rules for various payload activities currently addressed through experimental licensing, and radio links between space stations on-orbit and launch vehicles.[112]

NATIONAL TELECOMMUNICATIONS AND INFORMATION ADMINISTRATION

The White House Office of Telecommunications Policy administered frequency assignments for federal uses until 1977, when that authority was delegated to the Commerce Department.[113] The NTIA was created in 1978 and

---

[107]   *Id.* at 6724–25.

[108]   *Allocation of Spectrum for Non-Federal Space Launch Operations*, Report and Order and Further Notice of Proposed Rulemaking, 2021 FCC LEXIS 1541, ¶ 17–20 (2021).

[109]   *Id.* at ¶ 26.

[110]   *Id.* at ¶ 37–137.

[111]   *Id.* at ¶ 83.

[112]   *Id.* at ¶ 139–145.

[113]   Spectrum 101, *supra* note 36, at 13.

tasked with radio-spectrum management, 'which included frequency alloca-tion and assignment,' as well as 'service as Secretariat to the Interdepartment Radio Advisory Committee (IRAC).'[114]

The NTIA Organization Act codified the NTIA's responsibilities, which include assigning frequencies to federal government users, establishing pol-icies for spectrum assignment allocation and use, and providing departments and agencies with guidance 'to assure that their conduct of telecommunica-tions activities is consistent with these policies.'[115] The NTIA sets forth regu-lations for federal use of the radio spectrum within its Manual of Regulations and Procedures for Federal Radio Frequency Management (NTIA Manual).[116]

Federal Spectrum Management

The Communications Act of 1934 divided authority over spectrum between the executive branch for federal uses and the FCC for non-federal uses.[117] The Act provides for the functions of developing classes of radio service, allocating frequency bands to the various services, and authorizing frequency use.[118] However, the Act does not mandate specific allocations of bands for exclusive federal or non-federal use; all such allocations stem from agreements between the NTIA and the FCC.[119] Put simply, there are no statutory 'federal' or 'non-federal' bands.[120]

The NTIA and the FCC are required to work together to ensure that spectrum policy decisions promote efficient use of the spectrum consistent with both U.S. economic interests and national security requirements.[121] To accomplish goals of economic benefits balanced with national security needs, the chairperson of the FCC and the Assistant Secretary for Communications

---

[114] *A Short History of NTIA*, NAT'L TELECOMM. AND INFO. ADMIN, https://www.ntia.doc.gov/legacy/opadhome/history.html#:~:text=The%20National%20Telecommunications%20and%20Information%20Administration%20(NTIA)%20was,and%20the%20Commerce%20Department's%20Office%20of%20Telecommunications%20(OT) (last visited Dec. 19, 2021).

[115] Pub. L. No. 102-538, 106 Stat. 3533 (1992) (codified at 47 U.S.C. 901 et seq.).

[116] NAT'L TELECOMM. AND INFO. ADMIN., MANUAL OF REGULATIONS AND PROCEDURES FOR FEDERAL RADIO FREQUENCY MANAGEMENT (Sept. 2017 eds., 2017) [*hereinafter* NTIA Manual].

[117] Spectrum 101, *supra* note 36, at 13.

[118] *Who Regulates the Spectrum*, NAT'L TELECOMM. AND INFO. ADMIN., https://www.ntia.doc.gov/book-page/who-regulates-spectrum (last visited Dec. 19, 2021).

[119] *Id.*

[120] *Id.*

[121] Spectrum 101, *supra* note 36, at 13.

and Information, NTIA, signed a memorandum of understanding (MOU) in January 2003 that formalized their longstanding cooperative relationship.[122]

In accordance with the NTIA Manual, 'each Government agency decides, in the light of policies, rules, regulations, frequency allocations, and the availability of frequencies, whether, what, and how many mission requirements can be fulfilled by using telecommunications systems.'[123] Once an agency has determined its spectrum needs and conducted coordination with other involved agencies, it applies to the NTIA Office of Spectrum Management (OSM), Spectrum Services Division (SSD), for consideration by the Frequency Assignment Subcommittee (FAS) of the IRAC.

Commercial Access to Federal Spectrum

Applications for access to federal spectrum use by non-federal users, such as commercial spaceflight operators, are submitted to the FCC in accordance with FCC regulations, as described above. However, the NTIA maintains responsibility for coordinating those requests with other federal users. In planning operations that may involve federal spectrum, it is critical that space operators engage with the NTIA to pre-coordinate their requests.

QUESTIONS FOR REVIEW

1. The U.S. is the only country that bifurcates spectrum licensing into federal use and non-federal use, with the NTIA having jurisdiction over radio stations 'belonging to and operated by' the USG. The NTIA sits within the Department of Commerce. Do you see any potential challenges with Commerce essentially having ultimate authority over governmental uses of the radio-frequency spectrum?

2. What is the relationship between the FCC and the ITU?

3. What is the role of the FCC in orbital debris mitigation? How might that be challenging for licensing large constellations?

4. A recent FCC auction of spectrum for 5G reportedly conflicted with NOAA's use of adjacent spectrum for weather forecasting. In fact, the U.S. Navy considered it a national security concern, and meteorologists argued that weather forecasting would be jeopardized, imperiling the lives of millions of people who depend on accurate forecasts of floods, hurri-

---

[122] *FCC and NTIA Memorandum of Understanding on Spectrum Coordination,* NAT'L TELECOMM. AND INFO. ADMIN. (JAN. 31, 2003), https://www.ntia.doc.gov/other -publication/2003/fcc-and-ntia-memorandum-understanding-spectrum-coordination.

[123] NTIA Manual, *supra* note 116.

canes, winter storms, and tornadoes. If you were an FCC commissioner, what factors would you consider in determining which use of the spectrum is in the greater 'public interest'?

5.   What is the role of the FCC and the NTIA in launch and reentry activities and how are those different from licensing in-space activities?

10. Space operations and the U.S. Department of Defense

Ruth awoke with her heart racing. 'That was so real,*' she thought. Her dream started innocently enough; she was walking through a park on a Sunday afternoon. Children were chasing each other; a little boy was piloting his new drone. Suddenly, the park turned into a battlefield with mortars exploding around her. The sound was deafening. As she ran away from the turmoil and tumult of the fighting, she found herself in a modern, air-conditioned office building. She saw men with short-cropped hair and Hawaiian shirts, poring over their computer screens. She looked out the window at the building next door and gazed wistfully upwards at the clear, blue sky. She heard a loud whistling sound, and the hairs on her arms started to stand up. Suddenly, a rocket crashed into the neighboring building's roof, causing an explosion.*

'What a stressful way to wake up,' she thought, 'especially on this one day, when I can sleep in.' The firm was closed for Veterans Day. She had stayed up late watching Saving Private Ryan *again. Her dream felt like WWIII, which got her thinking, 'What role does space play in national security? What does the Defense Department do in space? And what about all of those three-letter agencies – do they have their own satellites too?' She grabbed her space law textbook, her first espresso, and headed for her comfy chair.*

The 2020 U.S. National Space Policy asserts that outer space has become a warfighting domain as a result of competitors seeking to challenge U.S. and allied interests in space.[1] In order to maintain a 'secure, stable, and accessible space domain,' the U.S. endeavors to adapt its national security organizations, policies, doctrine, and capabilities to deter hostilities, demonstrate responsible behaviors, and, if necessary, defeat aggression and protect U.S. interests in space.[2]

This chapter addresses the activities of the U.S. Department of Defense (DoD) in outer space. It describes the DoD's national security functions and provides a general description of the DoD's space activities and authorities.

---

[1] The National Space Policy, 85 F.R. 81755 § 5.3.a (Dec. 9, 2020) [*hereinafter* 2020 NSP].

[2] *Id.*

It next provides a general overview of the myriad U.S. Government (USG) military and intelligence community (IC) agencies that have some connection to the DoD in outer space, including the Space Force and Space Command. Finally, it explains the key national space policies, directives, and strategies applicable to the U.S. DoD as of the publication of this book.

SPACE OPERATIONS AND CAPABILITIES

Generally speaking, the DoD performs seven key space operations: space control; space situational awareness; position, navigation and timing (PNT); intelligence, surveillance, and reconnaissance (ISR); satellite communications; environmental monitoring; missile warning; nuclear detonation detection; spacelift; and satellite operations.[3] These space capabilities enable the military to perform the joint functions in all domains as described below.[4]

Space Control

There are two forms of space control: offensive and defensive.[5] The objective of both is to ensure freedom of U.S. action in space and, when directed, to defeat efforts to interfere with U.S. or allied space systems.[6] Hence, space control can be thought of as a means to ensure unfettered freedom to operate in space, which, according to the 2020 National Space Policy, the U.S. regards as a vital national interest.[7]

The Space Force's Capstone Publication, *Spacepower: Doctrine for Space Forces* (*Spacepower*), refers to the space control concept using slightly different terminology and without emphasizing the word 'control.' In *Spacepower*, freedom of action in space is ensured through 'combat power projection' consisting of 'defensive operations' and 'offensive operations.'[8] It explains, '[d]efensive operations enhance control by protecting and preserving U.S.

---

[3]   Chairman, J. Chiefs of Staff, Joint Publication 3-14, *Space Operations* (April 10, 2018), https://www.jcs.mil/Portals/36/Documents/Doctrine/pubs/jp3_14ch1.pdf?ver=-zw88OCRWcvI913jycR-uQ%3D%3D [*hereinafter* JP 3-14].

[4]   'Joint operations' is the general term used to describe military actions conducted by two or more military services as opposed to individual military services. *See* Chairman, J. Chiefs of Staff, Joint Publication I: *Doctrine for the Armed Forces of the United States* xi (Mar. 25, 2013), https://www.jcs.mil/Portals/36/Documents/Doctrine/pubs/jp1_ch1.pdf?ver=2019-02-11-174350-967.

[5]   JP 3-14, *supra* note 3, at II-2.

[6]   *Id.*

[7]   2020 NSP, *supra* note 1, § 3.

[8]   U.S. SPACE F., SPACEPOWER: DOCTRINE FOR SPACE FORCES 36 (Space Capstone Pub., 2010) [*hereinafter* Spacepower].

freedom of action in the space domain.'[9] 'When warranted,' however, 'offensive operations are designed to achieve a relative advantage by negating an adversary's ability to access, or exploit the space domain and are therefore essential to achieving space superiority.'[10]

Defensive operations preserve friendly space capabilities before, during, and after an attack.[11] They may be active or passive, and may apply to each segment of the space system – the space system itself, the ground station, or the link that joins them.[12] Active measures may be either reactive after an adversary attack, or proactive 'to seize the initiative once an attack is imminent.'[13]

Passive defensive measures, by contrast, attempt to improve survivability through system and architectural attributes.[14] These measures include camouflage, concealment, and deception; spacecraft maneuverability; self-protection; orbit diversification; communications security; dispersal of space systems; and hardening across the three segments of the space system.[15] Robust defensive space control capabilities contribute to deterrence, influence enemies' perceptions of U.S. space capabilities, and reduce enemies' confidence of success in disabling or interfering with those capabilities.[16]

Offensive space control operations seek to achieve space negation; that is, measures designed to deceive, disrupt, deny, degrade, or destroy space systems or services.[17]

- **Deceive** refers to measures designed to mislead an adversary, such as through spoofing, which deceives a receiver by introducing a fake signal with erroneous information.[18]
- **Disrupt** refers to measures designed to temporarily impair an adversary's use of a space system, usually without physical damage.[19]

---

[9]   *Id.*

[10]   *Id.*

[11]   *Id.*

[12]   *Id.*; *see* JP 3-14, *supra* note 3, at II-3.

[13]   *Spacepower, supra* note 8, at 36.

[14]   *Id.*

[15]   JP 3-14, *supra* note 3, at II-3; *see also Spacepower, supra* note 8, at 36.

[16]   JP 3-14, *supra* note 3, at II-3.

[17]   *Id.* at II-2.

[18]   *Space Threats*, Def. Intelligence Agency 9 (Jan. 2019), https://www.dia.mil/Portals/27/Documents/News/Military%20Power%20Publications/Space_Threat_V14_020119_sm.pdf.

[19]   JP 3-14, *supra* note 3, at II-2.

- **Deny** refers to measures designed to temporarily eliminate an adversary's access to a space system, usually without physical damage to the affected system.[20]
- **Degrade** refers to measures designed to permanently impair (either partially or totally) the adversary's use of a system, with some physical damage.[21]
- **Destroy** refers to measures designed to permanently eliminate the adversary's use of a system, usually with physical damage to the affected system.[22]

Deliberate offensive and defensive actions to ensure friendly use and prevent adversarial use of position, navigation, and timing (PNT) information through coordinated employment of space, cyberspace, and electromagnetic warfare (EW) capabilities are called navigation warfare (NAVWAR).[23]

Space Situational Awareness and Space Domain Awareness

Space situational awareness (SSA) and the related concept of space domain awareness play an important part in ensuring a 'secure, stable, and accessible space domain.'[24] Achieved through cooperation with interagency, international, and commercial entities, space domain awareness allows the DoD to 'characterize and attribute potentially threatening behavior' in space, according to the National Space Policy's national security space sector guidelines.[25] The sector guidelines also assign the DoD the role of providing to the Department of Commerce and other relevant agencies, as needed, SSA information 'that supports national security, civil, and human space flight activities, planetary defense from hazardous near-Earth objects, and commercial and allied space operations.'[26]

SSA is defined within the DoD as 'the requisite foundational, current, and predictive knowledge and characterization of space objects and the operational environment upon which space operations depend.'[27] Achieved through a combination of space-based and ground-based sensors, SSA incorporates

---

[20]　*Id.*
[21]　*Id.*
[22]　*Id.*
[23]　*Id.* at II-3.
[24]　2020 NSP, *supra* note 1, at 81769.
[25]　*Id.*
[26]　*Id.* at 81771.
[27]　JP 3-14, *supra* note 3, at II-1.

'understanding of the space capabilities and intent of those that pose a threat to our space operations and space capabilities.'[28] The USG has also defined SSA as 'the knowledge and characterization of space objects and their operational environment to support safe, stable, and sustainable space activities.'[29]

The DoD has statutory authority to enter into SSA sharing agreements with foreign governments and nongovernmental entities.[30] U.S. Space Command (USSPACECOM) and its predecessor, U.S. Strategic Command (USSTRATCOM), have concluded more than 100 SSA sharing agreements with various entities and foreign governments.[31] However, the 2019 National Defense Appropriation Act placed new statutory restrictions on the DoD's SSA sharing activities.[32] Starting January 1, 2024, the Secretary of Defense may only share SSA information with non-U.S. government entities if sharing is deemed necessary for national security.[33] This amendment roughly coincides with the policy direction set forth in Space Policy Directive-3, *National Space Traffic Management Policy* (SPD-3), which established the goal of transferring responsibility for the publicly releasable portion of the DoD catalog and for administering an open architecture data repository to the Department of Commerce, allowing the DoD 'to focus on maintaining access to and freedom of action in space.'[34]

Currently, and until these changes occur, USSPACECOM provides three levels of SSA services:[35]

- Basic – provides positional data on more than 16,000 satellites to registered users through a public website: www.space-track.org.[36]
- Emergency – notifies satellite operators when reportable criteria for a conjunction are satisfied at no cost and with no agreement necessary.[37]

---

[28]   *Id.*

[29]   Space Policy Directive 3: National Space Traffic Management Policy, 83 F.R. 28969 § 2(a) (June 18, 2018) [*hereinafter* SPD-3].

[30]   10 U.S.C. § 2274 (2018).

[31]   *See* USSPACECOM Pub. Affairs, *USSSPACECOM Adds Portugal – a Strategic NATO Ally – to SSA Data Sharing Cadre*, U.S. Space Command (July 15, 2020), https://www.spacecom.mil/MEDIA/NEWS-ARTICLES/Article/2274759/usspacecom-adds-portugal-a-strategic-nato-ally-to-ssa-data-sharing-cadre/ (noting that Portugal is the 117th partner with an SSA agreement).

[32]   John S. McCain National Defense Authorization Act for Fiscal Year 2019, Pub. L. No. 115-232 (codified as amended in scattered sections).

[33]   10 U.S.C. § 2274(a)(2) (2018).

[34]   See discussion of SPD-3, infra, Section IV.C.

[35]   *SSA Sharing & Orbital Data Requests (ODR)*, Space-Track.Org, https://www.space-track.org/documentation#/odr (last visited Oct. 17, 2021).

[36]   *Id.*

[37]   *Id.*

- Advanced – available to those who enter into an aforementioned sharing agreement authorized under 10 U.S.C. § 2274.[38]

Although joint doctrine on space operations was updated in October 2020 and continues to use the term SSA exclusively, an alternate term, space domain awareness (SDA), is becoming increasingly common. SDA encompasses the effective identification, characterization, and understanding of any factor associated with the space domain that could affect space operations and thereby impact the security, safety, economy, or environment of the U.S.[39] While the 2020 National Space Policy uses both terms, all references to SDA are limited to the national security sector guidelines, suggesting that SDA is preferred in a context of threats to security as opposed to the context of safety.[40]

Position, Navigation and Timing (PNT)

Along with terrestrial navigation systems, the DoD's global positioning system (GPS) helps provide PNT capabilities. PNT systems provide users with geolocation, navigation, and time reference services.[41]

Today's GPS constellation, which operates in medium-Earth orbit (MEO), comprises 31 satellites, not including decommissioned on-orbit spares.[42] The satellites broadcast a signal carrying a time code marked by the satellite's atomic clock. Receivers can then calculate their own location by measuring the relative time delay of signals broadcast by at least four different satellites.[43] GPS provides global coverage; due to the number of satellites in the GPS constellation and their orbital configuration, a GPS receiver is always in view of at least four GPS satellites.

The 1991 Gulf War has been called the 'first space war' as a result of a 16-satellite GPS constellation, though not yet fully operational, that enabled the U.S. military to conduct rapid maneuvers through the desert terrain.[44] The utility of GPS was in its infancy; for example, if bombs were guided at all during the Gulf War, they were laser-guided, not GPS-guided. Since then, GPS 'has fundamentally shifted the way U.S. forces locate and destroy targets, plan

---

[38]   *Id.*

[39]   *Spacepower, supra* note at 8, at 38.

[40]   2020 NSP, *supra* note 1, § 5.3.

[41]   JP 3-14, *supra* note 3, at II-3.

[42]   Nat'l Coord. Off. Space-Based Positioning, Navigation, & Timing, *Space Segment*, GPS.Gov (July 12, 2021), https://www.gps.gov/systems/gps/space/.

[43]   Larry Greenemeier, *GPS and the World's First 'Space War'*, Sci. Am. (Feb. 8, 2016), https://www.scientificamerican.com/article/gps-and-the-world-s-first-space -war/.

[44]   *Id.*

operations, control both material and war-fighting assets, synchronize effects, and guide troops and remotely piloted aircraft home.'[45]

Early in its development, the DoD envisioned GPS as a dual-use service. Today, civil society reliance on GPS is such that 'an extended outage of GPS, or extended period of spoofed or manipulated GPS signals, could cause severe economic losses and put lives at risk.'[46]

The Secretary of Defense is directed by statute to provide for sustained GPS capabilities for military purposes.[47] The same statute directs the Secretary of Defense to provide GPS operations for peaceful civil, commercial, and scientific uses on a continuous worldwide basis and free of direct user fees.

The U.S. previously employed a technique called selective availability to globally degrade the civilian GPS signal.[48] A 1996 Presidential Decision Directive established the goal of encouraging acceptance and integration of GPS into peaceful civil, commercial and scientific applications worldwide; and encouraging private sector investment in and use of GPS technologies and services.[49] In furtherance of this goal and upon the determination that national security would be minimally impacted, President Clinton announced that selective availability would be discontinued on May 1, 2000.[50] Beginning in 2007, GPS satellites have been built without the selective availability feature, making permanent the 2000 policy decision to discontinue the use of selective availability.[51]

GPS provides two levels of services: standard and encrypted.[52] The standard service is the service provided to all users through an unencrypted signal. The encrypted service signal – known as Military Code or M Code – enhances

---

[45]   Lt. Gen. Ellen Pawlikoswki, Lt. Gen. Doug Loverro & Col. Tom Chrisler, *Space: Disruptive Challenges, New Opportunities, and New Strategies*, 6 STRATEGIC STUD. Q. 27, 33 (2012).

[46]   Space Policy Directive 7: The United States Space-Based Positioning, Navigation, and Timing Policy § 3(a)(i) (January 15, 2021), https://trumpwhitehouse.archives.gov/presidential-actions/memorandum-space-policy-directive-7/ [*hereinafter* SPD-7].

[47]   10 U.S.C. § 2281 (2018).

[48]   *See* Press Statement, President Bill Clinton, Improving the Civilian Global Positioning Systems (GPS) (May 1, 2020), https://clintonwhitehouse3.archives.gov/WH/EOP/OSTP/html/0053_4.html [*hereinafter* Clinton GPS Press Statement].

[49]   Presidential Decision Directive NSTC-6: U.S. Global Positioning System Policy (March 28, 1996), https://fas.org/spp/military/docops/national/gps.htm.

[50]   Clinton GPS Press Statement, *supra* note 48.

[51]   Off. Space Com., *Selective Availability Feature Eliminated from GPS III Satellites*, NOAA (Sept. 18, 2007),
https://www.space.commerce.gov/selective-availability-feature-eliminated-from-gps-iii-satellites/.

[52]   JP 3-14, *supra* note 3, at II-4.

anti-jamming and anti-spoofing capabilities and is used by the DoD, authorized U.S. government agencies, and some U.S. allies.[53]

Intelligence, Surveillance, and Reconnaissance (ISR)

Space-based ISR is the collection of intelligence through the integration of sensors, assets, and systems for gathering data and information on an object or an area of interest.[54] As described further below, space-based ISR assets may be operated by military, nonmilitary, or intelligence community (IC) organizations and offer the ability to collect intelligence over areas where U.S. access may otherwise not be permitted.[55] International cooperation in space-based ISR collection activities also builds partnership capacity in support of national security objectives and multinational operations while improving interoperability and resiliency.[56]

Satellite Communication

Satellite communication (SATCOM) allows for establishing telecommunications connections independent from a terrestrial communications infrastructure.[57] DoD SATCOM comprises both DoD-owned as well as commercially owned resources. SATCOM provides a way to transmit voice, data, video, and imagery

Military satellite communications (MILSATCOM) include those systems owned and operated by the DoD. It consists of three bands: narrowband, wideband, and protected band.[58]

> • **Narrowband** SATCOM operates in the ultrahigh frequency (UHF), L-, and S-bands to provide secure data and voice communications that are less susceptible to adverse weather conditions or dense foliage.[59]

---

[53]   *Id.*

[54]   *Id.*

[55]   *Id.*

[56]   *Id.*

[57]   *Id.* at II-5; Chairman, J. Chiefs of Staff, Instruction 6250.01F, *Department of Defense Satellite Communications* A-3 (Feb. 26, 2019), https://www.jcs.mil/Portals/36/Documents/Library/Instructions/CJCSI%206250.01F.pdf?ver=2019-03-18-121700 -237 [*hereinafter* CJCSI 6250.01F].

[58]   CJCSI 6250.01F, *supra* note 57, at A-1.

[59]   *Id.*; Off. Chief Info. Officer, Instruction 8420.02, *DoD Satellite Communications (SATCOM)* 30 (Nov. 25, 2020), https://www.esd.whs.mil/Portals/54/Documents/DD/issuances/dodi/842002p.pdf?ver=Yn9vTMmEmry8GZbCpCUgPA%3D%3D [*hereinafter* DoDI 8420.02].

- **Wideband** SATCOM operates in the C-, X-, Ku-, and Ka-bands and provides substantial worldwide capacity for high-quality voice, imagery, video, and data.[60]
- **Protected** SATCOM systems operate in the extremely high frequency (EHF) Ka-, Q-, and V-bands and have the greatest level of protection against disruption.[61] Protected SATCOM capabilities can defeat, for example, jamming or scintillation through frequency hopping or increased power, respectively.[62] The protected band is used, among other things, for the nuclear command, control, and communications (NC3) mission set.[63]

Environmental Monitoring

Environmental monitoring supports military operations by giving commanders information about meteorological and oceanographic factors that can affect military operations, particularly in oceanic regions where terrestrial-based monitoring capabilities are limited.[64] Data may come from non-DoD satellites, such as those operated by NASA or the National Oceanic and Atmospheric Administration (NOAA).[65] Environmental monitoring also entails monitoring the space environment, such as detecting solar events, radiation, and other aspects of space weather that could affect the operation of satellites.[66]

Missile Warning and Nuclear Detonation Detection

The space-based missile warning capability supports the North American Aerospace Defense Command (NORAD) in its mission to warn national leaders of a missile attack.[67] It relies on space-based sensors like overhead persistent infrared (OPIR) sensors for the initial indication of a missile launch, and on ground-based radar to provide confirmation and follow-on information.[68] Nuclear detonation detection relies on an integrated network of space- and ground-based sensors to provide persistent surveillance of critical regions in

---

[60] JP 3-14, *supra* note 3, at A-1.

[61] *Id.* at A-2.

[62] DoDI 8420.02, *supra* note 59, at 31.

[63] JP 3-14, *supra* note 3, at A-2.

[64] *Id.* at II-6.

[65] *Id.*

[66] *Id.*

[67] *Id.* at II-7.

[68] *Id.*

order to detect nuclear detonations, as well as to inform national leaders of a detonation's location, yield, and height of burst.[69]

Spacelift

Spacelift refers to the ability to launch satellites into space and entails securing access to space through the deployment, sustainment, and reconstitution of satellite constellations.[70] The DoD uses commercial launch services to the maximum extent practical.[71] A key aspect of spacelift operations is federal launch range operations, which provide launch support, prelaunch testing, and launch, as well as planning for spacecraft and launch vehicle recovery services.[72]

Satellite Operations

Satellite operations encompass the operations of the spacecraft itself, colloquially known as the satellite bus, and the payload(s) on the spacecraft. Military satellite operations also include the ground segment that contributes to monitoring and operating DoD satellites and payloads.[73]

Rendezvous and proximity operations (RPO) involve two space objects that are intentionally brought close together.[74] On-orbit servicing (OOS) for inspections, repair, or upgrades to satellites requires RPO capability.[75] In 2017 the Defense Advanced Research Programs Agency (DARPA), a DoD agency whose mission is to pursue and invest in breakthrough technologies for national security, provided the seed money to establish an independent consortium for the execution of rendezvous and servicing operations (CONFERS) program with commercial industry partners.[76] The objective was to address

---

[69] *Id.*

[70] *Id.* at II-8.

[71] *Id.; see* 2020 NSP, *supra* note 1, § 5.3(e)(5) (directing the DoD to provide affordable and timely space access for national security purposes while using commercial space capabilities and services to the maximum practical extent).

[72] JP 3-14, *supra* note 3, at II-8.

[73] *Id.*

[74] *Id.* at II-9.

[75] *Id.*

[76] Ana Saplan, *Consortium for Execution of Rendezvous and Servicing Operations (CONFERS)*, DARPA, https://www.darpa.mil/program/consortium-for-execution-of-rendezvous-and-servicing-operations (last visited Oct. 20, 2021); *About Us*, DARPA, https://www.darpa.mil/about-us/about-darpa (last visited Oct. 20, 2021); *see generally* Dep't Def, Directive, *Defense Advanced Research Projects Agency (DARPA)* (Incorporating Change 1, Sept. 22, 2017), https://irp.fas.org/doddir/dod/d5134_10.pdf.

the lack of technical and safety standards for on-orbit robotic servicing that involve RPO capability. CONFERS released guiding principles for commercial RPO and OOS in 2018.[77] RPO may extend the life of satellites, including military satellites, but it also poses a counterspace threat. RPO activities could be used aggressively to cause physical damage to, steal parts from, or grapple a satellite.

DOD'S SPACE FUNCTIONS

In recent decades, space has had a 'wide-ranging impact on every element of war,' to include the impact of GPS on targeting and guiding troop movements, the impact of satellite communications on controlling remotely piloted aircraft, the impact of weather satellites on route and operations planning, the impact of space-based imagery on target identification, and the impact of overhead persistent infrared reconnaissance satellites on missile warning and battlespace awareness.[78] In doctrinal terms, each of the aforementioned space capabilities contributes to the joint force's ability to perform 'joint functions,' which are defined as a group of tasks and systems (people, organizations, information, and processes) united by a common purpose, and which commanders use to accomplish missions in all domains.[79] The DoD's seven joint functions are command and control; intelligence; fires; movement and maneuver; protection; sustainment; and information.[80]

Command and Control

Command and control (C2) encompasses the exercise of authority and direction by a commander over assigned forces to accomplish a mission.[81] Space

---

[77]   *Guiding Principles for Commercial Rendezvous and Proximity Operations (RPO) and On-Orbit Servicing (OOS)*, CONSORTIUM EXECUTION RENDEZVOUS & PROX. OPS. (Nov. 7, 2018), https://www.satelliteconfers.org/wp-content/uploads/2018/11/CONFERS-Guiding-Principles_7Nov18.pdf.

[78]   Lt. Gen. Ellen Pawlikowski, et al., *Space: Disruptive Challenges, New Opportunities, and New Strategies*, 6 STRATEGIC STUD. Q. 27, 33 (2012), https://www.airuniversity.af.edu/Portals/10/SSQ/documents/Volume-06_Issue-1/Pawlikowski.pdf.

[79]   JP 3-14, *supra* note 3, at II-1.

[80]   *Id.*; *see generally* J. Chiefs of Staff, Joint Publication 3-0, *Joint Operations* (Incorporating Change 1, Oct. 22, 2018), https://www.jcs.mil/Portals/36/Documents/Doctrine/pubs/jp3_0ch1.pdf (discussing the joint functions in Chapter III) [*hereinafter* JP 3-0]; J. Chiefs of Staff, Joint Publication 1, *Doctrine for the Armed Forces of the United State* at I-18 (Incorporating Change 1, July 12, 2017), https://www.jcs.mil/Portals/36/Documents/Doctrine/pubs/jp1_ch1.pdf [*hereinafter* JP 1].

[81]   JP 3-14, *supra* note 3, at II-9.

capabilities play an important role in enabling command and control in every domain. For example, SATCOM enables secure communications, ensuring plans and orders can be conveyed to all forces.[82] PNT enables linkage among command-and-control networks by providing highly accurate timing signals.[83] If these space capabilities are threatened, SSA helps commanders to better understand those threats.[84] Missile warning capabilities allow commanders to know whether an enemy has launched a missile.[85]

Intelligence

Intelligence is distinct from information. 'Information on its own may be of utility to the commander,' according to Joint Publication 2-0, *Joint Intelligence*, 'but when related to other information about the [operating environment] and considered in light of past experience, it gives rise to a new understanding of the information, which may be termed "intelligence."'[86]

Space-based intelligence may come from satellites owned and operated by the intelligence community (IC), as discussed further below, and may also come from commercially owned satellites or from foreign partners.

Fires

Fires is the doctrinal term for the use of weapons and other systems to create specific effects on a target.[87] Space operations support fires in all domains through intelligence, PNT, and communication capabilities.[88] Space-based PNT, for example, enables guided munitions that reduce collateral damage in comparison with non-guided munitions, whereas SATCOM enables communications and reconnaissance data.[89] In the space domain, the fires function includes space control operations that may create a desired effect on an enemy space system, thereby providing the possibility of deterring threats or deescalating a crisis.[90]

---

[82] *Id.*

[83] *Id.* at II-10.

[84] *Id.* at II-9.

[85] *Id.* at II-10.

[86] J. Chiefs of Staff, Joint Publication 2-0, *Joint Intelligence* at I-1 (Oct. 22, 2013), https://www.jcs.mil/Portals/36/Documents/Doctrine/pubs/jp2_0.pdf [*hereinafter* JP 2-0].

[87] *Id.* at II-13.

[88] *Id.* at II-14.

[89] *Id.*

[90] *Id.* at II-13.

Movement and Maneuver

The movement-and-maneuver function includes moving or deploying forces to gain positional advantages.[91] Space capabilities enable movement and maneuver in terrestrial operations. For example, PNT enables navigation, SATCOM enables communications while on the move, and environmental monitoring allows commanders to consider advantageous or adverse weather conditions when making decisions and planning routes.[92] Satellites can be moved to take advantage of differing orbital characteristics. In addition, space launch is considered a form of movement because of the role it plays in deploying, sustaining, and reconstituting satellite constellations in support of operations.[93] Movement and maneuver in the link segment includes methods such as frequency hopping along the electromagnetic spectrum or shifting users to other satellites.[94] In the ground segment, it includes using deployable mobile systems or backup locations to ensure redundancy if primary ground segments become disabled.[95]

Protection, Sustainment, and Information

The protection function entails protection of space operations to ensure space systems perform as designed and the use of space operations to protect joint operations in all domains.[96]

The sustainment function is the provision of logistics and services required to maintain and prolong operations.[97] Space operations are sustained through spacelift, satellite operations, force reconstitution through the repositioning or augmentation of satellites, and support to human spaceflight.[98] Space operations and the information function are 'mutually reinforcing.'[99] Space enables the delivery of information through, for example, satellite communications, whereas the use of information supports space capabilities such as space control.[100]

---

[91] *Id.* at II-14.
[92] *Id.* at II-15.
[93] *Id.*
[94] *Id.*
[95] *Id.* at II-15.
[96] *Id.* at II-15–16.
[97] *Id.* at II-17.
[98] *Id.*
[99] *Id.* at II-18.
[100] *Id.*

SPACE ACTORS

U.S. Space Command

Pursuant to the Goldwater Nichols Act of 1986, the military services are responsible for organizing, training, and equipping forces, while organizations established by the president called unified combatant commands are responsible for using those forces to conduct operations.[101] Combatant commands are assigned responsibility over either an area or function.[102] Geographic combatant commands, such as U.S. Central Command (USCENTCOM), are assigned responsibility over a particular geographic area, whereas functional combatant commands, such as USSTRATCOM, have transregional responsibilities and may conduct operations in various geographic areas in coordination with the appropriate geographic combatant command(s).[103]

USSPACECOM conducts DoD space operations. USSPACECOM delivers combat and combat support capabilities to enable offensive and defensive space operations and space support to joint operations in all domains.[104] A functional command in its first incarnation, USSPACECOM is now a geographic combatant command. Its geographic area of responsibility is defined as 'the area surrounding Earth at altitudes equal to, or greater than, 100 kilometers (54 nautical miles) above mean sea level,' although there is no indication that the U.S. regards this demarcation as defining the delimitation between airspace and outer space for the purposes of international law.[105]

USSPACECOM has two subordinate commands: the Combined Force Space Component Command (CFSCC) and Joint Task Force Space Defense (JTF-SD).[106] CFSCC plans, integrates, conducts, and assesses global space operations in order to deliver combat-relevant space capabilities to other com-

---

[101] Goldwater-Nicholas Department of Defense Reorganization Act of 1986, Pub. L. No. 99-433, 100 Stat. 992 (Oct. 1, 1986).

[102] *See* JP 3-0, *supra* note 80, at IV-5.

[103] JP I, *supra* note 80, at III-7.

[104] 2020 NSP, *supra* note 1, at § 5.3.c.; *see* Frank A. Rose, *Order From Chaos: Re-establishing U.S. Space Command is a Great Idea*, Brookings (Jan. 7, 2019), https://www.brookings.edu/blog/order-from-chaos/2019/01/07/re-establishing-u-s -space-command-is-a-great-idea/. During the period where space operations did not belong to a dedicated command, they were conducted by USSTRATCOM, the functional combatant command that, then and now, also conducts the nuclear mission.

[105] JP 3-14, *supra* note 3, at I-2.

[106] U.S. Space Command, *Organization and Subordinate Commands*, U.S. Space Command Dep't Def, https://www.spacecom.mil/Organization/ (last visited Nov. 6, 2021).

batant commands, coalition partners, and the nation.[107] One of the functions of the CFSCC, which includes the Combined Space Operations Center (CSpOC) located at Vandenberg Space Force Base in California, is to provide SSA services.[108] JTF-SD conducts space superiority operations to deter aggression, defend U.S. and allied interests, and defeat adversaries throughout the continuum of conflict.[109]

Space Force

Until 2019, the Air Force was the lead service performing the role of organizing, training, and equipping forces for the space mission, although other services like the Army also provided space capabilities. With the enactment of the Fiscal Year 2020 National Defense Authorization Act on December 20, 2019, Air Force Space Command was redesignated the U.S. Space Force, thus creating a new military branch.[110] A part of the Department of the Air Force – not unlike the way the Marine Corps is a part of the Department of the Navy – the Space Force is now the primary branch of the U.S. armed services responsible for organizing, training, and equipping forces capable of projecting power in, from, and to space; protecting the freedom of operation in, from, and to the space domain; and enhancing the lethality and effectiveness of the Joint Force.[111] Over time, the DoD plans to consolidate most, if not all, space missions throughout the armed services within the Space Force.[112]

The creation of a space force or space corps as an independent service was not a novel idea, but SPD-4 directed the Secretary of Defense to submit a legislative proposal 'that would establish the United States Space Force as a new armed service within the Department of the Air Force.'[113]

---

[107] *Id.*

[108] *SSA Sharing & Orbital Data Requests (ODR)*, SPACE-TRACK.ORG, https://www.space-track.org/documentation#/odr (last visited Nov. 6, 2021).

[109] *Id.*

[110] National Defense Authorization Act for Fiscal Year 2020, Pub. L. 116-92, §§ 951 *et seq.*, 1333 Stat. 1198 (2019).

[111] 2020 NSP, *supra* note 1, at § 5.3.c.

[112] STEPHEN M. MCCALL, CONG. RESEARCH SERV. IF 11495, DEFENSE PRIMER: THE UNITED STATES SPACE FORCE 1 (2021). Defense agencies, such as NRO, are not currently expected to become part of the Space Force. *See* Theresa Hitchens, *Battle for NRO Takes Shape As Space, Air Force Grapple With Acquisition*, BREAKING DEFENSE (Apr. 22, 2020), https://breakingdefense.com/2020/04/battle-for-nro-takes-shape-as-space-air-forces-grapple-with-acquisition/.

[113] Space Policy Directive 4: Establishment of the United States Space Force, 84 Fed. Reg. 6049 (Feb. 19, 2019) [*hereinafter* SPD-4]; *see also* H.R. Rep. No. 115-200, at § 1601 (2017) (calling for the establishment of a space corps within the Department of the Air Force); HON. DUANE P. ANDREWS ET AL., REPORT OF THE COMMISSION TO ASSESS

Support Agencies

National Reconnaissance Office (NRO)

The NRO is responsible for the development, launch, and operation of satellites and related processing facilities to collect intelligence and information to support governmental needs.[114] The Under Secretary of Defense for Intelligence and Security exercises authority over the Director of the NRO.[115] The NRO is also a member of the IC and subject to the oversight of the Director of National Intelligence (DNI).[116]

The NRO operates U.S. reconnaissance satellites, which are important for collecting intelligence such as geospatial intelligence (GEOINT) and measurement and signature intelligence (MASINT).[117] NRO space capabilities support activities such as missile warning, monitoring of arms control agreements (hence, NRO satellites are often referred to as 'national technical means' satellites, derived from references in arms control agreements to national technical means of verification), access to denied areas, and the planning and execution of military operations.[118]

National Geospatial Intelligence Agency (NGA)

The NGA is a defense agency and a member of the IC.[119] Its missions include providing geospatial intelligence to the Department of Defense in support of national security objectives, supporting safety of navigation through the provision of geospatial information, and supporting the geospatial intelligence

---

UNITED STATES NATIONAL SECURITY SPACE MANAGEMENT AND ORGANIZATION 81 (Jan. 11, 2001) (recommending the eventual creation of a space corps within the Department of the Air Force).

[114] Dep't Def., Directive 5105.23, *National Reconnaissance Office (NRO)* ¶ 4 (Incorporating Change 1, June 28, 2011) [*hereinafter* DoD 5105.23]; *see also* Dep't Def., Directive 5100.01, *Functions of the Department of Defense and Its Major Components* at Enclosure 7 ¶ 1.7.(d). (Incorporating Change 1, Sept. 17, 2020) [*hereinafter* DoD 5100.01]; JP 3-14, *supra* note 3, at III-6; United States Intelligence Activities, as amended, 3 C.F.R. 1981 Comp., p. 200 § 1.7.(d) (Dec. 4, 1981) [*hereinafter* EO 12333].

[115] DoDD 5105.23, *supra* note 114, at ¶ 5.a.

[116] *Id.*, at ¶ 5.c.; EO 12333, *supra* note 114, at § 1.d.(d).

[117] JP 3-14, *supra* note 3, at A-4; Dep't Def., Instruction 5105.58, *Measurement and Signature Intelligence (MASINT)*, at Enclosure 2 ¶ 5.b (Incorporating Change 2, Sept. 24, 2020).

[118] JP 3-14, *supra* note 3, at III-6.

[119] *Id.* at A-2; 10 U.S.C. § 441(a) (2018); EO 12333, *supra* note 114, at § 1.7.(e); Dep't Def., Directive 5105.60, *National Geospatial Intelligence Agency (NGA)* § 5(a), (b), (e) (July 29, 2009).

(GEOINT) requirements of other federal agencies.[120] GEOINT is defined by statute as 'the exploitation and analysis of imagery and geospatial information to describe, assess, and visually depict physical features and geographically referenced activities on or about the earth. Geospatial intelligence consists of imagery, imagery intelligence, and geospatial information.'[121] These three elements are also defined by statute.[122] NRO imagery satellites are one source of GEOINT. The NRO acquires, launches, and operates the satellites, but the NGA has the statutory responsibility for analyzing and disseminating the images acquired by the NRO satellites.[123]

Defense Intelligence Agency (DIA)

The Defense Intelligence Agency (DIA) is a DoD agency and a part of the IC.[124] The DIA's mission is to 'satisfy the military and military-related intelligence requirements of the Secretary of Defense and Deputy Secretary of Defense, the Chairman of the Joint Chiefs of Staff, and the DNI, and provide the military intelligence contribution to national foreign intelligence and counterintelligence.'[125] This mission includes gathering intelligence of various sources, including human intelligence (HUMINT), measurement and signature intelligence (MASINT), and counterintelligence.[126]

The DIA's space-related functions also include coordinating space-based intelligence collection policies among agencies having responsibilities for those systems.[127] The DIA developed and released in 2019 an unclassified report, *Challenges to Security in Space*, which describes adversary capabilities that pose an increasing threat to the free use of space.[128]

The DIA, along with the NGA, also contributes to navigation warfare (NAVWAR). Both are responsible for assessing threats to U.S. and allied PNT

---

[120] 10 U.S.C. § 442(a),(b),(d) (2018); 50 U.S.C. § 3045(a) (2018).

[121] 10 U.S.C. § 467(5) (Supp. II 2021). The definition was amended with the passage of the FY21 NDAA to add 'or about' before the Earth, reinforcing how the NGA's GEOINT mission is not limited to the surface of the Earth. *See* National Defense Authorization Act for Fiscal Year 2021, Pub. L. 116-283, 134 Stat. 4054, § 1621(f)(2) (2021) [*hereinafter* NDA FY21].

[122] 10 U.S.C. § 467(2)–(4) (Supp. II. 2021).

[123] *See* 50 U.S.C. § 3038(b)(2) (2018).

[124] Directive 5100.01, *supra* note 114, at Enclosure 7.1.d.(8).

[125] Dep't Def., Directive 5105.21, *Defense Intelligence Agency* ¶ 4 (Mar. 18, 2008).

[126] *Id.* at ¶¶ 4.1, .2, .5, .6.; JP 3-14, *supra* note 3, at A-3. MASINT is defined as 'information produced by quantitative and qualitative analysis of physical attributes of targets and events to characterize, locate, and identify them.'

[127] JP 3-14, *supra* note 3, at A-3.

[128] Def. Intelligence Agency, Challenges to Security in Space (2019).

and NAVWAR capabilities and for providing intelligence to the military in support of NAVWAR capabilities.[129]

National Security Agency (NSA)

The National Security Agency/Central Security Service (NSA/CSS) is a unified organization structured to provide for the signals intelligence (SIGINT) mission of the U.S. and to ensure the protection of national security systems for all departments and agencies of the U.S. government.[130] The NSA/CSS is a defense agency, a designated combat support agency, and a member of the IC.[131] SIGINT is intelligence produced by exploiting foreign communications systems and noncommunications emitters.[132] SIGINT that identifies an activity of interest can be used to cue GEOINT sensors to target a particular location to confirm that activity. Conversely, GEOINT can detect changes that can cue SIGINT collections against new targets.[133]

National Air and Space Intelligence Center (NASIC)

The National Air and Space Intelligence Center (NASIC) is an Air Force field operating agency (FOA) subordinate to the Air Force Deputy Chief of Staff for Intelligence, Surveillance, Reconnaissance and Cyber Effects Operations (AF/A2/6).[134] The NASIC's mission is to 'create integrated predictive intelligence in the Air, Space, and Cyberspace domains.'[135] Among its responsibilities are to serve as a 'National Planning & Direction, Collection, Processing & Exploitation, Analysis, and Dissemination node' that collects and analyzes data and information from multiple intelligence sources, including SIGINT, MASINT, and GEOINT.[136] Put another way, the NASIC 'assesses foreign air and space threats' and, in collaboration with other IC elements, functions as an 'all-source intelligence integrator for intelligence relating to suspected purposeful interference and electromagnetic attack' on space systems.[137] Reportedly, the Space Force will establish a dedicated National Space

---

[129] Dep't Def., Instruction 4650.08, *Position, Navigation, and Timing and Navigation Warfare* § 2.8–9 (Incorporating Change 1, Dec. 30, 2020).

[130] JP 2-0, *supra* note 86, at III-3.

[131] DoD 5100.01, *supra* note 114, at Enclosure 7 ¶¶ 1.d.(15), 2; 10 U.S.C. § 193 (2018); EO 12333, *supra* note 114, at § 1.7(c); Dep't Def., Directive 5100.20, *National Security Agency/Central Security Service (NSA/CSS)* ¶¶ 5.4-b., e. (Jan. 26, 2010).

[132] JP 2-0, *supra* note 86, at B-5.

[133] *Id.*

[134] Dep't A.F., Air Force Mission Directive 24, *National Air and Space Intelligence Center (NASIC)* ¶ 1, 2 (Sept. 22, 2016).

[135] *Id.* at ¶ 1.

[136] *Id.* at ¶ 3.3.

[137] JP 3-14, *supra* note 3, at A-5.

Intelligence Center (NSIC) that will be co-located with NASIC and inherit NASIC's space and counterspace mission.[138]

Space Development Agency (SDA)

The Space Development Agency is a DoD agency established by the Secretary of Defense in 2019.[139] Established as an independent agency aligned under the Under Secretary of Defense for Research and Engineering, it is to become part of the Space Force by 2022.[140] Its mission is 'designing and rapidly deploying the National Defense Space Architecture, a threat-driven constellation of small satellites that deliver critical services to our warfighters in space.'[141] The National Defense Space Architecture is a 'resilient military sensing and data transport capability via a proliferated space architecture primarily in Low Earth Orbit.'[142] Put another way, the Space Development Agency plans to develop a constellation of 'hundreds to thousands' of satellites – a proliferated LEO architecture that will enable both resiliency and global persistence – with the ability to detect, track, and calculate a 'fire control solution' for targets like mobile missile launchers, ships, and hypersonic glide vehicles.[143]

---

[138] Scott Maucion, *As New Member of IC, Space Force is Looking for a Clearer Picture of Orbit and Beyond*, FED. NEWS NETWORK (Jan. 2, 2021), https://federalnewsnetwork.com/defense-main/2021/01/as-new-member-of-ic-space-force-is-looking-for-a-clearer-picture-of-orbit-and-beyond/; Thomas Gnau, *General Confirm Wright-Patt Will Get Space Intelligence Center*, DAYTON DAILY NEWS (Nov. 18, 2020), https://www.daytondailynews.com/news/breaking-general-confirms-wright-patt-will-get-space-intelligence-center/UNCL7VKPABAULPOBRJSVX4YZPI/.

[139] DoD 5100.01, *supra* note 114, at Enclosure 7 ¶ 1.d.(20).

[140] Sec'y Def., Memorandum, Establishment of the Space Development Agency (Mar. 12, 2019); *see* NDA FY21, *supra* note 121, at § 1601(d) (directing the Secretary of the Air Force to transfer the Space Development Agency from the Office of the Secretary of Defense to the Space Force effective October 1, 2022).

[141] *What Does SDA Do?* in *Frequently Asked Questions*, SPACE DEV. AGENCY, https://www.sda.mil/home/about-us/faq/ (last visited Nov. 7, 2021).

[142] *About Us*, SPACE DEV. AGENCY, https://www.sda.mil/home/about-us/ (last visited Nov. 7, 2021).

[143] *Id.*; Dr. Derek Tournear, Director, Space Development Agency, Keynote Address at the SmallSat Symposium (Feb. 11, 2021), https://www.sda.mil/direct-from-smallsat-symposium-dr-derek-m-tournear-director-space-development-agency-keynote-address/.

POLICIES

2021 Interim National Security Strategy

Shortly after taking office, President Biden issued interim national security strategic guidance that included brief references to outer space, to include the direction that '[w]e will explore and use outer space to the benefit of humanity, and ensure the safety, stability, and security of outer space activities.' In addition, it states, '[w]e will lead in promoting shared norms and forge new agreements on emerging technologies, space, cyberspace, health and biological threats, climate and the environment.'[144]

2020 National Space Policy

The 2020 National Space Policy (NSP) was issued on December 9, 2020, superseding the 2010 National Space Policy.[145] It expressly listed the current applicable national space policy documents, some of which are described further in this section.[146]

According to the 2020 NSP, the U.S:

> considers the space systems of all nations to have the right to pass through and conduct operations in space without interference. Purposeful interference with space systems, including supporting infrastructure, will be considered an infringement of a nation's rights.[147]

This assertion reiterates similar or identical assertions expressed in numerous previous National Space Policies.[148] The U.S. does not elaborate on what

---

[144] JOSEPH R. BIDEN JR., PRESIDENT, RENEWING AMERICA'S ADVANTAGES: INTERIM NATIONAL SECURITY STRATEGIC GUIDANCE 17-8 (Mar. 2021), https://www.whitehouse.gov/wp-content/uploads/2021/03/NSC-1v2.pdf.

[145] 2020 NSP, *supra* note 1.

[146] *Id.* at § 1.

[147] *Id.* at § 2.6.

[148] *See* Presidential Directive/NSC-37: National Space Policy ¶ 1(d) (May 11, 1978), https://aerospace.csis.org/wp-content/uploads/2019/02/PD-NSC-37-Carter -National-Space-Policy-11-May-1978-Redacted.pdf ('Purposeful interference with operational space systems shall be viewed as an infringement upon sovereign rights'); National Security Decision Directive No. 42: National Space Policy ¶ I(2)(d) (July 4, 1982), https://aerospace.csis.org/wp-content/uploads/2019/02/NSDD-42-Reagan -National-Space-Policy.pdf ('Purposeful interference with space systems shall be viewed as infringement upon sovereign rights'); NASA Historical Ref. Collection, File No. 012605, National Space Policy Directive 1: National Space Policy, at 'Goals and Principles' (Nov. 2,1989) ('Purposeful interference with space systems shall be

'rights' may be violated by purposeful interference in this or other policies, but the context suggests it may be Article I of the 1967 Outer Space Treaty.[149]

The 2020 NSP includes guidelines for each of the three space sectors: the civil sector, the commercial sector, and the national security sector. The national security sector guidelines emphasize the importance of synchronicity between the DoD and the IC and assigns responsibilities for them to pursue cooperatively, including the promotion of norms of behavior for responsible space activities in coordination with the Secretary of State.[150]

Space Policy Directives

In 2017, the National Space Council was revived, which had been established in 1989 but became dormant after 1993.[151] The National Space Council issued several Space Policy Directives (SPD). Of these, SPD-2, SPD-3, SPD-4, and SPD-7 have notable impact on DoD space operations.[152]

Space Policy Directive-2, *Streamlining Regulations on Commercial Use of Space*, directed a review of the Federal Aviation Administration (FAA) launch and reentry licensing regulations and NOAA's remote-sensing regulations to promote economic growth, protect national security, and encourage American leadership in space commerce.[153] The FAA issued final, revised regulations in December 2020[154] and NOAA issued a revised rule in May 2020.[155]

---

viewed as an infringement on sovereign rights); *2006 NSP*, at 'Introduction', para 3 ('Purposeful interference with space systems shall be viewed as an infringement on sovereign rights').

[149] Treaty on Principles Governing the Activities of States in the Exploration and Use of Outer Space, Including the Moon and Other Celestial Bodies, *opened for signature* Jan. 27, 1967, 610 U.N.T.S. 205., T.I.A.S. No. 6347, Art. I. (declaring outer space 'shall be free for exploration and use by all States.')

[150] 2020 NSP, *supra* note 1, at § 5.3.(d).ii.8.

[151] Reviving the National Space Council, 82 Fed. Reg. 31429 (June 30, 2017); Establishing the National Space Council, 54 Fed. Reg. 17691 (Apr. 20, 1989). *See* DANIEL MORGAN, CONG. RESEARCH SERV. REPORT R44712, THE NATIONAL SPACE COUNCIL (Dec. 12, 2016) (providing some history of the National Space Council).

[152] The Space Policy Directives are available online at https://www.space.commerce .gov/policy/.

[153] Space Policy Directive 2: Streamlining Regulations on Commercial Use of Space, 83 Fed. Reg. 24901 (May 24, 2018) [hereinafter SPD-2]; Land Remote Sensing Act of 1992, 51 U.S.C. 60101 *et seq.* (2018).

[154] Streamlined Launch and Reentry License Requirements, 85 Fed. Reg. 79566 (Dec. 10, 2020) (to be codified in scattered sections of 14 C.F.R.).

[155] Licensing of Private Remote Sensing Space Systems, 85 Fed. Reg. 30790 (May 20, 2020) (to be codified at 15 C.F.R. Part 960).

Space Policy Directive-3, *National Space Traffic Management Policy*, endeavored to contribute to the ability of the U.S. to 'enhance safety and ensure continued leadership, preeminence, and freedom of action in space.'[156] SPD-3 directed that the DOD be relieved of some of the burden of providing SSA data to the public by moving that responsibility to the Department of Commerce.[157]

Space Policy Directive-4, *Establishment of the United States Space Force*, provided for the establishment of the Space Force by the end of 2019.[158] SPD-4 also devoted a section to the relationship between the DoD and IC, calling for mechanisms to enhance collaboration 'to increase unity of effort and the effectiveness of space operations.'[159]

Space Policy Directive-7, *United States Space-Based Position, Navigation, and Timing Policy*, was issued after the 2020 National Space Policy.[160] Among other things, SPD-7 directs the Secretary of Defense to develop and modernize GPS; encourage the use of GPS national security services by allied military forces to facilitate interoperability between U.S. and allied forces and capabilities; and maintain the commitment to discontinue the use of Selective Availability.[161]

The 2018 National Space Strategy

The National Space Strategy, issued on March 23, 2018, is publicly available only as a factsheet issued by the White House.[162] This strategy 'recognizes that our competitors and adversaries have turned space into a warfighting domain' and 'affirms that any harmful interference with or attack upon critical components of our space architecture [...] will be met with a deliberate response at a time, place, manner, and domain of our choosing.'[163] The 2020 National Space Policy affirmed that the 2018 National Space Strategy remains current.

---

[156] SPD-3, *supra* note 29, at § 1.

[157] *Id.* at § 5.a.(ii).

[158] SPD-4, *supra* note 133.

[159] *Id.* at § 8.

[160] SPD-7, *supra* note 46.

[161] *Id.* § 7.

[162] EXEC. OFFICE OF THE PRESIDENT, FACT SHEETS, PRESIDENT DONALD J. TRUMP IS UNVEILING AN AMERICA FIRST NATIONAL SPACE STRATEGY (Mar. 23, 2018).

[163] *Id.*

The 2018 National Defense Strategy

The DoD's 2018 National Defense Strategy has become well known for reorienting national defense priorities for the 'reemergence of long-term strategic competition' by 'revisionist powers.'[164] Its broad scope does not focus on space except to observe that both space and cyberspace are 'warfighting domains' and the DoD 'will prioritize investments in resilience, reconstitution, and operations to assure our space capabilities.'[165]

The 2020 Defense Space Strategy

The 2020 Defense Space Strategy (DSS) declares 'Space is a domain that has reemerged as a central arena of great power competition, primarily with China and Russia,' and 'China and Russia have weaponized space as a way to deter and counter a possible U.S. intervention during a regional military conflict.'[166] It is notable for introducing a concept of spacepower that incorporates the civil and commercial sector in addition to the national security sector. Spacepower, it says, is 'the sum of a nation's capabilities to leverage space for diplomatic, information, military, and economic activities in peace or war in order to attain national objectives.'[167]

Space Force Space Capstone Publication

Following the release of the 2020 DSS and its new conception of spacepower, the Space Force released its inaugural Space Capstone Publication, *Spacepower* (SCP).[168] *Spacepower* identifies national spacepower and military spacepower as distinct concepts. National spacepower is 'the totality of a nation's ability to exploit the space domain in pursuit of prosperity and security.'[169] It is 'comparatively assessed as the relative strength of a state's ability to leverage the space domain for diplomatic, informational, military,

---

[164] DEP'T DEF., SUMMARY OF THE 2018 NATIONAL DEFENSE STRATEGY OF THE UNITED STATES OF AMERICA: SHARPENING THE AMERICAN MILITARY'S COMPETITIVE EDGE 2 (2018), https://dod.defense.gov/Portals/1/Documents/pubs/2018-National -Defense-Strategy-Summary.pdf.

[165] *Id.* at 6.

[166] DEP'T DEF., DEFENSE SPACE STRATEGY SUMMARY 3 (June, 2020), https:// media.defense.gov/2020/Jun/17/2002317391/-1/-1/1/2020_DEFENSE_SPACE _STRATEGY_SUMMARY.PDF.

[167] *Id.* at 2.

[168] U.S. SPACE FORCE, SPACEPOWER: DOCTRINE FOR SPACE FORCES (Space Capstone Pub., June 2020).

[169] *Id.* at xii.

and economic purposes.'[170] Military spacepower is 'the ability to accomplish strategic and military objectives through the control and exploitation of the space domain.'[171] According to *Spacepower*, the three cornerstone responsibilities of military space operations are to:

- preserve freedom of action in space;
- strengthen and transform the effectiveness of the joint force; and
- provide U.S. national leadership with independent options capable of achieving strategic effects.[172]

QUESTIONS FOR REVIEW

1. What are offensive and defensive space control operations? Regarding the latter, what is the difference between active and passive? Can you give examples?
2. How has space technology changed the way war is waged on the ground for the U.S.?
3. The Space Force is commonly seen as the 'face' of space security affairs, but it is not the only domestic space actor in the security domain. What others are there and what are their relationships with the Space Force?
4. Although different, space safety and security often overlap. What are the differences between the two, and what are examples of collaboration between civilian agencies and the DoD to serve national security purposes? Do these collaborations exist to serve non-national-security-related objectives?
5. What are the DoD's space functions and how do they aid in achieving the cornerstone responsibilities of military space operations?

---

[170] *Id.* at 13.
[171] *Id.* at 21.
[172] *Id.* at 28.

11. Additional USG agencies involved in spaceflight activities

Ruth is feeling so grateful for the good weather they have been having in D.C. this week. As she runs along the Rock Creek trail, she starts thinking about the day ahead. The international client that submitted a bid for a NASA contract was pleased with the firm's work and asked them to continue advising on their U.S.-based operations. The partner told her that the client finds the myriad of agencies that intervene in space matters so confusing that they would like a memo outlining the roles of the different U.S. agencies involved with regulating space activities.

Ruth agrees with the client – there are a lot of cooks in the proverbial kitchen. If all goes well and no other client calls with an unexpected crisis or urgency, she'll finalize and send the memo by the end of the day.

INTRODUCTION

This chapter examines four U.S. government agencies – the Department of State, U.S. Coast Guard, U.S. Geological Survey, and Department of Energy – that are involved with U.S. governmental and commercial space activities. While these agencies are not primarily responsible for overseeing U.S. space activities, they play important and different roles.

DEPARTMENT OF STATE

The U.S. State Department (State) is the department of the executive branch with responsibility for U.S. foreign policy and international relations. The Secretary of State is the adviser to the president on foreign affairs. State exercises the Constitutional Article II 'foreign affairs' power of the executive branch. As with the many policy issues within its purview, State has two major concentrations related to space: (1) the peaceful uses of outer space; and (2) space security. The two pertinent bureaus focused on these issues are the Bureau of Oceans and International Environmental and Scientific Affairs (OES) and the Bureau of Arms Control, Verification and Compliance (AVC).

Bureau of Oceans and International Environmental and Scientific Affairs

OES is responsible for 'carr[ying] out diplomatic and public diplomacy efforts to strengthen American leadership in space exploration, applications, and commercialization by increasing understanding of, and support for, U.S. national space policies and programs.'[1] OES represents the U.S. in various international fora to promote and negotiate outcomes that are consistent with U.S. interests. It leads the U.S. delegation to the United Nations Committee on the Peaceful Uses of Outer Space (COPUOS).

OES also encourages foreign entities to purchase and utilize U.S. space capabilities, systems, and services.[2] In carrying out that function, OES supports bilateral and multilateral cooperation in civil and commercial space and high-technology activities, including supporting the International Space Station, as well as collaboration in global navigation satellite systems such as GPS, the International Thermonuclear Experimental Reactor (ITER), and nanotechnology. Policy issues in which OES provides its perspective include remote sensing, space traffic management, space weather, orbital debris, and the use of nuclear power sources in space.[3]

While it is not a regulatory agency, OES, together with State's Office of the Legal Adviser, also participates in interagency reviews involving U.S. foreign policy interests and international treaty obligations. State participates with other USG agencies in reviewing launch licenses and other U.S. commercial space activities as well as interagency reviews related to regulatory revisions, and national policy directives.

For example, in accordance with the Commercial Space Launch Act (CSLA), '[t]he FAA reviews a license application to determine whether it presents any issues affecting U.S. national security or foreign policy interests, or international obligations of the United States.'[4]

A U.S. spaceflight entity might also seek support from State regarding recovery of personnel or hardware from a spacecraft that returns to Earth on foreign soil or at sea. When such an instance occurs, OES may provide coor-

---

[1]   *Office of Space Affairs*, Department of State [hereinafter State], (last visited July 26, 2021), https://www.state.gov/bureaus-offices/under-secretary-for-economic-growth-energy-and-the-environment/bureau-of-oceans-and-international-environmental-and-scientific-affairs/office-of-space-affairs/.

[2]   *Id.*

[3]   *Kenneth Hodgkins*, Wilson Center (last visited July 26, 2021), https://www.wilsoncenter.org/person/kenneth-hodgkins

[4]   The FAA licensing regime, including the interagency review, is elaborated further in Chapter 7.

dination with the foreign government. The U.S. spaceflight entity provides information to support State's diplomatic efforts as it coordinates with the foreign government regarding where the personnel or hardware are located.

PRACTICE TIP

A commercial entity submitting a launch license or payload review that involves a new or unique activity should consider engaging directly with State to provide information ahead of the official, FAA-run interagency review.

Those efforts align with obligations under the Agreement on the Rescue of Astronauts, the Return of Astronauts and the Return of Objects Launched into Outer Space (the 'Rescue Agreement')[5] as well as the Convention on International Liability for Damage Caused by Space Objects (the 'Liability Convention'). For example, the Rescue Agreement generally provides that if personnel of a spacecraft land in another State's territory, that State Party must 'immediately take all possible steps to rescue them and render them all necessary assistance.'[6] When U.S. space objects are discovered on foreign soil, State will similarly coordinate requests for assistance in recovering those items. Should space objects cause damage that is subject the Liability Convention, State would get involved in resolving the claim.

State also supported NASA in concluding the Artemis Accords to facilitate international partnerships in pursuit of U.S. foreign policy interests.

Office of Emerging Security Challenges

The State Department's Office of Emerging Security Challenges (ESC) within the Bureau of Arms Control, Verification and Compliance (AVC) leads the development of positions to enhance space security. It is one of seven offices within AVC. The other office that engages in space issues is the Office of Multilateral and Nuclear Affairs, which leads policy efforts to develop, negotiate, and implement nuclear arms control and disarmament agreements and commitments, including ongoing engagement with UN-related disarmament. The State Department characterizes AVC's role as building 'cooperation among allies and partners in order to control the threat posed by weapons of

---

[5]   Agreement on the Rescue of Astronauts, the Return of Astronauts, and the Return of Objects Launched into Outer Space [*hereinafter* Rescue Agreement] (1968), 672 U.N.T.S. 119; 19 U.S.T. 7570; 7 I.L.M. 149 (1968), art. 2.

[6]   *Id.*, Article 2.

mass destruction, their means of delivery, space and cyber capabilities, and conventional weapons.'[7]

Directorate of Defense Trade Controls

The State Department's Directorate of Defense Trade Controls' (DDTC) mission is to '[Ensure] commercial exports of defense articles and defense services advance U.S. national security and foreign policy objectives'[8] in accordance with the Arms Export Control Act[9] and Executive Order 13637.[10] To that end, the DDTC implements the International Traffic in Arms Regulations (ITAR),[11] including the United States Munitions List (USML),[12] to oversee the export and temporary import of defense articles and services. Commercial space companies (and USG agencies) must comply with the ITAR or face significant repercussions for violations, including civil and criminal penalties.

U.S. GEOLOGICAL SURVEY

The U.S. Geological Survey (USGS) is required by the federal government to provide and archive remotely sensed data such as Landsat imagery. Since 1972, the Landsat series of Earth observation satellites have been imaging Earth's land surface. As discussed in Chapter 8, Landsat is a joint effort between NASA and the USGS to provide information to inform research and decision-making focused on natural resources and the environment.

The National Space Policy of 2020 directs the Secretary of the Interior, through the Director of the USGS, to conduct research on Earth's 'land, land cover, and inland surface waters, and manage a national global land surface

---

[7] *Bureau of Arms Control, Verification and Compliance*, State (last visited July 26, 2021), https://www.state.gov/bureaus-offices/under-secretary-for-arms-control-and-international-security-affairs/bureau-of-arms-control-verification-and-compliance/.

[8] The Directorate of Defense Trade Controls (DDTC), State (last visited July 26, 2021), https://www.pmddtc.state.gov/ddtc_public?id=ddtc_public_portal_about_us_landing.

[9] 22 U.S.C. § 2778.

[10] Exec. Order No. 13637, 3 C.F.R. 13637 (Mar. 8, 2013).

[11] 22 C.F.R. §§ 120–130.

[12] The USML is Part 121 of the ITAR and consists of 'articles, services, and related data that are designated as defense articles or defense services pursuant to sections 38 and 47(7) of the Arms Export Control Act.' *See, Understand the ITAR and Export Controls*, State (last visited July 26, 2021), https://www.pmddtc.state.gov/ddtc_public?id=ddtc_public_portal_itar_landing.

data archive and its distribution.'[13] In undertaking that research and archive management, the USGS is mandated to enhance land surface observations from space by utilizing international and commercial partnerships as well as relevant remote-sensing information[14] that can appropriately be obtained from national security space systems.[15]

U.S. COAST GUARD

The U.S. Coast Guard supports commercial and government space launch and reentry activities by issuing notice to mariners[16] (NOTMAR) to protect the public. Commercial space vehicle operators are required to coordinate with the Coast Guard to receive a license from the FAA.[17] The USCG also provides security at sea for U.S. governmental launches and landings of crewed missions to space. The USCG warns boaters who find themselves on the water to stay back if they find themselves near a space operation. USCG will at times restrict vessel movement in sensitive areas to protect responders, astronauts, and the space vehicle itself.

Additionally, if a launch or reentry operator is using a maritime vessel to support its operations (i.e., for launch, landing or recovery), the vessel and operations are subject to USCG regulations in Title 46 of the Code of Federal Regulations.

USCG authorities may be relevant to future U.S. space policies,[18] including the Coast Guard's broad search and rescue authority[19] as well as the mariner's

---

[13] National Space Policy of the United States of America, Dec. 9, 2020, p. 26, https://trumpwhitehouse.archives.gov/wp-content/uploads/2020/12/National-Space -Policy.pdf.

[14] Regulation of commercial remote-sensing systems is addressed in Chapter 8.

[15] Coordination is required with the Secretary of Defense and Director of National Intelligence, as are other measures, in order to utilize information from national security space systems. *See, supra* note 16.

[16] Notices to mariners provide timely marine safety information (such as a pending rocket launch or spacecraft return in a particular area) as well as the correction of navigation charts, to ensure the safety of life at sea. *See, Maritime Safety Information*, National Geospatial-Intelligence Agency (last visited July 26, 2021), https://msi.nga .mil/NTM.

[17] Further details regarding FAA licensees' coordination with the USCG to secure launch licenses, as well as the issuance of NOTMARs, are addressed in Chapter 7.

[18] Michael Sinclair, *The Future of the U.S. Coast Guard is in Outer Space*, The Brookings Institution (Oct. 15, 2020), https://www.brookings.edu/blog/order-from -chaos/2020/10/15/the-future-of-the-u-s-coast-guard-is-in-outer-space/.

[19] 14 U.S.C. § 521(b): 'The Coast Guard may render aid to individuals and protect and save property at any time and at any place at which Coast Guard facilities and personnel are available and can be effectively utilized.'

affirmative legal duty to render assistance.[20] Those policies align with the U.S. commitments under the Outer Space Treaty and the Rescue Agreement and could prove increasingly relevant.

DEPARTMENT OF ENERGY

The Department of Energy's (DOE) Office of Nuclear Energy is responsible for 'maintaining the infrastructure to develop, manufacture, test, analyze, and deliver' the systems that provide the power for deep space exploration (DSE) spacecraft, such as Cassini and Voyager.[21] These systems, called radioisotope power systems (RPSs), work by converting the heat from decaying plutonium-238 into electricity.[22]

For space activities, the DOE can provide two types of system: ones that provide electricity, such as radioisotope thermoelectric generators (RTGs), and others that are small heat sources called radioisotope heater units (RHUs), which keep spacecraft warm in harsh, cold environments.[23] The advantage of RPSs is that they can work in the harshest conditions in space *for decades* and have numerous advantages over other satellite power sources. RPSs 'are ideal for missions where distance from the sun, extreme closeness to the sun, or sheer duration make other power sources, such as solar panels, untenable. Furthermore, the heat from natural radioactive decay can also be harnessed in its own right to protect instruments from the extreme cold of deep space....'[24]

Space Policy Directive-6 (SPD 6), on the National Strategy for Space Nuclear Power and Propulsion, was issued on the basis that the ability to use space nuclear power and propulsion (SNPP) 'safely, securely, and sustainably is vital to maintaining and advancing [U.S.] dominance and strategic leadership in space.'[25] SPD 6 defined SNPP to 'include [RPSs] and fission reactors

---

[20]   46 U.S.C. § 2304(a)(1): 'A master or individual in charge of a vessel shall render assistance to any individual found at sea in danger of being lost, so far as the master or individual in charge can do so without serious danger to the master's or individual's vessel or individuals on board.'

[21]   *Space and Defense Power Systems*, Office of Nuclear Energy, Department of Energy (last visited July 26, 2021), https://www.energy.gov/ne/nuclear-reactor-technologies/space-power-systems.

[22]   *Id.*

[23]   *See,* Steven A. Mirmina and David J. Den Herder, *Nuclear Power Sources and Future Space Exploration,* 6 Chicago J. of Int'l L. 1 (2005), https://chicagounbound.uchicago.edu/cjil/vol6/iss1/11.

[24]   *Id.*

[25]   Space Pol. Dir. No. 6, 85 Fed. Reg. 82873 (Dec. 16, 2020), https://www.federalregister.gov/documents/2020/12/21/2020-28272/national-strategy-for-space-nuclear-power-and-propulsion. *See also,* Jeff Foust, *White House releases space*

used for power or propulsion in spacecraft, rovers, and other surface elements.'[26] SPD 6 directed the Secretary of Energy to 'support development and use of SNPP systems to enable and achieve the scientific, exploration, national security, and commercial objectives of the United States.'[27]

SPD 6 followed the *Presidential Memorandum on Launch of Spacecraft Containing Space Nuclear Systems*, which established the guidelines and launch authorization process for federal government launches and FAA-licensed commercial launches of nuclear power systems, including SNPP systems.[28] The launch process for the spacecraft containing nuclear systems follows a three-tiered process on: (1) the systems characteristics; (2) the level of potential hazard; and (3) national security considerations.[29] Specifically, a launch will be tiered depending on the level of radioactive quantities and the probability of radiation exposure to the public in the event of an accident during launch or subsequent operation.[30]

QUESTIONS FOR REVIEW

1. Why is the U.S. Coast Guard involved with space activities and how might its involvement increase as commercial spaceflight activities increase?

2. When space vehicle debris is discovered in a foreign country's jurisdiction, what is the State Department's role and what treaty provisions might apply to the situation?

3. Export control is a thorny subject with the ITAR regulations overseen by the Department of State and the Commerce Control List overseen by the Department of Commerce. Do you think export control facilitates the space industry? Why is it difficult to find the appropriate balance between national security and economy?

4. Consider this hypothetical situation: A private U.S. adventure company launches tourists into space; its spacecraft parachutes down safely into U.S. waters, where the tourists are rescued safely and returned to land by

---

nuclear power strategy, SPACENEWS (Dec. 16, 2020), https://spacenews.com/white-house-releases-space-nuclear-power-strategy/.

[26] *Id.*

[27] *Id.*

[28] For a discussion of the historic approach to space nuclear launch approvals for RPS and the recommendations that supported the 2019 Presidential Memorandum and SPD 6, see Reina Buenconsejo, Bhavya Lal, Susannah Howieson, Jonathan Behrens, and Katie Kowal. *Launch Approval Process for the Space Nuclear Power and Propulsion Enterprise*, Institute for Defense Analysis Science & Technology Policy Institute (Sept. 2019).

[29] *Supra* note 31, at § 4.

[30] *Id.* at § 5(a)–(c).

the Coast Guard. Should the USCG send the adventure company a bill for its services? Why or why not? On the one hand, the USG has a preexisting duty to rescue personnel of a spacecraft under the Rescue Agreement; on the other hand, why should the U.S. taxpayer foot the bill for these space tourists to be rescued? Is that some form of subsidization of the adventure company? If so, should that company arrange for its own, private, rescue services for its customers?

PART IV

Substantive legal issues in outer space law

12. Environmental issues in outer space

Avoiding another tragedy of the commons

Thanksgiving is a big deal for Ruth's family. This year she took four consecutive days off. She left her work phone and laptop in the office (gasp!), and it's been absolute bliss. Thanksgiving Day was filled with delicious homecooked food and excellent conversation with her family.

Her family was especially interested in her thoughts on the Russian anti-satellite test earlier that month. They had peppered her with questions like, 'Where will the debris fall? Can they really just blow stuff up in space? What about the stuff that falls back to Earth – is it a safety or environmental risk?'

Ruth awed them with stories about bus-sized Russian rocket debris falling to Earth and the trash left by Apollo astronauts on the Moon. They had no idea that there was a sports car in space or that a fleck of paint in space moves with enough velocity to crack a Space Shuttle windshield.

INTRODUCTION

Numerous environmental issues are implicated by modern space activities, including space debris generation from collisions, discarded stages and dead satellites; ocean pollution from expended launch vehicles and deorbited spacecraft; lunar surface pollution; and potential contaminates being carried from or to Earth. This chapter will provide a brief overview of principles of international environmental law that apply in outer space followed by an examination of various environmental issues arising from space activities.

INTERNATIONAL ENVIRONMENTAL LAW

International environmental law (IEL) is generally accepted as originating in Trail, Canada, a small, smelting town. The details of the 1941 *Trail Smelter* arbitration are a fascinating read in their own right,[1] but, in short, a private

---

[1]   Jaye Ellis, *Has International Law Outgrown Trail Smelter?*, in *Transboundary Harm in International Law: Lessons from the Trail Smelter Arbitration*, eds. Rebecca Bratspies & Russell Miller, Cambridge U. Press, at 56–65 (2006).

company in Canada smelting lead and zinc was producing thousands of tons of airborne sulfur pollution monthly. Originally, it utilized 150-foot-tall smokestacks to disperse the pollution. After Canadian farmers in the area complained, the smelter installed smokestacks 409 feet tall,[2] pushing the pollution higher up into the atmosphere. While this was welcomed by the neighboring farmers, it allowed the air pollution to drift across the Canadian border to pollute farms and cause damage in Washington state. In the resulting international arbitration, the Canadian government accepted responsibility for the actions of its private entity and provided U.S. farmers with compensation.

There are a few takeaways from *Trail Smelter*. First, it may be the first time that air pollution was ever determined by an international tribunal to be a compensable cause of damages. At that time, it did not violate international law to create air pollution. Second, *Trail Smelter* may be the first time that the *polluter pays principle* was applied internationally. Finally, and most importantly, the arbitral decision incorporated into modern international law the Roman law principle of *sic utere tuo ut alienum non laedas*.[3] In the context of international relations, it means that one nation's sovereign right to use its territory however it pleases is limited by the obligation not to cause harm to another nation or to areas beyond the limits of national jurisdiction.

The key principles of IEL are applicable to outer space in several ways. First, Article III of the Outer Space Treaty (OST) provides that 'States Parties to the Treaty shall carry on activities in the exploration and use of outer space, [...] in accordance with international law.' As IEL is part of international law, States Parties to the OST are obliged to observe it in their exploration and use of outer space. Another fundamental principle of IEL is that States should not cause damage beyond their borders.[4] Other principles of IEL may also be

---

[2]   Bratspies, *Id.* at James Allum, *An Outcrop of Hell': History, Environment, and the Politics of the Trail Smelter Dispute.*

[3]   You can use your property only insofar as it does not injure another. Note the implicit (new) limitation on a State's sovereignty.

[4]   Principle 21 of the 1972 Stockholm Declaration provides that 'States have in accordance with the Charter of the United Nations and the principles of international law, the sovereign right to exploit their own resources pursuant to their own environmental policies, and the responsibility to ensure that activities within their jurisdiction or control do not cause damage to the environment of other States or of areas beyond the limits of national jurisdiction.' Stockholm Declaration on the Human Environment, in *Report of the United Nations Conference on the Human Environment*, UN Doc. A/CONF. 48/14 (1972) [hereinafter Stockholm Declaration]. This principle was restated 30 years later in Principle 2 of the Rio Declaration on Environment and Development, in *Report of the United Nations Conference on Environment and Development*, UN Doc. A/CONF. 151/26 (Vol. 1), Annex I (1992) [hereinafter Rio Declaration], as well as in the GA Res. 37/7, Word Charter for Nature, art. 21(d) (Oct. 28, 1982).

applicable to outer space activities, including the precautionary principle;[5] sustainability;[6] duty of cooperation; common but differentiated responsibilities;[7] and intergenerational and intragenerational equity.[8]

SPACE DEBRIS

Before 1957, there were no human-made objects in space. The U.S.S.R. launched Sputnik 1 on October 4, 1957, and Sputnik 2 on November 3, 1957. Sputnik 1 burned reentering Earth's atmosphere on January 4, 1958, and Sputnik 2 burned up on April 14, 1958, after about 2,500 orbits.[9] Space

---

[5]   'The point of the precautionary principle is to anticipate and avoid environmental damage before it occurs.' Mary Stevens, *The Precautionary Principle in the International Arena*, 2 Sustainable Dev. L. & Policy, at 13–15 (2002). The precautionary principle urges caution when scientific evidence is lacking; while some assert that it hinders progress, others argue that measures with potential for widespread and irreversible damage should not be taken until they have been proved safe. The U.S. sometimes calls this the 'precautionary approach.' It is based on Principle 15 of the Rio Declaration, which states: 'In order to protect the environment, the precautionary approach shall be widely applied by States according to their capabilities. Where there are threats of serious or irreversible damage, lack of full scientific certainty shall not be used as a reason for postponing cost-effective measures to prevent environmental degradation.'

[6]   'The long-term sustainability of outer space activities is defined as the ability to maintain the conduct of space activities indefinitely into the future in a manner that realizes the objectives of equitable access to the benefits of the exploration and use of outer space for peaceful purposes, in order to meet the needs of the present generations while preserving the outer space environment for future generations.' *See*, Guidelines for the Long-term Sustainability of Outer Space Activities, in *Report of the Committee on the Peaceful Uses of Outer Space*, A/74/20, Aug. 20, 2019.

[7]   Common but differentiated responsibilities (CBDR) establishes that all States have some responsibility to address environmental destruction, but some States have a greater responsibility for its origins and greater technological capabilities for its cleanup. CBDR was established formally in Article 3(1) of the United Nations Framework Convention on Climate Change, in *Treaty Series*, Vol. 1771, at 107 (May 9, 1992).

[8]   *See generally*, LOTTA VIIKARI, THE ENVIRONMENTAL ELEMENT IN SPACE LAW: ASSESSING THE PRESENT AND CHARTING THE FUTURE, BRILL NIJHOFF (JUNE 15, 2008); and BROWN WEISS, MAGRAW, ET AL., INTERNATIONAL LAW FOR THE ENVIRONMENT, WEST ACADEMIC PUBLISHING (DEC. 8, 2015). Intergenerational equity refers to preserving the environment for future generations. *See, inter alia,* STEVEN A. MIRMINA, THE TIME IS ALWAYS RIGHT TO DO WHAT IS RIGHT, 51 GJIL 1, 9 AT FN 34 (2019).

[9]   For its part, the U.S. attempted to launch a satellite on December 6, 1957, which exploded when its fuel tanks ruptured, damaging both the satellite and the launch pad. The U.S. successfully launched its first satellite (Explorer 1) on January 31, 1958, about six months before the creation of NASA on July 29 of that year.

debris challenges are a cost of the many benefits arising from human-derived activities in space.

While it must be acknowledged that some creation of space debris is inevitable in outer space operations, in the first few decades of space exploration, satellites were designed with little thought given to the creation of space debris. Historically, satellite operators have abandoned spacecraft parts in orbit and have caused both operational and fragmentation debris.[10] Some of those objects have included lens covers, separation bolts used to lock fixtures in place, auxiliary motors, various shrouds, and objects merely dropped or discarded during human space missions. Fragmentation debris has numerous causes, including accidents, malfunctions, weapons testing, experimentation,[11] and intentional self-destruction.[12]

---

[10]   President Ronald Reagan's update of the U.S. National Space Policy on 5 January 1988 was the first White House declaration to address specifically the topic of orbital debris and to recognize the need for its mitigation to preserve near-Earth space for future generations. This presidential decree affirmed that 'All space sectors will seek to minimize the creation of space debris. Design and operations of space tests, experiments and systems will strive to minimize or reduce accumulation of space debris consistent with mission requirements and cost effectiveness.' In 1995, the U.S. created an Interagency Report on Orbital Debris, led primarily by the Department of Defense (DOD) and NASA to undertake a comprehensive assessment and survey of the debris issue, and a report was published by Office of Science and Technology Policy, with recommendations to develop guidelines and a strategy for orbital debris mitigation. NASA and the DOD began more focused work with other space agencies around the world to create the Inter-Agency Debris Coordination Committee (IADC), which drafted the technical guidelines that are now observed by space agencies around the world today. For more details on how the IADC's work transformed into the UN Guidelines in effect today, see, STEVEN A. MIRMINA, *THE REGULATION OF ORBITAL DEBRIS THROUGH NATIONAL MEASURERS*, 29 AIR & SPACE L. 2, 137–147 (2004), https://kluwerlawonline .com/journalarticle/Air+and+Space+Law/29.2/AILA2004003.

[11]   For example, the U.S.'s infamous Project West Ford experiment was launched in May 1963. Over the protests of other countries, the U.S. launched 480 million 'needles' into outer space. The U.S. asserted that the needles would disperse in outer space and create a ring around the Earth which the U.S. could use to relay military communications to remote areas. It was an attempt by the U.S. military to mitigate concerns that the Soviets would cut the undersea cables the U.S. relied on to communicate with its forces overseas. Although many of these needles did burn up from solar radiation in a matter of years, even today, in 2021, the NASA orbital debris program office still is aware of dozens of these 'clumps' of needles that failed to disperse correctly. *See*, J.-C. Liou & Debi Shoots, *West Ford Needles – Where Are They Now?*, 17 Orbital Debris Quarterly News 4, NASA (2013), https://orbitaldebris.jsc.nasa.gov/quarterly-news/ pdfs/odqnv17i4.pdf.

[12]   Comm. on Transp. Rsch. and Dev., Nat'l Sci. and Tech. Council, Interagency Report on Orbital Debris, at 3 (1995). The appendix to this report lists the history of

The Danger of Space Debris

Operational satellites and spacecraft often have the ability to avoid debris objects with sufficient warning. Debris larger than ten centimeters, or about the size of a softball, can be detected, monitored, and tracked from the ground, which allows for warnings ahead of possible collisions. However, the chief concern about these objects is that they may further disintegrate and potentially create millions of fragments.[13] Certain types of debris, such as bits of insulation, solid fuel fragments, and paint flakes, are degraded by solar heating and radiation and split into smaller components.

Unfortunately, tiny debris pieces can cause serious damage and pose a risk to human lives in space.[14] 'At orbital velocities, even a fleck of paint is powerful enough to damage a space shuttle. In its first 75 shuttle flights, NASA has replaced 60 cockpit windshields – at $40,000 per window – because of pitting from debris.'[15] In 2016, the ISS cupola was damaged by a piece of debris that the U.S. and ESA concluded was no more than a few thousandths of a millimeter across.[16] As recently as June 2021, *USA Today* reported that the Canadian arm on the ISS, 'the Canadarm-2,' was damaged when hit by orbital debris.[17]

---

on-orbit fragmentations and their probable causes. The latter are diverse and include propulsion or electrical causes, general unknown causes, and deliberate explosions.

[13]   The possibility of space debris colliding with other objects in space, creating a domino effect of ever-increasing numbers of collisions and further debris, is known as the Kessler syndrome. This could eventually create a belt of debris that could make it impossible for any space object to operate in, or even pass through a particular orbit. *See*, FRANCIS LYALL & PAUL B. LARSEN, *SPACE LAW: A TREATISE*, ROUTLEDGE, at 271 (2d ed. 2018).

[14]   Isobel Whitcomb, *How do tiny pieces of space junk cause incredible damage?*, Live Science (Mar. 14, 2021), https://www.livescience.com/tiny-space-junk-damage .html; and Nicholas L. Johnson, *National Research on Space Debris and Impact Hazards*, in presentation to Scientific and Technical Subcommittee (STSC), U.N. Comm. on the Peaceful Uses of Outer Space (COPUOS) (Feb. 2003).

[15]   Robert Lee Hotz, *The Orbiting Junkyard: Shuttle Endeavour's Near Miss With Abandoned Satellite Underscores Dangers of Space Debris*, L.A. Times (Mar. 28, 1996), https://www.latimes.com/archives/la-xpm-1996-03-28-me-52292-story.html.

[16]   Mary Beth Griggs, *Tiny Debris Chipped a Window on the Space Station*, POPULAR SCIENCE (May 12, 2016), https://www.popsci.com/paint-chip-likely-caused -window-damage-on-space-station/.

[17]   Rachael Nail & Christine Fernando, *'Lucky strike': International Space Station's robotic arm survives after being hit by space junk*, USA Today (June 2, 2021), https:// www.usatoday.com/story/news/nation/2021/06/02/iss-hit-space-debris-robotic-arm -canadarm-2-survives-space-junk/7503517002/. 'The [Canadian] space agency said more than 23,000 objects the size of a softball or larger are tracked 24/7 to avoid collisions. Smaller objects, including rock or dust particles and flecks of paint from satellites, are too small to be monitored.'

The greatest cause of space debris has been the intentional destruction of satellites in orbit. In 2007, China used an anti-satellite (ASAT) weapon to destroy one of its own aging weather satellites, Fengyun-1C, creating more than 3,000 pieces of debris larger than a softball that will remain in orbit for hundreds of years.[18] On March 27, 2019, India conducted a similar ASAT test with its 'Mission Shakti.' Like China, India used a kinetic kill vehicle.[19] India's prime minister saw India's ability to shoot down 'a live satellite 300 kilometers away in space, [as] an unprecedented achievement' and 'registered its name as a space power.'[20] In November 2021, Russia conducted its first hit-to-kill test, using a missile to destroy Cosmos 1408, a defunct Soviet satellite creating at least 1,500 trackable pieces of debris in low orbit.[21] The Indian and Russian events created debris that threatened human lives on the International Space Station (ISS). In reaction, NASA administrators respectively characterized the events as 'unacceptable'[22] and 'irresponsible.'[23] The 2021 test was criticized by countries, companies and organizations around the world.[24] These and previous ASAT tests[25] have been the subject of international discussions, including

---

[18]   'But one thing is for sure: the Chinese ASAT test is the largest debris-generating event in Earth orbit ever recorded.' Mark Williams Pontin, *China's Antisatellite Missile Test: Why?*, MIT Tech. Rev. (Mar. 8, 2007), https://www.technologyreview.com/2007/03/08/226350/chinas-antisatellite-missile-test-why/. The authors hope that the global community will eventually make illegal the intentional destruction of satellites creating long-lived debris, such as through the use of ASAT weapons.

[19]   Marco Langbroek, *Why India's ASAT Test Was Reckless*, THE DIPLOMAT.COM (Feb 8, 2020), https://web.archive.org/web/20190506215045/https://thediplomat.com/2019/05/why-indias-asat-test-was-reckless/.

[20]   Sanjeev Miglani & Krishna N. Das, *Modi hails India as military space power after anti-satellite missile test*, REUTERS.COM (Mar. 27, 2019). https://www.reuters.com/article/us-india-satellite/modi-hails-india-as-military-space-power-after-anti-satellite-missile-test-idUSKCN1R80IA.

[21]   Shannon Bugos, *Russian ASAT Test Creates Massive Debris*, ARMS CONTROL ASSOCIATION (December 2021), https://www.armscontrol.org/act/2021-12/news/russian-asat-test-creates-massive-debris.

[22]   *Sarah Lewin, India's Anti-Satellite Test Created Dangerous Debris, NASA Chief says* (Apr. 1, 2019), https://space.com/nasa-chief-condemns-india-anti-satellite-test.html.

[23]   *NASA Administrator Statement on Russian ASAT Test* (Nov. 15, 2021), NASA, https://nasa.gov/press-release/nasa-administrator-statement-on-russian-asat-test.

[24]   Lewin, *supra* note 22.

[25]   It is worth noting that Russia, China and India are not the only countries that have intentionally destroyed satellites in outer space. The U.S. and the U.S.S.R. conducted dozens of ASAT tests going back to the 1950s, with the U.S. conducting military operation 'Burnt Frost' as recently as February 2008. *See generally*, David Koplow, *ASAT-isfaction: Customary International Law and the Regulation of Anti-Satellite Weapons*, 30 MICH. J. INT'L L. 1187, 1208–11 (2008–2009). For more information on ASATs, see Chapter 13.

at the UN-supported Group of Government Experts (GGE), which attempted to create a report on practical measures to prevent a space arms race.[26]

In addition to posing a threat to humans and spacecraft in space, orbital debris poses a threat to humans and property on Earth and in Earth's atmosphere. The likelihood of a serious impact is mathematically low, but the consequences could be high. On average, orbital debris enters and burns up in the Earth's atmosphere on a daily basis. Most parts of the space object cannot survive the intense heat of reentry, which has increasingly been by design.[27] Components that do survive are most likely to land either in oceans and other bodies of water or in remote or thinly populated areas due to Earth's natural makeup.[28] As the number of objects launched to orbit increases, continued efforts to mitigate the proliferation of space debris are necessary to protect humans as well as national and commercial assets in space.

Mitigating Space Debris

In 2001, the U.S. Government issued a set of Orbital Debris Mitigation Standard Practices (ODMSP) to 'limit the generation of new, long-lived debris by the control of debris released during normal operations, minimizing debris generated by accidental explosions, the selection of safe flight profile and operational configuration to minimize accidental collisions, and post mission disposal of space structures.'[29] In 2018, Space Policy Directive 3 (SPD-3) called for updating the ODMSP to address '[r]apid international expansion of space operations and greater diversity of missions.'[30] To facilitate consistency across USG agencies involved in space activities, SPD-3 called for NASA to coordinate updates with the Departments of State, Defense, Commerce, and

---

[26]   Brian Weeden & Victoria Samson, *Op-ed: India's ASAT test is wake-up call for norms of behavior in space*, SPACE NEWS (Apr. 8, 2019), https://spacenews.com/op-ed-indias-asat-test-is-wake-up-call-for-norms-of-behavior-in-space/.

[27]   As materials technology has improved and operators increasingly consider end-of-life plans during designing spacecraft, there has been an increase in a phenomenon called 'design for demise.' Design-for-demise is the intent to fabricate a spacecraft that will completely burn up upon reentry, thereby reducing the risk of damages or human casualties.

[28]   The Earth is 71% water, and its land masses include large, unpopulated areas such as the Canadian tundra, the Australian outback, the deserts of Africa and the steppes of Siberia.

[29]   *Debris Mitigation*, Astromaterials Rsch. and Exploration Sci. Orbital Debris Program Office, NASA, https://orbitaldebris.jsc.nasa.gov/mitigation/ (last visited Dec. 13, 2021).

[30]   Space Policy Directive 3: National Space Traffic Management Policy, 83 Fed. Reg. 28969 (June 18, 2018), https://www.federalregister.gov/documents/2018/06/21/2018-13521/national-space-traffic-management-policy [*hereinafter* SPD-3].

Transportation as well as the Director of National Intelligence and the FCC.[31] The resulting ODMSP 2019 update includes improvements to the original objectives, additional standard practices, and new sections to 'address operating practices for large constellations, rendezvous and proximity operations, small satellites, and other classes of space operations.'[32]

At the international level, in the 1990s, like-minded spacefaring nations joined together to form the Inter-Agency Space Debris Coordination Committee (IADC) as an international forum with membership from space agencies and authorized governmental or intergovernmental entities, 'for the coordination of activities related to the issues of human-made and natural debris in space.'[33] Through the IADC, experts representing the members meet regularly to exchange information on orbital debris research and to identify debris mitigation options. In 2002, the IADC reached consensus and published the initial version of the *IADC Space Debris Mitigation Guidelines* to be considered during the planning and design of spacecraft and launch vehicles, with the goal of minimizing or eliminating the generation of debris during operations. The IADC Guidelines address four areas of concern: (1) limitation of debris released during normal operations; (2) minimization of the potential for on-orbit breakups; (3) post-mission disposal; and (4) prevention of on-orbit collisions. The IADC published Revision 2 of its guidelines in March 2020 with updates to address 'objects passing through the LEO region.'[34]

In addition to international guidelines and domestic regulation to limit the creation of space debris, efforts are under way to develop in-space tech-

---

[31] Within the U.S., each federal agency with regulatory oversight of commercial space activities, including the FAA for launch and reentry; the FCC for communications and broadcast satellites; and NOAA for remote-sensing satellites, levies orbital debris mitigation requirements through the regulations that govern that agency's licensing process. *Id.* at Section 6(b).

[32] *U.S. Government Orbital Debris Mitigation Standard Practices, November 2019 Update*, Preamble, https://orbitaldebris.jsc.nasa.gov/library/usg_orbital_debris _mitigation_standard_practices_november_2019.pdf.

[33] In 2020, members of the IADC included the Italian Space Agency (ASI), Centre National d'Etudes Spatiales (CNES), China National Space Administration (CNSA), Canadian Space Agency (CSA), German Aerospace Center (DLR), European Space Agency (ESA), Indian Space Research Organisation (ISRO), Japan Aerospace Exploration Agency (JAXA), Korea Aerospace Research Institute (KARI), National Aeronautics and Space Administration (NASA), State Space Corporation (ROSCOSMOS), State Space Agency of Ukraine (SSAU), and United Kingdom Space Agency (UKSA). *What's IADC*, Inter-Agency Space Debris Coordination Comm. (IADC), https://www.iadc-home.org/what_iadc (last visited Dec. 17, 2021).

[34] Inter-Agency Space Debris Coordination Comm., *Space Debris Mitigation Guidelines*, IADC (Mar. 2020), https://orbitaldebris.jsc.nasa.gov/library/iadc-space -debris-guidelines-revision-2.pdf.

nologies that can actively remove debris from space. SPD-3 recognized the promise of such technology and called for the U.S. to 'pursue active debris removal [(ADR)] as a necessary long-term approach to ensure the safety of flight operations in key orbital regimes.'[35] ADR is at the very cutting edge of our current technological means. There are various governmental and private initiatives to develop capabilities to remove debris. In parallel with those efforts, progress is necessary on the policy and legal front to facilitate a future with widespread ADR.

There is no dispute that a company engaged in ADR can remove or service a satellite with the agreement of its owner. The trickier legal question is whether a satellite servicer can remove a space object without such consent. Under OST Article VIII, a State that registers a space object 'shall retain jurisdiction and control over such object, and over any personnel thereof, while in outer space or on a celestial body.' Given the breadth and explicit wording of this provision, it is unlikely that any property in space can ever be considered abandoned. Thus, in this regard, space law is distinct from maritime law, which encourages individuals who rescue the ships of others to be reimbursed for their costs.[36]

Moreover, under the Liability Convention, launching States are absolutely liable for damages caused by their space objects to the surface of the Earth. If an ADR rescue mission goes awry, a private entity could cause liability on behalf of its launching State under the OST, further complicating approval for ADR activities. Contractual arrangements between owners of nonfunctional space objects or their launching States, and companies performing ADR services could be structured to address potential liability concerns. Recall that Article V of the OST allows for 'apportionment agreements' among launching States in which they 'may conclude agreements regarding the apportioning among themselves of the financial obligation in respect of which they are jointly and severally liable.' Once the technical and engineering issues are worked out, if structured appropriately, bilateral agreements could solve the thorny legal concerns.

Beyond Orbital Debris: Mega Constellations

At the beginning of 2019, there were approximately 1,100 active satellites in orbit. In the last two years, that number has increased nearly four-fold.[37] If the

---

[35]   SPD-3, *supra* note 30, at Section 5.

[36]   The 'law of salvage' is a concept found in maritime law that gives a reward to someone 'salving' another person's ship or cargo in danger at sea.

[37]   *UCS Satellite Database*, Union of Concerned Scientists (last updated Sep. 1, 2021), https://www.ucsusa.org/resources/satellite-database.

planned deployment of multiple large satellite constellations comes to fruition, an exponential increase could occur.[38] A handful of ambitious companies want to launch tens of thousands of satellites into space to spread the benefits of the Internet to the more than 3 billion people around the globe who lack access to high-speed Internet – benefits such as commerce, telemedicine, and agriculture.[39]

Setting aside challenges, such as avoiding conjunctions, that may arise from the sheer number of satellites, they are disrupting Earth-based astronomical observations – perhaps the oldest of all sciences.[40] Astronomers are concerned that the effects of tens of thousands of satellites could permanently alter the night sky.[41]

Operators are attempting to mitigate the glare from these constellations, ranging from darkening the materials from which they are made, to altering the configuration of the spacecraft.[42] For example, one company's satellites are 'rolled' during certain orbital phases to reduce the area of the spacecraft illuminated by the sun. Additionally, communication between observatories and spacecraft operators could limit unpredicted transits that would interfere with observation times. Currently, these efforts are the result of goodwill and a cooperative spirit, but these challenges may result in future policy and legal changes.[43]

---

[38] Nathaniel Scharping, *The future of satellites lies in the constellations*, Astronomy. com (June 30, 2021), https://astronomy.com/news/2021/06/the-future-of-satellites-lies -in-giant-constellations.

[39] Recall that there are no telephone wires strung across the expansive deserts of the world, or the rainforests, or the steppes – thus, the only hope of telecommunications for these populations is via satellite.

[40] *SpaceX's Satellite Swarm: Could It Hurt Astronomy?*, Nat. Pub. Radio (Nov 13, 2013), https://www.npr.org/2019/11/12/778483584/spacexs-satellite-swarm-could-it -hurt-astronomy.

[41] Numerous factors contribute to the satellites' effect on optical astronomy. For mega-constellations below 600 km, satellites are sunlit during twilight and dawn, but during the middle of the night, they enter the Earth's shadow and darken. This twilight brightness impacts sciences that require observations during those times, such as searches for near-Earth objects. Additionally, the low orbit and high brightness at twilight times can make these lower satellites visible to unaided-eye observation. For constellations above 600 km, satellites are illuminated even at night, always impairing astronomy.

[42] Chaneil James, *Dark-coated Starlink satellites are better but not perfect, say astronomers*, PHYSICS WORLD (Jan. 13, 2021), https://physicsworld.com/a/dark-coated -starlink-satellites-are-better-but-not-perfect-say-astronomers/.

[43] Jeff Foust, *Viasat asks FCC to perform environmental review of Starlink*, SpaceNews (Dec. 28, 2020), https://spacenews.com/viasat-asks-fcc-to-perform -environmental-review-of-starlink/.

OCEAN POLLUTION

Launching objects into space has environmental impacts on Earth's oceans, as can the reentry of spacecraft. Rockets are designed with multiple stages: generally speaking, in a nominal launch, the first stage ignites and lifts the rocket stages and payload off the pad. When the fuel in the first stage is consumed, it separates and falls back to Earth while the second stage ignites and propels the payload into orbit. The stage that deploys the payload will either deorbit or enter a parking orbit, staying in Earth's orbit as space debris, until, after months or years, Earth's gravity pulls it back and it mostly or entirely burns up in the atmosphere.

The rocket stages that fall back to Earth during the launch phase have all, until recently, fallen into the ocean where they sink and are rarely recovered.[44] For example, most launches from Kennedy Space Center/Cape Canaveral in Florida involve rocket stages splashing down in the Atlantic Ocean off the coast of Florida. The Pacific Ocean is home to a giant spacecraft cemetery between New Zealand and Antarctica.[45] Known as Point Nemo, it is the part of the ocean furthest away from any land mass.[46] Since 1971, the U.S., Europe, Russia, and Japan have sunk more than 263 spacecraft in this cold, dark, watery grave.[47] While recent advances in rocket reusability have resulted in fewer rockets discarded in the ocean, the majority of rocket launches are still expended in the ocean.[48]

Based on the laws of physics and gravity, spacecraft and rocket upper stages left in orbit will return to Earth and largely burn up in the atmosphere. In fact, bringing spacecraft back from LEO is considered the most environmentally

---

[44]   But see, billionaire Jeff Bezos' expedition to recover Saturn V rocket engines from 4km deep under the Atlantic Ocean: *Apollo rocket engines recovered by Bezos team*, BBC.com (Mar. 21, 2013), https://www.bbc.com/news/science-environment-21880147.

[45]   To be more precise, it is about 3,000 miles east of New Zealand and 2,000 miles north of Antarctica. If you were alone on a boat in Point Nemo, the closest humans to you would be those flying overhead on the ISS.

[46]   Point Nemo is also known as the Oceanic Pole of Inaccessibility or the South Pacific Ocean Uninhabited Area (SPOUA).

[47]   Vito de Lucia & Viviana Iavicoli, *From Outer Space to Ocean Depths: The Spacecraft Cemetery and the Protection of the Marine Environment in Areas Beyond National Jurisdiction*, 49 Cal. West. Int'l. L. J. 346, 347 (2019).

[48]   Keith Wagstaff & Devin Coldewey, *SpaceX Makes History: Falcon 9 Launches, Lands Vertically*, NBC News (Dec. 22, 2015), https://www.nbcnews.com/tech/innovation/spacex-makes-history-successfully-launches-lands-falcon-9-rocket-n483921.

responsible action, as it keeps LEO free of debris.[49] Further, reentering spacecraft over unpopulated areas protects the human environment. However, Point Nemo (or by one of its technical names: the Oceanic Pole of Inaccessibility; or the South Pacific Ocean Uninhabited Area (SPOUA)) is also the home of various ocean life, including: whales, octopuses, sponges, squids, and sea stars.[50]

International Law

International law is not silent on the intentional dumping of trash in the ocean.[51] The London Convention aims to prevent pollution of the sea by dumping of waste and other matter. Article III (a)(i) of the London Convention defines dumping as 'any deliberate disposal at sea of wastes or other matter from vessels, aircraft, platforms or other man-made structures at sea.' One could assert that aiming a spacecraft or a rocket stage at the ocean constitutes 'deliberate disposal at sea'; and a derelict spacecraft seems to fit within the scope of the terms 'wastes' or 'other matter.' The third criterion is 'vessels, aircraft...or other man-made structures at sea.'[52] A spacecraft could be considered a 'man-made structure' disposed at sea.

Upon further analysis, however, spacecraft operators are not violating the London Convention for their rocket or spacecraft disposal activities. The Ocean Dumping Act represents the U.S. implementation of the London

---

[49]   The currently proposed approach for decommissioning the ISS is the execution of a controlled, targeted deorbit into a remote ocean area. *Decommissioning Plan*, in *Final Tier 2 Environmental Impact Statement for International Space Station*, NASA, at pg. 2–19 (May 1996), https://ntrs.nasa.gov/archive/nasa/casi.ntrs.nasa.gov/19960053133.pdf.

[50]   Kiona Smith-Strickland, *This Watery Graveyard Is the Resting Place for 161 Sunken Spaceships*, Gizmodo.com (May 14, 2015), https://gizmodo.com/this-watery-graveyard-holds-161-sunken-spaceships-1703212211.

[51]   Convention on the Prevention of Marine Pollution by Dumping of Wastes and Other Matter, entry into force Aug 30, 1975, 1046 U.N.T.S. 120 (London Convention).

[52]   For present purposes, we are omitting the storied legal discussion of why a spacecraft would not be considered a vessel under U.S. law under 1 U. S. C. § 3. For those wanting to pursue that line of inquiry, *see*, *Lozman v. Rivera Beach*, 568 U.S. 115 (2013), where the Supreme Court overturned nearly 200 years of precedent regarding the term 'vessel.' According to the Supreme Court, an object is a vessel if a reasonable observer would conclude that the structure is designed to carry people or things over water. However, 'over water' does not mean 'above the water' (like in an airplane or spacecraft); rather it means upon the water. Otherwise, governance of aircraft and spacecraft could conflict with maritime law.

Convention.[53] The Act specifies that 'in the case of a United States department, agency, or instrumentality, no person shall transport from any location any material for the purpose of dumping into ocean waters.'[54] Space launches and reentries are not considered transporting material for the purpose of dumping into ocean waters. Rather, the purpose of the launch vehicle is to transport the spacecraft into outer space. The same argument applies regarding the London Convention's prohibition on 'deliberate disposal of waste at sea.' The London Convention was addressing the indiscriminate disposal of wastes at sea that could create human health hazards. The London Convention was not aimed at activities (such as space exploration) which may incidentally have secondary effects that cause ocean pollution.

Apart from the London Convention, Article 192 of the UN Convention on the Law of the Sea (UNCLOS) states unequivocally that: 'States have the obligation to protect and preserve the marine environment.'[55] That duty extends to territorial seas and areas beyond national jurisdiction.[56] UNCLOS defines pollution as 'the introduction by man, directly or indirectly, of substances or energy into the marine environment...which results or is likely to result in such deleterious effects as harm to living resources and marine life....'

Conceding that spacecraft plummeting into the ocean satisfy the first two criteria – they are (1) introduced by humans and (2) are in the marine environment – without more specific factual information, it is difficult to conclude that 'such deleterious effects as harm to living resources and marine life' would result.[57] Under this cursory analysis, the disposal of derelict spacecraft and spaceflight vehicles into the ocean does not appear to violate international law.

---

[53] Formally known as the Marine Protection, Research, and Sanctuaries Act, 33 U.S.C. § 1401 (1972) (Ocean Dumping Act).

[54] 33 U.S.C. § 1411(2).

[55] *See*, United Nations Convention on the Law of the Sea, Part XII, Dec. 10, 1982, 1833 U.N.T.S. 397.

[56] The International Court of Justice ('ICJ') has stated the 'existence of the general obligation of States to ensure that activities within their jurisdiction and control respect the environment of...areas beyond national control is now part of the corpus of international law relating to the environment.' Legality of Nuclear Weapons, Advisory Opinion, 1996 I.C.J. 226, ¶ 29.

[57] According to the NASA Environmental Assessments (*see, supra* note 49), the marine effects would be 'negligible,' because of the dilutive effects of both the quantity of ocean water, as well as with the understanding that spacecraft breakups are not localized in one area – rather, a spacecraft burning up on reentry could be spread out over a path literally thousands of miles long.

U.S. Law

The U.S. National Environmental Protection Act (NEPA) requires federal agencies to thoroughly consider the consequences of their proposed actions significantly affecting the quality of the human environment.[58] Federal agencies implement NEPA through extensive regulations governing their activities or the activities they license; for example, NASA for USG civil spaceflight activities and operations; the DOD for military spaceflight activities and operations; and the FAA for licensing commercial launch and reentry activities and operations. As part of any spaceflight projects, the starting point for an environmental review process is whether it qualifies for a categorical exclusion determination (CATEX), and if not, then an environmental assessment (EA) is undertaken, which may dictate a full environmental impact statement (EIS).[59] The type of review is determined by the significance of the proposed action's impact on the human environment.[60] The review does not require the result that is the best for the environment, nor does it prohibit actions with adverse environmental effect. Environmental concerns are balanced with social, economic, and technical impacts as well as national policy goals or security interests.

A review of several NASA EAs for launches from Kennedy Space Center provided minimal information concerning the environmental effects of dropping rocket stages into the ocean. Those EAs focus on changes in air and drinking water quality, along with the effects on the environment if the launch fails and include a single paragraph concerning the offshore environment.[61]

---

[58]   National Environmental Policy Act, 42 U.S.C. §§ 4321–22. In fact, the term 'major federal action' includes both actions as well as the failure to act, both of which are reviewable by courts or administrative tribunals under the Administrative Procedure Act or other applicable law as agency action. 40 C.F.R. § 1508.18.

[59]   *National Environmental Policy Act Review Process,* U.S. Environmental Protection Agency (EPA), https://www.epa.gov/nepa/national-environmental-policy -act-review-process.

[60]   *Id.*

[61]   This paragraph is almost identical in seven different mission EAs ranging from 1997 to 2020. *See, e.g., Ocean Environment,* in *Earth Observing System: Final Programmatic Environmental Assessment,* NASA, at 4–18 (1997), https://code200 -external.gsfc.nasa.gov/250/sites/code250/files/250/docs/nepa-eosfinalpea1997.pdf ('Toxic concentrations of metals would not be likely to occur due to the slow rate of corrosion in the deep ocean environment and the large quantity of water available for dilution.') ('Concentrations in excess of the maximum allowable concentration of the compounds for marine organisms would be limited to the immediate vicinity of the spent stage…due to the small amount of residual propellants and the large volume of water available for dilution.'). This conclusion (almost verbatim) was repeated in EAs from 1999, 2000, 2005, 2006, 2008, and as recently in the Mars 2020 EA. *See, Offshore Environment,* in *Final Environmental Impact Statement for the Mars 2020 Mission,*

That paragraph mentions the possible release of residual propellants into the ocean and the rate of metallic corrosion.[62] Multiple EAs state that any toxic concentration of propellant will be limited to the immediate vicinity of the rocket stage and will quickly disperse.[63] Also, NASA reports that is unlikely to find toxic concentrations of metals due to the slow rate of corrosion in the ocean and the large amount of water for dilution.[64] There is almost no further information available regarding the effect of jettisoned rocket stages on the ocean environment.[65] The reviewed EAs conclude that spent rocket stages and other jettisoned rocket parts do not have significant environmental impacts in accordance with U.S. environmental law.

Pursuant to the NEPA, when the EA indicates that there are no significant impacts identified, the decision is documented as a finding of no significant impact (FONSI). On the other hand, if the EA is performed and there could possibly be a significant impact on the human environment, the decision is documented as a notice of intent and an environmental impact statement is required. The regulatory requirements for an EIS are more detailed and rigorous than the requirements for an EA, often taking multiple years to complete. The process includes a scoping process during which the lead federal agency and the public collaborate to define the range of issues and potential alternatives to be addressed in the EIS. It also has strict timelines for public review and comment.[66]

There are three federal agencies that oversee NEPA implementation:

- The Council on Environmental Quality (CEQ) – the CEQ is responsible for ensuring that all executive branch agencies comply with NEPA.

NASA, at 4–9 (2014), https://mars.nasa.gov/mars2020/files/mep/Mars2020_Final_EIS .pdf ('Metal parts would eventually corrode, but toxic concentrations of the metals would not be likely because of the slow rate of the corrosion process and the large volume of ocean water available for dilution.').

[62] *Id.*

[63] *Id.*

[64] *Id.*

[65] For example, EAs from the New Horizons and the Genesis missions mention residual RP-1 fuel that would rise to the surface of the water and evaporate 'within hours.' *See, e.g.*, *Final Environmental Impact Statement for the New Horizons Mission*, NASA (2005), https://www.nasa.gov/sites/default/files/atoms/files/nh-feis_vol1_0 .pdf.

[66] While this is just a general overview, far more detailed information regarding NASA's process to comply with NEPA are provided in *NASA Procedural Requirement (NPR) 8580.1A, Implementing the National Environmental Policy Act and Executive Order 12114*, Environmental Mgmt. Div., NASA (Aug. 1, 2012), https://nodis3.gsfc .nasa.gov/displayDir.cfm?t=NPR&c=8580&s=1A.

- The Environmental Protection Agency (EPA) – the EPA reviews NASA's environmental impact statement (EIS) documents and environmental assessment (EA) documents. The EPA notifies the public by publishing its reviews of these documents in the Federal Register.
- U.S. Institute for Environmental Conflict Resolution – added to NEPA in 1998, this entity has the duty of resolving conflicts concerning the environment between federal agencies and the public.

AVOIDING HARMFUL FORWARD AND BACKWARD CONTAMINATION

OST Article IX explicitly brings some notions of international environmental law explicitly into the Treaty's text by emphasizing cooperation and due regard. Specifically, Article IX provides that, in the exploration and use of outer space, 'States Parties to the Treaty shall be guided by the principle of co-operation and mutual assistance and shall conduct all their activities in outer space [...] with due regard to the corresponding interests of all other States Parties to the Treaty.' Article IX requires States to undertake consultations with States that could be affected before conducting potentially harmful activities in outer space.[67]

In addition, OST Article IX requires that States conduct their exploration activities in outer space 'so as to avoid harmful contamination [of outer space] and also adverse changes in the environment of the Earth resulting from the introduction of extraterrestrial matter.' And so, Article IX presents the concepts known as forward and backward contamination. Forward contamination refers to earthlings contaminating other celestial bodies, while backward contamination is the introduction of extraterrestrial matter to Earth. These efforts are often referred to as 'planetary protection,' the goal of which is protecting solar system bodies from contamination by Earth life and protecting Earth from possible life forms that may be returned from other solar system bodies.

Apollo Missions and Lunar Pollution

On the 50th anniversary of Apollo's 1969 lunar landing, the Smithsonian Institute's National Air and Space Museum projected a life-size Saturn V rocket onto the Washington Monument. It was a reminder of the incredible and

---

[67] This is likely the one provision of the OST that is most ignored by States Parties. This provision serves as a good counter to those scholars who contend that the OST reflects customary international law.

inspiring accomplishment. Amidst the attention that the celebrations garnered were discussions recounting details about the astronauts' time on the Moon and items that were left behind.[68]

Over the course of the Apollo program, the 12 astronauts who walked on the Moon left behind about 400,000 pounds of space exploration detritus, including: lunar landers, moon buggies, several Hasselblad cameras, TV cameras, backpacks, five American flags, two golf balls and bags of human waste.[69]

Was NASA violating OST Article IX by causing 'harmful contamination?' The short answer is no. NASA's chief historian Dr. Bill Barry explained that when the Apollo missions were designed, they deliberately chose not to bring back unneeded equipment to save space and conserve fuel in the return capsule. The missions were designed to get the crew safely to the Moon, retrieve samples, and return them to Earth safely.[70] Perhaps surprisingly, some scientists now cannot wait to get their hands on the 96 bags of human vomit and excrement that were left behind. From a scientific perspective, learning the lunar fate of the 1,000-plus different microbe species that live in the human gut opens a new era of scientific inquiry. Given the Moon's brutal environment, scientists want to know how resilient the discarded microbes are and whether they might survive interstellar travel and potentially seed the universe.[71] It is fully expected that, in the conduct of space exploration, some waste will be produced. OST Article IX requires States Parties to conduct activities in outer space 'so as to avoid their harmful contamination.' Note that not all contamination violates Article IX – only 'harmful' contamination is prohibited, and it is not defined.[72]

---

[68]   Reuters Fact Check, *Fact Check-Apollo 11 astronauts left their space boots on the moon*, Reuters (Aug. 10, 2021), https://www.reuters.com/article/factcheck-apollo -boots-idUSL1N2PH26C.

[69]   Chabeli Herrera, *Cosmic golf balls, 96 bags of poop: What Apollo astronauts left on moon*, The Detroit News (July 8, 2019), https://www.detroitnews.com/story/ news/nation/2019/07/08/apollo-astronauts-moon-trash/39665887/. *See also*, Justin Culp, *Lunar Legacy Project*, Lunar Legacy Project, https://spacegrant.nmsu.edu/ lunarlegacies/artifactlist.html.

[70]   Laura Geggel, *How Much Trash is on the Moon?*, Live Science (Mar. 2, 2018), https://www.livescience.com/61911-trash-on-moon.html.

[71]   Brian Resnick, *Apollo astronauts left their poop on the moon. We gotta go back for that sh*t: What 50-year-old dirty diapers can teach us about the potential origins of life on Earth*, Vox.com (July 12, 2019), https://www.vox.com/science-and-health/ 2019/3/22/18236125/apollo-moon-poop-mars-science.

[72]   See also the discussion of planetary protection and forward contamination below.

Committee on Space Research

On the international level, the Committee on Space Research (COSPAR), an interdisciplinary scientific committee of the International Council of Science (ICSU) to promote at an international level scientific research in space, with emphasis on the exchange of results, information and opinions, and to provide a forum, open to all scientists, for the discussion of problems that may affect scientific space research. COSPAR grew out of concerns that 'spaceflight missions to the Moon and other celestial bodies might compromise their future scientific exploration.'[73]

COSPAR's *Planetary Protection Policy* includes technical requirements intended to serve as international standards and as a guide to compliance with OST Article IX.[74] In short, COSPAR generally divides the universe into five different categories depending on the likelihood a particular celestial body would contribute to the discovery of the origins of life.[75] These categories range from Category I, which has zero likelihood of interfering with 'understanding the process of chemical evolution or the origin of life,' and therefore, 'no protection of such bodies is warranted, and no planetary protection requirements are imposed.'[76] At the other extreme are Category V missions, which comprise all Earth return missions, the highest degree of concern, absolute prohibition of destructive impact upon return, as well as the need for sample containment throughout the return phase.[77] The COSPAR guidelines do not change if a mission is performed by robots or by humans, which makes decontamination of the launch vehicle (and any persons aboard it) challenging. There seems to be an understanding that human missions will indeed carry microbial populations that will differ from those of robotic explorers.

---

[73] *COSPAR's Planetary Protection Policy*, Comm. On Space Rsch., Int'l Council for Sci. Unions (2017), https://cosparhq.cnes.fr/assets/uploads/2019/12/PPPolicyDecember-2017.pdf.

[74] *See*, Rep. of the Comm. on the Peaceful Use of Outer Space on its Sixtieth Session, COPUOS, June 7–16, 2017, U.N. Doc. A/72/20.

[75] *COSPAR Policy on Planetary Protection*, Comm. On space Rsch., Int'l Council for Sci. Unions, at 1 (June 17, 2020), https://cosparhq.cnes.fr/assets/uploads/2020/07/PPPolicyJune-2020_Final_Web.pdf. Examples of Category I missions would be orbiters or flybys or NASA's Ulysses mission to study the north and south pole of the Sun. (For more information on Ulysses, see *Ulysses*, Jet Propulsion Lab., NASA, https://www.jpl.nasa.gov/missions/ulysses (last visited Dec. 20, 2021)).

[76] *Id.* Other Category V missions included all the Apollo missions, JAXA's Hayabusa missions, and various asteroid and comet sample returns.

[77] The levels of detail and characterization are far more scientifically precise than laid out in this general overview.

NASA's Planetary Protection Policies

NASA, like all major space agencies around the world, has an office dedicated to governing NASA's planetary protection efforts.[78] It controls forward contamination of other celestial bodies by Earth organisms in order to be certain that, if extraterrestrial life is ever found, that it did not originate on Earth to begin with. Moreover, it has a duty to preclude backward contamination of Earth by extraterrestrial life to prevent potentially harmful consequences for humans and the biosphere of the Earth.[79]

In July 2020, NASA updated its planetary protection policies to acknowledge some of the realities of space exploration. Most of the Moon will remain in Category I, except for the polar regions, which could contain water ice, as well as those Apollo lunar landing sites, which could contain biological materials – these would both be Category II. The administrator of NASA stated: 'NASA is changing its thinking on how we're going to go forward to the moon. Certain parts of the moon, from a scientific perspective, need to be protected more than other parts of the moon from forward biological contamination.'[80] Regarding human missions to Mars, a planet with greater planetary protection requirements than the Moon, the requirements include setting strict limits on the level of terrestrial contamination that some individuals had asserted are incompatible with human missions.[81] It is important to note that NASA's directives only apply to NASA missions or those in which NASA participates.[82] They do not apply to missions by commercial companies or by other space agencies.

---

[78]   Since NASA is not a regulatory agency, its planetary protection requirements are not regulations governing U.S. commercial entities. However, because NASA is consulted in the commercial licensing process, U.S. entities seeking a license to conduct novel activities often consult NASA's guidelines.

[79]   More information about NASA's Planetary Protection activities, *see, Planetary Protection*, Office of Planetary Protection, Office of Safety and Mission Assurance, NASA, https://sma.nasa.gov/sma-disciplines/planetary-protection/ (last visited Dec. 13, 2021).

[80]   Jeff Foust, *NASA implements changes to planetary protection policies for moon and Mars missions*, SPACENEWS (July 20, 2020), https://spacenews.com/nasa-implements-changes-to-planetary-protection-policies-for-moon-and-mars-missions/.

[81]   'We can't go to Mars with humans if the principle that we're living by is that we can't have any microbial substances with us, because that's just not possible.' *Id.*

[82]   Note that the COSPAR Planetary Protection Guidelines are also frequently observed by other nations as well. China claims to have followed similar procedures as NASA takes when it recently landed its Tianwen-1 rover mission on Mars. *See*, Meghan Bartels, *Here's what we know about planetary protection on China's Tianwen-1 Mars mission*, Space News (Feb. 25, 2021), https://www.space.com/china-tianwen-1-mars-mission-planetary-protection.

Foreign and Commercial Missions and Pollution

In February 2019, Space IL, an Israeli not-for-profit institution, launched a small robotic lander and lunar probe to the Moon's surface. This historic event was intended to inspire Israeli students to pursue STEM education and careers. However, one of the mission participants, the Arch Foundation, is alleged to have snuck small, microscopic life forms, known as tardigrades, onto the spacecraft.[83] The founder of the Arch Foundation later referred to himself as a 'pirate,' stating, '[w]e didn't tell them we were putting life in this thing…[s]pace agencies don't like last-minute changes. So we just decided to take the risk.'[84]

Tardigrades are notoriously good at survival – they can endure extreme heat, cold, radiation, years of dehydration and exposure to the space environment.[85] However, experts deemed them 'likely to be of minimal environmental impact.'[86] This alleged deception gave rise to significant discussion regarding responsibility for the voracity of information regarding payloads as well as U.S. and international law implications. It highlighted the fact that international guidelines and standard practices are only effective when people and entities act in good faith. The Arch Foundation's actions were met with disapproval throughout the space community, which made it clear that such 'piracy' is not acceptable practice.

Other U.S. commercial entities that have applied to the FAA for missions to the Moon have looked to NASA's guidelines since the U.S. has not specifically adopted regulations governing possible contaminates from commercial activities.[87] While no U.S. commercial missions have yet been conducted,

---

[83] Loren Grush, *Why Stowaway Creatures on the Moon Confound International Space Law*, THEVERGE.COM (Aug. 16, 2019), https://www.theverge.com/2019/8/16/20804219/moon-tardigrades-lunar-lander-spaceil-arch-mission-foundation-outer-space-treaty-law (noting that '[a]lmost no one knew…[the Tardigrades] were on board until a recent report in Wired revealed they had been added to the mission last minute – and without any governmental approval'); *See also*, Daniel Oberhaus, *A Crashed Israeli Lunar Lander Spilled Tardigrades on the Moon*, WIRED.COM (Aug. 5, 2019), https://www.wired.com/story/a-crashed-israeli-lunar-lander-spilled-tardigrades-on-the-moon/; and Kameron Virk, *Tardigrades: 'Water bears' stuck on the moon after crash*, BBC.COM (Aug. 7, 2019), https://www.bbc.com/news/newsbeat-49265125.

[84] Chris Taylor, *'I'm the first space pirate!' How tardigrades were secretly smuggled to the moon*, MASHABLE.COM (Aug. 8, 2019), https://mashable.com/article/smuggled-moon-tardigrade/.

[85] Carolina Chavez et al., *How tardigrades survive the extreme*, eLifesciences (Oct 1, 2019), https://elifesciences.org/digests/47682/how-tardigrades-survive-the-extreme.

[86] Grush, *supra* note 83.

[87] Jeff Foust, *Moon Express wins U.S. government approval for lunar lander mission*, SPACE NEWS (Aug. 3, 2016), https://spacenews.com/moon-express-wins-u-s-government-approval-for-lunar-lander-mission/.

there are some interesting concepts proposed for launch in the very near future, including sending sentimental memorabilia to the Moon. Such items might include sand from a favorite beach, a lock of hair, a fraternity pin, a company logo, or a pet tag.[88] The company offering these deliveries has a contract with NASA to deliver cargo to the Moon, but as of the date of this writing, NASA is not buying all the spacecraft's capacity, which will leave room for private items. There are also companies marketing the 'service' of delivering human cremated remains, 'cremains,' to the Moon.[89]

While one might ask how the U.S. could license such activities, recall that until authority for granting mission authorizations is delegated by Congress, these activities would flow through the FAA's payload review process. That interagency review process determines whether the proposed payload would jeopardize public health and safety, safety of property, U.S. national security or foreign policy interests, or international obligations of the United States.[90] While there may not be an explicit domestic or international obligation against launching human remains to the lunar surface, it remains to be seen whether the U.S. will grant approvals for some of the ideas being proposed for space-flight. Perhaps the State Department might claim that foreign policy interests are impacted and object to the FAA issuing a launch license.[91]

QUESTIONS FOR REVIEW

1. In this chapter, we learned that only 'harmful contamination' is to be avoided in conduct of space activities. How is 'harmful' defined? Do you think that is the right standard? Why or why not?

2. In the discussion of the London Convention, we learned that it is not against the law to pollute the ocean with spacecraft, if the intention of the

---

[88] *See, Immortalize Your Keepsake on the Moon*, Astrobotic, https://www.astrobotic .com/lunar-delivery/send-to-the-moon/ (last visited Dec. 13, 2021). The details of their 'delivery service to the moon' are available on their website. *See, Terms and Conditions*, Astrobotic, https://www.astrobotic.com/moon-box/terms (last visited Dec. 13, 2021).

[89] *Indica-Noodle Fabiano*, Celestis Memorial Spaceflights, https://www.celestis .com/participants-testimonials/indica-noodle-fabiano/ (last visited Dec. 13, 2021).

[90] See discussion above regarding the FAA's legal authority to review payloads at.

[91] While commercial activities in orbit and on the lunar surface will only be increas-ing, it may be worth noting that the activities that have caused the greatest pollution to the outer space environment to the present have been caused by national militaries and space agencies. Nevertheless, in areas such as the lunar South Pole, where we know that many space agencies and commercial entities are making plans to set up lunar bases (due to the presence of ice and other minerals in permanently shadowed craters), it will be extremely important that activities are conducted with due regard for other operators.

polluter was to launch an object into space. Does that make sense? Do you think that designing a rocket specifically to splash in the ocean at launch or spend eternity resting on the ocean floor upon return from space should be permitted under the law?

3. If an individual invests time and money to remove a piece of space debris from orbit, should they be entitled to a reward? What do you think of the idea of creating a pool of money based on user fees, out of which people who remove space debris are compensated? Would this work? Is this equitable?

4. Do you think that some agency of the U.S. Government should have the authority to regulate what U.S. nationals do on the Moon and Mars? If so, which agency? Do you think Congress needs to make such statutory authorization clearer? What U.S. 'foreign policy interest' would be served by setting limits on the conduct of U.S. nationals in areas beyond national jurisdiction?

13. National security and military uses of outer space

Ruth leans back on her chair, absentmindedly playing with her wine glass as she listens to her friends' animated conversation about the latest binge-worthy TV series. Laura turns to her and asks, 'Have you watched Space Force yet? I know you've been really busy, but I just finished it yesterday and I have so many questions!' Ruth smiles. Laura is also a bit of a 'space nerd,' and her enthusiasm is contagious.

'That one I have seen, as a matter of fact!' She replies. She hasn't had to deal with the intersection of space law and war for work, but after watching the series, her interest had been piqued and she had done some research on the subject.

'Do you reckon war in space is possible?' Laura asks. 'I remember there is a scene where both the U.S. and China set up military bases on the Moon. In fact, one of the taglines of the show is "Boots on the moon!" – they even made a Ben & Jerry's ice cream flavor in honor of that line! Is that something that could happen?'

Laura continues, 'I thought space was some sort of sanctuary of peace, like Antarctica – no weapons allowed, right? Can satellites be attacked with weapons from Earth? If so, how do countries protect their space technology?'

'And what about that scene where that gigantic Chinese satellite flies by the Space Force satellite and destroys it?' Jane interjects. 'Does that constitute an act of war? And if so, is there a space treaty or something that deals with warfare? Can the U.S. do anything to retaliate?'

Ruth leans forward and smiles, 'Let's order another round and I'll tell you all about it!'

SPACE AS THE ULTIMATE HIGH GROUND

Since the dawn of the space age, national security has been a key component in the use and exploration of space. The space domain's strategic and technological importance has made it essential to our everyday lives and a critical necessity for national defense and security.[1] Accordingly, many nations are preparing for the eventuality that space may become a future theater of conflict.[2] As a result, it is especially important for any space lawyer to understand the legal implications of the national security and military uses of outer space. After providing a short history of the military uses of outer space, this chapter will discuss the delicate balance between the peaceful uses of outer space and the concept of national security, the differences between outer space militarization and weaponization, and finally, the laws of war applicable to outer space.

Historical Context

Space exploration began during the height of the Cold War. The first forays beyond the Kármán line[3] were motivated by the U.S. and the Union of Soviet Socialist Republics (U.S.S.R. or Soviets) desires to achieve political, economic and military supremacy in space.[4] As U.S. President Johnson said, 'control of space means control of the world.'[5]

On October 4, 1957, the U.S.S.R. shocked the world by successfully launching Sputnik 1 into Earth's orbit. The Western Bloc grew concerned about

---

[1] PRICEWATERHOUSECOOPERS, DEPENDENCE OF THE EUROPEAN ECONOMY ON SPACE INFRASTRUCTURES: POTENTIAL IMPACTS OF SPACE ASSETS LOSS (2017), https://op.europa.eu/en/publication-detail/-/publication/e5450aac-0d4d-11e8-966a -01aa75ed71a1/language-en/format-PDF/source-80710841.

[2] Countries, such as the U.S. and France, have made moves to establish space commands and NATO has declared outer space an 'operational domain' for the alliance. *See* Victor Mallet, France Follows US to Set Up Military Space Command, FIN. TIMES (July 14, 2019), https://www.ft.com/content/a479bcb6-a628-11e9-984c-fac8325aaa04; *NATO's Approach to Space,* NATO (Oct. 23, 2020), https://www.nato.int/cps/en/natohq/topics_175419.htm.

[3] The Kármán Line is an imaginary line at about 100 km, or 62 miles, high and represents an attempt to approximate a boundary between Earth's atmosphere and outer space, primarily for legal and regulatory purposes. *See* FRANCIS LYALL & PAUL B. LARSEN, SPACE LAW: A TREATISE 147 (2d ed. 2018). According to NOAA, 'In theory, once this 100 km line is crossed, the atmosphere becomes too thin to provide enough lift for conventional aircraft to maintain flight.' *See* Nat'l Env't Satellite, Data, & Info. Serv., *Where is Space?*, NOAA (Feb. 22, 2016), https://www.nesdis.noaa.gov/news/where-space.

[4] LYALL & LARSEN, *supra* note 3, at 447.

[5] President Lyndon B. Johnson, Statement of Democratic Leader Lyndon B. Johnson to the Meeting of the Democratic Conference (Jan. 7, 1957).

the possibility of being attacked from outer space,[6] as the Soviets effectively demonstrated their intercontinental ballistic missile (ICBM) capabilities.[7]

In May 1958, the U.S. Air Force tested a nuclear-tipped, air-launched ballistic missile named Bold Orion.[8] Then, in August and September of that same year, the U.S. conducted high-altitude nuclear detonations over the south Atlantic Ocean, codenamed Operation Argus. Those gave rise to the first non-kinetic ASAT targeting space technology by creating a radiation belt produced by a nuclear detonation in the void of space.[9]

The fear of converting outer space into a new stage for warfare prompted the creation of the United Nations (UN) Committee on the Peaceful Uses of Outer Space (COPUOS).[10] In 1960, U.S. President Eisenhower presented two ideas to the UN that would become essential pillars of the international space legal regime:

1. Outer space should be preserved for peaceful use and developed for the benefit of all mankind;[11] and
2. Outer space should not be subject to claims of sovereignty.[12]

---

[6] The Western Bloc was a coalition of countries formed by the U.S. and its allies, and the Bloc opposed the U.S.S.R. and its allies (the Eastern Bloc) during the Cold War.

[7] VANNEVAR BUSH, MODERN ARMS AND FREE MEN: A DISCUSSION OF THE ROLE OF SCIENCE IN PRESERVING DEMOCRACY 116–17 (1949); *see* P.J. Blount, *Space Security Law*, OXFORD RES. ENCYCLOPEDIA PLANETARY SCI. (June 4, 2018).

[8] A single solid rocket stage was launch from a B-47 bomber. Brian Weeden, *Through a Glass, Darkly: Chinese, American, and Russian Anti-satellite Testing in Space*, SECURE WORLD FOUND. (Mar. 17, 2014), https://swfound.org/media/167224/through_a_glass_darkly_march2014.pdf ('Eight tests of this version were conducted between May 26, 1958, and June 19, 1959, during which the missiles reached apogees near 100 kilometers (62 miles) during their flights.').

[9] C.B. JONES ET AL., DEF. NUCLEAR AGENCY, DNA 6039F, OPERATION ARGUS 1958 (Apr. 30, 1982). Operation Argus was conducted to establish a proof of theory that a very high-altitude nuclear detonation could produce phenomena of potentially significant military importance by interfering with communications and weapons performance. The Argus nuclear tests grew out of an idea conceived of by physicist Nicholas Christofilos. In late 1957 and early 1958, he examined the possibility that a nuclear detonation at an extremely high altitude would create an artificial radiation belt in the upper regions of the Earth's atmosphere. 'It was theorized that the radiation belt would have military implications, including degradation of radio and radar transmissions, damage or destruction of the arming and fuzing mechanisms of ICBM warheads, and endangering the crews of orbiting space vehicles that might enter the belt.'

[10] *Id.*

[11] President Dwight D. Eisenhower, Address before the Fifteenth General Assembly of the UN (Sept. 22, 1960).

[12] Matthew T. King, *Sovereignty's Gray Area: The Delimitation of Air and Space in the Context of Aerospace Vehicles and the Use of Force*, 81 J. AIR L. & COM. 485 (2016). Eisenhower promoted space as a sanctuary less out of idealism and more as the

Competition between the U.S. and U.S.S.R. to achieve strategic and technological dominance during the Cold War heavily influenced the language of the Outer Space Treaty (OST).[13] COPUOS drafted the OST primarily to serve as an arms control treaty.[14] While the OST aims to encourage the use of the space domain for 'peaceful purposes,'[15] it utilizes language broad enough to encompass national security and military interests. The OST preserved the rights for nations to defend their national security. However, after several Soviet ASAT tests in the 1970s, the U.S. no longer viewed space as a sanctuary, but rather as a contested domain.[16] This shift in policy was emulated across the world, resulting in a space environment that is largely viewed as contested, congested, and competitive.[17]

In 1990, the U.S. invasion of Iraq, known as the first Gulf War, earned the moniker of being the first 'space war' due to the significant reliance on space technology.[18] The U.S. military and coalition allies relied on satellite imaging and telecommunications to provide clear communication channels and updated, high-resolution maps of the area, which allowed the U.S. and its allies to plan troop movements, accurately identify targets and analyze the terrain to identify water sources or trafficability.[19] Since then, military doctrine

---

best method to protect American satellites in space. Robin Dickey, *The Rise and Fall of Space Sanctuary in U.S. Policy*, AEROSPACE CORP. (Sept. 2020), https://aerospace.org/sites/default/files/2020-09/Dickey_SpaceSanctuary_20200901.pdf.

[13] Treaty on Principles Governing the Activities of States in the Exploration and Use of Outer Space, Including the Moon and Other Celestial Bodies, *opened for signature* Jan. 27, 1967, 610 U.N.T.S. 205, T.I.A.S. No. 6347 [*hereinafter* OST]. For more information on the OST, see Chapter 3.

[14] LYALL & LARSEN, *supra* note 3, at 4453–54. U.S. President Lyndon Johnson termed the OST as 'the most important arms control development since the Limited Test Ban Treaty of 1963.' President Lyndon B. Johnson, Statement by the President Announcing the Reaching of an Agreement on an Outer Space Treaty (Dec. 8, 1966).

[15] *See* OST, *supra* note 13, at Preamble.

[16] Memorandum from Brent Scowcroft to President Ford, Soviet Anti-Satellite Capability (Apr. 26, 1976), https://aerospace.csis.org/wp-content/uploads/2019/02/Scowcroft-memo-US-ASAT-Apr-1976.pdf ('The Soviet test of an anti-satellite interceptor last week, the second such test in the last two months, has emphasized the need to reexamine our posture in space and the vulnerability of our space assets.').

[17] Roger G. Harrison, *Unpacking the Three C's: Congested, Competitive, and Contested Space*, 11 ASTROPOLITICS 123 (2013).

[18] Dale Stephens & Cassandra Steer, *Conflicts in Space: International Humanitarian Law and Its Application to Space Warfare*, 40 ANNALS AIR & SPACE L. 71, 73 (2015).

[19] Sharon Watkins Lang, *SMDC History: 25 Years Since First 'Space War'*, U.S. ARMY (Jan. 20, 2016) https://www.army.mil/article/161173/smdc_history_25_years_since_first_space_war.

– particularly in the U.S. – fully accepts that future wars will be fought from, through or even in space.[20]

China's 2007 ASAT test and emerging counterspace capabilities from other countries such as Russia and India consolidated the view of space as a contested domain.[21] Nations were prompted to accept the real possibility of a conflict in space and concomitantly seek to protect their assets therein.[22] Some space actors now consider the development of counterspace technologies as a necessary achievement, a badge of accomplishment that allows them entry to the exclusive 'club' of advanced spacepowers.[23]

PEACEFUL PURPOSES AND NATIONAL SECURITY INTERESTS

International Peace and Security: The Goal of the Space Law Regime

The OST preamble expresses signatories' commitments to maintaining peace and security in outer space[24] as did the UN General Assembly resolution that preceded it.[25] However, maintaining peace and security is neither new nor unique to the outer space regime. Rather, it is an outgrowth of the UN Charter,[26] which outlines its central purpose in Article 1(1):

> To maintain international peace and security, and to that end: to take effective collective measures for the prevention and removal of threats to the peace, and for the suppression of acts of aggression or other breaches of the peace, and to bring about

---

[20]   Chairman, J. Chiefs of Staff, Joint Publication 3-14, *Space Operations* I-1 (Apr. 10, 2018, Incorporating Change 1) [*hereinafter* Joint Pub. 3-14] ('We must assume future war on earth will extend into space. We will need to "fight through" attacks on our space assets and capabilities and continue to provide the space support our warfighters need and have come to expect.').

[21]   DEF. INTELLIGENCE AGENCY, CHALLENGES TO SECURITY IN SPACE 20–1, 28–9 (2019).

[22]   *Id.*

[23]   After India's direct-ascent ASAT test in 2019, Prime Minister Modi lauded the demonstration: 'India has made an unprecedented achievement today (...) India registered its name as a space power.' *See* Sanjeev Miglani & Krishna N. Das, *Modi Hails India as Military Space Power After Anti-satellite Missile Test*, REUTERS (Mar. 27, 2019), https://www.reuters.com/article/us-india-satellite/modi-hails-india-as-military-space-power-after-anti-satellite-missile-test-idUSKCN1R80IA?feedType=RSS&feedName=worldNews.

[24]   Blount, *supra* note 7, at 11; *see* OST, *supra* note 13, at Preamble and art. III.

[25]   G.A. Res. 1348 (XIII), U.N. GAOR, 13th Sess., Supp. No. 18b U.N. Doc. A/4090 (Dec. 13, 1958), *op. cit. supra* note 15.

[26]   Charter of the United Nations and Statute of the International Court of Justice, June 26, 1945, 59 Stat. 1031; 33 U.N.T.S. 993 [*hereinafter* 'UN Charter'].

by peaceful means, and in conformity with the principles of justice and international law, adjustment or settlement of international disputes or situations which might lead to a breach of the peace.[27]

The OST expressly references the UN Charter in Article III:

> States Parties to the Treaty shall carry on activities in the exploration and use of outer space, including the Moon and other celestial bodies, in accordance with international law, including the Charter of the UN, in the interest of maintaining international peace and security and promoting international cooperation and understanding.

The drafters of the OST deemed it particularly important to transpose onto future space activities the general prohibition of the use of force, established by Article 2(4) of the UN Charter.[28] As such, the concept of 'peaceful purposes' serves to highlight the intrinsic link that exists between the international space legal regime and the goals of international peace and security.

The Concept of 'Peaceful Purposes'

The limitation that outer space be used for 'peaceful purposes' appears twice in the OST. First, in the non-binding, or hortatory, preamble, which states that there is a 'common interest of all mankind in the progress of the exploration and use of outer space for peaceful purposes.' The second reference is in Article IV, which establishes that '[t]he Moon and other celestial bodies shall be used by all State Parties to the Treaty exclusively for peaceful purposes.'[29]

The term 'peaceful purposes' is now generally understood to mean non-aggressive use, rather than non-military.[30] That interpretation, however,

---

[27] *Id.* Art. 1.

[28] Jackson Nyamuya Maogoto & Steven Freeland, *Space Weaponization and the United Nations Charter Regime on Force: A Thick Legal Fog or a Receding Mist*, 41 Int'l Law 1091, 1095 (2007). The prohibition to use force and its exceptions will be further analyzed below.

[29] It should be noted that OST Art. IV does not explicitly establish the limitation of exclusive use for peaceful purposes for the void of outer space as it does for the Moon and other celestial bodies. However, this obligation can be inferred from the applicability of general international law to the space domain, established in Art. III. The use of force is prohibited under general international law, particularly under UN Charter Art. 2(4).

[30] Shannon Orr, *Peace and Conflict In Outer Space*, 30 PEACE RES. 52, 58 (1998); Bhupendra Jasani & Maria A. Lunderius, *Peaceful Uses of Outer Space-Legal Fiction and Military Reality*, 11 SECURITY DIALOGUE 57, 58 (1980).

was not always so clear-cut. Different treaty signatories almost immediately interpreted the term to mean different things.[31]

While negotiating the OST, the U.S. and the Soviets shared the same interpretation of 'peaceful purposes' to mean 'non-aggressive.'[32] This interpretation is consistent with a nation's inherent right of self-defense.[33] Both countries were developing military reconnaissance satellites.[34] Therefore, it is not surprising that the two superpowers agreed on an interpretation that enabled military uses.[35]

However, several other countries initially opposed this view. Japan, for example, interpreted the concept of 'peaceful purposes' to refer to a strictly nonmilitary use of space, which, at that time, would not allow satellites to engage in routine communications, weather forecasting, or reconnaissance activities.[36] The 1969 Diet resolution established 'the principle of peaceful use of space' as the bedrock of Japan's space policy, consistent with Article 9 of the Japanese Constitution, which renounces war as a sovereign right of the nation and the threat or use of force as a means of settling international disputes.[37] However, this restrictive interpretation would have greatly limited the use of space. Considering those limitations, countries that initially opposed the U.S. position on 'peaceful uses' have reconsidered their views,[38] even enacting specific domestic laws permitting such reinterpretation.[39]

---

[31] JOAN JOHNSON-FREESE, SPACE AS A STRATEGIC ASSET 108 (2007).

[32] Jasani & Lunderius, *supra* note 30, at 57.

[33] Jackson Nyamuya Maogoto & Steven Freeland, *op. cit. supra* note 28, at 1099.

[34] At the same time, the U.S. was also pursuing anti-ballistic missile (ABM) technology systems because of the threat that the U.S.S.R. was developing orbital bombardment systems. President Johnson announced in a 1964 speech that, 'To insure that no nation will be tempted to use the reaches of space as a platform for weapons of mass destruction we began in 1962 and 1963 to develop systems capable of destroying bomb-carrying satellites.' *See* Laura Grego, *A History of Anti-Satellite Programs*, UNION CONCERNED SCI. (2012).

[35] Maogoto & Freeland, *supra* note 28, at 1100–1101.

[36] Paul Kallender & Christopher W. Hughes, *Hiding in Plain Sight? Japan's Militarization of Space and Challenges to the Yoshida Doctrine*, 15 ASIAN SECURITY 180 (2018); Maeda Sawako, *Transformation of Japanese Space Policy: From the 'Peaceful Use of Space' to 'the Basic Law on Space'*, 7 ASIA PAC. J. JAPAN FOCUS 1 (2009). Japan has significantly changed its view and interpretation of the concept of 'peaceful uses' and the types of activities this principle allows in space, in no small part due to national security concerns brought about by North Korean activity and, in recent years Chinese activity. *See* Paul Kallender, *Japan's New Dual-Use Space Policy: The Long Road to the 21st Century*, 88 ASIE.VISIONS 1, 9–10 (Nov. 2016).

[37] Sawako, *supra* note 36.

[38] JOHNSON-FREESE, *supra* note 31 at 108.

[39] Kallender, *supra* note 36, at 34 ('Japan has managed to fundamentally reorient its space policy from fundamentally anti-military use to one that supports hard domes-

The U.S. position reflects the assertion that:

[a]ll nations have the right to explore and to use space for peaceful purposes and for the benefit of all humanity, in accordance with applicable law. Consistent with that principle, the U.S. will continue to use space for national security activities, including for the exercise of the inherent right of self-defense.[40]

Widespread State practice supports the U.S. position, and, as such, outer space is now filled with satellites used for military purposes such as intelligence-gathering, reconnaissance, navigation, targeting over battlefields, early warning of missile and air attacks, or military communications. Those activities are usually conducted without protest from the international community.[41]

Beyond the Wording of the OST: Military Competition in Space

Despite the OST's early intent to control arms in space,[42] the space environment is far from being weapons-free. Spacefaring nations' vested interests in protecting their assets in outer space led to the development of ASAT technology, almost as soon as States began developing the very first satellites.[43] The few limitations on nations' military activities in outer space are those found in international law, including the UN Charter, and those stipulated in OST Articles III and IV.

Since the UN Charter forbids the use of force in space,[44] spacefaring nations seek space control as a military strategy against their competitors and potential enemies.[45] States have invested in intelligence, surveillance and reconnaissance

---

tic national security and regional security goals.'); *see* Sawako, *supra* note 36, at 4. The Japanese Basic Space Law enacted in 2008 lifted the ban on the use of space technology for military purposes, thus officially reinterpreting the meaning of 'peaceful purposes' in the OST to enable national security-related activities in space.

[40]   The National Space Policy, 85 Fed. Reg. 81755 § 5.3.a (Dec. 9, 2020).

[41]   Michael N. Schmitt, *International Law and Military Operations in Space*, 10 MAX PLANCK Y.B. U.N. L. 89, 102 (2006).

[42]   LYALL & LARSEN, *supra* note 3, at 453–454; *see* British Pathé, *Space Treaty (1967)*, YOUTUBE (Apr. 13, 2014), https://www.youtube.com/watch?v=ncphbeoPJ8I&feature=youtu.be.

[43]   David A. Koplow, *ASAT-isfaction: Customary International Law and the Regulation of Anti-Satellite Weapons*, 30 MICH. J. INT'L L. 1187, 1200–01 (2009).

[44]   *See* UN Charter, *supra* note 26, at Art. 2(4) ('All Members shall refrain in their international relations from the threat or use of force against the territorial integrity or political independence of any state, or in any other manner inconsistent with the Purposes of the United Nations.').

[45]   JOHNSON-FREESE, *supra* note 31, at 109.

(ISR) technologies since modern militaries rely heavily on space assets – and space assets are potential targets. The U.S. has the most operational satellites in orbit, followed by China and then Russia.[46] These are not all military satellites. Most of them, around 95%, are dual-use – valuable to both the civil and military communities.[47] The more technologically capable a State's dual-use assets are, the more threatened competitor nations feel, resulting in spacefaring nations finding themselves in constant technological one-upmanship.[48]

WEAPONIZATION OF OUTER SPACE

Militarization vs. Weaponization: A Crucial Distinction

Space has been militarized since the very beginning of space exploration.[49] However, militarization is not synonymous with weaponization. The militarization of outer space involves the use of space-based technologies for supporting military operations on Earth, such as command and control, communication, monitoring, early warning, and navigation activities.

On the other hand, the weaponization of space is generally understood to refer to the placement of implements of war in orbit that can destroy or disable assets either in outer space or on Earth's surface.[50] Ground-based systems designed or used to attack space-based assets, such as direct-ascent ASATs, are also considered space weapons by many, although they are not technically part of the weaponization of space since they are not placed in orbit.[51]

Some scholars assert that space is already weaponized.[52] OST Article IV provides the only international legal restrictions on the weaponization of

---

[46]   As of January 1, 2021, those numbers were respectively: US: 1,897; China: 412; and Russia: 176. However, those numbers are changing rapidly. *UCS Satellite Database*, UNION CONCERNED SCI. (Sept. 1, 2021), https://www.ucsusa.org/resources/satellite-database.

[47]   JOHNSON-FREESE, *supra* note 31, at 30.

[48]   Joan Johnson-Freese & David Burbach, *The Outer Space Treaty and the Weaponization of Space*, 75 BULLETIN ATOMIC SCI. 137 (2019).

[49]   JOAN JOHNSON-FREESE, HEAVENLY AMBITIONS 13 (2009) [*hereinafter* Heavenly Ambitions]; JOHNSON-FREESE, *supra* note 31, at 83; Johannes Wolff, *'Peaceful Uses' of Outer Space Has Permitted Its Militarization: Does It Also Mean Its Weaponization?* 3 U.N. INST. DISARMAMENT RES., DISARMAMENT FORUM 5 (2003).

[50]   Dio H. Tobing & Olivia N. Maryatmo, *Celestial Anarchy: States' Right to Self-Defense in Outer Space*, 4 JURIS GENTIUM L. REV. 9, 11 (2016).

[51]   Todd Harrison, *International Perspectives on Space Weapons*, CTR. STRATEGIC & INT'L STUDIES 4 (May 2020); *see* Péricles Gaspani Alves, *Prevention of an Arms Race in Outer Space: A Guide to the Discussions in the Conference on Disarmament*, U.N. INST. DISARMAMENT RES. 14 (1991).

[52]   Heavenly Ambitions, *supra* note 49, at 13.

space.[53] Article IV forbids the placement of nuclear weapons or weapons of mass destruction – commonly understood to comprise nuclear, chemical, and biological weapons[54] – in orbit around the Earth, on celestial bodies, or stationing them in outer space.[55] It also prohibits the testing of 'any type of weapons and the conduct of military maneuvers on celestial bodies.' The space treaties do not offer any other explicit prohibition regarding the placement of other types of weapons in space,[56] nor do they prohibit the launching of weapons from Earth to target an asset in space.[57]

Types of space weapons

A wide variety of ASAT and counterspace technologies can be deployed from land, sea, air, or space. Those can be classified into four groups:[58]

1. Kinetic physical – these systems can disable or destroy a satellite by means of striking it directly or exploding in its close proximity. They can be direct-ascent (launched from Earth) or co-orbital.
2. Non-kinetic physical – they can have physical effects on satellites and ground stations without needing to make physical contact. They can be used to permanently or temporarily blind or dazzle a satellite's sensors,

---

[53]   Johnson-Freese & Burbach, *supra* note 48, at 137.

[54]   The term 'weapon of mass destruction' is generally reserved for nuclear, chemical, and biological arms. The term was first used in 1937 by the Archbishop of Canterbury regarding the use of aerial bombardment and explosive weapons during the Spanish Civil War and the Second Sino-Japanese War in China. In 1948, the UN tasked a committee to analyze the concept of WMD. That committee concluded: '[WMD are] (…) atomic explosive weapons, radioactive material weapons, lethal chemical and biological weapons, *and any weapons developed in the future which have characteristics comparable in destructive effect to those of the atomic bomb or other weapons mentioned above.*' It is this broader definition of WMD – not limited to nuclear, chemical and biological weapons – that was accepted by the international community at the time of the drafting of the OST. *See* W. Seth Carus, Defining Weapons of Mass Destruction 6–7 (2012); Commission for Conventional Armaments Res., U.N. Doc. S/C.3/32/Rev.1 (Aug. 12, 1948). During the Senate ratification hearing of the Outer Space Treaty, Deputy Secretary of Defense Cyrus Vance defined WMD as, 'chemical and biological weapons (…) or any weapon which might be developed in the future which would have the *capability of mass destruction such as that which would be wreaked by nuclear weapons.*' Jeffrey A. Murphy, *The Cold Vacuum of Arms Control in Outer Space: Can Existing Law Make Some Anti-Satellite Weapons Illegal?* 68 Clev. St. L. Rev. 125, 143 (2019).

[55]   *See* OST, *supra* note 13, at Art. IV.

[56]   Stephens & Steer, *supra* note 18, at 74.

[57]   Johnson-Freese & Burbach, *supra* note 48, at 137.

[58]   Koplow, *supra* note 43, at 1208; *see also,* Todd Harrison et al., Ctr. Strategic & Int'l Studies, Space Threat Assessment 2021 (2021).

or damage a specific sensitive location, such as a fuel tank. Examples include lasers, high-powered microwaves (HPM), and electromagnetic pulse (EMP) weapons.

3. Electronic – these weapons have the ability to target the means by which space systems transmit and receive data by jamming or spoofing radio frequency (RF) signals.
4. Cyber – these weapons do not target the transmission signals, but rather they target the data itself, as well as the systems that use this data.

The Issue of ASAT Testing

Setting aside James Bond movies, the use of space weapons has been relatively limited.[59] The U.S.S.R. installed a cannon, the Kartech R-23M, on its Almaz space station in the 1970s and fired it in 1975.[60] The Soviet cannon was not an ASAT, but actions such as this one have contributed to something of a 'tolerance' for conventional weapons in outer space, as a result of States declining to condemn such actions as illegal.

The most notable type of ASAT testing, which has generated the most controversy in the international community, is the use of direct-ascent missiles. Four countries – the U.S., Russia, China, and India – have successfully conducted such tests, carrying out kinetic kill operations against another space object. In all instances, the targeted object belonged to the State conducting the test.

In 2007, China conducted a highly criticized ASAT test: China launched a missile that successfully collided with a non-operational Chinese weather satellite, Fengyun-1C (FY-1C), at an altitude of 863 km (534 miles).[61] Its noto-

---

[59]   One recent example included the French-Italian satellite ATHENA-FIDUS, which in 2017 was allegedly the target of ISR operations by the Russian satellite known as Olymp-K or Luch. The Russian satellite flew close enough to the ATHENA-FIDUS to provoke a protest from France, with French Minister of the Armed Forces Florence Parly accusing Russia of committing '*an act of espionage.*' See John Leicester, '*Espionage:' French Defense Head Charges Russia of Dangerous Games in Space*, Defense News (Sept. 7, 2018), https://www.defensenews.com/space/2018/09/07/espionage-french-defense-head-charges-russia-of-dangerous-games-in-space/.

[60]   Anatoly Zak, *Here Is the USSR's Secret Space Cannon*, Popular Mechanics (Nov. 16, 2015), https://www.popularmechanics.com/military/weapons/a18187/here-is-the-soviet-unions-secret-space-cannon/; see Mark Felton Productions, *Soviet Space Gun – The Armed Space Station*, YouTube (Jan. 24, 2019), https://www.youtube.com/watch?v=WXRAsxHgOm4.

[61]   Brian Weeden, *2007 Chinese Anti-Satellite Test Fact Sheet*, Secure World Found. (Nov. 23, 2010), https://swfound.org/media/9550/chinese_asat_fact_sheet

riety stems from the inordinate amounts of space debris it created – a cloud of more than 3,000 tracked pieces, the largest ever.[62]

The U.S. reacted by labelling the test, and its consequences, as 'regrettable,' 'very troubling,' and 'destabilizing,' and criticized that it was 'inconsistent with the spirit of cooperation that both countries aspire to in the civil space area.'[63] The European Union's condemnation was even stronger and expressed that 'such a test is inconsistent with international efforts to avert an arms race in outer space.'[64] In the face of China's actions, the EU 'call[ed] upon all signatory States [of the OST] to abide by their commitment to exercise their space activities in accordance with international law and in the interest of maintaining international peace and security.'[65] Japan also expressed concern in light of the Chinese demonstration. Prime Minister Shinzo Abe stated that the use of ASAT, particularly against other States' spacecraft, could constitute a violation of international law, in particular the OST.[66] Notably, China's action was not labelled as 'illegal' in countries' responses.

While China was criticized, those criticisms were insufficient to deter other nations from conducting similar tests, including those utilizing kinetic weapons. The U.S. shot down a former U.S. reconnaissance satellite in 2008.[67] In 2019 India conducted its own test (dubbed 'Mission Shakti,' which means 'power' or 'strength' in Sanskrit) to destroy one of its own satellites, Microsat-R, in an orbit less than 300 kilometers high.[68] In November 2021, Russia conducted its first hit-to-kill test, after having previously tested its Nudol anti-ballistic missile to conduct fly-bys, without targeting a specific

---

_updated_2012.pdf. As of mid-September 2010, the U.S. military's Space Surveillance Network (SSN) had tracked a total of 3,037 pieces of debris from this event, 97% of which has remained in orbit. Scientists estimate more than 32,000 smaller pieces.

[62]   *Id.*

[63]   Koplow, *supra* note 43, at 1238.

[64]   *Id.*

[65]   Rüdiger Lüdeking, Deputy Comm'r Arms Control & Disarmament, Ger. Fed. Gov't, Statement on Behalf of the European Union at the Conference on Disarmament, U.N. Doc. CD/PV.1048 (Jan. 24, 2007).

[66]   Manuel Manriquez, *Japan's Space Law Revision: the Next Step Toward Re-Militarization?*, NUCLEAR THREAT INITIATIVE (Jan. 1, 2008), https://www.nti.org/analysis/articles/japans-space-law-revision/.

[67]   The U.S. claimed that the purpose of this operation, 'Operation Burnt Frost,' was not to test any ASAT capabilities, but rather to protect populated areas from the satellite's unused supply of hydrazine propellant. The satellite was hit at an altitude of 247 km, which meant that the debris from the test burnt up relatively quickly in the Earth's atmosphere.

[68]   Brian Weeden & Victoria Samson, *Global Counterspace Capabilities: An Open Source Assessment*, SECURE WORLD FOUND. (Apr. 2021), https://swfound.org/counterspace.

object, but nevertheless demonstrating Russia's direct-ascent ASAT capabilities. The U.S. harshly criticized Russia's actions, deeming them reckless and irresponsible, and contrary to Russia's proposal for a Draft Treaty on the Prevention of the Placement of Weapons in Outer Space (PPWT).[69]

Not all ASAT weapons involve physically impacting a satellite with a missile. Other counterspace measures include non-kinetic, electronic, and cyber: examples include the ejection of unknown objects from Russian satellites,[70] and the orbital maneuvers by Russian inspector satellites to follow U.S. spy satellites and European communications satellites.[71] Meanwhile, some have claimed that China has been developing directed energy weapons for counterspace use; that Iran has demonstrated an electronic warfare capability to interfere with commercial satellite signals; and that North Korea has been developing two counterspace weapons technologies: electronic and cyber.[72]

MILITARY CONFLICT AND OUTER SPACE

The Nature of Military Space Operations

Outer space was first utilized during World War II, when Nazi Germany fired a V-2 rocket through space to London.[73] Today, modern warfare depends on outer space. Military space applications include satellite communications, positioning, navigation and timing (PNT), meteorology, environmental monitoring, space situational awareness as well as ISR.[74]

Sovereign states establish their own national space policies and decide their own national security postures and strategies.[75] Given this reality, an under-

---

[69] Press Statement, Antony J. Blinken, U.S. Dep't State, Russia Conducts Destructive Anti-Satellite Missile Test (Nov. 15, 2021).

[70] U.S. Space Command Pub. Affairs Office, Russia Conducts Space-based Anti-satellite Weapons Test, U.S. SPACE COMMAND (July 23, 2020), https://www.spacecom.mil/MEDIA/NEWS-ARTICLES/Article/2285098/russia-conducts-space-based-anti-satellite-weapons-test/ ('U.S. Space Command has evidence that Russia conducted a non-destructive test of a space-based anti-satellite weapon.').

[71] Loren Grush, *A Russian Satellite Seems to be Tailing a US Spy Satellite in Earth Orbit*, VERGE (Jan. 31, 2020), https://www.theverge.com/2020/1/31/21117224/russian-satellite-us-spy-kosmos-2542-45-inspection-orbit-tracking.

[72] *See* Weeden & Samson, *supra* note 7; *see also* HARRISON ET AL., *supra* note 59.

[73] Howard Kleinberg, *On War in Space*, 5 ASTROPOLITICS 1 (2007).

[74] Intelligence, surveillance, and reconnaissance. Dale Stephens, *Military Space Operations and International Law*, JUST SECURITY (Mar. 2, 2020), https://www.justsecurity.org/68815/military-space-operations-and-international-law/.

[75] Certain countries, such as the U.S., have developed detailed operational strategies. The U.S. distinguishes between offensive space control operations (OSC), which consist of negating adversaries' use of space through measures that deceive, disrupt,

standing of how the laws of war apply to outer space is recommended. Legal issues (such as applying the law of armed conflict (LOAC)) become more complex as the lines that separate State and non-State actors in space become increasingly blurred.[76]

The Law of War Applicable to Outer Space

OST Articles I and III make clear that the use and exploration of outer space shall be carried out 'in accordance with international law' and the UN Charter. The International Court of Justice (ICJ) has clarified that the established principles and rules of international humanitarian law (IHL) applicable in armed conflict apply 'to all forms of warfare and to all kinds of weapons, those of the past, those of the present and those of the future.'[77]

It is surprising to some that there are rules for waging war. Various reasons exist for these rules, but they generally boil down to protecting civilians from the impact of war and protecting the combatants.[78] Rules *jus ad bellum* (law for war) are the criteria to consider governing the justification for entering a war or for its avoidance. *Jus ad bellum* seeks to limit the use of force or the threat of force 'against the territorial integrity or political independence of any state, or in any other manner inconsistent with the Purposes of the UN.'[79] On the other hand, *jus in bello* (law in war), also known as LOAC or IHL, concerns the rules

---

degrade, deny, or destroy space systems or services. Defensive space control operations (DSC) consist of all active and passive measures taken to preserve friendly space capabilities from attack, interference, or unintentional hazards. For legal and policy purposes, the U.S. favors DSC; however, it considers interference with its space systems to be a violation of its sovereign rights that could merit taking all appropriate self-defense measures, including the use of force if necessary. *See* Joint Pub. 3-14, *supra* note 20, at I-1; *see also* The National Space Policy, *supra* note 40, at 3.

[76] Commercial companies frequently provide communication and imaging services to governments. For example, after the September 11 attacks, the National Imagery and Mapping Agency (NIMA) contracted with the U.S. company Space Imaging in 2001 for all of Space Imaging's satellite images of Afghanistan, captured by its satellite Ikonos. It was an exclusive contract, where the commercial entity sold that data only to the U.S. military. *See* James. A. Vedda, *Updating National Policy On Commercial Remote Sensing*, CTR. STRATEGIC & INT'L STUDIES 8 (2017), https://aerospace.org/sites/default/files/2018-05/CommercialRemoteSensing_0.pdf; Ricky J. Lee & Sarah L. Steele, *Military Use of Satellite Communications, Remote Sensing, and Global Positioning Systems in the War on Terror*, 79 J. AIR L. & COM. 69, 82 (2014).

[77] Legality of the Threat or Use of Nuclear Weapons, 1996 I.C.J. 226 ¶ 86 (July 6).

[78] GEOFFREY S. CORN ET AL., THE LAW OF ARMED CONFLICT. AN OPERATIONAL APPROACH 3 (2nd ed., 2019).

[79] UN Charter, *supra* note 26, at Art. 2(4). *See generally* KEIICHIRO OKIMOTO, THE DISTINCTION AND RELATIONSHIP BETWEEN *JUS AD BELLUM* AND *JUS IN BELLO* (2011).

Table 13.1   Law of war concepts applicable to military uses of outer space[1]

Jus ad bellum: law leading up to war	Jus in bello: law while engaged in war
Immediacy/imminence: No need to wait to be attacked; but nexus between the attack and self-defense.	**Distinction:** Only combatants and military objects may be attacked.
Necessity: Alternatives to the use of force must be exhausted.	**Proportionality:** Does the advantage gained outweigh the harm caused?
Proportionality: The force used must be proportional to neutralize or abolish the threat.	**Military necessity:** Is the attack required to defeat the enemy?
	Humanity: The weapon used may not contribute to unnecessary suffering.

[1]   Elaborated in detail below.

applicable once war has already commenced. It is concerned with the behavior of individuals and units toward combatants, noncombatants, property, and the environment during combat and occupation.[80]

While the rules and principles pertaining to both *jus ad bellum* and *jus in bello* predate the space age, they remain applicable to the space domain. The full *corpus* of the law of war, encompassing both the law of the use of force and IHL, is too vast to analyze in detail in this book; however, it is essential to understand how the core principles of *jus ad bellum* and *jus in bello* apply to space.[81]

Jus ad bellum: The Use of Force and Inherent Right of Self-Defense

Article 2(3) of the UN Charter affirms the duty of States to resolve international disputes by peaceful means.[82] Article 2(4) establishes the general

---

[80]   *Id*; *see generally* CORN ET AL., *supra* note 79. Conflicts can be international (between States), or non-international (involving non-State actors). Although both are important from an IHL perspective, this chapter will focus on State-to-State interactions.

[81]   The principles of IHL are distinction (discrimination), proportionality, military necessity, precautions, humanity (unnecessary suffering), and honor (chivalry). The latter two have not been analyzed in this chapter, as they regulate interactions with enemy combatants and do not directly relate to the use of weapons in space.

[82]   UN Charter, *supra* note 26, at Art. 2(3) ('All Members shall settle their international disputes by peaceful means in such a manner that international peace and security, and justice, are not endangered.').

prohibition on the use of force. States shall not 'threat[en] or use of force against the territorial integrity or political independence of any state, or in any other manner inconsistent with the Purposes of the UN.'[83] An exception to this rule is found in Article 51 of the UN Charter, which provides 'the inherent right of individual or collective self-defense if an armed attack occurs against a Member of the UN.' The right of self-defense is limited; it only exists 'until the Security Council has taken measures necessary to maintain international peace and security.' According to the ICJ, both the unilateral use of force and its exception in the case of self-defense against armed attack have reached the status of customary international law.[84]

In outer space, any direct damage suffered by space assets, setting aside human-tended assets such as a space station, would be considered damage or destruction of property. However, considering humankind's dependence on space technology, damage to a space asset could have devastating effects on persons on Earth, including their serious injury or death.[85] Effects 'that are not directly and immediately caused by the attack but are nevertheless the product thereof'[86] are just as important when considering whether an armed attack has occurred. According to the Tallinn Manual, any attacks that seriously injure or kill several persons or that cause significant damage to, or destruction of, property could suffice to be considered an armed attack.[87]

---

[83]   Article 2(4) of the UN Charter constitutes a step beyond its predecessor, the 1928 Kellogg-Briand Pact for the Renunciation of War as an Instrument of National Policy, which only forbade war and armed conflict. For more about the Kellogg-Briand Pact, see OONA A. HATHAWAY & SCOTT J. SHAPIRO, THE INTERNATIONALISTS: HOW A RADICAL PLAN TO OUTLAW WAR REMADE THE WORLD (2017). The use of force threshold is lower than that of an armed attack, according to most countries (although not the U.S.). *See* Christopher M. Petras, *The Use of Force in Response to Cyber-Attack on Commercial Space Systems – Reexamining Self-Defense in Outer Space in Light of the Convergence of U.S. Military and Commercial Space Activities*, 67 J. AIR L. & COM. 1213 (2002).

[84]   *See* Military and Paramilitary Activities in and Against Nicaragua (Republic of Nicaragua v. United States of America) 1986 ICJ 14 (June 27) [*hereinafter* Nicaragua v. U.S.].

[85]   For example, damaging a GPS satellite could cause aircraft to fly off course and crash, or an oil tanker to go off course and run aground, resulting in a catastrophic oil spill. Therefore, the consequences on Earth of such an attack must be considered.

[86]   Michael N. Schmitt, *Wired Warfare: Computer Network Attack and Jus in Bello*, 84 INT'L REV. RED CROSS 365 (2002).

[87]   As a general illustrative analogy for the space law practitioner, the Tallinn Manual on the International Law Applicable to Cyber Operations ('Tallinn Manual'), in line with what the ICJ determined in the *Nicaragua* case, states that '[w]hether a cyber operation constitutes an armed attack depends on its scale and effects.' *Id.* (discussing rule 71 – Self-defence against armed attack; that standard may prove instructive in the field of space law).

A detailed, factual analysis of the legality regarding a 'use of force' constituting an armed attack would be extremely fact-dependent and is beyond the scope of this book. However, some helpful guidelines follow. Attacks that disrupt services termed as essential or which incapacitate critical infrastructure could trigger the right to use self-defense.[88] The International Committee of the Red Cross (ICRC) has underscored that the disruption, damage, destruction or disabling of space objects on which safety-critical civilian activities and services essential to civilian survival rely would risk significant humanitarian consequences on Earth.[89] Further, the disruption of military capabilities, such as missile detection abilities, communication with soldiers on the battlefield, or incapacitation of the air defense system could also constitute an armed attack.[90] To exercise the right to self-defense, a State must satisfy the three-prong test of: immediacy, necessity, and proportionality.[91]

Immediacy and imminence

A State may only use force to exercise its right of self-defense 'if an armed attack occurs' against it.[92] A State may act in self-defense after an armed attack occurs, within some reasonable proximity in time (or immediacy) to the hostile act. This immediacy to respond is important since the passage of time presumably diminishes the need for self-defense, and a delayed response may look more like revenge or reprisal, which is not permissible.[93]

However, it is not necessary to wait until the attack has occurred: if an attack is imminent, the potential victim State has the right to take anticipatory action to defend itself, if the requirements of the *Caroline* test are met.[94] U.S.

---

[88]   Critical infrastructures include 'those used for, inter alia, the generation, transmission and distribution of energy, air and maritime transport, banking and financial services, e-commerce, water supply, food distribution and public health – and the critical information infrastructures that increasingly interconnect and affect their operations.' G.A. Res. 58/199 (Jan. 30, 2004).

[89]   Int'l Comm. Red Cross, Humanitarian Consequences and Constraints Under International Humanitarian Law (IHL) Related to the Potential Use of Weapons in Outer Space, working paper submitted to the Group of Governmental Experts on Further Practical Measures for the Prevention of an Arms Race in Outer Space, U.N. Doc. GE-PAROS/2019/WP.1 (Mar. 18, 2019) [*hereinafter* ICRC Working Paper].

[90]   Nils Melzer, *Cyberwarfare and International Law*, U.N. Inst. Disarmament Res. (2011), https://unidir.org/files/publications/pdfs/cyberwarfare-and-international -law-382.pdf.

[91]   Nicaragua v. U.S., *supra* note 86, at ¶ 237; *see*, Yoram Dinstein, War, Aggression and Self-Defence 249–252 (6th ed., 2017).

[92]   UN Charter, *supra* note 26, at Art. 51.

[93]   Corn et al., *supra* note 79, at 22.

[94]   The *Caroline* was an American steamship assisting Canadian rebels in their fight for independence against the British. When the British learned this, they seized

Secretary of State Daniel Webster explained that anticipatory self-defense should be limited to cases that 'show a necessity of self-defense, instant, overwhelming, leaving no choice of means, and no moment for deliberation.'[95] Today, the *Caroline* test is adapted to 'modern-day capabilities, techniques, and technological innovations.'[96] Thus, according to the most widely accepted interpretation, 'imminence' means the last possible window of opportunity to stop an armed attack.[97] This can be immediately before the attack in question or, in some cases, and considering the rapid advances in the field of technology, long before it occurs.[98]

Necessity

The use of force should always be a last resort. All peaceful means of dispute resolution must have been exhausted or otherwise not feasible. Necessity also means that the defensive measure must be limited to what is necessary to avert or terminate the ongoing attack.[99]

Proportionality

The principle of proportionality requires that the amount of force used in self-defense be similar to the threat to which it responds. Any harm caused must not be appreciably greater than the harm that would occur if the threat were not intercepted with force.[100] Proportionality does not mean parity

---

the *Caroline* in American waters, set it aflame, and sent it over Niagara Falls. Anthony Clark Arend, *International Law and the Preemptive Use of Military Force*, 26 WASH. Q. 89, 96 (2003).

[95] Letter from Daniel Webster, U.S. Sec'y of State, to Henry Fox, British Minister in Washington (Ap. 24, 1841), in *British and Foreign State Papers* 1138 (1857).

[96] Remarks of John O. Brennan, Assistant to the President for Homeland Sec. & Counterterrorism, Program on Law and Security, Harvard Law School (Sept. 16, 2011).

[97] GEOFFREY S. CORN ET AL., ASPEN TREATISE FOR NATIONAL SECURITY LAW: PRINCIPLES AND POLICY 105 (2nd ed. 2019).

[98] Ryan J. Hayward, *Evaluating the Imminence of a Cyber Attack for Purposes of Anticipatory Self-Defense*, 117 COLUM. L. REV. 399, 414 (2017); *see* TALLINN MANUAL 2.0 ON THE INTERNATIONAL LAW APPLICABLE TO CYBER OPERATIONS at Rule 73 (Michael N. Schmitt ed., 2017) ('By this standard, a State may act in anticipatory self-defence against an armed attack, whether cyber or kinetic, when the attacker is clearly committed to launching an armed attack and the victim State will lose its opportunity to effectively defend itself unless it acts [immediately].').

[99] Elizabeth Wilmshurst, ILP WP 05/01, *Principles of International Law on Use of Force in by States in Self-Defence*, CHATHAM HOUSE (Oct. 2005).

[100] This definition corresponds to *jus ad bellum* proportionality, and is different from *jus in bello* proportionality, under which there is a prohibition on only those attacks that cause incidental loss of civilian life that is excessive in relation to the concrete and direct military advantage anticipated. *In bello* proportionality will be discussed below.

between a response and the harm already suffered from an attack, since punishment and retaliation are not the objectives of self-defense.[101] The weapons used in self-defense need not be the same as those used in the attack.

Jus ad bellum proportionality serves two purposes: (1) to identify the situations in which the use of force is permissible; and (2) to determine the intensity and the magnitude of the forcible action. When assessing the proportionality of a measure, many different aspects must be taken into consideration, which can vary significantly. Here are just a few:

- the location of the target, for example, whether it is in a heavily populated orbit;
- the ease with which it can be protected;
- its proximity to civilian persons or property;
- its use, for example, whether it supports critical infrastructure;
- effects of the attack, for example, whether the space object will be destroyed or only temporarily disabled; and
- long-term effects of the attack, for example, whether the attack will cause space debris, thus putting other space assets beyond the targeted object at risk.

Jus in bello Principles of Armed Conflict (IHL)

The *jus in bello* principles that apply to space are distinction, proportionality, military necessity, and humanity (or avoidance of unnecessary suffering).[102] The first three of these principles have been identified by the ICJ as the 'cardinal principles' contained in the *corpus* of IHL,[103] and they, along with the fourth principle, which several authors consider to be essential as well,[104] must be carefully examined when engaging an opponent in the context of an armed conflict. As is the case with *the jus ad bellum* principles, these are general principles, and any genuine analysis would occur on a fact-specific, case-by-case basis.

Distinction/discrimination
Parties to an armed conflict must distinguish at all times between civilian and military objectives[105] and direct their attacks only against military objectives.

---

[101] Wilmshurst, *supra* note 103.

[102] Legality of the Threat or Use of Nuclear Weapons, *supra* note 78, at ¶78.

[103] *Id.*

[104] CORN ET AL., *supra* note 79, AT 50.

[105] Article 48 of the 1977 Additional Protocol I (API) provides: '[T]he Parties to the conflict shall at all times distinguish between the civilian population and combatants.'

Those are objects, as indicated by Article 52 Additional Protocol I (API), 'which by their nature, location, purpose or use make an effective contribution to military action and whose total or partial destruction, capture or neutralization, in the circumstances ruling at the time, offers a definite military advantage.'[106]

Considering that most assets in outer space are dual-use, this is not an easy analysis. If a civilian object is making an effective contribution to military actions, it could lose its protection under international law and becomes a legitimate target.[107] This same principle applies to dual-use assets.[108] Any harm to the civilian population due to the object's dual-use nature would have to be considered when assessing the proportionality of the attack.[109]

Note that the principle of distinction, as codified in API Article 48,[110] does not forbid all collateral damage or effect on civilians and civilian objects; only effects that are 'excessive in relation to the concrete and direct military advantage anticipated.'[111] If a user cannot control or reliably predict where the effects of the weapon may be felt, it fails the discrimination test.[112] Even when a weapon appears to be very discriminating, such as a direct-ascent kinetic ASAT, which can be directed with a very high degree of precision to a particular target, its indirect effects, such as the creation of space debris in

---

Protocol Additional to the Geneva Conventions of 12 August 1949, and Relating to the Protection of Victims of International Armed Conflict (Protocol I), June 8, 1977, 1125 U.N.T.S. 3 [*hereinafter* Protocol I].

[106] API has not been ratified by several States, including the U.S. Nevertheless, the distinction principle is considered CIL, and is recognized by several military manuals. *See* JEAN-MARIE HENCKAERTS & LOUISE DOSWALD-BECK, 1 CUSTOMARY INTERNATIONAL HUMANITARIAN LAW 3 (2005).

[107] Daniel Porras, *Shared Risks: An Examination of Universal Space Security Challenges,* U.N. INST. DISARMAMENT RES. 12 (2019).

[108] Christopher Greenwood, *Customary International Law and the First Geneva Protocol of 1977 in the Gulf Conflict,* in THE GULF WAR 1990–91 IN INTERNATIONAL AND ENGLISH LAW 63, 73 (Peter Rowe ed., 1993) ('If an object is a military objective, it may be attacked (subject to the requirements of the principle of proportionality which are discussed in the next section), while if it is a civilian object, it may not be attacked. There is no intermediate category of "dual use" objects: either something is a military objective, or it is not.').

[109] Office of Gen. Counsel, U.S. Dep't Def., Law of War Manual § 5.6.1.2. (Dec. 2016) [*hereinafter* Law of War Manual].

[110] INT'L COMM. RED CROSS, COMMENTARY ON THE ADDITIONAL PROTOCOLS OF 8 JUNE 1977 TO THE GENEVA CONVENTIONS OF 12 AUGUST 1949 at 598 (1987) (this basic rule applies to all parties to a conflict, whether or not they have signed API, due to its status as a customary rule).

[111] Protocol I, *supra* note 107, at Art. 51(5)(b). This also relates to proportionality in *jus in bello*, further analyzed below.

[112] Koplow, *supra* note 43, at 1244–45.

the case of kinetic ASATs, must also be taken into account when conducting the discrimination analysis.[113]

Proportionality

Attacks that are expected to cause a disproportionate loss of civilian life, injury to civilians, damage to civilian objects, or a combination thereof, and would be excessive in relation to the concrete and direct military advantage anticipated, are prohibited.[114] One must also account for the attack's secondary effects, considering both the space domain and effects felt on Earth.[115] For example, a kinetic energy ASAT launched against a satellite in LEO could be more devastating than a satellite in GEO, due to the space debris generated. Moreover, completely disabling a dual-use satellite that provides services to both military personnel and civilians would be less proportionate than partially disabling it, or somehow denying access to the satellite's military users while allowing civilians to continue to enjoy its services.

Military necessity

This principle 'justifies the use of all measures needed to defeat the enemy as quickly and efficiently as possible that are not prohibited by the law of war.'[116] For example, could a kinetic anti-satellite weapon be considered indispensable during an armed conflict in space? That depends on whether there exist alternative methods to kinetic energy impactors that would respect the environment of outer space and avoid the creation of space debris. If a State can effectively neutralize an enemy's satellite while avoiding the creation of long-lasting orbital debris and its harm to the peaceful space activities of future generations of civilians and neutral States, the LOAC principle of necessity would prohibit the use of kinetic ASAT technology.[117]

---

[113] Michel Bourbonniere, *Law of Armed Conflict (LOAC) and the Neutralisation of Satellites or Ius in Bello Satellitis*, 9 J. CONFLICT & SEC. L. 43, 65 (2004). Article 51(4)(c) API prohibits weapons the effects of which cannot be limited as required by the Protocol. Protocol I, *supra* note 107, at Art. 51.

[114] Int'l Comm. Red Cross, *Humanitarian Consequences and Constraints Under International Humanitarian Law (IHL) related to the Potential Use of Weapons in Outer Space*, Working paper submitted to the Group of Governmental Experts on Further Practical Measures for the Prevention of an Arms Race in Outer Space (March 2019), https://undocs.org/GE-PAROS/2019/WP.1.

[115] CORN ET AL., *supra* note 79, at 59.

[116] Law of War Manual, *supra* note 111, at § 2.2.

[117] Koplow, *supra* note 43, at 1248.

Humanity (or precaution, or unnecessary suffering)

When conducting military operations, constant care must be taken to spare the civilian population and civilian objects, with a view to avoiding, if not minimizing, incidental civilian casualties and damage to civilian objects.[118] The loss of satellite-based services, even if temporal, could have devastating consequences on Earth. An attorney advising on the decision to employ a kinetic weapon against a satellite might consider use of the weapon either at a very high altitude in an unpopulated orbit, or alternatively a very low orbit, where debris would enter the atmosphere shortly after impact; however, that attorney should also consider use of an alternative weapon system that does not rely on kinetic force.

QUESTIONS FOR REVIEW

1. If space is to be used for 'peaceful purposes,' how can military operations be carried out in Earth's orbit or on celestial bodies?
2. Are States allowed to perform reconnaissance from space? Could this provoke another State to target the first State's reconnaissance satellite? If so, how can the first State protect its assets in outer space from attack?
3. Is it ever okay to use force against another country's satellite? If so, when?
4. Could a space asset that is used to assist a war on Earth be attacked?
5. Are there any specific elements that have to be taken into consideration when using force against a space asset? Are they the same irrespective of whether the use of force happens during peacetime or during an armed conflict?
6. If Country A collaborates on a space mission with Country B that is at war with Country C, can Country C attack Country A's space assets? Why or why not?

---

[118] Protocol I, *supra* note 107, at Article 57(2)(ii).

14. Planetary defense

Avoiding the fate of the dinosaurs

Ruth has just received an abrupt call from her senior partner. One of the firm's most important – and most irascible – clients, someone whose whims were capricious but too lucrative to ignore, had questions that touched on space law.

During the night, the client's country house had been struck by a piece of a falling meteorite. The plummeting space rock had penetrated the roof of a garage, and some farm implements were damaged; one tractor was beyond repair. The client was outraged – he is clearly looking for someone to blame and sue. He is asking whether NASA, or perhaps the Space Force, could be held responsible for their failure to protect his property from this outrageous assault.

The senior partner directs Ruth to research the whole problem of asteroid–Earth collisions – how often do they occur, how damaging are they, and what can be done about them? He instructs Ruth that because this litigious client's pockets are deep, and his ire is fully engaged, she should explore the field fully, and prepare a comprehensive written report. By the time she is finished, perhaps the client's immediate zeal for a lawsuit will have tempered, but he will still want to know all that he can about this bizarre event.

INTRODUCTION

Planetary defense is an arcane and ominous topic, exploring the idea that we might someday discover that a large asteroid is on a collision course with Earth – a catastrophe that has occurred repeatedly in the past and is statistically certain to happen again at some unknown point in the future.[1] Practitioners

---

[1] *See*, NASA, *Will an Asteroid Ever Hit Earth? We Asked a NASA Scientist*, YouTube (Aug. 25, 2021), https://youtu.be/cBG1KYa95JY (Interview with Dr. Kelly Fast, NASA Planetary Defense Expert) ('Yes, asteroids have hit Earth over the course of its history, and it will happen again.').

in the field, led by NASA's Planetary Defense Coordination Office,[2] have labored for years to detect, identify, track, and characterize the potential dangers, and to begin to construct an effective response. This whole problem, of course, lies 99.9999% within the realm of science and technology, but there are interesting, underexplored legal dimensions too.

HISTORICAL IMPACTS

There are millions of asteroids and similar celestial bodies, presenting a dazzling array of sizes, structures, composition, and other characteristics. Most of these cosmic intruders stay far away, in the main asteroid belt between the orbits of Mars and Jupiter. But as gravity, collisions, and other forces exert their cumulative effects, many have come to adopt more eccentric obits, some of which draw them uncomfortably close to Earth.[3]

Some asteroids are huge: Ceres, for example, is nearly 1,000 kilometers across.[4] Others are tiny, making them virtually impossible to detect and track. Some asteroids are relatively intact, spherical bodies, while others have highly irregular shapes or may consist essentially of piles of rubble, loosely bound together by gravity. Some are stone-like while others are more metallic or carbonaceous; some are binary mini-systems, with two bodies orbiting each other. Each of these characteristics can influence the ability to detect and divert the incoming mass.[5]

---

[2]   NASA, *Planetary Defense*, https://www.nasa.gov/planetarydefense (last visited Dec. 20, 2021). *See also*, European Space Agency, *Space Mission Planning Advisory Group*, https://cosmos.esa.int/web/smpag (last visited Dec. 20, 2021) (the international structure for organizing several states' planetary defense operations); FRANCIS LYALL & PAUL B. LARSEN, SPACE LAW: A TREATISE (2d ed., 2018), p. 234–39; European Space Agency, *Risky Asteroids*, http://www.esa.int/Safety_Security/Risky_asteroids (last visited Dec. 20, 2021).

[3]   INTERAGENCY WORKING GROUP FOR DETECTING AND MITIGATING IMPACT OF EARTH-BOUND NEAR-EARTH OBJECTS, U.S. SCI. & TECH. COUNCIL, NATIONAL NEAR-EARTH OBJECT PREPAREDNESS STRATEGY AND ACTION PLAN 2 n.1 (2018), https://www.whitehouse.gov/wpcontent/uploads/2018/06/National-Near-Earth-Object-Preparedness-Strategy-and-ActionPlan-23-pages-1MB.pdf [https://perma.cc/YP54-REX5]; NASA Office of the Inspector General, N*ASA's Efforts to Identify Near-Earth Objects and Mitigate Hazards*, 1 (Sep. 15, 2014), https://oig.nasa.gov/docs/IG-14-030.pdf [https://perma.cc/P8A7-8Y7M].

[4]   *See*, NASA, *Asteroid Fact Sheet*, https://nssdc.gsfc.nasa.gov/planetary/factsheet/asteroidfact.html (last visited Dec. 20, 2021).

[5]   DAVID A. KOPLOW, *EXOATMOSPHERIC PLOWSHARES: USING A NUCLEAR EXPLOSIVE DEVICE FOR PLANETARY DEFENSE AGAINST AN INCOMING ASTEROID*, 76 UCLA J. OF INTL LAW & FOREIGN AFFAIRS 76, 83–85 (SPRING 2019); NAT'L ACAD. OF SC., COMM. TO REVIEW NEAR-EARTH-OBJECT SURVEYS AND HAZARD MITIGATION

CELESTIAL BODIES LEXICON

- **Asteroid:** solid, inert, irregularly shaped natural body orbiting the sun that is too small to be classified as a planet or dwarf planet.
- **Meteoroid:** small asteroid, less than one meter in size. A *meteor* is an asteroid or meteoroid that enters the Earth's atmosphere, burning and glowing as it vaporizes. If part of the body survives that passage, the fragment is referred to as *meteorite*.
- **Comet:** composed of rock and ice, typically a few kilometers in size, which elliptically orbits the sun. As it approaches the sun, the heat on the body's nucleus, or *coma*, causes a gaseous and dusty release, the *tail*.
- **Near-Earth object (NEO)** or near-Earth asteroid (NEA): approaches within 0.3 astronomical units of the Earth's orbit (about 45 million kilometers).
- **Potentially hazardous object (PHO)** or potentially hazardous asteroid (PHA): approaches within 0.05 astronomical units (7.5 million kilometers) of the Earth's orbit and is larger than 140 meters in size.
- Asteroid types:
  - C – carbonaceous, the most common;
  - M – metallic, the least common;
  - S – silicate or stony.
- **Bolide** or fireball: meteor that glows unusually brightly in the sky as it traverses or explodes. A super bolide is brighter still.

We know that the Earth is continuously pelted by small asteroids, usually with no discernable effect – these include the 'shooting stars' that routinely illuminate the night sky. Most incoming asteroids burn up completely in the atmosphere; larger, denser fragments that survive that passage will, statistically, tend to fall into the oceans or into vast, unpopulated wilderness areas. A few hardy specimens each year are retrieved by scientists, museums, or souvenir-hunters. There is no conclusive proof that any human being has ever been struck by a falling asteroid, but occasions of minor or even major property damage have been reported.[6]

As these space intruders pass through the atmosphere, they are consumed by friction, generating trails of dust that gradually percolate down to the surface.

STRATEGIES, DEFENDING PLANET EARTH: NEAR-EARTH-OBJECT SURVEYS AND HAZARD MITIGATION STRATEGIES 51, 52–53 (2010), https://www.nap.edu/read/12842/chapter/6#53 [*hereafter* National Academy].
  [6]   National Academy, *supra* note 5, at 12.

In fact, scientists calculate that the Earth continuously gains weight through that process – totaling an incredible 100 tons per day – indicating the enormous quantity of asteroids that regularly intersect the planet's orbital path.[7]

Occasionally, larger asteroids penetrate Earth's protective atmosphere and impact the surface. Historically, the most consequential asteroid collision, the Chicxulub event, occurred some 66 million years ago, off what is now the Yucatan Peninsula in the southern Caribbean Sea. That asteroid measured some 10–15 kilometers across; it impacted with sufficient force that it triggered abrupt environmental shocks resulting in the extermination of the dinosaurs and 75% of all the other plant and animal species then living on Earth.[8]

Even in the modern era, asteroid encounters have demonstrated overwhelmingly powerful effects. In 1908, above the central Russian area of Tunguska, an asteroid variously estimated as between 30 and 100 meters in diameter exploded about 5–10 kilometers above the surface. There were no known witnesses in that sparsely populated region, but 80 million trees were flattened over 2,000 square kilometers by force of the blast.[9]

A more recent, smaller asteroid encounter over the Siberian city of Chelyabinsk in 2013 exerted much less power, but was much more thoroughly documented, thanks to the profusion of car dashboard cameras in Russia, which recorded the luminous streak across the sky.[10] That asteroid, measuring perhaps 20 meters in diameter, exploded in the atmosphere at 30–50 kilome-

---

[7] *Id.* (noting that 'the average amount of material accreted daily to Earth is estimated to be in the range of 50 to 150 tons of very small objects').

[8] *Asteroid Dust Found in Crater Closes Case of Dinosaur Extinction*, UT NEWS (Feb. 24, 2021), https://news.utexas.edu/2021/02/24/asteroid-dust-found-in-crater -closes-case-of-dinosaur-extinction//; CHICXULUB CRATER, *About the Chicxulub Crater*, http://www.chicxulubcrater.org/ (last visited Dec. 20, 2021) [https://perma .cc/88PP-CARR]; Roff Smith, *Here's What Happened the Day the Dinosaurs Died*, NAT'L GEOGRAPHIC (June 11, 2016), https://news.nationalgeographic.com/2016/ 06/what-happened-day-dinosaurs-died-chicxulubdrilling-asteroid-science/ [https:// perma.cc/W2KB-V8N7].

[9] Natalia A. Artemieva & Valery V. Shuvalov, *From Tunguska to Chelyabinsk via Jupiter*, 44 ANN. REV. EARTH & PLANETARY Sci. 37 (2016); Melissa Hogenboom, *In Siberia in 1908, A Huge Explosion Came Out of Nowhere*, BBC NEWS (July 7, 2016), http://www.bbc.com/earth/story/20160706-in-siberia-in-1908-a-huge -explosion-came-out-ofnowhere [https://perma.cc/CW3F-7CJV]; Luca Gasperini et al., *The Tunguska Mystery – 100 Years Later*, Sci. AM. (June 30, 2008), https://www .scientificamerican.com/article/thetunguska-mystery-100-years-later/ [https://perma .cc/WM74-2E2E].

[10] *Moment meteor exploded over Russian city*, BBC News (Oct. 16, 2013), https://www.bbc.com/news/av/world-europe-24553733; SciShow, *The Chelyabinsk Meteor: What We Know*, YouTube (Jan. 8, 2014), https://www.youtube.com/watch?v= JB2eoQfOGBA.

ters height, with a force estimated as equivalent to 400–500 kilotons of TNT equivalent – 30 times the power of the nuclear weapons detonated at the end of World War II. Due to the altitude of the burst, the asteroid did not carve a sizeable impact crater, but it generated a shock wave that damaged 7,200 buildings on the ground and injured 1,500 people, mostly by flying glass from the shattered structures.[11]

In general, a bigger, denser asteroid would be expected to cause more substantial damage on Earth. A celestial body wider than approximately 140 meters in diameter could cause severe 'regional' consequences, afflicting thousands of square kilometers. A larger object, say 1 kilometer across, would cause devastation on a global scale. At 10 kilometers, a Chicxulub-scale asteroid could be an extinction-level catastrophe.[12]

Such a large asteroid impact would likely trigger a monumental series of intertwined ecological crises. Earthquakes, volcanoes, wildfires, and severe windstorms – localized and remote – would be prolonged and ghastly. An impact causing the sudden evacuation of a crater would thrust tons of rock and dirt into the atmosphere, some of which could remain aloft for months, obscuring sunlight and triggering a drastic drop in global temperatures. That would be devastating to plant life and ultimately to life up the food chain, too. If the asteroid struck in the ocean, it could generate a tsunami with enormous height and power, inundating coastal areas, many of which are densely populated.[13]

---

[11] *Five Years after the Chelyabinsk Meteor: NASA Leads Efforts in Planetary Defense*, NASA (Feb. 15, 2018), https://www.nasa.gov/feature/five-years-after-the -chelyabinsk-meteor-nasa-leads-efforts-in-planetary-defense (noting that the explosion 'released the energy equivalent of around 440,000 tons of TNT and generated a shock wave that blew out windows over 200 square miles and damaged some buildings,' in addition to injuring hundreds of people); Artemieva & Shuvalov, *supra* note 9; Don Yeomans & Paul Chodas, *Additional Details on the Large Fireball Event over Russia on Feb. 15, 2013*, CTR. FOR NEAR EARTH OBJECT STUD. (Mar. 1, 2013), https:// cneos.jpl.nasa.gov/news/fireball130301.html_[https://perma.cc/76LE-R276.

[12] Dave Mosher, et al., *How large asteroids must be to destroy a city, state, country, or the planet*, BUSINESS INSIDER (Jun. 30, 2018), https://www.businessinsider .com/asteroid-sizes-that-can-damage-cities-states-planet-2018-6; *Planetary Defense Frequently Asked Questions*, NASA, https://www.nasa.gov/planetarydefense/faq.

[13] John C. Kunich, *Planetary Defense: The Legality of Global Survival*, 41 A.F.L. REV. 119, 123–25 (1997) (describing diverse catastrophic effects of large asteroid impacts); Edward Bryant, Tsunami: The Underrated Hazard 169, 172–80 (3d ed. 2008) (calculating that if the Chicxulub asteroid had fallen into deep water, it could have generated a tsunami 4.6 kilometer high; in reality, it was probably 200 meters tall); Clemens M. Rumpf et al., *Asteroid Impact Effects and Their Immediate Hazards for Human Populations*, 44 GEOPHYSICAL RES. LETTERS 3433 (2017).

ASTEROID DETECTION

Despite best efforts by NASA and other nations' space agencies, we do not know where all the large asteroids are; we often do not see asteroids coming our way; and we may therefore have little advance warning about whether, when, and where an asteroid might strike and about how grave the effects might be.

Spotting asteroids is not an easy task. They tend to be small and dark, hard to pick out of the night sky, even with multiple types of advanced ground-based and orbiting telescopes. Special difficulties are posed by those that approach the Earth from the general direction of the Sun (which impedes observation) or those that are on unusual trajectories, departing from the plane on which most of the solar system orbits.[14]

Even more difficult to anticipate are the rare visitors from outside the solar system, such as the mysterious Oumuamua, which was suddenly detected in 2017. Oumuamua is approximately 230 meters long and was first observed only after it had already whizzed past Earth at 90,000 kilometers per hour, with a nearest approach of 24 million kilometers, a relatively close call on the cosmic scale.[15]

NASA experts and their international colleagues, accompanied by legions of university and private astronomers, are assiduously in search of the asteroid population. In 2019, their efforts discovered 2,433 asteroids, and in 2020, they found 2,961 more, bringing the total known inventory to 24,850.[16]

---

[14] Miriam Kramer, *Incredible Technology: How to Find Dangerous Asteroids*, SPACE.COM (Oct. 21, 2013), https://www.space.com/23277-dangerous-asteroids -incredible-technology.html; Will Dietrich-Egensteiner, *Detecting and Deflecting a Killer Asteroid*, Popular Mechanics (Oct. 25, 2013), https://www.popularmechanics .com/space/a9586/detecting-and-deflecting-a-killer-asteroid-16084695/.

[15] Donald K. Yeomans, Near-Earth Objects: Finding Them Before They Find Us 7, 125–127 (2013); Phil Davis, *Ten Things: Mysterious 'Oumuamua*, NASA Sci. (July 2, 2018), https://solarsystem.nasa.gov/news/482/10-things-mysterious-oumuamua/ [https://perma.cc/TS26-65PL]; *Small Asteroid or Comet 'Visits' from Beyond the Solar System*, NAT'L AERONAUTICS & SPACE ADMIN, https://www.nasa.gov/ feature/jpl/smallasteroid-or-comet-visits-from-beyond-the-solar-system [https://perma .cc/VF2T-2M8G].

[16] *Twenty Years of Tracking Near-Earth Objects*, NASA Jet Propulsion Laboratory (Jul 23, 2018), https://www.jpl.nasa.gov/news/twenty-years-of-tracking-near-earth -objects (as of 2018, there were 18,000 known NEOs and the discovery rate aver- aged about 40 per week); Steve Goldstein, *Why 2020 Was a Stellar Year for Hunting Asteroids*, KJZZ.ORG, https://kjzz.org/content/1661820/why-2020-was-stellar-year -hunting-asteroids (estimating that there are 25,000 near-Earth asteroids that are 140 meters in diameter and larger); *Discovery Statistics Cumulative Totals*, NASA

Congress has required NASA to discern and catalog the entire population of larger asteroids. Beginning in 1994, NASA was mandated to find and catalog 90% of the asteroids larger than one kilometer in size; NASA fulfilled that task in 2010. In 2005, Congress further directed the agency to find 90% of all asteroids larger than 140 meters by 2020; that mission is now approximately 50% finished, and the predicted completion date is still 30 years away.[17]

Once a potentially hazardous object is detected and identified, the best human efforts are likely to be able to anticipate only a certain probability of an Earth impact, until many additional measurements are available. Even then, the asteroid's nature and composition may still be incompletely known, making damage threat predictions similarly indefinite.[18]

PREVENTING AN ASTEROID IMPACT

Even if earthlings were somehow fortunate enough to gain appreciable advance notice of a likely asteroid impact, the world has very little ability to do anything effective in response to the problem – there are no techniques and no equipment designed, tested, and built for this purpose.

There are numerous candidate technologies for addressing planetary defense – some of them promising, but most of them currently confined to the drawing board stage. Perhaps the simplest, or most intuitively obvious, concept is the kinetic impactor. This scheme relies upon sending a spacecraft (the heavier the better) to intersect and collide with the incoming asteroid, with the concussion altering its current trajectory through space. Striking the asteroid head-on would slow it down a bit; knocking it from behind would speed it up – and either approach could alter the crucial timing of the asteroid's intersection with

---

Jet Propulsion Laboratory (Feb. 10, 2021), https://cneos.jpl.nasa.gov/stats/totals.html (noting that 27,355 NEOs have been found as of October 31, 2021).

[17] National Aeronautics and Space Administration Authorization Act of 2005, Pub. L. No. 109-155, 119 Stat. 2895, 2922 (2005) (codified as amended at 42 U.S.C. § 16691 (2010)); NASA Inspector General, *supra* note 3, at page iii, https://oig.nasa.gov/audits/reports/FY14/IG-14-030.pdf (warning that 'In addition to limited personnel, the NEO Program lacks a plan with integrated milestones, defined objectives, and cost and schedule estimates to assist in tracking and attaining Program goals').

[18] *See,* Richard P. Binzel, *The Torino Impact Hazard Scale,* 48 PLANETARY & SPACE Sci. 297, 297 (2000) (observing inherent uncertainties in estimating a distant NEO's trajectory, leading to representations of an 'error ellipse' to describe where it might impact Earth); David Farnocchia et al., *Orbits, Long-Term Predictions, and Impact Monitoring,* in ASTEROIDS IV 815 (Patrick Michel et al. eds., 2015); Steve Chesley and Paul Chodas, *Impact Risk Estimation and Assessment Scales,* in HANDBOOK OF COSMIC HAZARDS AND PLANETARY DEFENSE 651 (Joseph N. Pelton & Firooz Allahdadi eds., 2015).

the Earth's orbital pathway, so when the two flight lines cross, the Earth is not at the conjunction point.[19]

NASA is currently undertaking an unprecedented experiment to validate the kinetic impactor theory. The Double Asteroid Redirection Test (DART) Mission launched in November 2021 toward Didymos, a dual asteroid in which the primary body is approximately 780 meters across and its 'moonlet' is 160 meters in size. Eleven months later, and 11 million kilometers from Earth, the spacecraft will crash headlong into the Didymoon at 6.6 kilometers per second, perturbing its flight path around the larger partner. The change in velocity is expected to be only a fraction of 1%, but from that data, it should be possible to extrapolate how effective this type of kinetic interceptor could be in disrupting the pathway of a larger, more threatening asteroid.[20]

Another alluring alternative technology is the gravity tractor. Here, the hypothesis is that a spacecraft (again, the more massive, the better) would rendezvous with the asteroid, but instead of colliding with it, the spacecraft would assume a nearby parallel trajectory. The microgravity attraction between the two objects would incrementally pull them toward each other; the powered spacecraft would respond by sliding minutely away, and the asteroid would follow, in a tiny – but continuously repeated – movement. Over time, the asteroid would be pulled slightly off its original vector, and that motion could accrete into sufficient deflection to save the Earth.[21]

Still other creative proposals focus on depositing an engine of some sort onto the asteroid, to impart some movement to it, or on altering the color and

---

[19]   *Kinetic Impactor*, NASA (Mar. 16, 2015), https://www.nasa.gov/content/asteroid-grand-challenge/mitigate/kinetic-impactor (explaining that 'kinetic impaction involves sending one or more large, high-speed spacecraft into the path of an approaching near-earth object' with the goal of 'deflect[ing] the asteroid…away from the Earth's orbital path'); NEOSHIELD, *D7.5.3: NTP Kinetic Impactor Deflection Concept Report* 6–7 (July 19, 2013 report); Mingtao Li, et al., *Enhanced Kinetic Impactor for Deflecting Large Potentially Hazardous Asteroids via Maneuvering Space Rocks*, Scientific Reports (May 22, 2020), https://www.nature.com/articles/s41598-020-65343-z.

[20]   *Double Asteroid Redirection Test (DART) Mission*, NAT'L AERONAUTICS & SPACE ADMIN., https://www.nasa.gov/planetarydefense/dart [https://perma.cc/J2N2-U278]; Rob Landis & Lindley Johnson, *Advances in Planetary Defense in the United States*, 156 ACTA ASTRONAUTICA 394, 407 (2019).

[21]   *Gravity Tractor*, NAT'L AERONAUTICS & SPACE ADMIN. (Mar. 16, 2015), https://www.nasa.gov/content/asteroid-grand-challenge/mitigate/gravity-tractor; Daniel D. Mazanek et al., *Enhanced Gravity Tractor Technique for Planetary Defense* (4th IAA Planetary Defense Conference, IAA-PDC-15-04-11 (Apr. 13–17, 2015), https://selenianboondocks.com/wp-content/uploads/2015/05/IAA-PDC-15-04-11_Final.pdf [https://perma.cc/5DWM-H9WU]; Edward T. Lu & Stanley G. Love, *Gravitational Tractor for Towing Asteroids*, 438 NATURE 177 (2005).

reflectivity of the asteroid's surface, taking advantage of the differential way that sunlight energy may affect the asteroid's spin and thus its trajectory.[22]

But none of these alternatives has been experimentally validated, and some of them would be inapplicable against particular types of asteroids. (The kinetic impactor, for example, would be futile against an asteroid that consisted essentially of a cluster of gravity-linked flying rocks.) Just as important, all of these candidate techniques would be relatively slow in operation; they would require years or decades of advance warning, allowing time for the small, repeated effects to accumulate.

PLANETARY DEFENSE TECHNIQUES

- **Kinetic impactor:** A high-velocity spacecraft would ram into the asteroid, changing its flight path. This operation would require extremely precise guidance to strike a relatively small, fast-moving object. The heavier the spacecraft, the greater the effect would be. This technique would not be suitable against an asteroid that comprised a collection of loosely bound small objects. NASA's DART project will constitute an important operational test.
- **Conventional explosive:** A sub-surface chemical explosion would eject material from the surface of the asteroid, generating thrust in the opposite direction.
- **Nuclear detonation:** A nuclear explosive could be used in much the same fashion as a conventional explosive, to generate thrust in the asteroid, or to break it apart. Alternatively, the radiation from a nuclear explosion on the surface, or at a small distance, could vaporize surface material, imparting an opposite thrust.
- **Gravity tractor:** The intercepting spacecraft could hover alongside the asteroid, relying on the gravitational attraction to draw the asteroid toward the spacecraft, which would then maneuver slightly away from the dangerous original flight path. This effect could be enhanced if the

---

[22] National Academy, *supra* note 5, at 51, 72; J.P. Sanchez et al., *Multicriteria Comparison Among Several Mitigation Strategies for Dangerous Near-Earth Objects*, 32 J. GUIDANCE CONTROL DYNAMICS 121, 131–34 (2009); Dealing With the Threat to Earth From Asteroids and Comets, 58–59 (Ivan Bekey ed., 2009), https://iaaspace.org/product/dealing-with-the-threat-to-earth-from-asteroids-and-comets/; Steve Eckersley & Alistair Wayman, *D7.5.5: Laser Ablation Deflection Concept* (Aug. 6, 2013 report), in NEOSHIELD, D7.5.3: NTP Kinetic Impactor Deflection Concept Report; D.C. Hyland et al., *A Permanently-Acting NEA Mitigation Technique via the Yarkovsky Effect*, 48 COSMIC RES. 430 (2010).

spacecraft first lands on the asteroid and collects loose rocks, to increase the spacecraft's mass and magnify the resulting gravitational pull it could exert.

- **Ion beam:** A spacecraft would continuously fire ions onto the asteroid's surface, importing a small momentum change.
- **Laser ablation:** The spacecraft would fire a laser at the asteroid, vaporizing molecules on the surface; as they are ejected from the asteroid, they would impart a tiny reverse momentum.
- **Engines:** This would involve attaching a rocket engine to the asteroid, to propel it onto a different trajectory or to spin it faster than gravity could hold the asteroid's components together.
- **Reflectivity alteration:** This proposal would modify the light reflectivity of all or part of the asteroid by changing its surface color, through application of dust or pigmentation. These changes would alter the spin of the asteroid or affect the impact that sunlight would have on its flight path.

Attention naturally focuses, therefore, on the possibility of using a nuclear explosive device as a last resort for planetary defense. In one sense, this is a relatively mature technology. Humankind has conducted over 2,000 nuclear test detonations of widely varying size and performance characteristics, in a broad range of physical settings, including space. On a weight-to-yield basis, which is a vital consideration for a mission that requires spacelift and long-distance travel, nuclear explosions are enormously efficient.[23] However, nothing like using a nuclear explosion to divert a celestial body has ever been tried, and existing nuclear explosive devices were certainly not designed and optimized for any such purpose.

In Hollywood's several sensational asteroid-based disaster movies,[24] the climactic scene usually involves the hero emplacing a nuclear weapon onto a threatening asteroid and blowing it to smithereens, thereby rescuing the Earth

---

[23] National Academy, *supra* note 5, 76–79; M. Bruck Syal et al., *Nuclear and Kinetic Approaches to Asteroid Defense: New Numerical Insights* (46th Lunar and Planetary Science Conference, 2015); *Nuclear Weapon Effects in Space*, NAT'L AERONAUTICS & SPACE ADMIN., https://history.nasa.gov/conghand/nuclear.htm [https://perma.cc/T6QL-WBVG]; Douglas Birch, The Plans to Use Nuclear Weapons to Blow Up Incoming Asteroids, The Atlantic, October 16, 2013 (discussing the idea of collaboration between the U.S. and Russia on the concept of using a nuclear explosive device against an asteroid).

[24] Examples include METEOR (American International Pictures 1979) (starring Sean Connery and Natalie Wood); ARMAGEDDON (Touchstone Pictures 1998) (starring Bruce Willis, Ben Affleck, and Billy Bob Thornton); DEEP IMPACT (Paramount Pictures 1998) (starring Robert Duvall, Tea Leoni, and Morgan Freeman).

at the last possible moment. In reality, fracturing the asteroid in that manner would probably not be the most advantageous course. Most of the shattered, now highly radioactive, pieces would likely continue on their original trajectory toward Earth, potentially generating multiple, dispersed impact points that might inflict even more damage than a single, larger crater would cause.[25]

Instead, the favored concept now would detonate a nuclear device at some short standoff distance from the asteroid, using the resulting radiation energy to excite volatile molecules on the asteroid's surface. As these particles evaporate or sublimate off the surface, they would each impart a small, equal and opposite force nudging the asteroid in the reverse direction. Depending on the size and composition of the asteroid, several such detonations might be required to achieve the necessary displacement from the original trajectory.[26]

LEGAL IMPEDIMENTS TO A PLANETARY DEFENSE MISSION

Nuclear Weapons in Space

Use of a nuclear explosive device against an incoming asteroid would be technologically very challenging – but the legal obstacles for such an operation may be even greater. Several treaties address the possible use of a nuclear explosive device in space; each of these instruments is longstanding and has been joined by most of the countries that might be relevant to a planetary defense mission. Moreover, each of these international law implements is widely regarded as tremendously important – they are foundational for avoiding nuclear arms races and sustaining the world's fragile nuclear security structure. However, none of them was drafted with the asteroid danger in mind, and their specific application to this novel circumstance may be debated. Three treaties (in one case, a group of treaties) must be considered.

The first is the 1967 Outer Space Treaty (OST), addressed in other chapters of this book.[27] OST Article IV requires that 'States Parties to the Treaty

---

[25]   National Academy, *supra* note 5, at 84 (2010); Mark Strauss, *Helpful Tips for Nuking an Asteroid*, NAT'L GEOGRAPHIC (Aug. 3, 2015), https://news.nationalgeographic.com/2015/08/150803-space-nasa-asteroids-comets-nuclearweapons-defense/ [https://perma.cc/6XSF-WJ7W]; Bong Wie, *Hypervelocity Nuclear Interceptors for Asteroid Disruption*, 90 ACTA ASTRONAUTICA 146 (2012).

[26]   Bekey, *supra* note 22.

[27]   Treaty on Principles Governing the Activities of States in the Exploration and Use of Outer Space, including the Moon and Other Celestial Bodies, 18 U.S.T. 2410, 610 U.N.T.S. 205, 61 I.L.M. 386 (1967). *See,* Chapters 3 and 4.

undertake not to place in orbit around the Earth any objects carrying nuclear weapons or any other kinds of weapons of mass destruction, install such weapons on celestial bodies, or station such weapons in outer space in any other manner.'

This passage is sometimes ambitiously described as a comprehensive 'no nukes in space' dictate, but its actual coverage is significantly narrower. The provision addresses three specific activities: (1) placing a nuclear weapon or other weapon of mass destruction (WMD) into Earth orbit; (2) installing such a device on a celestial body; or (3) stationing one in space. While it is possible that a future planetary defense mission might run afoul of one of those three prohibitions, it may also be plausible to design the operation to dodge the Treaty's three key verbs – 'place,' 'install,' and 'station.'

Notably, Article IV is understood not to prohibit the 'transit' of space by a nuclear weapon, such as a warfighting device transported on an intercontinental ballistic missile (ICBM), which ascends out of its launcher, flies through space for 20 minutes or so, then descends back though the atmosphere to strike its terrestrial target halfway around the world. In the same way, a nuclear explosive device on a planetary defense mission that was boosted into and through space, flown directly to a rendezvous with an asteroid, and promptly detonated there – without ever orbiting the Earth, being installed on the asteroid, or being stationed in space – might escape the Treaty's coverage.

On the other hand, if the mission design called for emplacing the nuclear device onto the surface of the asteroid or, *a fortiori*, if it were lowered into a drilled borehole inside the celestial body, that might well be considered 'installing' the device, in violation of OST Article IV.[28]

Another important interpretive question is whether OST Article IV – which applies to a 'nuclear weapon' – might be considered inapplicable in a planetary defense mission, where the nuclear device might be characterized as something other than a 'weapon.' In one view, the ordinary use of the term 'weapon' would be limited to an implement employed for criminal, aggressive, or other hostile purposes. In contrast, when a nuclear explosive device is applied for a benign, humanity-saving function, to protect people instead of to target them, perhaps it is more properly regarded as a 'tool' rather than as a 'weapon,' and thus exempt from Article IV.[29]

---

[28] Note that the second paragraph of OST art. IV prohibits 'the testing of any type of weapon' on a celestial body, including an asteroid, so it would be illegal for a Treaty Party to practice the planetary defense routines in advance. The traditional testing protocols for routinely preparing a weapon and a technique before their operational deployment therefore could not be undertaken.

[29] *See*, James D. Rendleman & Brian D. Green, *Space Weapons According to Stewart*, in MONOGRAPH SERIES V: CONFLICTS IN SPACE AND THE RULE OF

This vocabulary debate might be a close call. A knife, for example, is a weapon when wielded to stab someone, but when used instead to slice an apple, it is characterized differently. Some authorities, therefore, have suggested that Article IV should be regarded as irrelevant to the possible use of a nuclear explosive device against an incoming asteroid.[30] The majority view, however, regards nuclear explosive devices as *sui generis*, holding that they are inherently and permanently weapons, regardless of their possible beneficial uses, and that the best reading of the Outer Space Treaty – the interpretation that would be most faithful to the agreement's object and purpose – would apply Article IV in full.[31]

The second treaty relevant here is the 1963 Limited Test Ban Treaty (LTBT), which requires its 125 Parties (including all the major spacefaring countries except China and France) 'to prohibit, to prevent, and not to carry out any nuclear weapon test explosion, or any other nuclear explosion, at any place under its jurisdiction or control…in the atmosphere; beyond its limits, including outer space.'[32]

Unlike the OST, the LTBT focuses on the nuclear detonation, rather than on the placement or location of the device, and it avoids the possible loophole

---

LAW 173 (Maria Manoli and Sandy Belle Habchi eds., 2018) (assessing that there is no generally accepted definition of 'space weapon'); LYALL & LARSEN, *supra* note 2, at 461 (suggesting that the drafters of the OST may not have contemplated a scenario involving a use of a nuclear device for planetary defense purposes); MICHAEL MINEIRO, *THE U.S. AND THE LEGALITY OF OUTER SPACE WEAPONIZATION*, 33 ANNALS OF AIR & SPACE L. 441, 446–48 (2008) (surveying various definitions of space weapon); JAMES A. GREEN, *PLANETARY DEFENSE: NEAR-EARTH OBJECTS, NUCLEAR WEAPONS, AND INTERNATIONAL LAW*, 42 HASTINGS INT'L & COMPARATIVE L. REV. 1 (2019).

[30] Planetary Defence Legal Overview and Assessment, Report by the Space Mission Planning Advisory Group (SMPAG) Ad-Hoc Working Group on Legal Issues to SMPAG, April 8, 2020, p. 28–32, https://www.cosmos.esa.int/documents/336356/336472/SMPAG-RP-004_1_0_SMPAG_legal_report_2020-04-08+%281%29.pdf/60df8a3a-b081-4533-6008-5b6da5ee2a98?t=1586443949723 [*hereinafter* Ad-Hoc Group].

[31] *See*, LEGAL ASPECTS OF NEO THREAT RESPONSE AND RELATED INSTITUTIONAL ISSUES: FINAL REPORT, Secure World Found. (Feb. 9, 2010), at 26, https://swfound.org/media/40426/legal_aspects_neo_response_institutional_issues_final_report.pdf [http://perma.cc/26Z8-QC5L]; 1 COLOGNE COMMENTARY ON SPACE LAW 79, 76–77 9 (Stephan Hobe et al. eds., 2009) (presenting the debate about whether the intended use of a nuclear device controls its designation as a weapon, and concluding that for nuclear devices, 'A "weapon" thus remains a "weapon" irrespective of whether it may be used for civilian uses.'); Koplow, *Exoatmospheric Plowshares*, *supra* note 5, at 111–17.

[32] Treaty Banning Nuclear Weapon Tests in the Atmosphere, in Outer Space and Under Water, *opened for signature* Aug. 5, 1963, 14 U.S.T. 1313, 480 U.N.T.S. 6964 (entered into force Oct. 10, 1963), art. I.1.

derived from the use of the term 'weapon.' This Treaty bans 'any' nuclear explosion in space, regardless of its intended or avowed benign purpose. The LTBT thus poses a direct, unavoidable impediment to any possible use of a nuclear explosive device for planetary defense.

Third, other treaties may also constrain effective international collaboration in the conduct of a nuclear planetary defense mission. The 1968 Nuclear Non-Proliferation Treaty, for example, prohibits most of its Parties (those known collectively as the non-nuclear-weapon States) from acquiring or receiving nuclear explosive devices or control over them, directly or indirectly.[33] Several regional 'nuclear-weapon-free-zone' treaties reinforce these constraints, requiring their Parties 'to refrain from engaging in, encouraging or authorizing, directly or indirectly, or in any way participating in the testing, use…or control of any nuclear weapon.'[34] Therefore, if multiple diverse countries were to collaborate in a nuclear-based planetary defense mission, the role of the non-nuclear-weapon States would have to be tightly constrained.

The newest treaty in this field is the Treaty on the Prohibition of Nuclear Weapons, which entered into force January 22, 2021. This ambitious instrument requires its Parties 'never under any circumstances' to test or use nuclear weapons or other nuclear explosive devices, and not to 'assist, encourage or induce, in any way, anyone to engage in any activity prohibited to a State Party under this Treaty.'[35] Here, too, any collaboration between a Party to the Treaty and a State carrying out a nuclear planetary defense mission would be barred, and even the act of requesting, endorsing, or authorizing such an operation would be impermissible.

Legal Liability for Mishaps in Space

The second major international legal problem arising in the planetary defense realm has nothing to do with reliance upon nuclear explosive devices. Instead, the issue is the financial liability for unintended consequences resulting from

---

[33] Treaty on the Non-Proliferation of Nuclear Weapons, July 1, 1968, 21 U.S.T. 483, 729 U.N.T.S. 169.

[34] Treaty for the Prohibition of Nuclear Weapons in Latin America and the Caribbean art. 1.1(a), Feb. 14, 1967, 634 U.N.T.S. 326 (entered into force Apr. 22, 1968).

[35] Treaty on the Prohibition of Nuclear Weapons (TPNW) art. 1.1.e, Sept. 20, 2017, 52 I.L.M. 347, https://www.un.org/disarmament/wp-content/uploads/2017/10/tpnw-info-kit-v2.pdf [https://perma.cc/2ENV-8ALJ]. As of 1 December 2021, the TPNW has 56 Parties and has been signed by an additional 30 States. None of the States that have nuclear weapons or their closest allies have joined the TPNW.

the mission. As described in Chapter 4, the 1972 Liability Convention[36] establishes a State's absolute liability to pay compensation for damage caused by its space objects to property or people on Earth's surface.[37]

Imagine a situation in which State X (or it could be a coalition of several States) responds to the global emergency posed by an incoming asteroid by mounting a planetary defense intervention. X does everything in a reasonable, appropriate fashion, exercising its best capabilities and operating in all good faith, to try to rescue the planet from the impending catastrophe. But suppose X's enterprise is only partially successful: it manages to change the asteroid's trajectory somewhat, but not sufficiently to make it miss the Earth altogether. Then, instead of striking State Y (where it would have impacted, if X had done nothing), the asteroid now hits – and devastates – State Z. Obviously, Y would be greatly relieved and grateful, while Z would be ruined.

The existing international legal framework requires that State X would face absolute liability for the damage inflicted by the asteroid on State Z – it was X's intervention that resulted in the harm, and it would be no excuse for X to demonstrate that it behaved flawlessly in all its planetary defense efforts. That financial responsibility could be immense – the asteroid might inflict massive harm to public and private property throughout Z. This financial burden could bankrupt X; more to the point, any such exposure would surely deter X from undertaking such a mission in the first place. No State would rationally volunteer to attempt such a rescue mission if the financial consequences for imperfect success could be so enormous.[38]

Possible Legal Solutions

So what is to be done about these legal obstacles – how can the legal community avoid the impediments established by the Outer Space Treaty, the Limited Test Ban Treaty, and the Nuclear Non-Proliferation Treaty and its successors (regarding the use of a nuclear explosive device in space) and those created by the Liability Convention (regarding possible tort damages)?

---

[36] Convention on International Liability for Damage Caused by Space Objects (Liability Convention), 24 U.S.T. 2389, 861 U.N.T.S. 187, 10 I.L.M. 965 (1972).

[37] Liability Convention, Articles III, IV.

[38] There is no specific obligation under international law for any particular State to undertake planetary defense actions. In general, States are free to explore and use space, but they are not required to do so. For self-protection, and as a humanitarian measure, States may feel compelled to try to act against an incoming asteroid, in the effort to avert a global or regional catastrophe, but the degree of overt international legal compulsion is limited, and in any event, different States may have starkly different capabilities for undertaking a planetary defense mission. *See*, Ad-Hoc Group, *supra* note 30, at 18–26.

At the most fundamental level, some people might express an instinct that if international law seems to erect an impenetrable barrier against rational, concerted action in the truly desperate circumstances of an incoming asteroid, the world should respond by simply ignoring or tossing aside the treaties. Those legal niceties, which were negotiated and brought into force years ago for totally different reasons, cannot be allowed to preclude concerted global action that is truly necessary to avoid a humanitarian catastrophe.

There is much to commend that perspective, but the world's legal, political, and social communities can do better than that – we should be able to find or invent a way to remain faithful to the principles of the rule of law and still empower a capacious response to an asteroid. We still have time to develop creative workarounds, preserving both the rules-based system of international order and our planetary defense opportunities.

Standard treaty law offers several suggestions here, none of them perfect. For example, treaties can be amended – but these particular instruments contain only relatively cumbersome provisions for such modifications. Also, a Party can withdraw from a treaty – but here, the key treaties require a significant delay before withdrawal can be effectuated. In addition, international law offers a variety of valid excuses for the non-performance of treaty obligations, and some of those (consent, necessity, and duress, for example) might seem to be available here – but on closer inspection, none of those 'circumstances that preclude the wrongfulness' of a Party's action is likely to be directly on point.[39]

Instead, the most promising recourse may be found through the UN Security Council. Under Chapter VII of the UN Charter, the Security Council possesses an extraordinary ability to create new international legal rights and obligations, and these authorities can take precedence over any contrary legal commitments that States may have assumed pursuant to prior treaties.[40] The applicable criterion is whether the provocation constitutes a 'threat to the peace,' which a life-threatening asteroid would readily satisfy.[41] The Security Council could then authorize a State or coalition of States to undertake a planetary defense mission employing a nuclear explosive device notwithstanding the obligations of the Outer Space Treaty, the Limited Test Ban Treaty, or any other contrary legal instrument. Similarly, the Security Council could in effect suspend the absolute tort responsibility that a State might incur pursuant to the Liability

---

[39] Draft Articles on Responsibility of States for Internationally Wrongful Acts, with Commentaries 169, Rep. of the Int'l Law Comm'n, 53d Sess., Apr. 23–June 1, July 2–Aug. 10, 2001, U.N. Doc. A/56/10, GAOR, 56th Sess., Supp. No. 10 (2001), G.A. Res. 56/83 (Dec. 12, 2001), *corrected by* A/56/49(Vol. I)/Corr.4; Ad Hoc Group, *supra* note 30, at 37–41; Koplow, *Exoatmospheric Plowshares*, *supra* note 5, at 127–34.

[40] *See*, UN Charter, art. 103.

[41] *Id.*, art. 39.

Convention, and instead establish some other, more equitable international mechanism for restoring any State devastated by a failed planetary defense effort.[42]

Of course, the Security Council could undertake such vigorous lawmaking only pursuant to unanimity among its five permanent members – China, France, Russia, the United Kingdom, and the U.S. – each of which possesses an unrestricted veto power. If the planet's leading nations do not see eye-to-eye on the need for an emergency planetary defense mission, the Earth is truly imperiled.

CONCLUSION

In sum, the problem of planetary defense has attracted increased attention, effort, and funding in recent years, but it is still far from a top priority for the United States or other countries. This sort of pernicious problem poses perhaps-insoluble difficulties for traditional public policy decision-making, as it is characterized by a wicked combination of factors: (a) it presents a novel, unfamiliar danger, outside the experience of any living persons; (b) it raises the specter of truly unimaginable global catastrophe; and (c) although it is statistically very likely to occur at some point in time, it is quite unlikely to occur at any particular moment (especially not foreseeably during the term in office of any contemporary governmental official).

That combination provides a formula for under-resourcing the problem, and there is little prospect that a viable, effective mechanism for diverting a threatening asteroid could be developed, tested, and deployed within the next several years. Whether that timetable exceeds that of the next large incoming asteroid is anyone's guess.

QUESTIONS FOR REVIEW

1. How serious is the danger of a major asteroid impacting the Earth, both in terms of the likelihood of an occurrence and in terms of the catastrophic harms it could inflict? What are the leading precedents?
2. How well are we able to identify, track, and characterize potentially hazardous asteroids; to predict the likelihood of an Earth impact; and to provide timely warning?

---

[42]   *See, e.g.,* Ad-Hoc Group, *supra* note 30, at 59–61; Koplow, *Exoatmospheric Plowshares, supra* note 5, at 142 (providing a sample draft UN Security Council resolution about planetary defense).

3. What tools and techniques might be available to divert an Earth-approaching asteroid? How mature are the relevant technologies? What factors would affect the effectiveness of each potential method?
4. What are the legal issues raised by a planetary defense mission? How can those be addressed?
5. What avenues does international law provide for circumventing the constraints of the relevant treaties, if a planetary defense mission becomes essential? What is the potential law-making role of the UN Security Council?
6. Do you think governments are providing sufficient funding for this high-risk, low-probability event? Why or why not?

Epilogue

Careers in space law

There are many paths to becoming a space law attorney. As Ruth did throughout this book, one can work at a 'big law' firm, which has a variety of practice areas assisting clients across the range of transactions that comprise the space industry. In fact, space lawyers frequently begin their careers by specializing in practice areas other than space law, such as government contracts, environmental law, employment litigation, intellectual property, or telecommunications. First and foremost, being a good lawyer is essential to becoming a good space lawyer.

Increasingly, there are opportunities in private space companies, from startups to Fortune 100 companies. Depending upon their size, companies may have either a singular general counsel or a large team of in-house lawyers who advise their clients on a wide set of legal matters while leveraging the work of outside counsel. Although there are examples of in-house hires right out of law school, companies more frequently hire attorneys with at least five years of experience.

Government service also offers career opportunities in space law, including hiring recent law school graduates as junior attorneys. Government agencies including NASA, the JAG Corps, and the Departments of Commerce, State and Defense all have Offices of General Counsel that hire attorneys in the space law field. Congressional committees with jurisdiction over space activities also employ lawyers. In certain cases, there may be loan repayment programs to support law graduates with high amounts of student debt in exchange for a certain number of years of government service.

If you are interested in pursuing a space law career, please consider the following suggestions. If you are still a student, good grades and good internships are important. A demonstrated interest in space law will distinguish your application. For example, if your school does not yet have a Space Law Society, you should start one. Your student note or upper-class writing paper offers an opportunity to write about a space law question and get it published. If your law school does not yet offer a Space Law course, advocate for adding it to the curriculum. In addition, participating in one of the Space Law Moot Court competitions will introduce you to fellow space law enthusiasts. For example, the Manfred Lachs moot court is a renowned space law competition whose final round is argued before three judges of the International Court of Justice in a different country every year. Traditionally, NASA has paid for the winning U.S. team to travel to the international competition. Other space agencies around the world do the same.

There are U.S. and international space law conferences that present law students, recent graduates and lawyers looking to shift into space law an excellent opportunity to network with space lawyers and identify mentors. Indeed, if you are a current law practitioner, much of the advice above applies – publish in the field, leverage your network, and consider an LL.M. However, you have an advantage over law students. Many government agencies, law firms, and private industry would prefer to hire an attorney with more experience. Working well on teams and communicating clearly are also key factors in your success as a space law attorney.

Given the growth of the space economy, the demand for attorneys knowledgeable about space law is on an upward trajectory. Congratulations on taking the first step by picking up this book. You have a future of exciting new possibilities, and an adventure awaits. *Ad astra!*

Index